Collected Papers on Suetonius

I0593104

'There can be no question about the standing of [Power's] scholarship and the contribution that he has made to Suetonian studies. Power is, I think, unique among modern Suetonians in that he works not just on the imperial *Lives* but on *De viris illustribus* and other "minor" works. His knowledge of Suetonian scholarship is encyclopaedic and it is demonstrated excellently throughout the work ... there is no likely competition to this volume from any living scholar.'

– David Wardle, University of Cape Town

This collection of essays by a leading authority on Suetonius, one of our most significant historical sources for the early Roman Empire, provides an in-depth examination of his works, whose literary value has in the past been overlooked.

Although Suetonius is well known for his *Lives* of emperors such as Caligula and Nero, he is rarely studied in his own right, aside from grammatical or textual commentaries. This is the first volume by an expert on the author to make him accessible to a wider audience, looking at his biographies not only of emperors but also poets, and discovering new contemporary evidence for Jesus from one of Suetonius' first-century sources. Other writers discussed include Homer, Sophocles, Catullus, Virgil, Horace, Curtius Rufus, Josephus, Plutarch, Pliny the Younger, Tacitus, Juvenal, and Cassius Dio. The book contains thirty-two papers in all, eleven of which are new, which examine Suetonius' neglected historical value and literary skills, and offer textual conjectures on both the *Illustrious Men* and *Lives of the Caesars*. It also has a new introduction and represents over a dozen years of research on an essential Latin source for Roman history.

Collected Papers on Suetonius provides an invaluable resource for students and researchers working on Suetonius. It also has broader significance for anyone studying Roman imperial history and culture, Latin literature, and classical historiography.

Tristan Power has taught Classics at Columbia University and is the co-editor of *Suetonius the Biographer: Studies in Roman Lives* (2014). He has also published on the Roman poet Catullus.

Collected Papers on Suetonius

Tristan Power

 Routledge
Taylor & Francis Group
LONDON AND NEW YORK

First published 2021
by Routledge
2 Park Square, Milton Park, Abingdon, Oxon OX14 4RN

and by Routledge
605 Third Avenue, New York, NY 10158

Routledge is an imprint of the Taylor & Francis Group, an informa business

© 2021 Tristan Power

British Library Cataloguing-in-Publication Data
A catalogue record for this book is available from the British Library

Library of Congress Cataloging-in-Publication Data
A catalog record has been requested for this book

ISBN: 9780367555658 (hbk)
ISBN: 9780367560010 (pbk)
ISBN: 9781003096030 (ebk)

Typeset in Sabon
by codeMantra

Matri meae

Contents

Preface

Suetonius is the most central author to our knowledge of Roman history not to have many resources for readers. This book collects eleven new papers on the biographer, together with twenty-one others that previously appeared in print but have since been revised, for a total of thirty-two chapters. It begins with a new introduction on his literary persona, as reflected in the letters on his early life from Pliny the Younger, and contains everything that I have written on Suetonius to date – besides what is already in the volume *Suetonius the Biographer*, where I provide an overview of the subject in my introduction.[1] All of the papers in the present book take a rather textual approach, examining specific passages of Suetonius' *Lives* that discuss Roman literature or history, with a detailed and at times grammatical focus on his writing style, and on the manuscript variants and emendations that form part of the basis of our modern editions of his works. Through such close readings, I present a reevaluation of Suetonius as a sophisticated and engaging biographer who often evokes poetry to underscore his moralistic points, rather than simply the derivative, unoriginal reporter of his sources that he was once thought.[2] Paradoxically, it is this literary side of Suetonius that is often the key to assessing his historical value, so that questions of history in his *Lives* are often inseparable from considerations of his style, sources, text, and literary embellishments, including previously undiscovered uses of the poets Homer, Sophocles, and Virgil.

To one of the first modern scholars of Suetonius in English, Gavin Townend, Suetonius was 'a conscientious, sensible and accurate reporter of the sources at his disposal ... the chance of a reliable version of the literary tradition

---

1 Power 2014b. For a modern biography of Pliny the Younger, see Gibson 2020.
2 On the interdependence of literary and textual studies in Latin literature, see e.g. Hunter and Oakley 2016; Kraggerud 2017, 4–5; on the main competing approaches to Suetonius as either too historical or too literary, Power 2014b, 18. A similar disparity is reflected in the scholarship of Livy; see Vasaly 2015, 31–2, 152 nn. 35–8 with bibliography; for a more balanced perspective on this historian, see Oakley 1997–2005, 1.16–19. For the purpose of literary allusion in Tacitus, see Ash 2007, 24–6; in Plutarchan biography, Pelling 2020.

available to him is evidently greater with Suetonius than with a more creative and imaginative historian such as Tacitus.'[3] The general opinion of the biographer's literary style has long been that it is mediocre and artless compared to the more complex Roman authors Sallust and Tacitus, or the Greek biographer Plutarch.[4] Sir Ronald Syme himself, one of the great Classicists of the twentieth century, considered Suetonius 'merely an erudite compiler'.[5] Some scholars, such as Wallace-Hadrill, have thus compared the style of his *Lives* simply to the competent academic writing of ancient commentators and antiquarians.[6] This book combats such conclusions that the author's writing is entirely unadorned or lacking in technique. As the papers to follow demonstrate, he is, on the contrary, a clever writer whose literary skills have not been fully appreciated. These skills, as well as Suetonius' biographical interests and prose style, must be understood in order to interpret his text and the historical facts that he preserves. As Plutarch writes, in biography, it is the 'minor detail' (πρᾶγμα βραχύ, *Alex.* 1.2) that can often be the most revealing, and a number of my arguments on finer points have much wider implications for history.

The book will be of interest not only to historians but also to theological scholars, since it finds new extra-biblical evidence for Jesus (Chapter 29). Moreover, several misguided assumptions about Suetonius are overturned, such as the scandalous allegation that he made an overture to the emperor Hadrian's wife while he was Secretary of Correspondence (*ab epistulis*), where low-mindedness has been imputed to the author's own life even by his earliest readers in antiquity (Chapter 26), just as it has been attributed by some scholars to his biographies.[7] In the volume's last paper (Chapter 32) in particular, I challenge the view that the emperor Vitellius' death scene in Tacitus' *Histories* is necessarily a greater example of artistic invention than that in Suetonius' *Life* of the emperor, which has frequently been considered less creative in its use of the common earlier material than the parallel

---

3 Townend 1982a, xv. For Suetonius as 'enslaved to his sources', see D'Anna 1954, 208: 'per quanto riguarda lo stile, è succubo delle fonti'; Grant 1970, 33: 'scissors-and-paste technique'. Cf. also id. 1954, 118–20; Mouchová 1968, 13; Ektor 1980, 325; Goodyear 1982, 663; Ripat 2006, 325; Damon 2018, 125.

4 See e.g. Teuffel 1891–2, 2.201; Funaioli 1927, 25 = 1947, 178–9; Stuart 1928, 230; Ailloud 1931–2, 1.xlii; Garraty 1958, 54; Martin 1981, 37–8; Carter 1982, 8; Hurley 2011, xxiv–xxvi; Schulz 2019a, 362. Cf. also Buckwald 2020, 116: 'a relatively obscure Latin author', although this statement is at odds with the ensuing characterization of his *Lives* as 'remarkable portraits of historically prominent figures' (ibid.).

5 Syme 1958, 464 n. 1. See also id. 1980a, 110–11 = *RP* 3.1257: 'erudite compilation'; cf. Simcox 1883, 221: 'a popular compiler'. Against this view of Suetonius' biographies as 'mere compilation', see Lewis 1991, 3666.

6 Wallace-Hadrill 1983, 21–2, 25, 69, 197; Burke 1993, 7; Kaster 1995, xxxiv–xxxv; Burridge 2004, 181.

7 For Suetonius as writing with the 'relish' of a sensationalist, see e.g. Ogilvie 1980, 266; Crompton 2003, 102; Osgood 2019, 143; Damon 2020, 125, 136 n. 61; cf. Bradley 1978, 200–1; Burke 2019, 268: 'lurid'.

account in Tacitus. Suetonius' version has been dismissed by scholars as factual in a simpler way, yet paradoxically has thus been seen as more historically reliable. The presumption that the biographer takes less care in shaping his sources, which began most forcefully with Syme in his treatment of the two authors on this emperor, is not well founded. Consequently, it is shown by this paper among others (e.g. Chapter 9) that Suetonius' details for history are at times deceptively fictional and untrustworthy.

Part I of this book discusses Suetonius' biographies of famous Roman figures in his first published collection the *Illustrious Men* (*c.* AD 105–10), which he wrote before the *Lives of the Caesars* (*c.* AD 119–22). Part II then deals with his use of poetry in both of these works. The chapters in Part III offer notes on the author's text, and lastly, Part IV looks at Suetonius with regard to his historical sources and evidence. The references for the papers that are republished with additions and corrections in this volume are as follows:

Chapter 1	'Pliny, *Letters* 5.10 and the Literary Career of Suetonius', *JRS* 100 (2010), 140–62.
Chapter 2	'Two Acrostics by Late Republican Poets in Suetonius', *Athenaeum* 99 (2011), 509–14.
Chapter 3	'Calvus' Poetry in Suetonius and Pliny, *Letters* 5.3', *Athenaeum* 102 (2014), 543–5.
Chapter 5	'Juvenal, *Satires* 3.74 and Suetonius', *CW* 107 (2014), 399–403.
Chapter 6	'The Orator Memmius in Suetonius', *RhM* 155 (2012), 219–23.
Chapter 8	'Suetonius and the Date of Curtius Rufus', *Hermes* 141 (2013), 117–20.
Chapter 9	'Poetry and Fiction in Suetonius' *Illustrious Men*'. In De Temmerman and Demoen 2016, 217–39.
Chapter 11	'Pyrrhus and Priam in Suetonius' *Tiberius*', *CQ* 62 (2012), 430–3.
Chapter 12	'Claudius' Homeric Quotation', *Latomus* 70 (2011), 727–31.
Chapter 13	'Galba, Onesimus, and Servitude', *Eranos* 107 (2012–13), 38–40.
Chapter 14	'Priam and Pompey in Suetonius' *Galba*', *CQ* 57 (2007), 792–6.
Chapter 15	'Galba and Priam in Tacitus' *Histories*', *RhM* 157 (2014), 216–20.
Chapter 16	'The Servants' Taunt: Homer and Suetonius' *Galba*', *Historia* 58 (2009), 242–5.
Chapter 17	'Suetonius, *De grammaticis* 13.1', *CQ* 62 (2012), 886–8.
Chapter 19	'Augustus' Mime of Life (Suetonius, *Aug.* 99.1)', *CW* 107 (2013), 99–103.

In all cases, the newer versions are to be preferred, and the permission of the original editors to republish these studies is gratefully acknowledged. I have updated them with regard to both bibliography and text, so that they now follow Kaster's OCT.[8] This new Latin edition of Suetonius represents a sea change in our understanding of the transmission of his substantially extant *Lives* (that is, the *De uita Caesarum* and the *De grammaticis et rhetoribus* section of *De uiris illustribus*), and has superseded the formerly standard Teubner of Ihm.[9] Nevertheless, the studies in this volume challenge a further seven *loci* from Kaster's recension,[10] in which my conjectures on two passages (*Gramm.* 13.1, *Aug.* 99.1) have already been accepted. In many of the papers, I take my lead from the biographer himself, who was known to 'love brevity' (*amare breuitatem*, SHA, *Quad. Tyr.* 1.2).

It is a distinct pleasure to express here my thanks to those who commented on earlier drafts of the previously published material and kindly offered me advice when I was a student, particularly Professor D. Curley, Professor T. E. Duff, Professor R. K. Gibson, Professor S. P. Oakley, and Professor C. Pelling. I should also note that the late Nicholas Horsfall sent me a message of praise out of the blue upon the publication of my first article on Virgil in Suetonius (Chapter 14), which was meaningful to me at an early stage in my career, coming as it did from a great expert on this poet. I should likewise be remiss if I did not thank the reviewers of Routledge, who provided helpful suggestions on the work, as well as Amy Davis-Poynter and her staff at the press for their assistance in seeing the volume into print. As someone who works on a historical Latin text, I could not be more fortunate than to have had Stephen Oakley as my doctoral supervisor. I have benefitted greatly from his expertise and being challenged by him to try to master many different aspects of Suetonius. His wisdom and guidance have continued to point me in the right direction long after I ceased being his student. I am also indebted to Professor D. T. Steiner for my

8 Kaster 2016a.
9 Ihm 1907.
10 *Iul.* 49.2 (Chapter 18), *Claud.* 25.4 (Chapter 29), *Ner.* 29 (Chapter 20), *Ner.* 34.2 (Chapter 21), *Galb.* 20.1 (Chapter 18), *Vesp.* 23.1 (Chapter 23), *Dom.* 10.3 (Chapter 24).

position as Lecturer in Classics at Columbia University from 2017 to 2018, which allowed me to update the bibliography and finish my research for the new chapters, and to Professor D. S. Levene for getting some recent articles for me before I submitted the manuscript.

Finally, I am thankful to my parents, especially my mother, the dedicatee of this book, who most of all encouraged me to pursue my work on the great Roman biographer.

Tristan Power
New York
December 2020

Editions and Abbreviations

I print the Latin of the OCT by Kaster (2016a) for Suetonius with my own translations, unless otherwise stated. Abbreviations follow those of *The Oxford Classical Dictionary*, 4th ed. (Oxford, 2012), or else standard convention. Note also the following:

AAT	*Atti della Accademia delle scienze di Torino*
AC	*L'antiquité classique*
AClass	*Acta classica*
AE	*L'année épigraphique*
AFAM	*Anuari de filologia antiqua et mediaeualia*
AFLC	*Annali della Facoltà di lettere e filosofia dell'Università di Cagliari*
AIIS	*Annali dell'Istituto italiano per gli studi storici*
AIPhO	*Annuaire de L'institut de philologie et d'histoire orientales et slaves*
AJAH	*American Journal of Ancient History*
AJP	*American Journal of Philology*
AncSoc	*Ancient Society*
ANRW	*Aufstieg und Niedergang der römischen Welt*
AntTard	*Antiquité tardive*
AUMLA	*Journal of the Australasian Universities Language and Literature Association*
BICS	*Bulletin of the Institute of Classical Studies*
BJRL	*Bulletin of the John Rylands Library*
Blasph.	J. Taillardat, ed., *Suétone: Περὶ βλασφημιῶν, Περὶ παιδιῶν*. Paris, 1967.
C&S	*Cultura e scuola*
CB	*Classical Bulletin*
CIL	*Corpus inscriptionum Latinarum*
CJ	*Classical Journal*
ClAnt	*Classical Antiquity*
CP	*Classical Philology*

CQ	*Classical Quarterly*
CR	*Classical Review*
CRAI	*Comptes rendus des séances de L'académie des inscriptions et belles-lettres*
CSCA	*California Studies in Classical Antiquity*
CW	*Classical World*
DHA	*Dialogues d'histoire ancienne*
EClás	*Estudios clásicos*
EMC	*Échos du monde classique*
EPHE	*Annuaire de L'école pratique des hautes études*
FLP	*Fragmentary Latin Poets*
FRHist	*Fragments of the Roman Historians*
G&R	*Greece and Rome*
GFF	*Giornale filologico ferrarese*
GLP	*Graecolatina Pragensia*
Gramm.	R. A. Kaster, ed., *C. Suetoni Tranquilli De uita Caesarum libri VIII et De grammaticis et rhetoribus liber.* Oxford, 2016.
GRBS	*Greek, Roman and Byzantine Studies*
Hauthal	F. Hauthal, ed., *Acronis et Porphyrionis commentarii in Q. Horatium Flaccum*, vol. 2. Berlin, 1866.
Herz.-Schm.	R. Herzog and P. Schmidt, eds., *Handbuch der lateinischen Literatur der Antike*, 8 vols. Munich, 1989–.
Holder	A. Holder, ed., *Pomponi Porfyrionis Commentum in Horatium Flaccum.* Innsbruck, 1894.
HSCP	*Harvard Studies in Classical Philology*
ICS	*Illinois Classical Studies*
Ihm	M. Ihm, ed., *C. Suetoni Tranquilli opera*, vol. 1. Leipzig, 1907.
IJCT	*International Journal of the Classical Tradition*
JAH	*Journal of Ancient History*
JHS	*Journal of Hellenic Studies*
JIES	*Journal of Indo-European Studies*
JPh	*Journal of Philology*
JRS	*Journal of Roman Studies*
JThS	*Journal of Theological Studies*
LCM	*Liverpool Classical Monthly*
LEC	*Les études classiques*
MAT	*Memorie dell'Accademia delle scienze di Torino*
MCr	*Museum criticum*
MD	*Materiali e discussioni per l'analisi dei testi classici*
MH	*Museum Helveticum*
MIL	*Memorie dell'Istituto Lombardo*
MLQ	*Modern Language Quarterly*

Mooney	G. W. Mooney, ed., *C. Suetoni Tranquilli De Vita Caesarum libri VII–VIII: Galba, Otho, Vitellius, Divus Vespasianus, Divus Titus, Domitianus.* Dublin, 1930.
N&Q	*Notes and Queries*
NECJ	*New England Classical Journal*
NTS	*New Testament Studies*
OLD	P. G. W. Glare, ed., *Oxford Latin Dictionary*, 2 vols., 2nd ed. Oxford, 2012.
Op.	F. Della Corte, *Opuscula*, 14 vols. Genoa, 1971–2000.
PACA	*Proceedings of the African Classical Association*
Paid.	J. Taillardat, ed., *Suétone: Περὶ βλασφημιῶν, Περὶ παιδιῶν.* Paris, 1967.
PAPhS	*Proceedings of the American Philosophical Society*
PCA	*Proceedings of the Classical Association*
PCPS	*Proceedings of the Cambridge Philological Society*
PLLS	*Papers of the Langford Latin Seminar*
Poet.	A. Rostagni, ed., *Svetonio: De poetis e biografi minori.* Turin, 1944.
PP	*La parola del passato*
PVS	*Proceedings of the Virgil Society*
RAL	*Atti della Accademia nazionale dei Lincei*
RCCM	*Rivista di cultura classica e medioevale*
RD	*Revue historique de droit français et étranger*
RE	A. Pauly, G. Wissowa, and W. Krolls, eds., *Realencyclopädie der classischen Aletertumswissenschaft*, 86 vols. Stuttgart, 1893–2000.
REA	*Revue des études anciennes*
Reiff.	A. Reifferscheid, ed., *C. Suetoni Tranquilli praeter Caesarum libros reliquiae.* Leipzig, 1860.
REL	*Revue des études latines*
REMA	*Revue des études militaires anciennes*
RFIC	*Rivista di filologia e di istruzione classica*
RFP	*Revue française de psychanalyse*
RhM	*Rheinisches Museum für Philologie*
RIL	*Rendiconti dell'Istituto Lombardo*
Roth	C. L. Roth, ed., *C. Suetoni Tranquilli quae supersunt omnia.* Leipzig, 1858.
RP	R. Syme, *Roman Papers*, 7 vols., ed. E. Badian and A. R. Birley. Oxford, 1979–91.
RSA	*Rivista storica dell'antichità*
Sch.-Hos.	M. Schanz, ed., *Geschichte der römischen Literatur bis zum Gesetzgebungswerk des Kaisers Justinian*, 4 vols., rev. ed. C. Hosius and G. Krüger. Munich, 1914–35.
SCI	*Scripta classica Israelica*

SicGymn	*Siculorum gymnasium*
SIFC	*Studi italiani di filologia classica*
SKAW	*Sitzungsberichte der Kaiserlichen Akademie der Wissenschaften*
SLLRH	C. Deroux, ed., *Studies in Latin Literature and Roman History*, 17 vols. Brussels, 1979–2018.
SO	*Symbolae Osloenses*
SPh	*Studies in Philology*
StudUrb	*Studi urbinati*
SyllClass	*Syllecta classica*
TAPA	*Transactions of the American Philological Association*
TAPS	*Transactions of the American Philosophical Society*
ThZ	*Theologische Zeitschrift*
TLS	*Times Literary Supplement*
TRHS	*Transactions of the Royal Historical Society*
VChr	*Vigiliae Christianae*
Vita Hor.	G. Brugnoli, ed., *Suetonio: Vita di Orazio*. Rome, 1968.
Vita Verg.	G. Brugnoli and F. Stok, eds., *Vitae Vergilianae antiquae*. Rome, 1997.
VL	*Vita Latina*
WJA	*Würzburger Jahrbücher für die Altertumswissenschaft*
WZRostock	*Wissenschaftliche Zeitschrift der Universität Rostock*
ZAnt	*Živa Antika*
ZJKF	*Zprávy Jednoty Klasickaych Filologu*
ZPE	*Zeitschrift für Papyrologie und Epigraphik*

Introduction
Suetonius' Early Life in Pliny's *Letters*

As he states in *My Thoughts*, Montesquieu considered the two greatest masterpieces of ancient literature to be Plutarch's account of the assassination of Julius Caesar (*Caes.* 63–6), which Shakespeare used as a source for his play about the dictator, and the death scene in Suetonius' *Life* of the emperor Nero (*Ner.* 47–9), about which Montesquieu wrote: 'one is astonished to see Nero forced by degrees to kill himself, without any reason that constrains him, and yet so that he has no power to avoid it.'[1] The political philosopher's admiration for the latter biography was more fully expressed in his unfinished *Essay on Taste*, which was posthumously published in 1757 two years after Montesquieu's own death:

> Suetonius describes the crimes of Nero with a cold-bloodedness that surprises us, making us almost believe that he does not feel sufficient horror for what he describes; but he suddenly changes his style, and says: 'The universe having suffered such a monster for fourteen years, at last abandoned him' (*tale monstrum per quatuordecim annos perpessus terrarum orbis tandem desitituit*). This produces in the mind different kinds of surprise: we are surprised at the author's change of style; at the discovery of his different manner of thinking; at his method of relating in so few words one of the greatest revolutions that

---

1 Montesquieu 1879, 159 (my trans.). For Suetonius' death of Nero as one of his greatest passages, see Rolfe 1913, 220 n. 63; Steidle 1951, 93; Kendall 1965, 36; Townend 1967, 93; Bradley 1978, 243, 273; Goodyear 1982, 661; Baldwin 1983, 510; Wallace-Hadrill 1983, 11; Lounsbury 1987, 63; Sansone 1993, 179; Hägg 2012, 219; Hurley 2013, 40; 2014b, 29; Damon 2018, 112. However, honourable mention is given to the description of Vitellius' ascendancy (*Vit.* 7–8) by Pausch (2004, 287), while Oakley (2009b, 209) considers that emperor's death scene (*Vit.* 16–17) to rival any episode in Suetonius, even if Tacitus' version is generally considered superior; see below, Chapter 32. Translations of Suetonius and Pliny in this introduction are taken from the Loeb editions of Rolfe 1913–14 and Radice 1969, respectively.

ever happened. Thus the soul finds a vast number of different sensations that combine to move it, and inspire it with pleasure.[2]

This astute description of *un sang-froid* ('a cold-bloodedness') in Suetonius' writing from early modern Europe has found a counterpart in the judgement of subsequent critics right up to the present century, who have variously characterized the biographer's prose style as 'neutral', 'businesslike', 'deadpan', 'heartless', 'disenchanted', 'contempt', 'cool', 'dry', 'factual', 'absence of emotion', 'pedantic', and 'calm'.[3] The biographer's non-reactive, matter-of-fact tone is maintained throughout the *Caesars*, as he reports rather lewd and sometimes even quite gruesome details as though they were entirely unsurprising facts. Due to this impression of his writing style, Goodyear drew a connection between Suetonius' detached voice and what he saw as a vacuity in his thinking: 'he seems largely indifferent to niceties of style ... it is clear that he possesses no original mind.'[4]

However, as Montesquieu realized, behind the controlled iciness of Suetonius' published words, there was a passionate viewpoint, restrained into a carefully articulated position that can often surprise us by its uniqueness and specificity. After many pages of an apparently monotone and unmodulated authorial voice that gives the appearance of impartiality,[5] despite the subtle effects of occasionally varied sentence structure and prose rhythm, all of a sudden, he will startle us by interjecting a rather opinionated statement, which ironically belies the overall seemingly even-handed presentation of character in the biography up to that point. In this introduction, I shall examine how these conflicting impressions of the biographer are portrayed in the earliest source that we have for his own character, the surviving *Letters* of his friend and colleague Pliny the Younger. But first, we must assess the previous literary criticism on these two authors.

Pliny and Suetonius

Syme published a paper in 1960 that was rather questionably entitled 'Pliny's Less Successful Friends', in which he summarized what is known

---

2 The translation is adapted from Montesquieu 1777, 134. For the original French text, see id. 1879, 129. On this effect of Suetonius' style, cf. Simcox 1883, 214, describing the 'startling plainness' of the similar turning point at *Iul.* 76.1; also Grau 2017, 272–4. For the similarly cold-blooded style of Lucan, whose extant biography was written by Suetonius, see Bartsch 1997, 91–3; Williams 2017, 99–101. On the stylistic comparison between Suetonius and Joyce, see Power 2016, 288 n. 1; Buckwald 2020, 119–21.
3 Simcox 1883, 218; Rolfe 1913, 220 (also Butler and Cary 1927, viii; Wallace-Hadrill 1983, 19); Carney 1968, 11 (also Grant 1970, 335; Coleman 2011, 342); Southern 1970, 183 = 2004, 19; Grant 1979, 8; Lounsbury 1987, 103; Burke 1993, 70; Averintsev 2002, 26; Crompton 2003, 101; Damon 2014, 44; 2020, 132; Powell 2017b, 178, respectively.
4 Goodyear 1982, 662–3.
5 On Suetonius' authorial persona, see Dubuisson 2003; Duchêne 2016.

of Suetonius from the *Letters* of Pliny as bespeaking a hopelessly timid character:

> There was a certain Suetonius Tranquillus, born about the year 70, a man of studious tastes and hampered by doubts about the life and career he ought to elect. He thought of the bar, and was going to plead a case, but was frightened by a dream and begged Pliny to have the hearing postponed (I. 18). In the year 101 Pliny wrote on his behalf to Neratius Marcellus, and got him a military tribunate (III. 8). Neratius was governor of Britain at this time. But Suetonius did not want the post, and it was made over to one of his relatives. That was not all. He had been engaged in a piece of literary work, but was afraid to publish (V. 10) ... The notices in Pliny convey the strong impression that this man was not going to make his mark anywhere. Pliny had done his best.[6]

Later in the essay, Syme went further, referring to him as 'the scholarly and diffident Suetonius Tranquillus', which suggests that Pliny's portrayal of his friend was that of a stereotypically shy and insecure writer better suited to books than real life.[7] This caricature of Suetonius as indecisive and unsure of himself has since met with great opposition from experts on the biographer, who convincingly conclude that, on the contrary, Suetonius must have been an especially outgoing and public figure, on the basis of historical evidence such as the Hippo inscription, which records his official posts. These posts involved much more skill than that of the average Roman administrative bureaucrat, including eventually working directly with the emperor in high matters of governance, and even travelling with him abroad.[8]

---

6 Syme 1960, 364 = *RP* 2.479. This is a good example of what Lounsbury (2006, 79) described as 'the old abuse, the old condescension' that has long bedevilled Suetonian studies, even going so far as to call such scholars the 'enemies of Suetonius'; see id. 1991, 3778. Cf. Pelling 2015, 208 generally on Syme's 'knowing, seen-it-all-and-seen-through-most-of-it voice'.

7 Syme 1960, 377 = *RP* 2.493. Cf. id. 1981, 115 = *RP* 3.1347: 'A diffident character or hesitance to take decisions'; McDermott 1980, 494 on Plin. *Ep.* 5.10. See also Townend 1961, 102: 'his quiet and scholarly character'.

8 Baldwin 1983, 13; Bradley 1985, 264–5; 1991, 3712; Lounsbury 1986–7, 161; 1987, 9. On Suetonius' offices and what they seem to have entailed, see Houston 2014, 235–6, 240–2; also Davenport 2019, 466 on the very public nature of his appointment to the priesthood of Vulcan, which the biographer probably held under Trajan (although Davenport is confused, since this post was as *pontifex*, not *flamen* – little is known of Suetonius' flaminate; for conjectures on the latter, see Grosso 1959, 267 n. 21 with bibliography): 'When we consider the duties undertaken by the *flamen Volcanalis*, Suetonius the biographer becomes less of a solitary bookworm, and instead emerges as a vital participant in the religious life of the *sacra urbs*.' He was thus far more than a 'paper-pusher' (Geue 2020, 214). Bruun and Edmondson's (2015, 18) reading *[p]on[t(ifici)] Volca[n]i* in the inscription that was discovered at Hippo Regius in 1952 actually fits better with the position of the 'i' that can be seen on the fragment above it than the previous conjecture

Nevertheless, this evidence has not prevented Leach from attempting to perpetuate, and indeed advance, Syme's theory by proposing that Suetonius may never have published the work to which Pliny looks forward in *Letters* 5.10 at all, thanks to his supposedly 'diffident' character.[9]

Nor does this kind of charge against Suetonius stop there. It drove Syme himself to believe that the biographer's greatest work, the *Lives of the Caesars*, was not even of his own making, but entirely a response to the work of Tacitus, to whom the biographer allegedly viewed himself as unequal, and worthy only of writing a 'supplement'.[10] Such prejudice against Suetonius continues even today, with his original contributions attributed to his contemporaries, and the credit for his ingenuity removed to other writers who have long been considered more creative by scholars. It is still believed by some, for example, that his choice to write the *Caesars* may in fact have been inspired instead by the older biographer Plutarch – a speculation which, despite having not a shred of real evidence to support it, nonetheless serves to undermine the autonomy and individuality of Suetonius.[11] Such a reading of Suetonius' text finds another proponent in Roche, who interprets a passage in the author's *Life* of Domitian as motivated out of a need to 'correct' Pliny's *Panegyric*, which there is absolutely no evidence that he had even read, but which Roche thinks he must have greatly admired. He builds a similar case to Syme's, again using the presentation of Suetonius by Pliny:

> Pliny's letters attest to their respectful friendship over three decades. We glimpse the two men consulting on matters of rhetoric (*Ep.* 1.18). We observe Pliny reading Suetonius' work, and urging him to publish (*Ep.* 5.10). We are made privy to Pliny seeking advice from Suetonius about the etiquette of recitation (*Ep.* 9.34); and of Pliny's regard for the biographer as scholar (*Ep.* 10.94–5). It would be surprising, then, had Suetonius not been familiar with Pliny's speeches.[12]

---

[p]on[t(ifici)] Volca[nal]i by Marec and Pflaum (1952, 78), which was never certain; *pace* Townend 1961, 100 and n. 4. It has been argued by Wardle 2002 (also Pagán 2012b, 89; both anticipated by Marec 1954, 391–2; Townend 1961, 107) that this location in North Africa was the biographer's birthplace, but the town may have given him such an honour for any number of reasons; cf. Bruun and Edmondson 2015, 17.

9   Leach 2012, reviving Sherwin-White's (1966, 337–8) idea that this work was a volume of verse, which Suetonius is not even known to have written. *Contra*, see Reeve 2011, 209 n. 12; below, Chapter 1.

10 See below, Chapter 25. However, Tacitean scholarship has now accepted my argument in that chapter, first published in 2014, against the widespread belief in Suetonius' use of Tacitus, which had been tenaciously held by scholars for more than a century – a major reversal in its own right; see e.g. Shaw 2015, 89 n. 77; Ash 2018, 7 (and contrast the completely opposite position taken by her in her earlier commentary: ead. 2007, 30 n. 84).

11 See e.g. Hägg 2012, 240–1; Geiger 2014, 302; Schropp 2017; Gibson 2018, 404; cf. Desideri 2017, 316. *Contra*, see below, p. 199, n. 71 with bibliography.

12 Roche 2018, 147–8.

Like Syme, he then ventures out on a crumbing limb, arguing that Suetonius was 'an engaged reader of Pliny's speech':

> To allude to a text is to give to it or recognise its cultural authority. In the act of correcting Pliny's application of Domitian's famous utterance, Suetonius marks the *Panegyricus* as a privileged repository of information about the imperial past.[13]

The underlying assumption, as usual, is that Suetonius was acutely aware of his contemporaries, a view which espouses the influence of Syme's tired opinion that Suetonius was not his own man. It does not allow for the possibility that he could not have cared less for Pliny's speech, the publication of which in book form afforded no hot-blooded impulse whatsoever to procure a copy. After all, the literary respect, so obvious on the part of Pliny for Suetonius, may not have been mutual. We know for a fact that Pliny was a great reader of Suetonius' *Lives*, and even announced his forthcoming *Illustrious Men* in his own verses, because he tells us so (*Ep.* 5.10).[14] Apart from the biography of his uncle Pliny the Elder in that collection, which Suetonius might have written even if they had not been friends, what actual evidence is there at all that the biographer ever admired his writings in return? Some have tenuously hypothesized that Suetonius may have edited Book 10 of the *Letters*, which was posthumously published.[15] But beyond this pure speculation, there is no trace of Suetonius' awareness of Pliny's collection within his own oeuvre.

Roche's proposed reminiscence of Pliny's *Panegyric* in Suetonius, a tortuous 'window allusion', may be swiftly discounted.[16] He presumes that Suetonius alludes to an earlier allusion in the first place by Pliny to Suetonius' own source, the emperor Domitian, who is reported to have said that 'he had conferred [the senate's] power on both his father and brother, and that they had but returned him his own' (*et patri se et fratri imperium dedisse,*

---

13 Ibid. 159. Roche had previously been more restrained in his comparison of these two texts; contrast id. 2011, 9–10, 12–13.
14 My view as set out below in Chapter 1, which first appeared in 2010, that the *Illustrious Men* is indeed the work discussed by Pliny in *Letters* 5.10 has since been accepted in *The Cambridge Companion to Latin Love Elegy*; see Lee-Stecum 2013, 68, who follows my date of AD 105–10 for the biographical collection; cf. Elder and Mullen 2019, 273. The compelling evidence for my overall reconstruction of the chronology of Suetonius' works besides the *Caesars* has been questioned on misguided grounds by Wardle (2014, 3–4; cf. id. 2020, 72; Elder and Mullen 2019, 231; Whitton 2019a, 24, 99 n. 130), but here is not the place for a rebuttal, since I shall treat this subject fully elsewhere.
15 See e.g. Matthews 2010, 103–6; Gibson and Morello 2012, 252–3; Harrill 2017, 285; each with earlier bibliography.
16 On the term 'window allusion', which implies a secondary allusion to an intermediary source, see Thomas 1986, 188–9. For legitimate examples in Suetonius, see MacRae 2015; below, Chapter 14; in Pliny, Baraz 2012a, 110–13 on *Ep.* 1.18.

illos sibi reddidisse, Dom. 13.1). This is thought to recall Pliny's statement
to Trajan about that emperor's father: 'he gave you supreme power and you
returned it to him' (*ille tibi imperium dedit, tu illi reddidisti, Pan.* 6.4).
Since Roche spends much of his essay enumerating the reasons why readers might disbelieve him – including the more sensible conclusion that the
biographer is simply reporting a well-known saying by the subject of his
Life, to which Pliny independently alludes – and cites some of my own refutations of such allusions, it is unnecessary to rehearse fully here the general
weakness of his claim.[17] The difficulty lies in his attempt to identify an
intertextual relationship between Suetonius and the *Panegyric* without first
having a single strong allusion to establish that relationship as probable, if
not an explicit statement of the author's familiarity with the text in question. It is enough to repeat my paraphrase of Momigliano's old dictum that
even many bad allusions can never amount to one good one.[18] In contrast
to Pliny, who delighted in his friends' publications, Suetonius was cold-
blooded in his neglect of the fellow writers of his age, including his personal
acquaintances; in this matter, he was hardly 'diffident', but instead entirely
decisive and consistent.[19]

From this survey of the current *status quaestionis* on the relationship
between Pliny and Suetonius, one thing is clear: the letters themselves obviously warrant closer examination, in order that we might discover the
origin of Syme's incorrect notion of the biographer as a bookish and intim-
idated researcher susceptible to being awed by recent masterpieces, which
has resulted in so many misreadings of his text. Obliterating this misconception once and for all is an essential step before we can better understand
the biographer's writings without the distortion of bias. First of all, the
earliest Plinian letter that we have involving Suetonius, *Letters* 1.18, does
not describe a dream before his very first trial, as has often been baselessly
assumed by Syme and others.[20] He is not merely contemplating a life at the
bar, but already pleading cases at this point *c.* AD 96–7, being by now in
his late twenties.[21] Suetonius had almost certainly been a seasoned product of the declamatory schools (*scholae*), a specialized training beyond the

17 But see e.g. Chapter 15 below, first published in 2014, which goes uncited by Roche 2018.
    Roche's proposed allusion is accepted by Whitton 2019b, 339 n. 2.
18 Momigliano 1968–9, 429 = 1975, 98. Cf. below, pp. 184–5.
19 For Suetonius' preference, which was quite the opposite of Pliny's, for authors of earlier
    periods, see Gibson 2014. The recent historian Tacitus was also ignored by Suetonius; see
    below, Chapter 25.
20 Cf. Townend 1961, 99; Cizek 1977, 9. Syme had been anticipated in this false assumption
    by Macé 1900, 59–64; Mooney 1930, 5–6; Ailloud 1931–2, 1.v; Della Corte 1958, 11,
    229. Nor do I see how Duchêne (2016, 286) is able to infer from this letter that 'he tried
    his hand at the courts, but he does not seem to have been very good at it.' *Letters* 1.18 is
    further discussed below.
21 For the date of this letter, see Sherwin-White 1966, 27–8. Suetonius' date of birth *c.*
    AD 70 can be inferred from his own personal references (*Gramm.* 4.6, *Ner.* 57.2, *Dom.*
    12.2); see Hurley 2001, 2.

standard Roman education, as implied by the use of the term *scholasticus* for him in another correspondence from the same book of Pliny's *Letters* (1.24.4).[22] It is this latter text that has plainly caused the most confusion about Suetonius' personality, and to which we must now turn.

Letters 1.24

What has not yet been realized is that in *Letters* 1.24, Pliny pokes fun at Suetonius' name Tranquillus, creating wordplay on the 'tranquillity' of the idyllic country scene that he describes. This literary game may possibly have been noticed by a few astute readers, including Henderson, who makes the same pun himself in reference to this letter:

> Whether or not Suetonius could find a steer toward tranquillity in the property market, in 1.24 Pliny has turned the 'could-you-see-your-way note to a friend for a friend' routine into a compactly collusive sketch of the economics/ergonomics of life-style.[23]

We might also point to the much earlier lines on Suetonius in a nineteenth-century sonnet entitled 'Tranquillus' by de Heredia, which also takes its inspiration ultimately from Pliny's text:

> Here, far from Rome, he came each fall to see
> The softest, deepest blue the heavens can wear,
> And from his elms to reap the vintage there.
> His life flowed on in calm tranquillity.[24]

But to my knowledge, no one has yet explicitly proposed that this pun exists in the Plinian letter in the first place. Even though Woodman has perceived a pun on Tacitus' name in Pliny's word *silentium* in a different letter

---

22 See Lounsbury 1987, 19–21; Bradley 1991, 3706–7; de Coninck 1991, 3687; Méthy 2009, 223–4. More sceptical is Sherwin-White 1966, 141 (ad loc.). The epithet does not imply, contrary to Macé (1900, 51–3; cf. Townend 1961, 99–100; Cizek 1977, 35; Mehl 2011, 166; Elder and Mullen 2019, 226 n. 14), that Suetonius was a *grammaticus*; see Kaster 1995, xxii n. 3; Lefèvre 2009, 164 n. 211. To argue, as Damon (2014, 40) does, that the context of the letter in which it appears, where Pliny is in search of a country estate on Suetonius' behalf, hints that this appellation conveys the biographer's contentment with quiet learning is to put the cart before the horse: it is, after all, precisely because he is an advocate that he needs a respite from his public responsibilities, not because he seeks quiet that he is a *scholasticus*. I am no more convinced by Cova (1966, 85; cf. Hoffer 1999, 223–4) that the word evinces Pliny's 'sense of superiority' to Suetonius, which follows the same circular logic as Syme and Damon.

23 Henderson 2002, 30. See also his translation of *Ep.* 1.24 quoted below, n. 27.

24 de Heredia 1898, 71. Cf. the anonymous contemporary couplet on Philemon Holland's first English translation of Suetonius in 1606: 'Philemon with his translation does so fill us; / He will not let Suetonius be Tranquillus.' It is quoted by e.g. Duff 1916, 167.

addressed to that historian (*Ep.* 1.6.2),[25] the only time that such a pun on Suetonius' name in the collection has been suggested is by Hoffer, but with regard to *Letters* 5.10 (on which, more in a moment).[26] As it turns out, there is much textual evidence to support such linguistic allusion not only in *Letters* 1.24, but across Pliny's whole Suetonian correspondence.

Let us begin with the missive at hand. In this letter, Pliny acts as a middle-man for Suetonius, negotiating the purchase of a suburban villa on his behalf, and listing several desired qualities for the estate itself. Here is the pertinent sentence:

> in hoc autem agello, si modo arriserit pretium, Tranquilli mei *stomachum* multa *sollicitant*, uicinitas urbis, opportunitas uiae, mediocritas uillae, modus ruris, qui auocet magis quam distringat.

> There is indeed much about this property *to whet* Tranquillus' *appetite* if only the price suits him: easy access to Rome, good communications, a modest house, and sufficient land for him to enjoy without taking up too much of his time.

> (Plin. *Ep.* 1.24.3)

It is safe to claim that the italicized words have been universally misinterpreted by scholars and translators, who have taken them to mean 'rouse his appetite' (*OLD* s.v. *sollicito* 4b).[27] However, it is better construed in the sense of 'shake up' (1b). Suetonius, as portrayed here by Pliny, is not so much enticed, as worried. We may compare Horace's use of the exact same phrase: 'when abundant evils *turn* the anxious *stomach*' (*mala copia quando / aegrum* sollicitat stomachum, *Sat.* 2.2.43). Pliny's line should thus be rendered instead as 'there are many things that are *unsettling* my friend Tranquillus' *stomach*.' The qualities listed by Pliny are not points of attraction that the estate already holds, but rather the prospective buyer's demands. This makes better sense, because Pliny does not yet know anything about the estate, aside from hearing that a friend of the addressee Baebius has a modest one for sale. What he does know, however, is the kind of place sought by Suetonius and the concerns that are on his mind. Suetonius needs no rousing, for he has already been roused to impose conditions

---

25 Woodman 2009d, 32 = 2012, 244. For other proposed puns on names in Pliny, see Whitton 2010, 132; 2012, 356; 2013, 17, 67, 75; 2019a, 347.

26 Hoffer 1999, 213: 'even without dreams to scare him Suetonius is excessively cautious and diffident (5.10); a pun on his name Tranquillus, Mr. Calm, may lurk in the background.' Hoffer's proposal has been influential: e.g. Lefèvre 2009, 166 n. 219; Baraz 2012a, 114 n. 29.

27 Cf. Hoffer 1999, 221: 'appeal to the appetite of my friend Tranquillus'; Walsh 2006, 28: 'excite my friend Tranquillus' appetite'; Henderson 2002, 25: '*detranquillize* my friend Mr Calm's passions' (original italics); Leach 2012, 91: 'many features of the farm are suited to Suetonius' disposition.'

on his property search. The explicit mention of his name Tranquillus within this sentence is certainly not by coincidence, but it works for ironic effect, underscoring his friend's *un-calm* state.

This new reading now draws into question the meaning of the letter's ending, which is also the final passage of Pliny's Book 1:

> haec tibi exposui, quo magis scires, quantum esset ille mihi ego tibi debiturus, si praediolum istud, *quod commendatur his dotibus,* tam salubriter emerit ut paenitentiae locum non relinquat. uale.

> I am writing this to show you how much he will be in my debt and I in yours if he is able to buy this small estate *with all its advantages* at a reasonable price which will leave him no room for regrets.
>
> (Plin. *Ep.* 1.24.4)

Pliny places a second emphasis on Suetonius' express wish for an affordable purchase, in the hopes that Baebius will do his best to influence the owner's asking price. In light of our reinterpretation of the letter, the use of the relative clause *quod commendatur his dotibus* within the conditional protasis represents not so much what Pliny knows to be inherently true ('all *its* advantages'), but rather what he *hopes* is true. A more pointed translation might even be '*so long as it has these* advantages', since, as we have said, Pliny thus far knows only that it is a small estate (*agellus*). He relies on Baebius to ensure that it is graced with the attributes he mentions, and falls within Suetonius' economic range. Besides the clichéd themes in this letter of a writer's idyllic country house and an equestrian's modest home,[28] there is also the suggestion of Suetonius as a conscientious rather than casual buyer, with many needs that must be met, as brought out by our new reading. Suetonius is by no means shown to be pleased by the estate's tranquil attractions, as Plinian scholars have presumed. Rather, he is cool-headed and calmly fixed on particular goals.

This pun on Suetonius' name Tranquillus can also be supported by the word's associations as an adjective in both these authors. Pliny refers elsewhere in his *Letters* to the 'peaceful time' (*tranquillitati saeculi, Ep.* 10.3a.2) of the emperor Trajan, and Suetonius likewise reserves his only two uses of this word for his biography of Augustus, whose reign was similarly distinguished by its peace: once for the peaceful old age to which his grandfather lived (*Aug.* 2.2), and again for the emperor's calm expression (79.1).[29] Syme argued that Suetonius by the same token may have owed his name to being born

---

28 See, respectively, Leach 2012, 91–2; Armstrong 2012, 67. The houses or country villas of famous writers are also ironically a biographical theme in Suetonius; see Gibson and Morello 2012, 227; below, pp. 54–5. For imperial residences as revelatory of humbleness in the *Caesars,* see Siwicki 2020, 254–5; below, pp. 54–5 on *Aug.* 72.1.

29 Howard and Jackson 1922, s.v. *tranquillus.* On Augustus' peaceful era, see e.g. de Souza 2008, 76–106.

at the start of the peaceful rule of Vespasian.[30] Pliny seems to evoke the more specific idea of tranquil repose in the estate letter when he claims that scholars such as Suetonius wish to purchase farms in order to 'clear their head, refresh their eyes' (*releuare caput, reficere oculos, Ep.* 1.24.4), and several of the other appearances of *tranquillus* in the *Letters* are in similar contexts of retirement and leisure (*Ep.* 2.1.4, 3.7.9, 4.23.4, 7.25.2), or else refer to pleasant weather (2.17.27, 8.20.6) or a person's calm disposition (3.20.4). The easygoing scene of a simple country lifestyle in *Letters* 1.24 is thus ironically juxtaposed with Suetonius' less than tranquil approach to his property search, and our new reading of *Letters* 1.24 bolsters the view that this theme is a literary game by Pliny.

Letters 1.18 and 3.8

Just as *Letters* 1.24 makes a joke about the excessive concern of a man named Tranquillus, with the phrase *Tranquilli mei stomachum multa sol-licitant* certainly containing a humorous pun on Suetonius' name, *Letters* 1.18 takes as its subject Suetonius' agitation from a bad dream. So Pliny writes of Suetonius as 'disquieted' (*perterritum*, §1) at the very start of the letter, a probable pun on *tranquillus* right at his initial introduction in the collection.[31] Pliny compares Suetonius' situation to circumstances from his own past, which he says could have 'distressed his mind' (*excutere mentem*, §3) in the same way. The close of the letter creates the same pun when Pliny writes that postponing the case is 'indeed a pain, but nonetheless possible' (*aegre quidem sed tamen potest*, §6). Ironically, the vexation here is Pliny's, not Suetonius', for he is the one who will have to arrange the adjournment, but he expresses his resentment through a pun that lends closure to the letter by echoing its beginning, with a last jibe at the addressee.[32] Pliny is reluctant to grant Suetonius' request, but he will do so if necessary.

---

30 Syme 1977, 44 = *RP* 3.1053. Suetonius' name has more recently been viewed as an indication that he was born earlier during the wars of AD 69, when peace was needed; see Ash 2016, 216. However, the name's appropriateness for the son of a man named Suetonius Laetus (*Otho* 10.1) may discount both arguments; see *OLD* s.v. *laetus* 5, 6a: 'prosperous', 'propitious', with Wallace-Hadrill 1983, 3. For Suetonius' date of birth, see above, n. 21.

31 See Noguerol 2003, 160; cf. Baraz 2012a, 114. The word is rare and emphatic in Pliny; see Hoffer 1999, 212.

32 On this device of closure in poetry, see Smith 1968, esp. 27, 163–6. As with many of Pliny's addressees, there is an implicit recognition here of the biographer's erudition with regard to the application of well-known verses – as confirmed by his interest in adapted Homeric quotations (Berthet 1978; Aparicio 2008), such as Augustus' reinvention of the scene where Hector reproves Paris for idling with Helen instead of fighting in battle (*Aug.* 65.4 ~ *Il.* 3.40) – when Pliny writes εἷς οἰωνὸς ἄριστος ἀμύνεσθαι περὶ πάτρης ('The singular best omen is to fight for one's country', *Ep.* 1.18.4 ~ *Il.* 12.243). In a way similar to Suetonius' dream itself, this line is especially pliable, not only having been used by Cicero (*Att.* 2.3.3–4; see Baraz 2012a, 110), but also famously misquoted by Pyrrhus (Plut. *Pyrrh.* 29.2). It was therefore even more widely famous than for its original context

A similar annoyance may be sensed in *Letters* 3.8, where Suetonius is witnessed requesting that Pliny transfer a military tribunate in Northern Britain to his relative Caesennius Silvanus.[33] Again, Pliny starts with the usual pun:

> facis pro cetera *reuerentia* quam mihi praetas, quod tam *sollicite* petis ut tribunatum, quem a Neratio Marcello clarissimo uiro impetraui tibi, in Caesennium Siluanum propinquum tuum transferam.

> You act in line with the usual *reverence* that you exhibit towards me when you ask so *anxiously* that a tribunate, which I procured for you from the illustrious man Neratius Marcellus, be transferred by me to your kinsman Caesennius Silvanus.
>
> (Plin. *Ep.* 3.8.1)

We are never told the reason for this request by Suetonius, so that Syme's inference of 'doubts about the life and career he ought to elect' seems baseless. If Suetonius had intimated any such reason, Pliny would no doubt have seized upon it in order to develop further his theme of alleged Suetonian disquiet, but significantly he does not. The biographer proudly tells us of his own father's holding of this very same imperial post during the tumultuous year of the four emperors (*Otho* 10.1), so that he must have had a good reason for declining it. No less relevant to point out is the detail that the appointment was arranged for Suetonius by Pliny, perhaps without the biographer's consent.

It therefore may not be that this incident reflects a change of mind by Suetonius, but rather the simple inconvenience of an untimely post that he had not sought in the first place. The biographer probably had other commitments at the time. Pliny's disavows any resentment, but he does not completely disguise his wish that Suetonius had accepted his gesture:

> mihi autem sicut iucundissimum ipsum te tribunum, ita non minus gratum alium per te uidere. neque enim esse congruens arbitror ... huic pietatis titulis inuidere ...

> Yet just as I would have been delighted to see you tribune, I am no less pleased to see another on your behalf. For I do not consider it right ... to begrudge the honour of this dutifulness ...
>
> (Plin. *Ep.* 3.8.2)

---

alone. I think it is fanciful to conclude that one of the aims of Pliny's Homeric allusion is to convey his social superiority to Suetonius; *pace* Fields 2020, 110. On Suetonius' own ironic inversions of epic poetry, see below, Chapters 11–12, 14–16, 23.

33 For annoyance in the tone of this letter, see Matthews 2010, 104–5; Leach 2012, 88–9, 92–3; Shelton 2013, 373, n. 125. It is lost on Davenport 2019, 275–6, who nonetheless rightly observes (326) that the biographer himself probably had little to gain from this post in terms of his career. For the location of the post, see Syme 1981, 106 = *RP* 3.1337; on Suetonius and Northern Britain, the preface to Power and Gibson 2014, v–vi.

The 'anxiousness' with which Suetonius wrote to Pliny may have been simply conventional, as Pliny seems to imply when he likens it to his typical displays of respect, while Pliny's tranquillity appears no less feigned. In reality, their positions were probably the opposite of what they appear in Pliny's characterization.[34] Pliny depicts the biographer as reluctant even to bother him, but a less subjective reading again yields a Suetonius who knows his own mind, much like his requirements for a country estate.

Pliny no doubt learned his lesson, and when he later writes to the emperor Trajan in *Letters* 10.94 to petition that the tax privileges of the *ius trium liberorum* be awarded to Suetonius, he is more likely doing so at his friend's explicit behest. The six letters of Pliny in which Suetonius figures reveal the biographer manoeuvring to get precisely what he wants: a delay in his court case (*Ep.* 1.18), a country villa with his specified conveniences and price (1.24), a transfer of an imperial post to a relative (3.8), an early promotion of his forthcoming work (5.10), recognition of his expertise in recitation (9.34), and a specially bestowed award of a tax exemption for his own household (10.94). Suetonius thus seems all too decisive in his desires, whereas it is Pliny who does not know whether to tell his friend to delay his court case or not, or whether to complement or threaten him so that he issues his publication. Pliny is the one who appears vexed and uncertain when it comes to Suetonius, not vice versa, and vexation is at any rate something of a *topos* in Pliny's *Letters*. It is important to remember that these letters are rather one-sided, and they often have more to do with Pliny than anything else. Suetonius' dream becomes an occasion to discuss Pliny's own first big case, and the Suetonius letters in general seem partly an opportunity for Pliny himself to have some literary fun at the expense of the biographer's name.

Letters 9.34

That the portrait of Suetonius' lack of calmness is anything more than wordplay projecting Pliny's own pains is a difficult proposition to accept. This emerges especially from the letter in which the epistolographer reverses the trope, *Letters* 9.34. In that letter, he begins by asking Suetonius to 'settle *my* anxiety' (*explica aestum* meum, §1) about whether or not to read his writings himself at a recitation, and this refrain recurs at the end of the letter as a closural device (§2).[35] Pliny creates an inversion of his first

---

34 This would seem to corroborate, at least in respect to the Suetonius letters, the overall thesis of Hoffer (1999) that real concerns generally underlie Pliny's optimistic authorial persona; cf. Strunk 2012 with bibliography on Pliny's 'pessimism'. It is hardly coincidental that the only letter addressed to Suetonius in which Pliny openly admits the opposite dynamic, *Letters* 9.34 (discussed below), falls within his 'darker' books. On Books 7–9 of the *Letters* as more revealing of Pliny's own troubles, see Gibson 2015.

35 For this device in poetry, see Smith 1968, 246.

letter to Suetonius in Book 1 about whether or not to try a case after a bad dream. The narrative of calming fears has come full circle, providing closure to Pliny's nine-book collection (since Book 10 is certainly independent of this cycle, whether or not it was edited by Pliny himself or posthumously by another hand such as Suetonius).[36] The additional detail of the possibility that the freedman whom Pliny considers employing to read his work might become 'unsettled' (*perturbatus*, §1) seems specifically designed by Pliny to play into his theme of disrupted and restored tranquillity that he develops throughout the letters on Suetonius; the pun is again palpably present at this point in the collection due to the addressee's sheer name at the top of the letter. At least in its published version, Pliny's artifice has taken on a life of its own, transcending his original need simply to know Suetonius' views on speaking style.[37]

Diffident or Cold-Blooded?

Suetonius is never described by Pliny in *Letters* 1.18, 1.24, or 3.8 as 'diffident', any more than he is so in *Letters* 5.10. In that letter, Pliny urges Suetonius to publish a long-awaited work, which the biographer is taking extra care in polishing. Much like the estate letter, it shows a Suetonius who is premeditated and calculated. In fact, Pliny even has to try to *instil* worry *in him* by joking threats. If anything, Suetonius is true to his name by being calm through undaunted perfectionism, rather than worrying. Syme characteristically overstated things when he claimed that Pliny's Suetonius is diffident, although Pliny no doubt plays on his name, perhaps taking his lead from one of his literary models, the poet Catullus, who also creates wordplay with his addressee's names.[38] In this context, the portrayal of his worries in these early books of the *Letters* is probably exaggerated for literary aims. We are overly beholden to Pliny for biographical information on the writers of his time,[39] and if we read between the lines for his facts rather than his artistic embellishment, we can give Suetonius much more credit as a shrewd professional than he has been afforded. Despite the pun on his name in the letter on his estate and other letters in the collection, Suetonius is shown, as in his own biographies, to be a rather cool customer.

---

36 On Book 10, see the references above, n. 15. Leach 2012, 96 sees a connection also back to another Suetonius letter: 'In Pliny's self-deprecating description of his own reading may well be a reprise of the *cunctator* of letter 5.10.'

37 However, the suggestion by Leach (2012, 95) that the scenario was entirely invented goes too far. Such readings were of great importance to Pliny; cf. *Ep.* 7.17, with Fantham 1999, 224–5.

38 See Hawkins 2011, 255. For Catullus as a model for Pliny, see below, p. 29, n. 35.

39 Cf. Griffin 1999, 141–2 = 2018, 250 on Tacitus. For discussions of Pliny and Suetonius, see the references in Gibson and Morello 2012, 304.

How much of Pliny's portrayal, then, should we take at face value as evidence for Suetonius? Without further context, we do not know, for example, whether Suetonius' dream was even real, or merely an excuse that allowed him to delay his case for some legal or political reason. Like Tacitus, Suetonius may offer us few glimpses of himself from his own works, but at least we may trust those works far more than Pliny as evidence for his life. The alleged diffidence in Pliny's portrait of Suetonius that was perceived by Syme is hard to reconcile with the writer who declares Julius Caesar 'rightly slain' (*iure caesus*, *Iul.* 76.1), and who calls Caligula no emperor, but instead a 'monster' (*monstro*, *Calig.* 22.1). Asking for advice is not antithetical to decisive judgement or clear-cut thinking, but rather a sign of prudence and a preference for consensus. It does not imply a lack of composure, any more than Pliny's seeking advice himself from Suetonius does in turn. As we have shown, the point of such jokes may actually be that Suetonius is often *too* calm, and Pliny wishes that he were otherwise. Suetonius may well have gone ahead with his court case (we certainly know that he published the *Illustrious Men*). But even if he did not proceed to trial, we cannot know the whole story. Sincerity has too often been assumed not only on the part of Pliny, but on that of Suetonius. Syme has regrettably over-influenced the way we have long seen Pliny, and the way we see Pliny has for too long determined how we read Suetonius. If we take the biographer's own writing at face value, it betrays a controlled persona, one which uses emotion sparingly to dramatic effect, especially in his justly famous death of Nero. His *Lives* themselves are thus probably a more reliable guide to his character, just as an emperor's writings are important to his biographical portrait in the *Caesars*. They say that style is the man, and Suetonius' style is cold-blooded.

Part I
Illustrious Men

1 Pliny, *Letters* 5.10 and the Literary Career of Suetonius[*]

The presumed chronology of Suetonius' works has always been centrally important to their interpretation. For example, Wallace-Hadrill builds his view of the *Lives of the Caesars* as ultimately the work of a 'scholar' on the belief that Suetonius first cut his teeth on minor scholarship and his collection of literary *Lives*, the *Illustrious Men*, before making his transition to imperial biography. In his view, the *Caesars* bear the mark of an author still interested in the scholarly themes of the *Illustrious Men*, and this order of composition can be held to explain much about the unique form and content of the *Lives* of emperors.[1]

However, the evidence for this view of the relationship between these two works has always been shaky, since the only firm date we have for Suetonius' works is the dedication of at least part of the *Caesars* sometime in 119–22.[2] No one has yet been able to prove that the *Illustrious Men* came first; scholars such as Syme simply assume it on a priori grounds: 'From that kind of erudite compilation, the transition seemed easy to biographies of emperors.'[3] Wallace-Hadrill bases his own viewpoint about the three phases of Suetonius' literary career on similar common sense:

> The book [*Illustrious Men*] is the fruit of long years of scholarly study, and ought to follow the bulk of the less demanding philological and antiquarian essays. In its wake, Suetonius could approach the *Caesars* with a mind already stocked with information; and this

[*] This chapter was first published in *JRS* 100 (2010), 140–62.

1 Wallace-Hadrill 1983, 43–66, 74–8, 92, 126–9, 132–3. The ancient *Life* of Virgil preserved by Donatus that is discussed in this chapter is generally accepted as that of Suetonius, with the exception of the interpolation at *Vita Verg.* 37–8, on which see Horsfall 1995, 3 with bibliography; cf. Power 2009, 302. All dates in this chapter are AD.

2 This is the period when Septicius Clarus was Prefect of the Praetorian Guard (SHA, *Hadr.* 9.5, 11.3), and when at least part, if not all, of the *Caesars* was dedicated to him, according to Lydus (*Mag.* 2.6). See Syme 1980b, 68–9 = *RP* 3.1283–5; Baldwin 1983, 39–41.

3 Syme 1980a, 110–11 = *RP* 3.1257; cf. id. 1958, 501.

is surely what he did, moving more or less directly from the lives of authors to Caesars.[4]

This reconstruction is made especially plausible if we think that publications aided Suetonius' rise through positions in the imperial service, and Wallace-Hadrill himself believes that Suetonius was promoted to his post *ab epistulis* sometime after Hadrian's assumption of power in 117 because of the *Illustrious Men*.[5]

Nevertheless, the reconstruction is open to valid criticism. First, very little is known about Suetonius' scholarly works, certainly not enough to characterize them all confidently as 'less demanding' than the two largely extant collections of *Lives*. Second, tangents between the two biographical collections, or between these and the scholarly works, could be explained in the opposite way too, that is, they represent the beginnings of Suetonius' interests in these topics, rather than their culmination; or, at any rate, research on a subject does not necessarily indicate prior publication on it.[6] The *Illustrious Men* could still have followed the *Caesars*.

In the first part of this paper, I wish to explore some allusions in a letter of Pliny the Younger written to Suetonius in either 105 or 106 (*Letters* 5.10) which establish that the composition of the *Illustrious Men* was well under way at that time. I shall then argue in the second part that Suetonius' award of the *ius trium liberorum* no later than 110 was probably due to a publication, which – since he was recently working on the *Illustrious Men* – is most likely that work. Finally, the paper's third part will draw an important implication from the discovery of this new date of the *Illustrious Men* for Suetonius' next publication, the *Caesars*: the latter may now have appeared in their entirety by 122, contrary to the widely held scholarly belief that only the first two *Caesars* were dedicated to Septicius Clarus during his Praetorian prefecture.

Letters 5.10

Scholars have long speculated on the possibility that Pliny's letter to the biographer Suetonius urging him to publish an unnamed work (*Ep.* 5.10)

---

4 Wallace-Hadrill 1983, 59; cf. ibid. 45: 'it might be a fair guess that he learnt his trade, so to speak, on Greek words, and gradually progressed to the accumulated learning evident in the *Caesars*.' For other speculations on the *Illustrious Men* as earlier than the *Caesars* based on a priori assumptions about the *Caesars*' larger scale and omission of details reported in the *Illustrious Men*, see e.g. Macé 1900, 300–1; Della Corte 1956, 94–5 = *Op.* 9.261–2; Syme 1958, 501; 1980a, 110–11, 124 = *RP* 3.1257, 1270; Townend 1982b, 1051; Lindsay 1994, 464; 1995a, 77; Bradley 1998, 6, 10; 2012, 1409; Bennett 2001, 136; Pausch 2004, 88, 238–9, 246; Paratore 2007, 193, 334 n. 63.

5 Wallace-Hadrill 1983, 7–8.

6 For this point, see Baldwin 1983, 383–4; Wardle 1994, 14–15; 1998a, 428–9.

actually refers to his *Illustrious Men.*[7] A possible allusion to Virgil in the letter may offer some help:

C. Plinius Suetonio Tranquillo suo s.

 libera tandem hendecasyllaborum meorum fidem, qui scripta tua communibus amicis spoponderunt. appellantur cotidie, efflagitantur, ac iam periculum est ne cogantur ad exhibendum formulam accipere. sum et ipse in edendo haesitator,[8] tu tamen meam quoque cunctationem tarditatemque uicisti. proinde aut rumpe iam moras aut caue ne eosdem istos libellos, quos tibi hendecasyllabi nostri blanditiis elicere non possunt, conuicio scazontes extorqueant. perfectum opus absolutumque est, *nec iam splendescit* lima sed *atteritur.* patere me uidere titulum tuum, patere audire describi legi uenire uolumina Tranquilli mei. aequum est nos in amore tam mutuo eandem percipere ex te uoluptatem, qua tu perfrueris ex nobis. uale.

Gaius Plinius to his friend Suetonius Tranquillus, greetings.

 Make good at last on the pledge of my hendecasyllables, which have promised your writings to our mutual friends. They are accosted every day, are met with demands, and are now in danger of being forced to comply with a legal instruction to produce it. I myself am also hesitant to publish, but you exceed my reluctance and lateness too. Therefore, either cease now your delays or take care that those very books of yours, which my hendecasyllables cannot elicit from you by flattery, are not wrenched out by abuse in scazons. The work is finished and complete, and *no longer begins to shine* from the file but *is being worn away*. Let me see your cover, and let me hear that my friend Tranquillus' books are being copied, read, and sold. It is fair that in such shared fondness I take the same delight from you as you enjoy from me. Farewell.

(Plin. *Ep.* 5.10)

---

7 See Macé 1900, 66–77; Rolfe 1913–14, 2.390; Sch.-Hos. 3.56; Ailloud 1931–2, 1.xiii; Rostagni 1944, viii–xi; Sanders 1944, 114; Paratore 1950, 739; Della Corte 1956, 94 = *Op.* 9.261; Brugnoli 1968a, 142–3; Cizek 1977, 14; McDermott 1971a, 93; 1980, 493 n. 39; Syme 1981, 115 = *RP* 3.1346; Shotter 1993, 6; Velaza 1993, 45; Stok 1994, 202; Herz.-Schm. 4.28; Lana 1998, 1031; Walsh 2006, xxvii, 331 (suggesting the whole *Illustrious Men* or perhaps only part of the collection). A different possibility was raised by Wallace-Hadrill (1983, 46–7), that the work mentioned by Pliny was in fact a compilation on Greek and Roman games – following Reifferscheid's (1860, 461–5) reconstruction of that work; cf. Mellor 1999, 147–8. However, our fragments of Suetonius on that topic do not fit well with the context of Pliny's letter. On Suetonius' work on games, see below, p. 58. Sherwin-White 1966, 338 erroneously favours a volume of verse, but concedes that no such volume by Suetonius is known; cf. above, p. 4, n. 9. For more sceptical views of *Letters* 5.10 as evidence for Suetonius' works, see e.g. Funaioli 1931, 598; Lindsay 1993, 15 n. 10.

8 Gamberini 1983, 528 convincingly defends *haesitator* against the conjectures *haesitantior* or *haesitabundus* proposed by Syme 1980c, 426 = *RP* 3.1233.

The words emphasized above recall the first lines of the *Georgics* following the proem:

> uere nouo, gelidus canis cum montibus humor
> liquitur et Zephyro putris se glaeba resoluit,
> depresso incipiat *iam* tum mihi taurus aratro
> ingemere et sulco *attritus splendescere* uomer.

> In early spring, when the icy liquid flows from the snowy mountains and the crumbling soil is softened by the western wind, let my bull then *already* begin to groan from the sunken plough, and my ploughshare *begin to shine, worn down* from the furrow.

(Verg. G. 1.43–6)

The arguments that support this allusion may be stated as follows.

a   In his *Letters*, Pliny frequently quotes from and alludes to Virgil's works, more often the *Aeneid*, but also sometimes the *Georgics* (e.g. *Ep.* 2.1.12 ~ *G.* 4.500–2, 523–7; *Ep.* 5.8.3 ~ *G.* 3.8–9; *Ep.* 9.2.3 ~ *G.* 4.206–8).[9] He was therefore very familiar with Virgil's poetry.

b   There is also an adjacent allusion to the *Aeneid* in this letter through Pliny's command *rumpe iam moras* (§2; cf. *Aen.* 4.569, 9.13),[10] and paired references to these two poems are something that Pliny likewise does in *Letters* 5.8 (§3; *G.* 3.8-9, *Aen.* 5.195).[11]

c   The clear echoes of the words *iam* (§§1, 2, 3), *splendesco*, and *attero* (§3) cannot be explained entirely by the *topos* of *limae labor et mora*,[12] because of the rare combination of the two verbs. Besides one phrase in Ammianus (*splendescit attritu*, 20.11.29), which may itself have been influenced by the Virgilian passage,[13] the combination occurs in extant Latin literature only in these two places.[14]

---

9 See Marchesi 2008, 193–4, 156, 237, respectively; also index locorum s.v. 'Virgil'. Pliny's use of Virgil was underestimated by Sherwin-White 1966, 5.

10 Syme 1980c, 426 = *RP* 3.1233; 1981, 115 = *RP* 3.1346.

11 See Marchesi 2008, 156–7, and below.

12 On this metaphorical *topos* in the letter, see Steidle 1951, 9 n. 2; Brugnoli 1968a, 29–30, cf. 50; Gamberini 1983, 217; Lounsbury 1987, 25, 144–5. Imagery of brightness, such as Pliny's *splendescit*, is customary within this metaphor; see Krostenko 2001, 254–5; and on Pliny's use of *splendesco*, also Gamberini 1983, 507. On the theme of *labor limae* in general, see Hor. *Ars P.* 291 (the *locus classicus*), with e.g. Nauta 2006, 35. Pliny may have partly in mind Quint. *Inst.* 10.4.4 on the dangers of too much revision; see Cova 1966, 52–3, comparing *Ep.* 9.35.2.

13 Ammianus also often alludes to Virgil's works, including the *Georgics*; see e.g. Amm. Marc. 14.11.34, 26.1.1, 31.4.6 ~ *G.* 2.105–6, with Kelly 2008, 292–3; also index locorum s.v. 'Virgil'. On Ammianus' use of Virgil, see also O'Brien 2006; 2007.

14 On the importance of unique textual echoes in establishing an allusion, see Hinds 1998, 19, 25–6.

d   There are similarities of context in these two passages, which are both about delayed beginnings. The delay in Virgil's description of activities already commencing (*incipiat iam ...*) has been viewed as a metaphor for the poet's delay in beginning the *Georgics* only after a formal proem. In other words, the passage on farming is also about a literary work: Virgil is commenting on his own late beginning.[15] Suetonius' delay of his own work by not yet publishing it therefore recalls the passage, and Pliny's metaphor of the *lima* for the literary craft parallels Virgil's metaphor of the ploughshare and furrow for the same idea.[16] Furthermore, both images of the 'furrow' and 'file' evoke freshness that comes from hard work: in Virgil freshness of the soil, and in Pliny literary freshness.[17]

Taken together, the points listed make it reasonably certain that Pliny alludes to the Virgilian lines. In fact, Pliny's allusion to this passage of the *Georgics* so as to connect its imagery explicitly with a literary work may even signal his recognition of Virgil's original double meaning, the implication of the poem itself behind the metaphor of the ploughshare. The point of the allusion is clear: Pliny emphasizes Suetonius' need to act by alluding to Virgil's own consciousness that the preparations have already been made for his poem, which must at last be properly begun. The next step is to ask what, if anything, the allusion can tell us about the work of Suetonius to which Pliny refers.

The first thing we ought to observe is that *Letters* 5.10 is part of a carefully designed epistolary collection, and also part of an artfully polished individual book within that collection (Book 5). Recent scholarship on Pliny has conceded that he almost certainly revised and edited his letters, and that an appreciation of the greater context of each letter, particularly the surrounding context of the individual book, can often enhance our understanding of the letter's meaning.[18] Moreover, scholars have demonstrated that Pliny often joins more than one letter, either by intratextual

---

15 See Batstone 1997, 135–7. On such metaliterary readings of the *Georgics*, see also e.g. Harrison 2007b, 138–49. In addition to the word *incipiat*, Virgil's *splendescere* is also worth noting, which does not mean simply 'shine' (as in *splendeo*), but rather '*begin* to shine'; see *OLD* s.v. *splendesco* 1a.

16 On Pliny's metaphor, see Gamberini 1983, 217; on Virgil's, Mynors 1990, 11 (ad loc.): 'you can still tell a good farmer by the shine on his tools.'

17 See Görler 1999, 277–8 on the Virgilian imagery. An allusion to the *Georgics* is also generally fitting in the context of the *lima*, since Virgil epitomized *limae labor et mora* especially while writing that poem; see Suet. *Vita Verg.* 22, with Horsfall 1995, 15–16.

18 For this kind of appreciation of Pliny's *Letters* in context, see esp. Marchesi 2008, 1–11, *passim*; also Henderson 2002 on Book 3; and more generally, Gibson and Morello 2012. On the polished revision of the *Letters*, cf. Ash 2003, 215; Mayer 2003b, 232–3.

cross-reference or through a shared allusion to another text, suggesting that they should be read and interpreted together.[19]

Bearing in mind this methodology for reading Pliny's work, let us see if understanding the Virgilian allusions of *Letters* 5.10 within the context of related letters in Book 5 can cast any light on our question. *Letters* 5.10 seems to be connected to a letter that comes just before it in Pliny's Book 5, *Letters* 5.8, which similarly contains the theme of delay and combines allusions to the *Georgics* and *Aeneid* within the same thought (§3), as noted briefly above (b).[20] In that case, however, the verses are explicitly quoted, and therefore would not fail to be in the recent memory of the reader of *Letters* 5.10, providing Book 5 is being read in order. There is also an explicit cross-reference in 5.10 to Pliny's own hesitance to publish (*sum et ipse in edendo* haesitator, *tu tamen* meam *quoque* cunctationem tarditatemque *uicisti. proinde aut rumpe iam* moras ... §2), which has most recently been discussed in *Letters* 5.8 (*cur ergo* cunctor? §5), and is even recalled in its final line (*cunctationis et morae*, §14). The fact that *Letters* 5.10 is placed so close to 5.8 and deals with the same subject of a delayed literary publication already suggests the two letters' correlation. However, their shared double allusion to the same Virgilian works makes it almost indisputable, suggesting that the two letters should in fact be read together.

The allusion to the *Georgics* in *Letters* 5.8 that parallels the one in 5.10 is worth briefly considering. Pliny again alludes to a delayed beginning, this time Virgil's second proem, the start of *Georgics* Book 3, where Virgil announces a future epic work (the *Aeneid*), which will be even greater than the present didactic poem; it is this next, rather different writing that will

19 See e.g. *Ep.* 5.8, which is recalled in 7.33 through the shared model of Cic. *Fam.* 5.12 (Sherwin-White 1966, 333; Marchesi 2008, 221–3); also *Ep.* 1.2 and 1.3 (*Aen.* 6.129); 1.12 and 1.13 (Catull. 8); 5.3.2 and 7.4.2 (Ter. *Hau.* 77); with Marchesi 2008, 26–36, 40–52, 80, respectively. See too ibid. 25–6 on letters paired through intratextual narrative connections, such as those to Tacitus on the death of Pliny's uncle (*Ep.* 6.16 and 20) – in both of which Pliny again has in mind Cic. *Fam.* 5.12; see Traub 1955, 229. For 6.16 and 6.20 as a pair, cf. Berry 2008, 301–2, 307. See also ibid. 302–3 for the connections of 6.15, 6.16, and 6.20 through the shared intertext of *Aeneid* 2. Hoffer 1999, 211–25 discusses Pliny's two letters about Suetonius in Book 1 (1.18 and 1.24) as similarly linked by theme.

20 Both letters also include legal humour: in one, Pliny seeks an adjournment (5.8.11), and in the other, he jests that his verses might be served with a writ (5.10.1); on the latter joke, see Sherwin-White 1966, 338. Furthermore, as with 5.8 (see the previous note), there is a letter in another book to which 5.10 also relates: the similar plea of 2.10 to Octavius Rufus; cf. Della Corte 1956, 93 = *Op.* 9.260. The same themes in 2.10 of hesitation to publish (*cunctatione*, §8; cf. *cunctationem*, 5.10.1), denied pleasure (*nobis uoluptate*, §2; cf. *nos ... uoluptatem*, 5.10.3), and especially personified verses (*ut errones aliquem cuius dicantur inuenient*, §3; cf. *cogantur ad exhibendum formulam accipere*, 5.10.1) are all recalled in 5.10, and the potential loss of Rufus' work through plagiarism is paralleled in 5.10 by the implied potential loss of Suetonius' work through theft (on this implication, see below). On Plin. *Ep.* 2.10, see Seo 2009, 569–73.

make him 'fly victorious on the lips of men' (*uictorque uirum uolitare per ora*, *Ep.* 5.8.3 = G. 3.9).[21] This sort of *recusatio* – 'Meanwhile ...' (*interea*, G. 40) – is an appropriate parallel to Pliny's own *recusatio* in *Letters* 5.8 – 'And so, in the meantime ...' (*ideoque interim*, §11) – where he contemplates a change from oratory to history, and ultimately decides to continue with the former for the time being.[22]

This preceding allusion to the *Georgics* in Book 5 may have other implications for both *Letters* 5.8 and 5.10. Pliny the Younger may also here be alluding to the preface to the *Natural History* of his uncle Pliny the Elder, particularly a section in which the Younger appears to have taken a great interest; it similarly is placed within the form of a letter and makes use of the same *topos* as in Virgil of an author advertising within a more modest genre a greater work of literature by himself:[23]

> uos quidem omnes, patrem, te fratremque, diximus opere iusto, temporum nostrorum historiam orsi a fine Aufidii. *ubi sit ea, quaeres. iam pridem peracta sancitur* et alioqui statutum erat heredi mandare, ne quid ambitioni dedisse uita iudicaretur.
>
> peracta sancitur *mss.*: per acta sancitum *Detlefsen*
>
> Indeed, all of you – your father [Vespasian], you [Titus], and your brother [Domitian] – I discuss in a finished work, having begun a history of our times from the end of Aufidius [Bassus]. *Where is this, you will ask. It is already seen through and enacted*, and had been specially placed in trust for my heir, so that my life could not be judged to have served a desire for favour.
>
> (Plin. *HN praef.* 20)

In this case, the work under discussion is already completed (*peracta*), although its publication will be delayed by the author. The problems that come with publishing a work of contemporary history, which are thereby avoided by Pliny the Elder, are also a theme in *Letters* 5.8 (§§12–14). What is more, the question *ubi est ea?* attributed to the Elder's addressee Titus (*quaeres*) may be seen to be recalled by the Younger's *cur ergo cunctor?* (5.8.5), which itself seems to indicate an expected question from the letter's recipient, as the following objection explicitly does: 'You will say: "You can rewrite your cases and compose history at the same time"' (*dices: 'potes*

---

21 For G. 3.8–9 as referring to the *Aeneid*, see e.g. Thomas 1988, 2.36–7, 39 (ad loc.). Virgil alludes in the first place to Enn. *Varia* 18, and revisits the allusion at *Aen.* 12.235; see Hinds 1998, 52–6.
22 For *Letters* 5.8 as a *recusatio* in this sense, see Baier 2003.
23 On this *topos* in this section of the Elder's preface, see Gibson 2011, 198–9, citing Janson 1964, 75–6. The same section of the preface is also evoked by Pliny in *Letters* 3.5, 5.6, 6.16, and 6.20; see Gibson 2011, 196–205; id. and Morello 2012, 224.

simul et rescribere actiones et componere historiam', §7).[24] In both passages, the reason for the delay is also preventative: the immediate answer to the rhetorical question takes the form of a negative purpose clause (*ne … iudicaretur, HN praef.* 20 ~ *ne … intercidat, Ep.* 5.8.6).

This rhetorical question posed in the voice of the reader of *Letters* 5.8, to which Pliny seems to allude in 5.10 by comparing Suetonius to the explicit example of himself (*meam quoque cunctationem*, §2 ~ *cur ergo cunctor? Ep.* 5.8.5), follows directly after an explicit comparison of himself with his uncle and the historical work mentioned in the Elder's preface:

> me uero ad hoc studium impellit domesticum quoque exemplum. auunculus meus idemque per adoptionem pater historias et quidem religiosissime scripsit. inuenio autem apud sapientes honestissimum esse maiorum uestigia sequi, si modo recto itinere praecesserint. cur ergo cunctor? egi magnas et graues causas. has, etiamsi mihi tenuis ex iis spes, destino retractare, ne tantus ille labor meus, nisi hoc quod reliquum est studii addidero, *mecum pariter intercidat*. nam si rationem posteritatis habeas, quidquid non est *peractum*, pro non incohato est.

> However, a familial precedent too beckons me to this endeavour. My uncle, who was also my father by adoption, wrote historical narratives, and very zealously. Moreover, I find that according to the philosophers it is most honourable to follow in the footsteps of one's ancestors, provided that they led by a righteous path. Why, then, do I delay? I have pleaded some great and important cases. These, though I have meagre hopes for them, I intend to rework, so that all that work of mine, for lack of adding this remaining attention, might not *equally perish with me*. For if we take account of posterity, whatever is not *seen through* is the same as never begun.

> (Plin. *Ep.* 5.8.4–7)

Pliny the Elder, who made sure his history was *peracta* (*HN praef.* 20), is brought to mind in this passage not only through the context of his being mentioned, the use of the same *topos* (both in the letter and in its intertext the *Georgics*) of a greater future work by the author, and the employment of a similar rhetorical question and answer, but also through the echo of the word *peractum*.[25] When one considers these connections of *Letters* 5.8

---

24 For Pliny's rhetorical structuring of this letter around Capito's expected questions, see Marchesi 2008, 162–3.

25 The word *incohato* in this passage may also have connotations of Pliny the Elder, since Gibson 2011, 194–5 shows that Pliny the Younger appears to allude to him in *Letters* 5.6 with regard to parts of his own villa *quae maxima ex parte ipse incohaui aut incohata percolui* ('which I myself *began* for the most part or completed from *what had been begun*', §41), since these parts were probably begun by the Elder; cf. Gibson and Morello 2012, 223. See also *Ep.* 6.16.9 on the Elder during the eruption of Mount Vesuvius: *quod*

to the Elder's preface, and the intratextual link of the Younger's cross-reference between 5.10 and 5.8, the double emphasis in 5.10 on Suetonius' work as 'finished and complete' (*perfectum ... absolutumque*, §3) recalls the Elder's work, which was not only unpublished too but similarly 'seen through and sanctified' (*peracta sancitur, HN praef.* 20).

The example of Pliny the Elder, whose unexpected death in the eruption of Vesuvius will be described by Pliny the Younger in Book 6 (and also famously recounted in Suetonius' *Illustrious Men*), is relevant here in *Letters* 5.8 to the Younger's point about his own need to finish his speeches, but also to 5.10, where he pleads with Suetonius to finish his work. It is the differences that are instructive: in the *Natural History*, the Elder gives advance notice of a work that has been completed and will certainly appear; in *Letters* 5.8, the Younger advertises a future work that he may not write, and decides to complete a different work; and in 5.10, he has already praised a work by Suetonius that has been completed, but which may not appear. The point of Pliny's comparison of these situations is that the Elder's work did not 'perish' (*intercidat*) with him, as Pliny's speeches and Suetonius' unnamed work still may do.

The concern in the above passage of *Letters* 5.8 for protecting one's writings from the same oblivion (*intercidat*) that awaits their author also echoes the very beginning of the letter (*occidere*):[26]

> C. Plinius Titinio Capitoni suo s.
>   suades ut historiam scribam, et suades non solus: multi hoc me saepe monuerunt et ego uolo, non quia commode facturum esse confidam – id enim temere credas nisi expertus – sed quia mihi pulchrum in primis uidetur non pati *occidere*, quibus aeternitas debeatur, aliorumque *famam* cum sua *extendere*.

> Gaius Plinius to his friend Titinius Capito, greetings.
>   You urge me to write history, and are not alone in urging: many have often advised me to do this, and I am willing, not because I should be confident in a satisfying result – for indeed you should hardly believe that unless you have experienced it – but because it seems to me an especially beautiful thing not to allow *to perish* those to whom immortality is owed, and *to increase the fame* of others along with one's own.
>   (Plin. *Ep.* 5.8.1)

This passage contains yet another allusion to a passage in Virgil, one which ironically emphasizes the glory of real action, not the mere glory of its telling:

---

studioso animo incohauerat *obit maximo* ('what *he had begun* with a scholarly spirit he ended with a brave one'); this dichotomy between writers (*studioso*) and the heroic characters within literary works (*maximo*) is particularly relevant to *Letters* 5.8; see below.
26 On this intratextual link within the letter, cf. Marchesi 2008, 163.

stat sua cuique dies, breue et inreparabile tempus
omnibus est uitae; sed *famam extendere* factis,
hoc uirtutis opus. Troiae sub moenibus altis
tot gnati cecidere deum, quin occidit una
Sarpedon, mea progenies; etiam sua Turnum
fata uocant metasque dati peruenit ad aeui.

Each man has his own day, and the time of life is brief and unrecover-
able to all; but *to increase one's fame* through deeds, this is a work of
virtue. Under the high walls of Troy so many children of the gods have
died – indeed, together with them my son Sarpedon fell; even Turnus is
called by his fates, and has reached the limits of the time he was given.

(*Aen.* 10.467–72)

The implied contrast with this Virgilian passage introduces a tension in the
letter between Pliny as a historian and as a character within a historical
work.[27] The resolution of the letter rests ultimately on neither alternative,
but rather on the importance of a completed *opus*, which for the time being
will be Pliny's speeches.[28]

What is particularly illuminating about *Letters* 5.8 with regard to 5.10 is
that, in addition to opting finally for being a writer (presently of speeches),
Pliny also appears to find a middle ground in this letter between writing
history and participating in it, just as he does in composing notes for Tacitus
in *Letters* 6.16 and 6.20.[29] The act of revision itself is portrayed as an important historical deed in 5.8, especially by Pliny's intratextual equating in
the above passages of the potential loss of his hard work as a writer (*tantus
ille labor meus*, §6) with the potential loss of the deeds represented by great
men's lives (*quibus aeternitas debeatur*, §1). A similar equating is evident in
5.10 through Pliny's allusion to the *Aeneid* (*rumpe iam moras!* §2; cf. *Aen.*
4.569, 9.13), which implies a comparison of Suetonius' act of publishing to
Aeneas' founding of Rome (retaining the original anagrammatic pun on
mora as *Roma*) and to his final battle with Turnus (cf. *praecipitatque* moras

---

27 See the discussion of Marchesi 2008, 151–70, and 154–5 on this allusion; cf. Ludolph
   1997, 73 and n. 225. For this tension between action and literary composition, cf. also
   Ep. 6.16.3 (on Pliny the Elder): *aut facere scribenda aut scribere legenda* ('either to do
   things worth recording or to record things worth reading'); and §9 (quoted above, n. 25).
28 Cf. Marchesi 2008, 162: 'It is neither heroic nor authorial endurance, but textual canon-
   ization that concerns Pliny'; also 163–4.
29 In those letters, Pliny is the witness of and participator in events within the narrative, the
   supplier of raw material for another's historical work, and (through the sheer polish of
   these letters) a rival historian himself – all in one; see e.g. Traub 1955, 226–32; Ash 2003;
   Augoustakis 2004–5; Tzounakas 2007, 52; Marchesi 2008, 171–89. Berry 2008 shows
   that Pliny is also a rival advocate to Tacitus, since these letters are no less comparable to
   oratory than to historiography.

omnis, opera omnia rumpit, 'and he draws to a close all *delays, ceases* all endeavours', *Aen.* 12.699).[30]

A second cross-reference of *Letters* 5.10 to another letter in Book 5 reinforces this importance of revision and the precariousness of unfinished works – a theme of such great importance that Pliny even devotes the end of the book to it.[31] Gibson and Morello notice that Pliny's phrase *perfectum opus* (5.10.3) is reminiscent of the phrase used in *Letters* 5.5 of Gaius Fannius' incomplete work at the time of his death: *opus imperfectum* (§2). In fact, the echo is even more extensive than this, and other correspondences in *Letters* 5.5, not only to 5.10 but to 5.8, may also be found:

> sed hoc utcumque tolerabile; grauius illud, quod pulcherrimum *opus imperfectum* reliquit. quamuis enim *agendis causis* distringeretur, scribebat tamen exitus occisorum aut relegatorum a Nerone et iam tres libros *absoluerat* subtiles et diligentes et Latinos atque inter sermonem historiamque medios, ac tanto magis reliquos perficere cupiebat, quanto frequentius hi lectitabantur. mihi autem uidetur acerba semper et immatura mors eorum, qui immortale aliquid parant. nam qui uoluptatibus dediti quasi in diem uiuunt, uiuendi causas cotidie finiunt; qui uero *posteros cogitant*, et *memoriam sui operibus extendunt*, his nulla mors non repentina est, ut quae semper *incohatum aliquid* abrumpat.

> But this is somehow bearable; more crushing is the fact that he left a most beautiful *work unfinished*. For although he was busy with *acting in cases*, he was nevertheless writing the deaths of those killed or exiled by Nero and had already *completed* three books that were in simple and accurate Latin, halfway between conversation and history; and the more widely these were being read, the more eager he was to turn out the rest. Yet it seems to me always distressing and untimely when those die who are preparing something immortal. For indeed those who are devoted to pleasures, as though living for the day, finish their reasons for living every day; but those who *think of posterity*, and *increase their remembrance through their works*, for them there is no death that is not too sudden, as it always cuts short *something begun*.

> (Plin. *Ep.* 5.5.2–4)

This passage's language (*posteros cogitant,* §4 ~ *rationem posteritatis habeas,* 5.8.7; *memoriam sui operibus extendunt,* §4 ~ *famam cum sua*

---

30 On these lines within the *Aeneid,* see Reed 2007, 109 and n. 15.
31 See *Ep.* 5.21.5 (on Julius Avitus): *quantum etiam scripsit! quae nunc omnia* cum ipso *sine fructu* posteritatis abierunt ('How much he even wrote! Now all of it *has disappeared along with him* without any benefit to *posterity*'); cf. 5.8.6 (quoted above): mecum *pariter intercidat*. On the theme of unfinished work in Book 5 generally, cf. also Gibson and Morello 2012, 222–3.

extendere, 5.8.1; *incohatum aliquid*, §4 ~ *quidquid ... incohato*, 5.8.7) and very topic are the same as those surveyed by us already in *Letters* 5.8; and in both letters Pliny juxtaposes legal cases with activities of writing (*agendis causis*, 5.5.3 ~ *egi ... causas*, 5.8.6). Moreover, the connection with 5.10 is even more complete if we read in parallel the two successive sentences of 5.5.2–3: opus imperfectum *reliquit ... tres libros* absoluerat (~ *perfectum opus absolutumque est*, 5.10.3). Pliny's distress in *Letters* 5.5 that a literary endeavour is often 'cut short' (*abrumpat*, §4) is also ironically counterbalanced in 5.10 by Pliny's command that the delays of Suetonius' literary endeavour be 'ceased' (*rumpe*, §2) – a word already highlighted through the allusion to Virgil discussed above. Pliny cautions that Suetonius must interrupt his delays before some unforeseen circumstance interrupts *him*, and that by not preventing his procrastination, he may be preventing his work itself. The biographer must choose between the two: *perfectum opus* or *opus imperfectum*.

With this earlier context of Book 5 in mind, we can now better interpret *Letters* 5.10. At the beginning of this chapter, I translated Pliny's line containing the allusion to the *Georgics* in *Letters* 5.10 as follows: 'The work is finished and complete, and *no longer begins to shine* from the file but *is being worn away*' (*perfectum opus absolutumque est, nec* iam splendescit *lima sed* atteritur, §3).[32] However, it now seems from our comparison with *Letters* 5.5 and 5.8 above that a better translation of *atteritur* would be 'is being squandered', that is, being pared down to nothing by Suetonius' metaphorical file.[33] The point of Pliny's earlier passages is that without the final act of publishing and circulating a text, all of the author's hard work is for nothing.

In this sense, an irony emerges when we contrast Virgil's original scene in the *Georgics* (1.43–6), where the polishing of the ploughshare from the earth is a sign of the farmer's (and according to Virgil's metaphor, the poet's) brilliant talent.[34] Whereas Virgil's lines appear in a text that has already been published and is well known, the toil of Suetonius may yet end up being in vain. Pliny reverses the order of the verbs, facilitating this new logic and the different sense of *attero*: Virgil's ploughshare is rubbed smooth (*iam ... attritus*), so it starts to shine (*splendescere*); Suetonius' work is no longer starting to shine (*nec iam splendescit*), so it is being wasted (*atteritur*). This interpretation renders more significant the emphasis by Pliny towards the

---

32 Radice 1969, 1.367 translates the line in a similar way: 'The work is already finished and perfect; revision will not give it further polish but only dull its freshness.' Cf. also the translation of Walsh 2006, 123: 'Your writings are fully developed and perfected; the file does not give them a bright sheen, but impoverishes them.'

33 *OLD* s.v. *attero* 3a: 'diminish (property, resources, etc.) by use, waste, fritter away'. Both Radice and Walsh seem to prefer 4c: 'diminish, impair (qualities, faculties, etc.)'; cf. the previous note.

34 See above (d) and nn. 16–17.

end of *Letters* 5.10 on actually seeing Suetonius' book in final form and knowing that it is in full production and circulation (*patere me uidere titulum tuum, patere audire describi legi uenire uolumina Tranquilli mei,* §3).

This combined reading of *Letters* 5.5, 5.8, and 5.10 suggests the importance of another intertext in Pliny's letter to Suetonius, Catullus 42:[35]

> adeste, hendecasyllabi, quot estis
> omnes undique, quotquot estis omnes.
> iocum me putat esse moecha turpis,
> et negat mihi nostra reddituram
> pugillaria, si pati potestis.
> persequamur eam et reflagitemus.
> quae sit, quaeritis. illa, quam uidetis
> turpe incedere, mimice ac moleste
> ridentem catuli ore Gallicani.
> circumsistite eam, et reflagitate,
> 'moecha putida, redde codicillos,
> redde, putida moecha, codicillos!'
> non assis facis? o lutum, lupanar,
> aut si perditius potes quid esse.
> sed non est tamen hoc satis putandum.
> quod si non aliud potest, ruborem
> ferreo canis exprimamus ore.
> conclamate iterum altiore uoce
> 'moecha putida, redde codicillos,
> redde, putida moecha, codicillos!'
> sed nil proficimus, nihil mouetur.
> mutanda est ratio modusque uobis,
> siquid proficere amplius potestis:
> 'pudica et proba, redde codicillos.'

Be here, hendecasyllables, as many as you are, all of you from all sides, however many you all are. A foul adulteress thinks that I am a joke, and refuses to return to me our writing-tablets, if you can suffer it. Let us pursue her and demand them back. Who is she, you ask. She is the one you see strutting foully, with a forced smile like a mime's on the face of a Gallic puppy. Surround her, and demand them back: 'Vile

---

35 On this poem as an intertext of *Letters* 5.10, see Roller 1998, 287–8 (anticipated by Brugnoli 1968a, 29 n. 40), who notes strong contextual similarities and structural echoes, as well as verbal ones at *Ep.* 5.10.1 (*hendecasyllaborum ~ hendecasyllabi,* Catull. 42.1) and *Ep.* 5.10.1 (*efflagitantur ~ reflagitate,* Catull. 42.10). For Catullus' great influence on Pliny generally, see Marchesi 2008, *passim,* esp. 39–95 with earlier bibliography. For many of Catullus' poems as originally sent to friends like letters, see Wiseman 1985, 126–7.

adulteress, return the writing-tablets, return them, vile adulteress, the writing tablets!' You do not care at all? O you filth, you brothel, or if you could be anything baser. But still it should not be thought that this is enough, because if nothing else is possible, let us force a blush from the dog's unfeeling face. Shout together again in a louder voice: 'Vile adulteress, return the writing-tablets, return them, vile adulteress, the writing tablets!' But we achieve nothing; she is not at all moved. Our plan and manner should be changed, if you can achieve anything more: 'Chaste and upright girl, return the writing-tablets.'

The poem is about the loss of Catullus' writing-tablets (*pugillaria*), which presumably contained nearly finished drafts, good enough to show to others but not yet copied onto papyrus.[36] The letter is a fitting epistolary model for Pliny: Catullus tries to recover his drafts from a young girl through insults, but the power of the insults is cleverly contrasted with the futility of his request for her to return the tablets, which she does not do.[37] If we are familiar with this original Catullan context, we may see an implication that Suetonius' own tablets could be stolen, and that he should set down his work in final form before such a fate befalls them; Suetonius' situation is no less precarious. Perils are threatening writings throughout this letter, from the legal actions against Pliny's verses to the abuse of Suetonius' own work by Pliny, and the intertext of Catullus 42 suggests in addition the potential theft of Suetonius' work and possibly other dangers.[38]

One last possible allusion in *Letters* 5.10 is worth examining that may draw all of Pliny's other allusions together and reveal the identity of Suetonius' unnamed work. A passage in Suetonius' biography of Virgil, which was part of his larger work *Illustrious Men*, reads as follows:

egerat cum Vario, priusquam Italia decederet, ut si quid sibi accidisset, Aeneida combureret; at is ita facturum se pernegarat. igitur in extrema ualetudine assidue *scrinia* desiderauit, crematurus ipse; uerum nemine offerente, nihil quidem nominatim de ea cauit. ceterum eidem Vario ac simul Tuccae scripta sua sub ea conditione legauit, ne quid ederent, quod non a se editum esset. edidit autem auctore Augusto Varius, sed

---

36 Regarding the content of the tablets in this poem, see e.g. Quinn 1973, 216–17 (on 42.4–5).

37 On this irony, see Selden 1992, 482–4. For other ironies in this poem, see Pelling 2002a, 177.

38 Other possibly implied threats to Suetonius' work may be those of fire and reuse, but these must be inferred from two other poems by Catullus, to which 42 seems tied (Catull. 36 and 95, respectively). Horace recognizes a connection between Catullus 36 and 42 through his combined allusions to both poems (*Carm.* 1.16); see Putnam 2006, 81–5. See also Farrell 2009, 172–3: 'it seems likely that destroying the poems is what the *moecha* of 42, like the *puella* of 36, has in mind' (173). Other poets such as Propertius (3.23) and Ovid (*Am.* 1.12) seem to have drawn instead on the connection with Catullus 95 in their own reinventions of Catullus 42; see Roman 2006, 360 and 366–7, respectively. On Catull. 95, see also Watson 2005.

summatim emendata, ut qui uersus etiam *imperfectos*, si qui erant, rel-
iquerit. quos multi mox supplere conati non perinde ualuerunt ob diffi-
cultatem, quod omnia fere apud eum hemistichia *absoluto perfectoque
sunt sensu*, praeter illud 'quem tibi iam Troia'.[39]

He had discussed with Varius, before leaving Italy, that if anything
were to happen to him, he should burn the *Aeneid*; yet he persistently
denied he would do so. Therefore, in his last sickness he called repeatedly for his *writing chests*, in order to ignite it himself; but when no
one brought them, he in fact stipulated no express wishes about the
work. However, to this same Varius and also Tucca he bequeathed his
writings under the condition that they not publish anything which had
not been published by him. Nevertheless, on the authority of Augustus Varius published it, but only lightly revised, so that even if there
were verses *unfinished*, he left them. Many soon tried to complete these
verses and were unequal to the task, due to the difficulty that practically all the half-lines in his work *have a complete and finished meaning*, except for one: 'whom now at Troy your [*Aen.* 3.340] ...'

(*Vita Verg.* 39–41)

In *Letters* 5.10 through the words *perfectum opus absolutumque est* (§3),
Pliny may be drawing Suetonius' attention to the example of the biographer's own subject matter, that of Virgil himself, whose half-lines were
imperfectos but also *absoluto perfectoque sunt sensu*, which would identify the *Illustrious Men* as the work under discussion.[40] Virgil's *Aeneid*
was both *imperfecta* and *perfecta*, and Suetonius' paradoxical use of both
words and the double emphasis that he adds to the latter make the phrase
absoluto perfectoque a memorable one in this passage.

Although the combination of the verbs *perficio* and *absoluo* (or of the
nouns *perfectio* and *absolutio*) is not unique,[41] the similarities of context
between Pliny and Suetonius are compelling. First, the subject of the Suetonian passage is the literary process behind Virgil's writing, which, as we
have shown, is also the subject of the allusion to the *Georgics* found in the

---

39 For the unlikelihood that this or any of Virgil's half-lines were intentional, or that he
would not have finished them had he lived, see Baldwin 1993. This story of Augustus
vetoing Virgil's wish is told more briefly by Pliny the Elder (*HN* 7.114) with no mention
of the *Aeneid*'s degree of completeness.

40 Other possible textual echoes of Suetonius' *Virgil* in Pliny's *Letters* are proposed by Stok
(1994, 196, 200 n. 30) and Marchesi (2008, 81 n. 44), but they are too general.

41 See e.g. Cic. *Inv. rhet.* 1.25, *Brut.* 137, *De or.* 1.130, 3.192, *Orat.* 207, *Acad. pr.* 55, *Div.*
2.150, *Fin.* 4.14, 5.24, *Off.* 3.3, *Tusc.* 2.22, 4.17; *Rhet. Her.* 2.18; Sen. *Ep.* 34.3; Plin.
HN 2.8, 22.117; Gell. *NA* 16.18.6. It is, however, the only such pairing (rather than
mere proximity) of these two words in Pliny's *Letters*, and in Suetonius; see Howard and
Jackson 1922, s.v.v. *absolutio, absoluo, perficio*. Although Howard and Jackson omit
Suetonius' *Virgil, Persius, Passienus Crispus*, and *Pliny the Elder*, the phrase cannot be
found in these *Lives*. See also Bayer 2002, 296.

same sentence of Pliny as the phrase *perfectum ... absolutumque*. Second, the precise context is a writer's hesitance to publish a literary work and the importance of publication to saving it from destruction, with an emphasis on the writing materials themselves (*scrinia*, *Vita Verg.* 39; cf. *istos libellos ... titulum ... uolumina*, *Ep.* 5.10.2–3). Of this very theme developed by Pliny in *Letters* 5.5, 5.8, and 5.10, that is, the disastrous fates that threaten un-published writings, there is perhaps no more salient example than the above anecdote about the *Aeneid*, which was arguably the most famous 'unfin-ished' work in antiquity.[42]

Therefore, while *perfectus absolutusque* is by no means an uncommon expression, the rarity of the shared context suggests allusion, since both scenes relate to the publication of a literary work. In Suetonius' *Virgil*, this combination of words refers to the completeness of Virgil's unfinished verses in sense as opposed to metre, and its use by Pliny in a sentence di-rectly after his mention of switching from his usual hendecasyllables to a metre that ends more abruptly (*hendecasyllabi ... scazontes*, *Ep.* 5.10.2),[43] together with echoes of Virgil's own poetical phrasing *attritus splendescere* (*G.* 1.46), might cause Suetonius to think of his own *Life* of the poet, in which he places great emphasis on Virgil's unfinished lines in the *Aeneid*. Suetonius even describes these unfinished lines, along with some of the po-et's temporary lines that were lacking in substance, earlier in the biography as produced through a negotiation between delay and completeness similar to that seemingly proposed to Suetonius by Pliny in *Letters* 5.10:

> ac ne quid impetum *moraretur*, quaedam *imperfecta* transmisit, alia leuissimis uersibus ueluti fulsit, quos per iocum pro tibicinibus inter-poni aiebat ad sustinendum *opus*, donec solidae columnae aduenirent.

42 See Griffin 1986, xv–xvi: 'It is worth observing that the survival of a visibly unfinished poem in antiquity is a very rare thing: ancient taste was not attracted by the romantic appeal of the fragmentary and suggestive but looked for perfection and completeness ... That the *Aeneid* was none the less accepted shows the high position which Virgil had at the time of his death, the expectation which the poem had aroused, and the immediate impression which it made on its first readers'; cf. Gransden 2004, 35. See also O'Hara 2010. On the unique anticipation for the *Aeneid*, see below.

43 By threatening to change from flattering hendecasyllables to insulting scazons, Pliny reverses Catullus' own reversal from insults to flattery, suggesting that his letter, like Catullus' poem, is an exercise in revision that mirrors its own subject matter: Catullus simulates the act of erasure on a writing-tablet by rearranging the words *moecha putida, redde* to *redde, putida moecha* (Catull. 42.11–12, 19–20), and eventually by altering two of the letters in *putida* to make it *pudica* (42.24); see Roman 2006, 354–5. In the same way, Pliny inverts Virgil's *incipiat iam ... attritus splendescere* (*G.* 1.45–6) into *nec iam splendescit ... sed atteritur* (*Ep.* 5.10.3) as discussed above, and will also change from hendecasyllables to scazons, which have a more unfinished sound. On the differences between these two metres, see e.g. Freudenburg 2001, 138; Watson 2006, 286–96. Pliny also revises Catullus' word *reflagitate* into *efflagitantur* (more suitable to the context, since Pliny is not demanding the return of tablets), and also his hendecasyllables, which are no longer the agents of the *flagitatio*, but its recipients. For other erasures of and ad-ditions to Catullus in this letter, see Roller 1998, 288.

And so as not *to delay* any of his momentum, some things he left *unfinished*, others he sustained, as it were, with very light verses, which he jokingly said were put in place as props to support *the work*, until the sturdy columns arrived.

(*Vita Verg.* 24)

If Virgil could not polish each verse to a perfect shine, he at least made certain that it would suffice with buttressing stop-gaps.[44] Through the closeness of contexts, and through the language of *Letters* 5.10 (*moras ... perfectum opus absolutumque*, §§2–3; cf. *moraretur ... imperfecta ... opus*, *Vita Verg.* 24), Pliny may be said to evoke both of these passages in Suetonius (*Vita Verg.* 24, 39–41), which are already linked within the *Life* through the recurring subject of Virgil's unfinished work.

Any discussion by Pliny of the extent of the 'finished' quality of a literary work, especially one for which a great amount of anticipation has been created, could conceivably make the reader think of the *Aeneid*, since as Suetonius tells us, that work was similarly praised and advertised in verse – 'Give way, Roman writers, give way Greeks: something greater than the *Iliad* is born' (*cedite, Romani scriptores, cedite Grai: / nescio quid maius nascitur Iliade*, Prop. 2.34.65–6) – and was expected anxiously even by the emperor Augustus (*Vita Verg.* 30–1). However, it is significant that Pliny revises the order of Catullus' abuse and flattery, and also his word *reflagitate* (Catull. 42.10) into *efflagitantur* (*Ep.* 5.10.1),[45] since this more closely resembles Suetonius' description of Augustus' demands for the *Aeneid*:

Augustus uero, nam forte expeditione Cantabrica aberat, *supplicibus* atque etiam *minacibus* per iocum litteris *efflagitaret*, ut sibi de Aeneide, ut ipsius uerba sunt, 'uel prima carminis ὑπογραφὴ uel κῶλον quodlibet' mitteretur.

Augustus in fact, for he happened to be away on a Cantabrian expedition, *demanded* with *entreaties* and even *threats* jokingly in letters

---

44 As Quintilian remarks in a passage (*Inst.* 10.4.4) that may also be partly in Pliny's mind (see above, n. 12) on the file polishing, rather than 'wearing away', a work: *sit ergo aliquando quod placeat aut certe quod sufficiat, ut opus poliat lima, non exterat.* It is noteworthy too that in the above passage of Suetonius, Virgil describes his own process of writing using the metaphorical term 'props' (*tibicinibus*), much like the (literal and) metaphorical 'ploughshare' (*uomer*) in the passage towards the start of the *Georgics*, which creates a 'shine' (*splendescere*, G. 1.46) indicative of the author's literary ability.

45 Albeit a more appropriate word; see above, n. 43. Although the verb *flagito* is common in Pliny's *Letters*, *efflagito* is rare, appearing only one other time (*efflagitatam*, *Ep.* 2.5.1) in a letter that borders on the same paradoxical notion of a work being both finished and unfinished: 'some part is thought finished even without the rest' (*existimatur pars aliqua etiam sine ceteris esse perfecta*, §12). See also Pliny's possible revision of Quintilian's *exterat* (*Inst.* 10.4.4) into *atteritur* (*Ep.* 5.10.3) so as to allude to the Virgilian passage (G. 1.45–6); cf. the previous note, and contrast *deterit* (*Ep.* 9.35.2).

that he should send him from the *Aeneid*, to use his own words, 'either the first draft of the poem or whatever section he pleased'.

(Vita Verg. 31)

Pliny's attempt to obtain Suetonius' work by flattering entreaties as well as the threat of slander (efflagitantur ... *caue ne eosdem istos libellos, quos tibi hendecasyllabi nostri* blanditiis *elicere non possunt,* conuicio *scazontes extorqueant, Ep.* 5.10.2) therefore recalls not only the situation of Catullus 42 but also the demands of Augustus in Suetonius' biography of Virgil for rough material, which is sought by two similar methods in the same humorous tone and would presumably have been sent, like Catullus' work, on writing-tablets.[46] More importantly, Augustus' attempts to see the tablets are no less futile, since just like the girl of Catullus 42, Virgil also seems not to have sent them.[47] Pliny's obvious allusions to Catullus 42, a poem which has associations of the extreme reluctance to send a literary work, might also therefore make Suetonius think of his *Virgil*. That Pliny the writer of letters would have taken a special interest in the epistolographic theme of this passage about Augustus seems probable. The scene may also be recalled by another intertext of *Letters* 5.10, Pliny the Elder's *Natural History*, in which the author denies an emperor's access to the complete literary work which is of great interest to him, and in which he is described, until after the author's death (*HN praef.* 20).

---

46 Augustus' use of Greek (*uel prima carminis* ὑπογραφὴ *uel* κῶλον *quodlibet*) would have lessened the force of any threats in this letter; on this use of Greek in letters, see Adams 2003, 330–5. As with the phrase *absolutus perfectusque,* the coupling of *supplex* and *minax* (or variations thereof) is not uncommon (e.g. *postulare multo minaciter magis quam suppliciter,* Livy 2.23.11; *suppliciter nec non et minaciter efflagitantes,* Suet. *Tit.* 5.2), or for that matter the coupling of *blanditia* and *conuicium* (e.g. *nec dic blanditias nec fac conuicia posti,* Ov. *Rem. am.* 507), but the contextual similarities again seem more than coincidence. The closeness of these two sets of opposing ideas is demonstrated by the ideas being interchangeable; see e.g. Tac. *Hist.* 1.35.2: *minantibus intrepidus, aduersus blandientis incorruptus.*

47 See the fragment of what appears to be Virgil's letter of response to Augustus in Macrob. *Sat.* 1.24.11: 'I have indeed received the frequent letters from you ... Regarding my Aeneas in fact, if I now had anything at all worthy of your ears, I should freely send it, but so great is the theme I have begun that I seem to myself to have entered upon so great a work almost by some mental defect, especially since, as you know, I am incorporating other much more useful studies in this work' (*ego uero frequentes a te litteras accipio ... de Aenea quidem meo, si mehercle iam dignum auribus haberem tuis, libenter mitterem, sed tanta inchoata res est ut paene uitio mentis tantum opus ingressus mihi uidear, cum praesertim, ut scis, alia quoque studia ad id opus multoque potiora impertiar*). On this letter in relation to Virgil's wish to burn the *Aeneid*, see e.g. Otis 1964, 1–4; and in relation to his tactfulness towards Augustus, e.g. Thomas 2001, 39–40; cf. Horsfall 1995, 18 n. 119, comparing Suet. *Aug.* 89.3: *componi tamen aliquid de se nisi et serio et a praestantissimis offendebatur* ('He [Augustus] took offence at anything being composed about him except seriously and by the most eminent writers').

These and the other very specific reminiscences of Suetonius' *Virgil* that we have discussed make the argument for direct allusion by Pliny, not to the tradition on Virgil in general, but to the text of this Suetonian biography, particularly persuasive. Pliny in his own jokingly threatening letter to Suetonius (cf. *minacibus per iocum litteris, Vita Verg.* 31) adopts not only the role of the messenger of the gods to Aeneas (*rumpe iam moras!*)[48] but also the role of Augustus to that hero's author Virgil (*efflagitantur ... blanditiis ... conuicio*). What is more, by thus equating the publications of both Virgil and Suetonius with the deeds of Aeneas, Pliny implies that in addition to literary endeavours, these are also important historical acts themselves worthy of recording – a blurring of distinctions which we have seen is a major theme of Pliny's Book 5, and one fittingly shared by Suetonius' *Illustrious Men.*

That Pliny may have seen at least part of the Suetonian work mentioned in *Letters* 5.10 is certainly plausible, since it was not uncommon during this period for writers to send each other sections from a work for critical comments prior to its wide publication.[49] Walsh sees a change in Pliny's attitude towards Suetonius beginning in Book 5, and believes that Suetonius may have even given readings of parts of the *Illustrious Men* by the time *Letters* 5.10 was written.[50] This conjecture more fully explains why their *communes amici* (*Ep.* 5.10.1) would have been excitedly enquiring about the collection, not merely because of its advertisement through Pliny's hendecasyllables but because excerpts of the *Lives* may have been copied for these readings and circulated among friends; such was a usual custom with forthcoming works.[51] Walsh's view lends credence to the possibility that in

---

48 Cf. Syme 1981, 115 = *RP* 3.1346 on this allusion: 'The over-powerful epic phrase softens the rebuke and conveys a humorous note.'

49 Cf. Iddeng 2006, 78. See e.g. Plin. *Ep.* 7.17.7 (*aliis trado adnotanda*), and Roller 1998, 293. Cf. Mayer 2001, 24–5 on the possibility that Tacitus may have sent Pliny selections from his *Dialogus*; also Edwards 2008, 37–9, 52–4.

50 Walsh 2006, xxvii. On public and private readings at Rome generally, see e.g. Wiseman 1985, 124–9; Habinek 1998, 103–21, 201–9; Roller 1998, 290–7. See also Parker 2009, 224 who notes that drafts of poetry were sometimes sent to those who had attended their reading; cf. Roller 1998, 293.

51 On this practice, see Parker 2009, 202–11, esp. 203–4 on the favouring of prose works as reading material for private social events. For readings creating subsequent eagerness for the work's written text, see e.g. Plin. *Ep.* 3.10.2, 5.3.10; cf. also 5.5 (to which 5.10 cross-refers; see above), where Fannius' desire to finish his work is based on positive responses to the books already in circulation (*tanto magis reliquos perficere cupiebat, quanto frequentius hi lectitabantur,* §3, quoted above). Pliny notably does not, as he does in §§6–7 of *Letters* 2.10 (which is otherwise very similar to 5.10; cf. above, n. 20), urge Suetonius at least to give readings, which is most easily explained by the possibility that he has already done so. Furthermore, in a later letter to Suetonius (*Ep.* 9.34), Pliny asks the biographer for advice on giving readings, as though he were rather experienced at it. If Suetonius has given readings of the *Illustrious Men*, this adds to the probability of an implied parallel in 5.10 with the *Virgil*, since Suetonius reports in that *Life* that Virgil too gave readings of the *Aeneid* before publication (*Vita Verg.* 32–4).

Letters 5.10, Pliny might be recalling the specific passages above from Suetonius' *Virgil* (24, 31, 39–41), since he would have seen the text and known that allusions to it would cohere well with the overall point of the letter and its other allusions: Suetonius' reluctance, like Virgil's, is unwarranted, since to the fresh eyes of others the work is finished.

Furthermore, the fact that Pliny already draws attention to the phrase *perfectum opus absolutumque est* through the intratextual link (to *Letters* 5.5) within Book 5 that we have already discussed seems to highlight its significance, annotating the allusion to Suetonius' biography of Virgil not only in *Letters* 5.10, but in 5.5. If we read *Letters* 5.10 together with 5.5, the Suetonian allusion is even more complete, especially if we recall the passage in the latter on Fannius' dream about Nero:

> Gaius quidem Fannius, quod accidit, multo ante praesensit. uisus est sibi per nocturnam quietem iacere in lectulo suo compositus in habitum studentis, habere ante se *scrinium* – ita solebat; mox imaginatus est uenisse Neronem, in toro resedisse, prompsisse primum librum quem de sceleribus eius ediderat, cumque ad extremum reuoluisse; idem in secundo ac tertio fecisse, tunc abisse. expauit et sic interpretatus est, tamquam idem sibi futurus esset scribendi finis, qui fuisset illi legendi: et fuit idem.

> In fact, Gaius Fannius foresaw much earlier what occurred. He appeared to himself through a dream at night lying on his couch, arranged into his state of study, holding before him his *writing chest* – as he was accustomed; soon he imagined that Nero arrived, sat down on the bed, took out the first book that he had published on his crimes, and read through all the way to the end; he did the same for the second and third, and then left. He was terrified and interpreted that his own writing would have the same ending as that emperor's reading: and it was so.
>
> (Plin. *Ep.* 5.5.5–6)

This passage contains the same focus on the physicality of the writing materials (*scrinium ... primum librum ... reuoluisse ... secundo ac tertio*, §5) as in Suetonius' *Virgil* (*assidue scrinia desiderauit, crematurus ipse; uerum nemine offerente ...* 39) as well as the other contextual similarity of an emperor determining for the writer a decision with regard to publication that is contrary to the writer's own wish, even though in Fannius' case the books are suppressed rather than published; the resemblance between the two situations of Pliny's Fannius and Suetonius' Virgil is nonetheless striking, especially when one considers this letter's emphasis on Fannius' work as *opus imperfectum* (§2). The one author was effectively forced by an emperor posthumously to publish, and the other was prevented by an emperor in a dream from doing so, which then forecasted his death. Pliny's syntax even suggests the usurpation of Fannius by Nero in a way similar to that of

Virgil by Augustus in Suetonius, since Nero's act of 'reading' effectively becomes Fannius' act of 'writing' (*idem* sibi *futurus esset* scribendi *finis, qui fuisset* illi legendi, *Ep.* 5.5.6), just as Augustus overshadows Virgil and also Varius in becoming literally the 'author' of the *Aeneid*, a point emphasized through the emperor's prominence in the word order (*edidit autem* auctore Augusto *Varius, Vita Verg.* 39).[52]

In this way, Pliny compares both Fannius and Suetonius to Virgil, connecting *Letters* 5.5 and 5.10 through a shared allusion as well as a cross-reference, but he also compares both Fannius and Virgil to Suetonius as implicit *exempla*. Fannius, like both Pliny the Elder and Virgil, is confronted by an emperor who wishes to read the work that has been written about him. In *Letters* 5.10, by assuming the role of the emperor (Augustus/Nero/Titus) eager to see the work of the writer of his deeds (Virgil/Fannius/Pliny the Elder), Pliny implies that what Suetonius has written has a specific bearing on him, perhaps because it describes his uncle and adoptive father Pliny the Elder, whom he is eager to see immortalized also by Tacitus' *Histories* in another letter (*Ep.* 6.16).[53] Pliny the Elder's own work was of interest to Titus as much for its portrayal of his father Vespasian (the actual emperor at the time) as for that of Titus (cf. *uos quidem omnes,* patrem, *te fratremque, diximus, HN praef.* 20). The implied similar relevance of Suetonius' work to Pliny the Younger may equally hint at the *Illustrious Men*. This understanding of *Letters* 5.10 may also uncover a meaning for the letter's ending (*aequum est nos in amore tam mutuo eandem percipere ex te uoluptatem, qua tu perfrueris ex nobis,* §3), which may refer not to Pliny's publications in general, but specifically to those about Suetonius, including this letter itself: just as Pliny has spread the fame of Suetonius in his hendecasyllables and in letters such as 5.10, so too Suetonius' work will spread the fame of Pliny's family. This personal significance of the work to Pliny may also explain Suetonius' extra care and delay in finally showing it to him in full, just as Virgil was hesitant to show Augustus a work which described his ancestors.

Through the interconnections of Book 5, Pliny the Younger in *Letters* 5.10 is able to suggest implicitly Catullus, Virgil, Pliny the Elder, Gaius

---

52 Through Pliny's appropriation of Catullus 42 in *Letters* 5.10, his own interest in Suetonius' work is also taken to the point of suggesting usurpation, since he tries to obtain the writing from Suetonius as if it were his own, as in Catullus' poem; on the implications of Pliny's great interest in Suetonius' work, see below.

53 Cf. Della Corte 1956, 94 = *Op.* 9.261; Gibson and Morello 2012, 222. On Pliny's concern for his uncle's fame in *Letters* 6.16, see Berry 2008, 299–301. For Suetonius' *Life* of Pliny the Elder, which formed part of his *Illustrious Men*, see Roth's edition of Suetonius (1858, 300–1). This particular concern of Pliny is one that Suetonius himself shared, since he immortalizes his own father Suetonius Laetus in the *Otho* (10.1). We may also compare Clarus' frequent pleas for Pliny to publish the *Letters* (*Ep.* 1.1), since Clarus himself was not a writer, and could only hope to be immortalized through the works of others; on this, see Hoffer 1999, 19.

Fannius, and himself all to Suetonius as edifying and cautionary examples of the perils of a literary endeavour and the need to finish one's work when the timing is right and the stage has been set. He builds up a network of allusions in Book 5; their associations are cohesive rather than dissonant, and their theme of the dangers that attend unpublished writing is pointed. He leaves his allusions not so ambiguous as to lose their precise meaning, but veiled enough to reward only the careful reader, and to preserve at all times the irony of his initial protestations that his *Letters* are anything more than mere compilation (*Ep.* 1.1).[54] However, Pliny's distinct references in *Letters* 5.10 to the hesitations behind Virgil's poetry that self-consciously delay the beginning of the *Georgics* and almost prevented the publication of the *Aeneid*, as well as to the joking demands of Augustus for Virgil's work through both entreaties and threats, strongly call to mind Suetonius' biography of that poet, making it likely that Pliny is indeed referring to the *Illustrious Men*. Virgil was the most obvious example in antiquity not merely of *labor limae*, but of the more specific *topos* of its *dangers* and the overcoming of those dangers. In *Letters* 5.8, Pliny compares his own delayed publication to the *Aeneid* (*uictorque uirum uolitare per ora*, §3), and it is therefore fitting that he would make the same comparison in the related letter about Suetonius' delayed work. To Syme, the fact that in *Letters* 5.10 Pliny refers to the *Illustrious Men* is 'the general and painless belief'.[55] However, the relatively solid evidence of allusions discussed in this part of the paper gives us something more substantial on which to hang that belief.

The Date of the *Illustrious Men*

If we can accept that these allusions in Pliny, *Letters* 5.10 convincingly support an identification of Suetonius' unnamed work in that letter with the *Illustrious Men*, a reasonable conjecture about the order of Suetonius' biographical collections can be drawn. As the original composition of all three of the letters discussed above – *Letters* 5.5, 5.8, and 5.10 – can be dated to 105–6,[56] it has long seemed to provide us only with a *terminus post quem* for Suetonius' first literary debut of significant note, but nothing more.[57] While at least part of the *Lives of the Caesars* can be pinned

---

54 On this irony, see e.g. Ash 2003, 213–14; Tzounakas 2007. Cf. references above, n. 18.

55 Syme 1981, 115 = *RP* 3.1346.

56 See Sherwin-White 1966, 34–5.

57 Pliny's distinction in *Letters* 5.10 with regard to circulation (*describi legi uenire uolumina Tranquilli mei ... eandem percipere ex te uoluptatem, qua tu perfrueris ex nobis*, §3) need not connote an initial publication, but only Suetonius' first work on a major scale. It is still possible that some of the antiquarian works had appeared before the *Illustrious Men*, but none for which a comparable amount of copies was produced and sold. This collection of literary biographies would have had an obviously wide appeal, and if we can take the entries in Jerome's *Chronicle* that probably derive from Suetonius as an indication of scope, each full copy must have run several books in length; for conjectures

securely to 119–22,[58] it could not previously have been said with any certainty whether the *Illustrious Men* were published earlier, contemporaneously, or later than that work. Although the possibility of a *terminus ante quem* of *c.* 118 being established for the *Illustrious Men* through allusions to them in Juvenal 7 has been accepted by some scholars,[59] the proposal does not stand scrutiny. These allusions are by no means certain, since a common source can too easily be posited for details on the grammarian Remmius Palaemon (*Gramm.* 23), on whom there was no deficiency of sources;[60] and Juvenal's logical, if hardly standard, combination of literary categories can be seen as a coincidence in light of the prominence of grammarians and rhetoricians at that time.[61] Unfounded too is the claim for the same boundary at the time of Pliny's death *c.* 113 simply because he seems not to have been included by Suetonius;[62] this argument is not cogent, since the biographer had apparently resolved not to go beyond Flavian authors.[63] However, the new evidence examined in this paper now validates much previous speculation about *Letters* 5.10 as providing a *terminus post quem* of 105–6 for the *Illustrious Men* in particular, and about the general relationship between this work and the *Caesars*.[64]

Nevertheless, the accepted chronology of these two works still requires adjustment, since it is often assumed that Suetonius was still occupied with the *Illustrious Men* during the last years of Trajan's reign, possibly owing his promotion as *ab epistulis* under Hadrian to its final publication over a decade after this letter was written.[65] So great an amount of time spent polishing a work which already by 106, and possibly as early as 105, was con-

---

on the work's exact scale, see e.g. Wallace-Hadrill 1983, 51–2; Velaza 1993, 38–40 with earlier bibliography.

58 See above, n. 2.

59 A Suetonian model for this satire was first suggested by Townend in an unpublished paper (summarized in Townend 1972b; cf. id. 1973, 152), and has since found some acceptance: Wallace-Hadrill 1983, 52; Braund 1988, 45–7, 212–13; Hardie 1990, 174–6, 203–4; Kaster 1995, xlix, 238–40; Uden 2020, 594.

60 See Kaster 1995, 232. The argument of Hardie 1990, 176 for direct allusions at Juv. 7.215–36 to Suet. *Gramm.* 23.1–6 is speculative: there are no verbal echoes, and two of the details are merely comparisons to Palaemon, while another is attributed to a teacher in general (*praeceptori*, Juv. 7.230).

61 On this prominence, see e.g. Kaster 1995, xxix; McNelis 2007; cf. Mayer 2001, 15 on rhetoricians. The matter is further complicated by the conjectural status of our categories for Suetonius' *Illustrious Men*, which are based simply on the existing *Lives* and the fragments in Jerome.

62 For this claim, see Roth 1858, lxxviii; Macé 1900, 69–76; Funaioli 1931, 598; Brugnoli 1968a, 59.

63 See Reifferscheid 1860, 422; Wallace-Hadrill 1983, 52–3 and n. 5. For Suetonius' appearing to have imposed a cut-off of the Flavian period for the subjects of the *Illustrious Men*, based on the existing *Lives* and fragments in Jerome, and on the similar cut-off in the *Caesars*, see Wallace-Hadrill 1983, 52–6.

64 See references above, nn. 1, 4, 7.

65 As proposed by Wallace-Hadrill; see above, p. 18, and below, n. 71.

sidered finished by Pliny severely strains acceptance. It now makes better sense that the publication of the *Illustrious Men* followed only a few years after the receipt of Pliny's letter.

Another conjecture may be ventured that would define the *terminus ante quem* for the *Illustrious Men* as not longer than five years after the original composition of *Letters* 5.10. Suetonius is seen in another letter of Pliny (*Ep.* 10.94), which was first written and sent in 110,[66] being introduced to Trajan as 'most upright, honourable, and learned' (*probissimum honestissimum eruditissimum*, §1). The letter asks for the privileges of the *ius trium liberorum* on Suetonius' behalf, which are then granted by Trajan in his reply to Pliny (*Ep.* 10.95). Although the first two of Pliny's words, *probissimum* and *honestissimum*, could be dismissed as language common in letters of recommendation, and therefore more reflective of Pliny himself than the recommendee,[67] the last word *eruditissimum* cannot, and seems to imply a literary reputation.[68] For example, Pliny uses this word also in a letter recommending Septicius Clarus' nephew, Erucius Clarus (*Ep.* 2.9.3), who is mentioned as a known literary figure by Gellius (*NA* 7.6.12, 13.18.2–3).[69]

Furthermore, the privileges of the *ius trium liberorum* could be awarded to literary men as rewards for publication. Pliny himself is one example of a writer who received this special status (*Ep.* 10.2), although the exact merits stated for it are unknown.[70] However, the parallel of Martial provides a fitting comparison for the similarly equestrian career of Suetonius.[71] Martial requested the same privileges in recognition of his writing (*si ... detinuere oculos carmina nostra tuos*, 'if our poems have caught your eyes', Mart. 2.91.3–4), and was granted them (2.92). The award appears to have been due to Martial's production of a book of epigrams celebrating the opening

---

66 For the date of this letter, see Sherwin-White 1966, 81, 689 (ad loc.); cf. Millar 2004, 38, 45.

67 See Saller 1982, 108. For letters of recommendation as extensions of the sender's own status, see also Rees 2007.

68 See Millar 1977, 90–1; also Macé 1900, 77, proposing the recent publication of the *Illustrious Men*, although he dates this letter incorrectly to 113 (cf. ibid. 49–50, based on Mommsen 1869, 43, 58 = 1906, 378, 393); contrast references above, n. 66. Cf. Rostagni 1944, x; Della Corte 1956, 94 = *Op.* 9.261; Paratore 2007, 193.

69 On this Clarus, see Sherwin-White 1966, 157; on Suetonius and Gellius, see below, p. 55. The same word *eruditissimus* is also used by Pliny the Younger to describe Pliny the Elder at *Ep.* 6.16.7, possibly as an allusion to the list of the latter's publications in *Ep.* 3.5, where the Younger refers to the *Natural History* as *opus diffusum eruditum* ('a learned and vast work', §6); see Gibson 2011, 203; and on *Ep.* 6.16 as connected to 3.5 more generally, Berry 2008, 301, 303, 305.

70 The suggestion of Eck (2000, 211–12) that both Pliny and Suetonius received these awards through the influence alone of those who interceded on their behalf is unconvincing; see below.

71 See Wallace-Hadrill 1983, 7, favouring a work on games by Suetonius (46–7) for this particular honour (cf. above, n. 7); Groot 2008, 33 n. 21, arguing instead for the *Illustrious Men*. Cf. also above, n. 68.

of the Flavian Colosseum in 80, which was later republished as part of his *Liber de spectaculis*.[72] Although some of Martial's books on spectacles from which the *Liber de spectaculis* was composed may have been for small occasions and therefore presented privately to the emperor,[73] this does not preclude the publication of the collection in honour of Titus' Colosseum, to which so many of the epigrams pertain.[74] Suetonius' privileges may very well likewise have been granted in recognition of the publication of part of the *Illustrious Men*, a work which demonstrated his wide-ranging erudition.[75] It is therefore likely that Pliny's description of Suetonius as *eruditissimum*, and Trajan's granting of this request signify the publication of some of the *Illustrious Men* no later than 110; and a more exact time period for at least the partial appearance of the work may thus be determined as 105–10.[76] Suetonius' literary reputation had by 110 reached farther than his inner circle, possibly due to the publication of this entire collection of biographies, but perhaps only the *Poets*.[77]

The Later Biographies of the *Caesars*

Let us now draw some conclusions from these new dates for the composition of Suetonius' later work, *Lives of the Caesars*. Given that at least part of the *Illustrious Men* had been completed and published by 110, this leaves at least nine years before any publication of the *Caesars*. One possibility is that, if we assume that only a partial appearance of the *Illustrious Men*

---

72 See Coleman 2006, lxxxiii–lxxxiv, and on the *Liber de spectaculis* as combined from previous smaller collections, xlv–lxiv, esp. liv–lvi for parts datable as late as 83–5. Cf. also C. A. Williams 2004, 4–5, 278–9 (on 2.92, suggesting, implausibly, the whole *Liber de spectaculis* as the poems mentioned by Martial).

73 Coleman 2006, lx–lxi.

74 See ibid. xlix, Table 4.

75 Suetonius' literary reputation may also have led to his appointment by Trajan to one of his first offices, as recorded by the Hippo inscription (*AE* 1953, 73), possibly *inter selectos* (*iudices*); see Townend 1961, 100, citing the parallel of Gell. *NA* 14.2.1.

76 The notion that the *Illustrious Men* could not have been published before 107, when the rhetorician Iulius Tiro, whose biography was included according to a later ancient index to the *Grammarians and Rhetoricians*, may still have been alive (see Funaioli 1931, 598 with earlier bibliography; also Kaster 1995, xxiv n. 9), depends on the assumption that this is the same man whose will was contested in that year (Plin. *Ep.* 6.31.7–12, with the date of Sherwin-White 1966, 391). This is only plausible if Wallace-Hadrill's conjecture about Suetonius' temporal boundaries within the work is incorrect (see above, n. 63), in which case Tiro would be the only known exception to this timeframe. Unconvincing too is the suggestion of Kaster (1995, 211) that *Gramm.* 20.2 implies Suetonius' holding of the post *a bibliothecis*, since Suetonius had a general interest in imperial offices, as evident from the *Caesars*, the *Illustrious Men*, and his mostly lost work *Institution of Offices* (for the fragments of this work, see Roth 1858, 302–3); see Wallace-Hadrill 1983, 74–8, 81–8; Wardle 2002, 462–3.

77 Cf. Walsh 2006, 331. For the likelihood that the *Poets* were the first part of Suetonius' *Illustrious Men*, cf. the edition of Reifferscheid 1860.

is signified by Suetonius' award of the *ius trium liberorum*, as discussed above, some of the following nine to twelve years may have been spent simply finishing the rest of this work. However, even if that were the case, this reconstruction still allows for considerably more time for the writing of the *Caesars* before 119–22, during which time we know that there was a publication of that work with a dedication to Septicius Clarus. The *Lives* of emperors may then have been begun by Suetonius a whole decade earlier than this publication of them (especially if the *Illustrious Men* – according to the second possibility – had been published by 110 in full), rather than merely a few years earlier at the time of Hadrian's assumption of power in 117. It is difficult to imagine that, if sections of the *Illustrious Men* were still unfinished in 110, the majority of the years unaccounted for would have been devoted to completing them.

If we assume that Suetonius had roughly a decade to write what he published of the *Caesars* in 119–22, then it is fair to conclude that this publication may have been of the whole *Caesars*, and not merely the first two books (*Divine Julius* and *Divine Augustus*) as argued by Townend more than half a century ago and still widely believed by scholars.[78] While it is still possible that other literary works or the duties of his earlier posts *a studiis* and *a bibliothecis* delayed Suetonius' work on the *Caesars* under Trajan, their full publication during Clarus' prefecture is now far more plausible. In this final part of the paper, some further objections to Townend's theory may be adduced.

Townend's theory that the last ten of the twelve *Caesars* were published after Suetonius' dismissal rests mainly on two pieces of evidence. First, Townend argues for contemporary allusions suggestive of a later date, which are easily discounted as unconvincing.[79] Second, Townend questions the scale and documentation in the later *Lives*, especially the seeming overreliance on the private letters of Augustus and no other emperor, since this research may have been conducted in restricted imperial archives during Suetonius' employment in the civil service, to which he lost access after his dismissal.[80] This decline in quality and the loss of access as its explanation were later accepted by Syme, who, however, argued that the loss originally occurred instead when Suetonius' travelled abroad with Hadrian to

---

78 Townend 1959; cf. Syme 1980b, 69 n. 54; Wallace-Hadrill 1983, 62; Birley 1984, 246; Bradley 1991, 3724 n. 102; Wardle 2002, 463 n. 6.
79 Townend 1959, 290–3; cf. id. 1967, 90; 1982b, 1055–6. Against these and other such allusions, see Wardle 1998a; Vlaardingerbroek 1999, 224–5.
80 Townend 1959, 286–8. For the belief that Augustus' letters were the fruit of Suetonius' privileged access to archives, see the bibliography cited in de Coninck 1980–1, 398 n. 71, to which add Fraenkel 1957, 17; Gascou 1984, 471–5, 498–502; 1994, 8–9, 17, 19; 2001, 160–1; Stok 2010, 108; Elder and Mullen 2019, 247, cf. 231. On Augustus' private letters generally, see Giordano 2000.

Germany in 121, a year before his dismissal by him in Britain.[81] Syme also believed that Suetonius may have simply lost interest in writing the *Caesars* after his dismissal.[82] Wallace-Hadrill agrees with Townend that there is a perceivable decline towards the end of the collection,[83] but suggests that it should be connected not to Suetonius' dismissal and a resulting loss of enthusiasm, but rather to his greater interest in the Principate's foundation, a period which would have been less well known to his audience.[84]

However, scholarship since Syme has greatly exposed the lack of foundation for this notion of a qualitative decline in the *Caesars*. Several scholars, including Wallace-Hadrill, have shown that some of the letters of Augustus in Suetonius may well have been circulated, even if they were not widely published like the collection of Augustus' letters to his grandson Gaius that is mentioned by Quintilian (*Inst.* 1.6.19) and Gellius (*NA* 15.7.3).[85] In fact, we may now revive an older point that not all of the letters of Augustus in the *Caesars* must have derived from imperial archives, since they are quoted also in Suetonius' *Virgil* and *Horace*,[86] which, given our new date for the *Illustrious Men*, were probably written before he held any of his high official offices. It is possible that at least one of the letters in the *Horace* had been published, since it is introduced by the verb *extant* (*Vita Hor.* 6).[87]

Yet even if Suetonius' remarks on the authenticity of a few of the letters based on handwriting (*Aug.* 71.2, 87.1) and his comments on Augustus' unique diction and orthography (87–8) suggest that he did personally inspect some originals, Pliny the Elder attests the widespread availability of documents written in Augustus' and Virgil's hands (*manus … Diui Augusti Vergilique saepenumero uidemus, HN* 13.83).[88] Moreover, there are simi-

---

81 Syme 1980a, 116–17, 121 = *RP* 3.1263–4, 1267–8; 1980b, 69 = *RP* 3.1284–5; 1981, 116–17 = *RP* 3.1348.

82 Id. 1981, 116–17 = *RP* 3.1348. Cf. also Venini 1988, 2146 n. 4.

83 Wallace-Hadrill 1983, 61–2. Cf. also Bradley 1978, 20–1; Pagán 2002, 253.

84 Wallace-Hadrill 1983, 94 n. 27; cf. 56–7, 66; Macé 1900, 361–9 and Crook 1969, 63, both cited by Wallace-Hadrill (62 n. 14); *pace* Sharrock and Ash 2002, 366, 369 and Konstan 2009, 461 n. 54, who attribute to Wallace-Hadrill instead the view of Syme (cf. above, n. 82). Wallace-Hadrill was anticipated also by McDermott 1969, 189.

85 See de Coninck 1980–1, 397–403; 1983, 45–57; 1991, 3690–2; Baldwin 1983, 47–8; Wallace-Hadrill 1983, 94–5; von Albrecht 1997, 1393; Hurley 2001, 9; Brandão 2009, 49–50.

86 Levi 1937, 14–18 = 1951, xliv–liv.

87 See Macé 1900, 123, and 168, comparing *Aug.* 3.2, 85.2, 94.6. However, the inference from this that the letters of Augustus in the *Caesars*, none of which are so introduced, may not therefore have been similarly in circulation like those in the *Illustrious Men* lacks cogency (*pace* Crook 1956–7, 22), since the other letters in the *Illustrious Men* are not prefaced in this way either (*Vita Verg.* 31, *Vita Hor.* 5).

88 Including probably their well-known and frequent correspondence to each other (cf. above, n. 47); for inspection of writings by Virgil and Augustus in their own hands, particularly Augustus' letters, cf. Quint. *Inst.* 1.7.20–2; *pace* Gascou 1994, 8–9 (cf. id. 1984, 471–2), who thinks that the familiarity with Augustus' handwriting in Pliny and

lar instances of private and unpublished first-hand material by the emperors themselves in the later *Lives*, most notably the memoirs of Tiberius (*Tib.* 61) and Claudius (*Claud.* 41.3), Nero's revised poems (*Ner.* 52), and Domitian's handbook on hair (*Dom.* 18.2). Nero's poems are even introduced by Suetonius with the phrase *uenere in manus meas* ('There have come into my hands', *Ner.* 52), which he also uses in the *Horace* (12) on the poet's spurious letters and poems; such material too, like Augustus' letters, may not have been the result of archival research.[89] In addition, Augustus' letters may have been the only ones by an emperor to be preserved because of their epistolary style, or Suetonius may have decided to use them so frequently to underscore the exemplary status of Augustus within the *Caesars*.[90]

The other aspects of declining quality that Townend sees in Suetonius' later *Caesars* can also be briefly addressed. Aside from Suetonius' generally greater interest in the early Principate discussed above, the smaller scale of the *Lives* of the second hexad can also be explained by the shortness of reigns in the case of the emperors of 69, to which we may compare Plutarch's equally short *Galba* and *Otho*;[91] and by the close proximity to Suetonius' own time in the case of the Flavian emperors, for whom the audience would have had recourse to much other available material.[92] Furthermore, Townend exaggerates the decline in the later part of the collection with respect to diligent research. In addition to the evidence for Suetonius' usual research at the beginning of the *Divine Vespasian* (1.3–4) conceded by Townend,[93] some further examples in the later *Lives* may be added (*Vit.* 1–2, *Vesp.* 16.3, *Dom.* 11.3).[94] Townend's view of an increase in the number of unnamed sources in these biographies due to a lack of

---

Quintilian is merely indirect. For Pliny the Elder's knowledge of Augustus' letters, see also *HN* 18.139; and Baldwin 1995, 62–3.

89 See Baldwin 1983, 48; cf. id. 2005, 309. However, Baldwin elsewhere suspects (2002, 41) that this phrase implies 'covert pride ... in the secretarial position that gave him access to papers denied to others'.

90 Suetonius was at any rate more interested in the period of the foundation of the Principate than in those closer to his own time; see above. See also Wallace-Hadrill 1983, 94–5 on the similar silence of Suetonius' contemporaries on the private letters of other emperors and the exemplary style of Augustus' letters. It was common for Roman rulers to destroy records, especially the papers of their predecessors; see e.g. Zadorojnyi 2006, 373, citing Plut. *Sert.* 27.4–5, *Eum.* 16.4, *Pomp.* 20.7–8; App. *B Civ.* 5.132; Dio Cass. 41.63.5–6, 52.42.8, 64.15.1, 67.11.1–2, 71.28.4, 71.29.1–2; Amm. Marc. 21.16.11; Zadorojnyi elsewhere adds (2005, 118 n. 30) App. *B Civ.* 1.115; Dio Cass. 43.13.2.

91 See Georgiadou 1988, 354–5; Duff 1999, 19–20.

92 See Mooney 1930, 15.

93 Townend 1959, 286.

94 See Bradley 1973, 262. See also *Ner.* 23.1, with Bradley 1978, 142 (ad loc.). Baldwin 1983, 43–6 (cf. id. 1997) pushes the evidence of the *Augustan History* (*Hadr.* 11.3) too far to presume an ongoing friendship between Hadrian and Suetonius following the latter's dismissal and a continued use of imperial archives, which is now unnecessary.

sources is also suspect,[95] since this appears to be a literary device having more to do with the fact that the later *Lives* are mostly negative portraits where Suetonius wishes to attack his subjects.[96] With these arguments refuted, we are now justified in no longer reading Suetonius' dismissal into the shape and quality of the *Caesars*.

In conclusion, although scholars have generally believed (previously without sufficient cause) that Suetonius' *Illustrious Men* came first in the chronology of his two mostly extant collections of *Lives*, the commonly agreed date for the work has been much later than that proposed in this paper. Since Suetonius probably published the *Illustrious Men* by 110, he may have been working on the *Lives of the Caesars* much earlier than scholars have thought, and possibly published them in their entirety before his dismissal in 122. The later *Caesars* should therefore no longer be seen as necessarily suffering from a lack of resources or the apathy of exile. This conclusion adds weight to the view that they are no less carefully created, and that the proportions, documentation, and polish of all of the *Caesars* may be exactly as intended.

---

95 Townend 1959, 288–90.
96 Cf. Bradley 1985, 263. On this device in Plutarch and Tacitus, cf. Pauw (1980, cited by Bradley), who shows how it is used to portray figures in worse light than the authors can honestly claim. Townend 1959, 289–90 appreciates this purpose with regard to Suetonius' generalizations from specific instances, but not in his deployment of unnamed sources, which, as he himself demonstrates (289), does not mean that real sources do not lie behind them. It is unnecessary to refute the over-subtle arguments on Suetonius' use of sources by Geue (2019, 32, 39–52; 2020, 214–21), who not only seems unaware of the earlier version of the present chapter, first published in 2010, but also fundamentally misinterprets the *Caesars* as though it were a work of Roman satire; for this unsuitable approach, cf. Cowan 2011, 308–10; Uden 2020, 595.

2 Two Acrostics by Late Republican Poets in Suetonius[*]

Volcacius Sedigitus

In his *Life* of Terence, Suetonius quotes three lines of iambic senarii from Volcacius Sedigitus' *De poetis* (fr. 4 Courtney), which contain a possible acrostic:[1]

de morte eius Volcatius **SIC** tradit

> Sed ut Afer populo sex dedit comoedias,
> Iter hinc in Asiam fecit. in nauim ut semel
> Conscendit, uisus numquam est: **SIC** uita uacat.

On his death, Volcacius **THUS** reports:

> But when Afer had presented six comedies to the people, he made a journey from here into Asia, and as soon as he stepped aboard the ship, he was never seen again: he **THUS** left life.
>
> (Suet. *Poet.* 39.86–9)

This acrostic would not be surprising in a work such as Volcacius' *De poetis*, which was especially influenced by Alexandrian scholarship in containing lists of poets and their works, discussing their authenticity and ranking them in order of merit.[2] Against the acceptance of this acrostic, a sceptic

---

[*] This chapter was first published in *Athenaeum* 99 (2011), 509–14.

1 I print Courtney's (1993) text of the verses, rather than that of Rostagni (1944), who prefers *set* to *sed*, and *ut nauem semel* to Wessner's (1902) *<in> nauem ut semel*, but neither affect my argument. La Penna 1996 offers the conjecture *Achaiam* for *Asiam*, to reconcile the conflicting version told by Porcius Licinius (Suet. *Poet.* 32.23–8) and Quintus Cosconius (Suet. *Poet.* 39.90–1) that Terence journeyed to Greece before dying in Arcadia (cf. Jer. *Chron.* Ol. 155.3).

2 See Volcacius' 'canon' (*De poetis*, fr. 1 Courtney) at Gell. *NA* 15.24, cf. 3.3.1; also Suet. *Poet.* 33-4.37-9 (*De poetis*, fr. 2 Courtney). For the influence of Alexandrian scholarship on Volcacius, see Courtney 1993, 96; cf. Citroni 2006, 214–15. For acrostics as indicative of the learning of Alexandria, see e.g. Smith 1997, 42. On ancient acrostics in general, see Courtney 1990.

could point to the shortness of the word *sic*, since the fewer the letters are, the greater the possibility is of a coincidence. However, what makes the case for this acrostic particularly strong is the word's repetition, both within the lines themselves (sic *uita uacat*) and in Suetonius' introduction of them (sic *tradit*). We may compare Virgil's acrostic MARS at *Aeneid* 7.601–4, which he appears to annotate by including the word *Martem* at the end of the third line: 'when they first move **MARS** into battles' (*cum prima mouent in proelia* **MARTEM**, *Aen.* 7.603).[3] As Horsfall writes on that Virgilian acrostic: 'this was an old Alexandrian game and however serious the passage, such an ornamentation is truly not grotesque.'[4] Volcacius' acrostic would underscore his final phrase *sic uita uacat* and the abrupt end to Terence's life. Courtney writes on this last line: 'Volcacius seems to hint at some dark mystery about the disappearance of Terence ... The callous curtness of this leaves room for our sinister suspicions'[5]; the acrostic SIC further emphasizes this mystery.

Suetonius may very well have been able to appreciate Volcacius' acrostic. In another part of the *Illustrious Men*, the biographer comments on an acrostic in a similar work by Volcacius' contemporary Aurelius Opillus:[6]

huius cognomen in plerisque indicibus et titulis per unam <L> litteram scriptum animaduerto, uerum ipse id per duas effert in parastichide libelli qui inscribitur Pinax.

I notice that his name has been written in several catalogues and titles with a single letter 'L', but he himself spells it with two in an acrostic in a short book entitled *Pinax*.

(*Gramm.* 6.3)

Furthermore, Suetonius has an interest in ciphers (*Iul.* 56.6, *Aug.* 88) and in linguistic puns (*Ner.* 33.1),[7] which demonstrates his awareness of even subtler forms of words in code. The fact that Suetonius chooses to introduce

---

3 On that acrostic, see Fowler 1983; Courtney 1990, 11; Morgan 1993a, 143, using the term 'verbal referent' to describe Virgil's *Martem*; see also Feeney and Nelis 2005, 644–5. For another annotated acrostic in Virgil, see e.g. *Ecl.* 9.34–9, with Grishin 2008; and for an annotated telestich, *G.* 4.562–5, with Schmidt 1983, 317; Carter 2002, 616–17.
4 Horsfall 2000, 391 (ad loc.).
5 Courtney 1993, 95.
6 On Opillus' *Pinax*, see Kaster 1995, xxxvii–xxxviii, 114–16.
7 In that passage, Suetonius shows his understanding of Nero's pun on the Greek word for 'fool' in reference to Claudius: 'He used to joke that he had ceased to "reside" [morari ~ μωρός] among men, lengthening the first syllable' (*morari eum desisse inter homines producta prima syllaba iocabatur*); see Warmington 1999, 60 (ad loc.). Cf. also *Aug.* 97.1, where an eagle lands on the first letter of Agrippa's name, which is taken to refer to Augustus; and 97.2, where lightning strikes the letter 'C' on a statue bearing the emperor's name 'Caesar', which is interpreted as signifying a hundred days (C = *centum*) and leaving *aesar*, the Etruscan word for 'god'.

the above verses by Volcacius with *sic tradit*, instead of, as he sometimes uses, *ita scribat* (*Poet.* 33.38) or *ita tradit* (*Gramm.* 10.2), may be more than mere *uariatio*. Suetonius' quotation of these lines in isolation so as to highlight the acrostic and his addition of a third *sic* may signal his recognition of Volcacius' poetical game.

Furius Bibaculus

In his *Life* of Valerius Cato, Suetonius quotes seven lines of hendecasyllables by Furius Bibaculus (fr. 85 Hollis), which contain another possible acrostic:

> CAtonis modo, Galle, Tusculanum
> TOta creditor urbe uenditabat.
> mirati sumus unicum magistrum,
> summum grammaticum, optimum poetam,
> omnes soluere posse quaestiones,
> *unum* deficere *expedire nomen.*
> en cor Zenodoti, en iecur Cratetis!

> CATO's Tusculan estate, Gallus, was just now being offered for sale by a creditor through the whole city. We were amazed that this unique teacher, greatest grammarian, and best poet could solve all literary questions, but failed *to put in order one name.* Behold the mind of Zenodotus, behold the energy of Crates!

> (*Gramm.* 11.3)

This acrostic would be suitable to the grammatical context of these lines, especially their mention of the Alexandrian scholar Zenodotus.[8] If they are a complete poem by Bibaculus, as seems likely[9] – or at least the initial fragment, as seems confirmed by the addressee's name in the first line (*Galle*) – then the acrostic is also in a prominent position, the beginning of the poem, making it all the more probable.[10]

We should have here a variation of the 'gamma-acrostic', in which horizontal and vertical spellings of the same word connect to form the shape of the Greek letter gamma (Γ), although in this case the vertical word is spelled by using the first two letters of each line, instead of the first letter

---

8 On Valerius Cato and his lost works generally, see e.g. Hollis 2007, 429.

9 Kaster 1995, 157 (on 11.3); cf. Hollis 2007, 137. Compare, for example, the length of Catullus 56, which is in the same number of hendecasyllables and is the only poem by Catullus to mention a Cato; it is also similarly structured around a pun (see below, n. 18).

10 Cf. Courtney 1990, 11 on Virgil's acrostic *Mars* at *Aen.* 7.601–4 (discussed above): 'this comes at a conspicuous place, the beginning of a new paragraph and an important turning-point in the narrative.'

alone.[11] Because of this second feature, perhaps the closest parallel is a Virgilian acrostic in the *Georgics*:[12]

> si uero solem ad rapidum lunasque *sequentis*
> *ordine respicies*, numquam te crastina fallet
> hora, neque insidiis noctis capiere serenae.
> luna reuertentis cum primum colligit ignis,
> si nigrum obscuro comprenderit aëra cornu,
> **MA**ximus agricolis pelagoque parabitur imber;
> at si uirgineum suffuderit ore ruborem,
> **VE**ntus erit: uento semper rubet aurea Phoebe.
> sin ortu quarto (namque is *certissimus auctor*)
> **PV**ra neque obtunsis per caelum cornibus ibit,
> totus et ille dies et qui nascentur ab illo
> exactum ad mensem pluuia uentisque carebunt,
> uotaque seruati soluent in litore nautae
> Glauco et Panopeae et Inoo Melicertae.

But if at the blazing sun and the phases of the moon *you look again as they follow in order*, tomorrow's hour will never deceive you, and you will not be seized by the traps of the calm night. When the moon first gathers its returning fires, if it embraces the dark air with its shadowy horn, a great shower will be expected for farmers and the sea; but if it is tinged with a maiden's red in its complexion, there will be wind: golden Phoebe always blushes from the wind. If, however, at its fourth rising (for that is the *most certain sign*) the moon is clear and goes through the sky with pointed horns, both that whole day and those which are born from that day to the month's completion will be free from rain and winds, and sailors safe on the shore will pay vows to Glaucus, Panopea, and Melicertes, son of Ino.

(Verg. G. 1.424–37)

Like Bibaculus' possible acrostic in Suetonius' *Grammarians*, Virgil's acrostic is also onomastic, suggesting the poet's full name: **PV**blius **VE**rgilius **MA**ro. However, it is more complicated for three reasons. First, it runs backwards instead of forwards: MA-VE-PV; second, lines are interspaced

11 For the term 'gamma-acrostic', see Morgan 1993a, 143 (on Aratus, *Phaen.* 783–7). For a more straightforward variation of this kind, see e.g. Apul. *Met.* 4.33, with Gore and Kershaw 2008. Although Apuleius uses single rather than paired letters, his word *mons* is spelled vertically in the nominative and horizontally in the genitive, just as in our Suetonian passage.

12 This acrostic was first detected by Brown 1963, 102–5. For the compelling arguments in its favour, see Katz 2007, 78 and 2008, 108–10, 115–16, each with bibliography.

between the letters (*at si uirgineum ... / ... / sin ortu quarto ...*); and third, the sets of letters merely begin the words, rather than fully spelling them out.

Nonetheless, in using two letters of a line instead of one, the acrostic provides a very good precedent for our acrostic in Suetonius. In the case of Virgil, his decision to form his acrostic in this way, and using every other line, may be explained by the acrostic of Aratus to which his own alludes, since it is also five lines long (*Phaen.* 783–7).[13] But this choice may equally owe something to the degree of difficulty in creating longer acrostics: Virgil may have been able to achieve his own 'signature' only in alternate lines, while maintaining his satisfaction with the content and style of the poetry; and a four-line acrostic spelling CATO would have been similarly more confining for Bibaculus.[14]

What is most important to note about Virgil's acrostic, however, is another very close similarity to ours: Virgil appears to annotate the acrostic through the phrases *sequentis / ordine respicies* (*G.* 1.424–5) and *certissimus auctor* (432), the last of which draws attention to the 'definite author' of the text, Virgil himself,[15] thus acting as a sort of 'Alexandrian footnote'.[16] Virgil's acrostic ensures the authenticity of his text, and his pun on *auctor* again points to this authenticity. In addition to the fact that Virgil's passage alludes to similar linguistic games in Aratus, including an acrostic, these annotations all but clinch the certainty of Virgil's acrostic.

A similar congruity between acrostic and subject matter is present in the lines of Bibaculus quoted by Suetonius, in which there is a humorous

13 See Brown 1963, 103. Virgil alludes both to an acrostic in Aratus' own passage on weather signs (ΛΕΠΤΗ, *Phaen.* 783–7) and to Aratus' 'signature' pun on his own name (ἄρρητον, *Phaen.* 2); see references in the previous note. There may also be a pun on Virgil's nickname *Parthenias* in the word *uirgineum* (*G.* 1.430; see Thomas 1988, 1.139 on *G.* 1.427–37) – which, at any rate, sounds like *Vergilius*; see Somerville 2010, 205 n. 18, 208. Further allusion to Aratus is suggested by Feeney and Nelis 2005, 645–6; and to Aratus' own model (the acrostic ΛΕΥΚΗ at the beginning of Homer, *Iliad* 24) in Virgil's word *nigrum* (*G.* 1.428) by Somerville 2010, 207–8. For allusions to other writers in this passage, see Thomas 1988, 1.140–1 (on *G.* 1.437).

14 With regard to the reverse order of Virgil's name, might this be related to his more general inversion of the order of passages in Aratus on which this part of the poem is modelled (*G.* 1.351–423 ~ *Phaen.* 909–1043; *G.* 424–63 ~ *Phaen.* 733–891)? On that inversion, see Thomas 1988, 1.127 (on *G.* 1.351–463). Some support for this idea has been added by Somerville 2010, 205–6, who finds this particular passage containing Virgil's acrostic (*G.* 1.427–37) to be a structural reversal of the one containing Aratus' (*Phaen.* 783–7); Somerville was anticipated to some extent by Brown 1963, 102.

15 See Feeney and Nelis 2005, 645–6 with earlier bibliography. On *sequentis ordine respicies*, cf. Somerville 2010, 204, who does not seem to be aware of Feeney and Nelis 2005.

16 On the Alexandrian footnote, see e.g. Hinds 1998, 1–2; cf. Wills 1996, 30–1 on 'external markers'. We might add that *auctor* may not only signal the 'author' Virgil whose name is spelled by the acrostic but also the author Aratus to whom Virgil alludes and, in its immediate context of weather signs, the acrostic itself as a sort of 'sign'; the word functions as an external marker of allusion, suggesting other 'signs' in the text. On Virgil's use of *auctor* to annotate an allusion, see below, p. 124, n. 10.

pun on *expedire nomen* to mean not only 'clearing his name' by settling a financial debt – literally, removing his name from the ledgers (*OLD* s.v. *expedio* 3) – but also the grammarian's profession of solving a *quaestio* by 'supplying the name' that answers it (*OLD* 6), since grammatical puzzles frequently revolved around names.[17] The phrase *expedire nomen* is thus the punch line to which Bibaculus' list of superlatives about Cato (*unicum magistrum, / summum grammaticum, optimum poetam, / omnes soluere posse quaestiones*) leads: despite all of these abilities, a single name caused him difficulty (*unum deficere expedire nomen*).[18] When we uncover a third implication, suggested by the ambiguity of this original joke, that Bibaculus too has 'supplied a name' within his lines of poetry, this additional meaning seems to reconfirm the acrostic, which may already be announced by the word's repetition within the lines (*Catonis*) in a 'gamma' construction.

My argument for this acrostic can therefore be supported through the analogy of Virgil's acrostic at *Georgics* 1.424–37, which is widely accepted,[19] despite being less obvious. If Bibaculus did intend the acrostic *Cato* in these lines, then the phrase *expedire nomen*, which is already a pun in at least one sense, would also be meant to annotate the acrostic in the same way as Virgil's *sequentis ordine respicies* and *certissima auctor*. Bibaculus' *expedire nomen* may be more of a punch line to his poem than has previously been thought. By 'working out the name' of Cato through his acrostic, and thereby doing what Cato cannot, Bibaculus may be cleverly one-upping the great grammarian and poet.

There are reasons to believe both that Bibaculus was capable of creating such an acrostic and that Suetonius was capable of understanding it. Earlier in this part of the *Illustrious Men*, the biographer quotes another line of verse from Bibaculus (fr. 83 Hollis) on the grammarian Orbilius that contains similar wordplay:[20]

---

17 For this pun, see Hollis 2007, 141–2 (ad loc.).

18 See Kaster 1995, 157 (on 11.3), comparing a similar list that prepares for a punch line in the other fragment of Bibaculus on Cato (fr. 84 Hollis), which is recorded by Suetonius just before this one (*Gramm.* 11.3): 'we are clearly meant to hear a note of hyperbole and irony in both poems.' In being hendecasyllables that lead to a pun, our poem by Bibaculus is often also compared to Catullus 26 on similar subject matter, and to Catullus 56, which is addressed to a Cato – probably the same writer (cf. above, n. 9); see e.g. Loomis 1969; Quinn 1973, 168–70 (on 26) and 253–5 (on 56); Hollis 2007, 127; Uden 2007, 10, n. 30. On the relationships between these poets, see Crowther 1971.

19 See e.g. Thomas 1988, 1.139 (on 1.427–37); Feeney and Nelis 2005, 645; Katz 2007, 78, n. 1; cf. id. 2008, 108; Somerville 2010, 204.

20 I am convinced by Hollis (2007, 136–7 with bibliography) that Suetonius does not misunderstand this line as implying that Orbilius suffered from memory loss, *pace* Kaster 1995, 136 (ad loc.). I take *memoria* as 'memory of him' (*OLD* s.v. *memoria* 5: 'What is remembered of a person ... repute'), rather than 'his memory' (*OLD* 1: 'The power or faculty of remembering').

uixit prope ad centesimum aetatis annum, amissa iam pridem memoria, ut uersus Bibaculi docet:

Orbilius ubinam est, litterarum *obliuio*?

He lived almost to one hundred years old, but memory of him had long since been lost, as Bibaculus' verse informs us:

Where is *Orbilius*, to whom literature is *oblivious*?

(*Gramm.* 9.6)

Bibaculus here puns on the word *obliuio* to suggest the grammarian's name *Orbilius*.[21] If this poet could produce such assonance with the name of one grammarian (*Orbilius* ~ *obliuio*), is it a stretch to think that he played also with the name of another through an acrostic, or that Suetonius would notice both? We have already mentioned in our discussion of Volcacius' acrostic that Suetonius was well aware of such linguistic games. Suetonius may have preserved these fragments of Bibaculus not only for their confirmation of certain facts but also as examples of the kinds of literary puzzles and games that were the stock in trade of the grammarians whose *Lives* he wrote.

---

21 See Kaster 1995, 136 (ad loc.): '*Oblivio*, chosen to frame the line with a play on O.'s name.'

3   Calvus' Poetry in Suetonius and Pliny, *Letters* 5.3[*]

Pliny justifies his own composition of erotic verses by claiming that many great men have spent their leisure time writing this kind of poetry:[1]

> an ego uerear – neminem uiuentium, ne quam in speciem adulationis incidam, nominabo – sed ego uerear ne me non satis deceat, quod decuit M. *Tullium*, C. Caluum, *Asinium Pollionem*, M. *Messalam*, Q. Hortensium, M. Brutum, L. Sullam, Q. Catulum, Q. Scaeuolam, Seruium Sulpicium, *Varronem*, Torquatum, immo Torquatos, C. *Memmium*, Lentulum Gaetulicum, *Annaeum Senecam* et proxime Verginium Rufum et, si non sufficiunt exempla priuata, Diuum Iulium, Diuum Augustum, Diuum Neruam, Tiberium Caesarem? Neronem enim transeo, quamuis sciam non corrumpi in deterius quae aliquando etiam a malis, sed honesta manere quae saepius a bonis fiunt. inter quos uel praecipue numerandus est *P. Vergilius*, *Cornelius Nepos* et prius *Accius Enniusque*. non quidem hi senatores, sed sanctitas morum non distat ordinibus.

Should I fear – I shall name no one alive, so as not to slip into seeming flattery – but should I fear that it should not sufficiently become me, that which became *Marcus Tullius*, Gaius Calvus, *Asinius Pollio*, *Marcus Messalla*, Quintus Hortensius, Marcus Brutus, Lucius Sulla, Quintus Catulus, Quintus Scaevola, Servius Sulpicius, *Varro*, Torquatus, nay the Torquati, *Gaius Memmius*, Lentulus Gaetulicus, *Annaeus Seneca*, and most recently Verginius Rufus, and, if civilian examples are not enough, Divine Julius, Divine Augustus, Divine Nerva, Tiberius Caesar? For I pass over Nero, even though I know that things sometimes done by the evil are not corrupted, but remain honourable for being more often done by the good. Among the latter, ranked especially high must be *Publius Virgil*, *Cornelius Nepos*, and earlier *Accius* and

---

* This chapter was first published in *Athenaeum* 99 (2011), 509–14.

1 Cf. Catull. 16; Plin. *Ep.* 4.14; and esp. Ov. *Tr.* 2.421–46, where Ovid defends his own purple passages by referring to Roman erotic verses by Memmius and Hortensius among others. See Marchesi 2008, 60, 74–5.

Ennius. These were not in fact senators, but moral virtue does not discriminate against social classes.

(Plin. *Ep.* 5.3.5–6)

Over a third of the men Pliny mentions (ten out of the twenty-six, here italicized) are thought to have been given their own *Lives* by Suetonius in his biographical collection the *Illustrious Men*: in the case of Virgil, the *Life* is extant; in that of the others, their inclusion is almost certain, either from fragments preserved by Jerome, or from Suetonius' use of research relating to the author, especially the author's own writings.[2] In this note, I wish to add another name as a likely subject of the *Illustrious Men*, that of Licinius Calvus, thus tipping the scale in favour of Pliny's drawing on that work as his source for this letter.[3]

Licinius Calvus appears three times in the *Lives of the Caesars* (*Iul.* 49.1, 73; *Aug.* 72.1), a relative frequency which already makes him a rather strong candidate. As Wallace-Hadrill writes: 'If we seek to extend Jerome's list, we should think in the first place of authors Suetonius knew and used ...'[4] Calvus is mentioned by Suetonius in the same literary circle as Memmius and Catullus (*Iul.* 73),[5] both of whom had *Lives* in the *Illustrious Men*, and appears most tellingly in a passage of the *Divine Augustus* on the humbleness of the emperor's home:

> habitauit primo iuxta {Romanum} forum supra Scalas anularias, in domo quae *Calui oratoris* fuerat, postea in Palatio, sed nihilo minus aedibus modicis Hortensianis {et} neque laxitate neque cultu conspicuis, ut in quibus porticus breues essent Albanarum columnarum et sine marmore ullo aut insigni pauimento conclauia.

> He first lived next to the Roman Forum above the Stairs of the Ring-Makers, in a house which had belonged to the *orator Calvus*, later on the Palatine, but in the equally modest home of Hortensius that was remarkable in neither space nor furnishing, so that inside there

2 See below, Chapter 6, arguing that Pliny's mention of Memmius' name in this list may be due to familiarity with his biography in the *Illustrious Men*; cf. Gibson 2014, 226–7, pointing to Pliny's rather uncharacteristic adoption of Suetonius' emphasis on the Ciceronian and Augustan periods in this letter, and on figures who are not known primarily as poets; cf. Sherwin-White 1966, 317 (ad loc.).
3 For Pliny's knowledge of Suetonius' *Illustrious Men*, see above, Chapter 1; also Gibson and Morello 2012, 222; Gibson 2014, 202–3, 227–8. On Pliny and poetry generally, see e.g. ibid. 91–2, 99–100, 186, 301; also 125 on his interest in Calvus as a poet; cf. Marchesi 2008, 59–62, 67–9; Gibson 2014, 205 n. 25, 223. Calvus' verses are also mentioned by Pliny at *Ep.* 1.16.5; cf. 4.27.4, quoting Sentius Augurinus.
4 Wallace-Hadrill 1983, 57–9 (quotation at 59); cf. Kaster 1995, xxix–xxxix.
5 On these three literary figures, see Hollis 2007, 91.

were short porticos of Alban columns and rooms devoid of any marble or patterned floor.

(Aug. 72.1)

These details may have been discovered in the composition of a biography of Calvus, rather than in research specifically for the *Augustus*. The same could not be said, for example, of the details reported in the *Tiberius* about the grants needed by the grandson of the orator Hortensius (*Tib.* 47), since they relate to the administration of the Principate (cf. *Aug.* 41.1; Tac. *Ann.* 2.37–8); in that case, a historical source is more likely than independent research for a biography.[6]

Moreover, Calvus is quoted by Gellius (*NA* 9.12.10), a later writer who was familiar with Suetonius' works (*NA* 9.7.3, 15.4.4), and may have derived his knowledge indirectly from the *Illustrious Men*.[7] Gellius definitely knew of Suetonius, since he uses him as a source for Ventidius Bassus (*NA* 15.4.4 = Suet. fr. 210 Reiff.). Gellius almost certainly draws on his *Illustrious Men* for his facts about the origin of rhetoric at Rome (*NA* 15.11.1–2 ~ *Gramm.* 25.2), and possibly for those about Pacuvius and Accius (*NA* 13.2.1–6 ~ Suet. fr. 13 Reiff.) and Plautus (*NA* 3.3.14 ~ Suet. fr. 7 Reiff.).[8] Gellius may also rely on Suetonius for a discussion of Cicero (*NA* 15.28.1–7), since he cites three sources used by Suetonius elsewhere in the *Illustrious Men*: Nepos, Fenestella, and Asconius (§§1, 4–5).[9] If Gellius draws on Suetonius for the orator Calvus too, it must have been from this same work.

To conclude, Suetonius almost certainly wrote the *Life* of Licinius Calvus in his *Illustrious Men*, a biography which would have contained political themes conducive to that collection, when one considers Calvus' close connections to Cicero and Caesar.[10] It was most likely placed in the *Orators*, rather than the *Poets*, since Suetonius cites him in the *Caesars* as an orator; we may contrast Quintilian (*Inst.* 10.1.115) and Tacitus (*Dial.* 18.1), both of whom considered him to be foremost a poet.[11] However, Suetonius would still have made some comment on the orator's poetical endeavours,

---

6 See Lindsay 1995b, 144–5; *pace* Herz.-Schm. 4.37.
7 Cf. Herz.-Schm. 4.30.
8 Kaster 1995, xlix–l; Holford-Strevens 2003, 166–7; *pace* Baldwin 1983, 408, 454–5.
9 Reifferscheid 1860, 423–4; Wallace-Hadrill 1983, 58.
10 See Gruen 1967. On the political focus of the *Illustrious Men*, see e.g. Treggiari 1969, 266; Wallace-Hadrill 1983, 59–61; Gibson 2014, 217, 222, 224; also below, Chapters 6–9.
11 This point is made in an unpublished paper by Townend, who also thought Calvus a likely subject of the *Illustrious Men*; for a summary, see Townend 1972b. The suggestion of Dugan 2001, 401–2 that a Suetonian biography of Calvus underlies Pliny, *Natural History* 34.166 (*Caluus orator*) is erroneous, since the *Natural History* was published in AD 77, less than a decade after Suetonius' birth.

just as he does for his grammarians (*Gramm.* 4.2, 11.2, 15.2, 18.2, 23.3, 24.4), for the rhetorician Pitholaus (*Iul.* 75.5), and for the Caesars (*Poet.* 43–4.115–121, *Vita Luc.* 17–19, *Iul.* 56.7, *Aug.* 85.2, *Tib.* 70.2, *Ner.* 52, *Dom.* 2.2).[12] The fact that Suetonius seems to have taken a particular interest in the recondite works of his biographical subjects, particularly the poetry of non-poets, adds to the strong likelihood that he is the source behind Pliny, *Letters* 5.3.[13] Nor does it hurt that we have established an eleventh Suetonian subject in Pliny's list of erotic poets.

12 For Suetonius' attention to the literary activities of his subjects in general, see Wallace-Hadrill 1983, 83–4; Lefebvre 2010.
13 Cf. Ov. *Tr.* 2.427–40, who appears to draw on his friend Hyginus' biographical writings for his catalogue of details about the real mistresses of erotic poets, including Calvus (431–2); see Wiseman 1969, 50–2, who suggests that Suetonius' *Famous Courtesans*, drawing too on Hyginus, was the source for the similar list at Apul. *Apol.* 10.2–5. If so, it is noteworthy that Apuleius in the same work discusses Calvus, not as a poet, but as an orator (*Apol.* 95.5) – possibly how Suetonius described him in discussing his mistress. On the *Famous Courtesans*, see Power 2014c.

4 Horace and the Gladiators Bithus and Bacchius

Bithus et Bacchius gladiatores optimi illis temporibus fuerunt, qui cum multos interemissent, commissi inter se mutuis uulneribus conciderunt.

Bithus and Bacchius were the greatest gladiators at that time who, after killing many men, were pitted together and died from each other's wounds.
(Porph. ad *Sat.* 1.7.20, p. 142 Hauthal)

This short but detailed scholium on Horace, *Satires* 1.7 by the ancient commentator Porphyrio explains how the previously undefeated gladiators Bithus and Bacchius finally slew each other in the arena during the poet's time. They appear to have been matched after beating a number of others, as implied by the words *multos interemissent*, so that each already had a reputation in his own right, making their deaths all the more significant. The tale was noteworthy because gladiatorial games did not necessarily result in a death, let alone two, but could instead end in a draw, or else with the loser spared for his bravery.[1] Porphyrio's note is similar to two other reports by the Horatian scholiasts Pseudo-Acro and Cruquius, who cite the biographer Suetonius as the source of this information:

Bithus et Bacchius gladiatorum nomina celebrata apud Suetonium Tranquillum sub Augusto.

Bithus and Bachhius are the names of gladiators celebrated by Suetonius Tranquillus in the reign of Augustus.
(Ps.-Acro ad *Sat.* 1.7.20, p. 138 Hauthal)

Bithus et Bacchius gladiatorum nomina celebrata apud Suetonium.

Bithus and Bacchius are the names of gladiators celebrated by Suetonius.
(Cruq. ad *Sat.* 1.7.20, ed. 1597, p. 383)

---

1 For the story, see Ville 1981, 322 n. 214; Coleman 2006, 169–70; Gowers 2012, 258 (ad loc.). This fatal confrontation between Bithus and Bacchius was known for being their last, but it may not have been their first, since rematches between gladiators were common; see Fagan 2011, 224–5.

Based on these briefer citations, Orelli assigned the above tale to Suetonius' lost antiquarian work *Shows and Contests of the Romans* (Περὶ τῶν παρὰ Ῥωμαίοις θεωριῶν καὶ ἀγώνων), and was later followed by Ritter,[2] as well as by Suetonius' own editors Roth (280) and Reifferscheid (Suet. fr. 196). In this paper, I shall argue that this fragment in fact belongs to a missing part of the author's *Illustrious Men*, not his scholarly work on Roman games.

The Greek title Περὶ τῶν παρὰ Ῥωμαίοις θεωριῶν καὶ ἀγώνων, which is listed in the *Suda* (τ 895), is likely an elaborate translation of the original Latin (perhaps *De Romanorum lusibus*, as proposed by Reifferscheid), whether or not it was a part of Suetonius' larger work *History of Games* (*Historia ludrica*, Gell. NA 9.7.3).[3] If indeed this Latin publication on games was anything like the extant fragments of Suetonius' similarly entitled *Games of the Greeks* (Περὶ τῶν παρ' Ἕλλησι παιδιῶν) and *Children's Games* (*De puerorum lusibus*) that have been edited together by Taillardat, it was in the form of a treatise that briefly defined different kinds of games, followed by quotations of famous writers on each game in the manner of a lexicon.[4] There would thus not have been room for a digression on Bithus and Bacchius in such a work, so that this anecdotal material seems the provenance more of a biographical than antiquarian work, much like the fragment of Suetonius from Diomedes' *Ars grammatica* (Suet. fr. 3 Reiff.) that I agree with Reifferscheid is better placed in the *Illustrious Men* than Roth's (280) previous idea of the *Games of the Romans*.[5] Certainly, many discussions of gladiators and imperial *spectacula* more generally may be found throughout the *Caesars*, and no doubt were also present in lost parts of the *Illustrious Men*. Porphyrio, our fullest and most trusted source for the tale, is known to have drawn elsewhere solely on Suetonius' *Life* of Horace from his *Illustrious Men* (Porph. ad Hor. *Epist.* 2.1), and there is no reason to think that he is following any different source here.

Would it not make better sense for Porphyrio again to have consulted the *Illustrious Men* in writing this note on Horace, rather than the *Games of the Romans* – hardly a probable main source for a commentator on poetry? We might compare, for example, the two stories about Nonius Asprenas and Aeserninus, the grandson of Asinius Pollio, which expand on

---

2 Orelli 1852, 134; Ritter 1857, 95.

3 Cf. Wardle 1993, 96; Power 2014c, 250 n. 63. For the Latin title, Wiseman 2014, 257 suggests the different possibility *De ludis scaenicis et circensibus*.

4 See Taillardat 1967. On Suetonius' lexicographical works, see Wallace-Hadrill 1983, 43–6.

5 Roth's conjecture on this fragment's location has since been accepted by Wiseman (2014, 261–4), who then ironically concedes (265 n. 41) that the next fragment on Pylades (Suet. fr. 4 Reiff.), despite its relevance to games, probably belongs to the *Illustrious Men* because it comes from Jerome, who mainly relied on that work. If Wiseman applied the same standard to our fragment above about the gladiators, he would arrive at the same conclusion, since, out of all Suetonius' works, Porphyrio is only known to have used the *Illustrious Men* as a source; see below, p. 87, n. 9.

a mention of the *lusus Troiae* in the *Life* of Augustus (*Aug.* 43.2). Editors of Suetonius are better placing the anecdote about Bithus and Bacchius in a lost part of the *Illustrious Men*, and possibly even in the suspected lacuna on the assured Horatian oeuvre in the *Life* of the poet as it stands (*Vita Hor.* 11). This lost section must have preceded the existing assessment of spurious attributions, perhaps arising out of a discussion of Horace's frequent and well-known use of language from gladiatorial combat in his verses, or the real-life interest in the games that his poetry evinces, particularly the present passage of *Satires* 1 where he adduces the mutual death of this pair of fighters. Horace refers to them as an *exemplum* of equally matched competitors, holding them forth as an analogy for the two excellent orators debating each other in his satire: *uti non compositum / melius cum Bitho Bacchius* ('just as Bacchius was no better pitted against Bithus', *Sat.* 1.7.19–20).[6] Since the *Life* of Horace that comes down to us is not likely to be the full biography, these two lines of poetry about two famous Roman deaths could easily have been quoted and explained by Suetonius in his original *Horace*, as he is generally accustomed to do with the verses in his *Lives*, especially in this particular biography (*Vita Hor.* 4, 8). The story about Bithus and Bacchius should therefore at least be included more plausibly as a lost fragment of the *Illustrious Men*, and quite possibly of the *Life* of Horace itself.

6 On these lines generally, see Courtney 2013, 112–13. Horace's tendency to use gladiatorial metaphors is examined by e.g. Bowditch 2001, 172–5; McCarter 2015, 26–34. For the lacuna at *Vita Hor.* 11, see below, p. 87, n. 11.

5   Juvenal, *Satires* 3.74 and Suetonius[*]

Juvenal's third satire mentions a contemporary rhetorician at Rome named Isaeus who had 'a quick wit, an excessive boldness, a ready and more rapid speech than Isaeus' (*ingenium uelox, audacia perdita, sermo / promptus et Isaeo torrentior*, Juv. 3.73–4). This rhetorician, still alive in the reign of Trajan, is also discussed by Pliny the Younger in one of his letters (*Ep.* 2.3), which is later quoted by a scholiast of Juvenal in the mid-fifth century AD: 'Isaeus, a Roman orator eloquent in all regards. Pliny the Younger says of him: "Despite the great reputation that had preceded him, Isaeus was found greater"' (*Isaeus Romae orator omnibus eloquentior. de hoc Plinius Secundus ait: 'magna Isaeum fama praecesserat, maior inuentus est'*, Schol. Iuv. 3.74).[1] The scholiast's work was later built upon by the humanist scholar Giorgio Valla, who expanded this entry in particular:

> Isaeus rhetor fuit Atheniensis, ut Probus inquit, illius temporis, cuius et Tranquillus meminit. alter Isocratis, ut ferunt, discipulus praeceptorque Demosthenis, ut quidam sentiunt, Atheniensis, ut alii, Chalcideus. sed Isaeum dixisse hunc credi par est, de quo Plinius in epistolis: 'magna Isaeum fama praecesserat, maior inuentus est.'

> Isaeus the rhetorician was an Athenian, as Probus says, from that [i.e. Domitian's] era, of whom Tranquillus too makes mention. Another was a pupil of Isocrates, as is well known, and Demosthenes' teacher, who some think was Athenian, others Chalcidian. It is right to believe that he [Juvenal] spoke of the same Isaeus about whom Pliny does in his letters: 'Despite the great reputation that had preceded him, Isaeus was found greater.'
>
> (Valla ad Juv. 3.74)[2]

This muddled note, which disambiguates the Isaeus of Juvenal's day from a much earlier writer of the same name, is a patchwork by Valla that draws on more than one supplementary source. Its first part, *Isaeus rhetor fuit*

---

* This chapter was first published in *CW* 107 (2014), 399–403.
1 On the date of this scholiast, see Cameron 2010.
2 For Valla's use here of *hic* with *qui*, see Adams 1995, 587–9.

Atheniensis, ut Probus inquit, illius temporis, was inherited en bloc from
L (= Leiden BPL 82), a manuscript of scholia from the tenth or eleventh
century habitually used by Valla.[3] To this line, Valla himself seems to have
added *cuius et Tranquillus meminit*[4] – although no doubt based on his own
direct knowledge of an original citation by 'Probus', whom he knew independently and who used Suetonius regularly – before probably deriving the
ensuing sentence *alter … Chalcideus* from the *Suda,*[5] and carrying over the
Plinian quotation on Isaeus' reputation from the earliest scholiast (quoted
above).

Valla clearly refers to some lost piece of Suetonius' *Illustrious Men,*[6] but
which one? Roth (272) assigned the fragment to the *Rhetoricians,* despite
Isaeus' absence from our extant ancient index for that section of the *Illustrious Men,* while Reifferscheid (Suet. fr. 49 Reiff.) proposed that it belongs
instead to the preface of Suetonius' section on orators, together with an
entry from Jerome on the early history of oratory: 'Nicetes, Hybreas, Theodorus, and Plutio were considered the noblest teachers of the Greek art
of oratory' (*Nicetes et Hybreas et Theodorus et Plutio nobilissimi artis
rhetoricae graeci praeceptores habentur,* Jer. *Chron.* Ol. 187.2 = Suet. fr.
48 Reiff.). Both editors follow Valla in reasonably presuming that Suetonius
wrote on the Domitianic Isaeus, because of the biographer's contemporaneity with the rhetorician. However, even as Valla tries to avoid confusing the
two Isaei, he certainly does so at least once by describing the rhetorician in
Juvenal as 'an Athenian', an error which was carried over from the scholia
in *L* that were used by Valla for this line, and for which the named source
'Probus' is ultimately responsible.[7] This conflation by Probus may be partly
explained by the Roman Isaeus' Assyrian birth and eventual Athenian

3 See Wessner 1931, 35, 243; Brugnoli 1963, 260. This manuscript appears in fact to have
   been copied from a ninth-century one (Cambridge, King's College 52), in which the gloss
   may have originated with Heiric of Auxerre's drawing on the same Probus who is used independently by Valla elsewhere (cf. Wessner 1931, xx–xxiii; see von Büren 2010; Grazzini 2011, xxiv–xxvi.

4 Champlin 1989, 109.

5 *Suda* ι 620: 'Isaeus is one of the Ten Orators, a pupil of Isocrates and the teacher of
   Demosthenes, and an Athenian by birth. But Demetrius says that he is from Chalcis'
   (Ἰσαῖος εἰς μέν ἐστι τῶν δέκα ῥητόρων, μαθητὴς δὲ Ἰσοκράτους, διδάσκαλος δὲ Δημοσθένους,
   Ἀθηναῖος τὸ γένος. Δημήτριος δὲ Χαλκιδέα φησὶν αὐτὸν εἶναι). On the *patria* of the Greek
   orator Isaeus, see Bollansée 1999a, 379 n. 3.

6 Cf. Jahn 1851, 202.

7 See Kaster 1995, 339–41: 'sober refs. to Suet. and the younger Pliny are preceded by
   the blundering description of Isaeus as *Atheniensis*' (quotation at 340); cf. Champlin
   1989, 109, who adduces Philostratus, *Lives of the Sophists* 1.20 for the Roman rhetorician's Assyrian birth and epigraphy for his retirement in Athens, but still opts for
   confusion with the Greek Isaeus on the part of Valla's Probus. For the unreliability of
   this Probus, who used Suetonius carelessly, see Jones 1986, 245, 249–51; Champlin
   1989, 105–7; and below, where I argue that neither is the reference to Suetonius quite
   so 'sober'.

citizenship,[8] which nevertheless do not negate the fact that he practised rhetoric at Rome, and would therefore probably not have been described overall as 'Athenian', unless he had been mistaken for the other Isaeus.

Valla's additional reference to Suetonius may in fact represent a second slip on the part of Probus, that is, Suetonius may have originally discussed the earlier Isaeus. It would not be the first time that Valla's Probus got it wrong using Suetonius as a source for Juvenal. In Valla's revised scholium on the orator Passienus Crispus, he similarly relies on Probus, who transfers the *patria* of one man named Crispus to another; Passienus Crispus is confused with Vibius Crispus, and his place of birth mistaken for Placentia, instead of Visellium: *Vibius Crispus Placentinus, ut inquit Probus ...* (Valla ad Juv. 4.81). Contrast the poet's earliest scholiast: *Crispus, municeps Viselliensis ...* (*Schol. Iuv.* 4.81 ~ Suet. fr. 71 Reiff.).[9] This example offers a perfect precedent for the same kind of confusion we witnessed over Isaeus, involving both the shared name and confused birthplaces of a pair of public speakers, and again with Valla following the same intermediate source for his imprecise Suetonian information. Considering the temporal boundary of the *Illustrious Men*, scholars have been right to be sceptical of Valla's testimony about a figure such as Juvenal's Isaeus, who lived beyond the reign of Domitian, being described in his work.[10] However, none have proposed that Suetonius himself somewhere mentioned the much earlier Greek orator Isaeus.

Like the two Crispi, the two Isaei were ripe for such confusion, especially because of the later Isaeus' ties to Athens, but the ultimate source on Isaeus, Suetonius, also lent himself to error, because he was contemporary with the one, and wrote on the other. This explanation coheres with the accepted temporal endpoint for the *Illustrious Men*, and the perfect place for the earlier Isaeus' mention would have been in the preface to Suetonius' *Orators*. I thus agree with Reifferscheid on the location of Suetonius' discussion of Isaeus, albeit a different man of that name. There is good reason to think that Suetonius would have included a brief summary of the origin and early development of the oratorical profession before the individual biographies

---

8 For the *patria* of the Roman Isaeus, see Aleshire 1991, 72; cf. the previous note. At Rome, he may have taught the emperor Hadrian; see Whitton 2013, 91 (on *Ep.* 2.3.1).

9 On this error by Valla's Probus, see Jones 1986, 249–50; Kaster 1995, 340. Less convincing is the suggestion of Champlin (1989, 110) that the mistake may be Valla's own, since Valla himself hailed from Placentia. For the different orator Vibius Crispus, see Rutledge 2001, 278–82; on Passienus Crispus, below, Chapter 7.

10 Brugnoli 1963, 260–1 suggests that the citation of Suetonius is erroneous, being merely inferred by Valla from Isaeus' appearance in Pliny (or else referring, not to Isaeus, but to 'Probus', whom he mistakes for the grammarian discussed by Suetonius at *Gramm.* 24). Townend 1972a, 377–8, 386 also distrusts the fragment, with appeal to the biographer's avoidance of contemporary figures; cf. Reeve 2011, 208. For Suetonius' chronological endpoint of the Flavian era for the lifespan of his subjects in the *Illustrious Men*, see above, p. 39; below, p. 80.

of his *Orators*; hence Reifferscheid's inclusion of Jerome's fragment on the four Greek teachers of oratory that we have already mentioned. Similar accounts precede Suetonius' sections on both grammarians (*Gramm.* 1.1–4.6) and rhetoricians (*Gramm.* 25.1–5), which include mention of the major figures in the early development of the grammatical profession going back to third century BC, such as Livius Andronicus, Ennius (*Gramm.* 1.1), Crates of Mallos (*Gramm.* 2.1), Lucius Aelius (*Gramm.* 3.1), Lutatius Daphnis, Octavius Teucer, Sescenius Iaccus, and Oppius Chares (*Gramm.* 3.5–6).

Although Suetonius does not go back further than the inception of these two professions at Rome, this may be explained by their relative novelty as respectable endeavours.[11] For oratory, however, Suetonius does appear to have begun with the Greeks, and also for poetry, as shown by a fragment from Isidore, however brief the Greek side of these summaries may have been: 'This kind of discourse, since it is composed in a certain form called *poiotēs*, was named a "poem", and its creators "poets"' (*id genus quia forma quadam efficitur, quae* ποιότης *dicitur, poema uocitatum est, eiusque fictores poetae*, Isid. *Etym.* 8.7.1–2 = Suet. fr. 2 Reiff.).[12] Since Hermippus wrote on the Greek orator Isaeus in the second book of his *Pupils of Isocrates* (frr. 45a–b), it is tempting to think that Suetonius cited him for the same Isaeus. If so, might this even have been one of the prefatory items in the *Illustrious Men* that Jerome had in mind when he wrote that among Suetonius' forerunners was the biographer Hermippus?[13]

It is often thought that Suetonius himself listed a sort of canon of predecessors in a digression on his genre of literary biography, which was simply reproduced by Jerome in the same manner.[14] However, the Christian author may just as easily have gleaned these names from the sources cited by Suetonius in the prefaces to his individual sections. This theory is certainly more in line with Suetonian style, which (at least in his extant beginnings) avoids self-conscious or rhetorical prefaces, or any comment on his literary purpose.[15] Citations, on the other hand, are generally plentiful in Sue-

---

11 Kaster 1995, xxv–xxix.
12 Cf. also the Greeks mentioned by Suetonius in the next note.
13 Jer. *De vir.* 2.821 Vallarsi = Suet. fr. 1 Reiff.: 'The same thing has been done on the Greek side by Hermippus the peripatetic, Antigonus Carystius, the learned man Satyrus, and, by far the most learned of all, Aristoxenus the musician ...' (*fecerunt hoc idem apud Graecos Hermippus peripateticus Antigonus Carystius Satyrus doctus uir et longe omnium doctissimus Aristoxenus musicus* ...). On this passage, see Stem 2012, 108–9 with bibliography.
14 See e.g. Stuart 1928, 192–4; Wallace-Hadrill 1983, 50; Geiger 1985, 32; Kaster 1995, xxv; Bollansée 1999a, 94–7; 1999b, 92–3, 100; Stok 2010, 108; Hägg 2012, 69.
15 On Suetonius as an unapologetic biographer, see Power 2014b, 13. For his informal prefaces in the *Caesars*, see below, Chapter 22, where it is argued that the beginning of the *Galba* acts as a preface to Book 7, and therefore could not have been a 'postscript' to the *Nero*; *pace* Georgiadou 2014, 256. My argument against Suetonius' alleged canon of his biographical precursors in this chapter, first published in 2014, has been challenged by

tonius' beginnings, where he seeks to establish authority with the reader through displays of erudition on the background of his subject and through the careful weighing of evidence, often naming his sources (e.g. *Vita Hor.* 1, *Poet.* 28–9.1–10, *Gramm.* 4.1, 4.3, 7.1, *Aug.* 2.3, *Tib.* 2.1, *Ner.* 1.2, *Vesp.* 1.4).[16] Jerome's own mention of Hermippus is more likely owed to such a citation, whether or not it was on Isaeus, than to a self-conscious discussion by Suetonius of his own task as a biographer. It therefore did not arise from an acknowledgement of a predecessor or source in any kind of formal preface to Suetonius' *Illustrious Men*, but rather from a more casual citation. The 'canon' of early literary biographers was Jerome's making.

In conclusion, it is easy to see how Suetonius' editors have been led astray in accepting the fragment on Isaeus, but since his *Illustrious Men* focused on authors who died no later than AD 96, it is implausible that it included a biography of the Roman rhetorician Isaeus who appears briefly in Juvenal, *Satires* 3. It is more probable that the Isaeus mentioned by Suetonius is the Greek orator of the fourth century BC, and a fitting place for his appearance would have been in the introductory chapters of the *Orators*, where Suetonius may have cited Hermippus as a source. Valla (or, rather, Valla's Probus) fares far worse in exhibiting his own research, erring not only in his confusion of the *patriae* of the two Isaei, where he commits the same kind of error in using Suetonius as he does with Passienus Crispus, but also in the careless reference *cuius et Tranquillus meminit*, which should have been attributed to the earlier Isaeus.

Marshall (2019, 121 n. 12), but his objection lacks cogency, as I shall demonstrate in a future discussion.

16 See below, p. 92, n. 33.

6 The Orator Memmius in Suetonius[*]

Of the many lost subjects of Suetonius' *Illustrious Men* that have been proposed by scholars, an unduly neglected name is Gaius Memmius, the orator who was praetor in 58 BC. No fragment of a biography of his has been preserved by Jerome, but Jerome's entries were compiled in haste (*tumultuarii operis*, *Chron. praef.* 2 Helm), and their use of Suetonius was selective and haphazard.[1] It is in recognition of this fact that both Wallace-Hadrill and Kaster survey writers who are mentioned or used as sources by Suetonius, although curiously neither mentions Memmius.[2] The orator appears several times in Suetonius' extant *Lives* (*Poet.* 36.60–2, *Gramm.* 14.1, *Iul.* 23.1, 49.2, 73), and is cited no less frequently as a source than, for example, Messalla Corvinus (*Gramm.* 4.2, *Aug.* 58.1–2, 74) and almost as many times as Asinius Pollio (*Gramm.* 10.2, 10.6, *Iul.* 30.4, 55.4, 56.4), both of whom were almost certainly included in Suetonius' *Orators* (see below).[3] In this note, I wish to offer some additional evidence in support of a Suetonian biography of Memmius. I shall conclude by venturing a conjecture on the *Life*'s content.

First, let us look briefly at a letter of Pliny the Younger, in which he lists notable figures who, according to him, were both virtuous and yet composed erotic verses:

> an ego uerear – neminem uiuentium, ne quam in speciem adulationis incidam, nominabo – sed ego uerear ne me non satis deceat, quod decuit M. Tullium, C. Caluum, Asinium Pollionem, M. Messalam,

* This chapter was first published in *RhM* 155 (2012), 219–23.

1 See e.g. Wallace-Hadrill 1983, 51–3; Viljamaa 1991, 3831 n. 21; Herbert-Brown 1999, 536.
2 Wallace-Hadrill 1983, 50–9: 'If we seek to extend Jerome's list, we should think in the first place of authors Suetonius knew and used …' (59); Kaster 1995, xxxi–xxxiii; cf. Viljamaa 1991, 3830–1. For Suetonius' biographical approach of reading his own subject's works, see Wallace-Hadrill 1983, 62.
3 Memmius is also cited as a source more than Pollio's son Asinius Gallus (*Gramm.* 22.3), who was likewise included in the *Orators* (Jer. *Chron.* Ol. 198.2 = Suet. fr. 68 Reiff.).

Q. Hortensium, M. Brutum, L. Sullam, Q. Catulum, Q. Scaeuolam, Seruium Sulpicium, Varronem, Torquatum, immo Torquatos, C. Memmium, Lentulum Gaetulicum, Annaeum Senecam et proxime Verginium Rufum et, si non sufficiunt exempla priuata, Diuum Iulium, Diuum Augustum, Diuum Neruam, Tiberium Caesarem? Neronem enim transeo, quamuis sciam non corrumpi in deterius quae aliquando etiam a malis, sed honesta manere quae saepius a bonis fiunt. inter quos uel praecipue numerandus est P. Vergilius, Cornelius Nepos et prius Accius Enniusque. non quidem hi senatores, sed sanctitas morum non distat ordinibus.

Should I fear – I shall name no one alive, so as not to slip into seeming flattery – but should I fear that it should not sufficiently become me, that which became Marcus Tullius, Gaius Calvus, Asinius Pollio, Marcus Messalla, Quintus Hortensius, Marcus Brutus, Lucius Sulla, Quintus Catulus, Quintus Scaevola, Servius Sulpicius, Varro, Torquatus, nay the Torquati, Gaius Memmius, Lentulus Gaetulicus, Annaeus Seneca and most recently Verginius Rufus and, if civilian examples are not enough, Divine Julius, Divine Augustus, Divine Nerva, Tiberius Caesar? For I pass over Nero, even though I know that things sometimes done by the evil are not corrupted, but remain honourable for being more often done by the good. Among the latter, ranked especially high must be Publius Virgil, Cornelius Nepos, and earlier Accius and Ennius. These were not in fact senators, but moral virtue does not discriminate against social classes.

(*Ep.* 5.3.5–6)

Almost half of the names in this catalogue (excluding the Caesars) are thought, based on evidence in Jerome and Donatus, to have had biographies by Suetonius: Ennius (Jer. *Chron.* Ol. 135.1, 153.1 = Suet. frr. 8–9 Reiff.), Accius (Ol. 160.2 = fr. 13 Reiff.), Virgil (*Vita Vergili*), Cicero (Ol. 168.3, 174.2, 175.2, 179.4, 184.2 = frr. 50–4 Reiff.), Asinius Pollio (Ol. 195.4 = fr. 59 Reiff.), Messalla Corvinus (Ol. 180.2, 188.3, 197.3 = frr. 60–2 Reiff.), Nepos (Ol. 185.1 = fr. 75 Reiff.), Varro (Ol. 166.1, 188.1 = frr. 83–4 Reiff.), and Seneca (Ol. 211.1 = fr. 86 Reiff.).[4] It is certainly possible that Pliny's list is influenced by, or engages with, Suetonius' choice of subjects in the *Illustrious Men*, since Pliny probably had first-hand knowledge of the work in late draft form by the time he was composing his

---

4 On the fragments of Jerome and their derivation from Suetonius, see Helm 1929, 3–12 (Ennius), 22–3 (Accius), 27–31 (Cicero), 70 (Asinius Pollio), 46–52 (Messalla Corvinus), 57–8 (Nepos), 23–4 (Varro), and 81–2 (Seneca). I am not convinced by Stroup 2010, 276 n. 3 that the Messalla mentioned by Pliny is instead Messalla Rufus, the consul in 53 BC. Pliny almost certainly means Messalla Corvinus, who is the Messalla cited in the works of Suetonius, and in Tacitus (*Ann.* 4.34.4); on Corvinus, see Martin and Woodman 1989, 180–1 (ad loc.).

fifth book.[5] Pliny perhaps mentions Memmius among other poets in this letter at least partly because of Memmius' biography in the Suetonian collection that he has recently read, and may even have been reminded of Memmius' verses by that work.

Another indication that Suetonius wrote the biography of Memmius is that he has (at least ostensibly) a similar respect for Memmius' speeches to that afforded by Cicero, who, unlike Quintilian, deemed them important enough to mention in his *Brutus*. Although Cicero claims that Memmius preferred Greek to Latin literature and that his oratorical skills were diminished by lack of practice due to his laziness (*tantum sibi de facultate detraxit quantum imminuit industriae, Brut.* 247), he nonetheless praises his style (*argutus orator uerbisque dulcis*, ibid.). Suetonius certainly knew and used this text (*Iul.* 55.1 ~ *Brut.* 261; *Iul.* 56.2 = *Brut.* 262),[6] and appears to have admired Cicero's views on literary matters.[7] Suetonius may be taking his lead from Cicero in considering Memmius worthy of citation in his *Lives*. Witness, for example, the following passage:

> omitto Calui Licini notissimos uersus:
>
> > Bithynia quicquid
> > et pedicator Caesaris umquam habuit.
>
> praetereo actiones Dolabellae et Curionis patris, in quibus eum Dolabella 'paelicem reginae, spondam interiorem regiae lecticae', at Curio 'stabulum Nicomedis et Bithynicum fornicem' dicunt. missa etiam facio edicta Bibuli quibus proscripsit collegam suum Bithynicam reginam eique antea regem fuisse cordi, nunc esse regnum. quo tempore, ut Marcus Brutus refert, Octauius etiam quidam ualitudine mentis liberius dicax conuentu maximo, cum Pompeium regem appellasset, ipsum reginam salutauit. sed C. Memmius etiam ad cyathum et uinum Nicomedi stetisse obicit cum reliquis exoletis pleno conuiuio accubantibus nonnullis urbicis negotiatoribus, quorum refert nomina. Cicero uero ...

> et uinum Y'O², *Rolfe, conieci*: eum *Salmasius, Kaster*: et ui M V L²δ: et uina G

I say nothing of the notorious lines of Licinius Calvus:

> Whatever Bithynia and the paramour of Caesar ever possessed.

---

5 Cf. Sherwin-White 1966, 317: 'it is possible that Pliny drew his list from a literary history.' For Pliny's knowledge of the *Illustrious Men*, see above, Chapter 1; on Suetonius and Pliny, *Letters* 5.3, see Gibson 2014, 226–7, who argues that Pliny's list especially resembles Suetonius' *Illustrious Men* in its focus on earlier and lesser-known figures, in contrast to the rest of Pliny's *Letters*. On Pliny's selection of names in this letter, see also Gibson and Steel 2010, 129–30.
6 Cf. also *Gramm.* 3.2 ~ *Brut.* 169 and 205–7, with Kaster 1995, 75–7.
7 See e.g. McDermott 1971b.

I leave aside the speeches of Dolabella and the elder Curio, in which Dolabella calls him 'the rival of the queen', 'the inner frame of the royal litter', while Curio calls him 'the tavern of Nicomedes' and 'the Bithynian brothel'. I also disregard the edicts of Bibulus in which he published that his colleague was the queen of Bithynia and that he was formerly pleased by a king, now by a kingdom. At that time, as Marcus Brutus reports, in a very large assembly a certain Octavius who was rather freely spoken because of mental illness, after addressing Pompey as king, saluted him as queen. But Gaius Memmius even charges that he bore the drinking-cup and wine of Nicomedes together with the rest of his boys at a full banquet attended by many of the town-merchants, whose names he reports. Indeed, Cicero ...

(*Iul.* 49.1–3)

Suetonius first employs rhetorical *praeteritio* (*omitto ... praetereo ... missa etiam facio* ...) with regard to the first three sources: the verses of Calvus, the speeches of Dolabella and Curio, and the edicts of Bibulus. The last of these calls Caesar 'the queen of Bithynia', to which Suetonius adds Brutus' similar story. Suetonius then makes a transition to Memmius and Cicero not only because of their more detailed and condemning accounts, but with an emphasis through the words *sed* and *uero* on the greater credibility of these figures.[8]

A similar contrast with Memmius as a more reliable source may be observed in the *Life* of Terence, where Suetonius follows his discussion of the common rumour (*non obscura fama*, *Poet.* 35.47) that Laelius and Scipio aided the poet in writing his plays first with support from verses by Terence himself, which he has reason to find suspect (*Poet.* 35.48–58). Suetonius then turns to quotations of Memmius and Nepos: 'Nevertheless, this rumour gained more strength, and all the way into later times. Gaius Memmius in a speech in his own defence says ... Nepos on high authority ...' (*quae tamen magis et usque ad posteriora tempora ualuit. C. Memmius in oratione pro se ait ... Nepos auctore certo ... Poet.* 35–6.59–63). Again, Memmius is thus paired with Nepos as a more legitimate source than the preceding citations in the *Terence*, just as he is with Cicero in the *Life* of Caesar.

The last piece of evidence for a biography of Memmius by Suetonius is a passage of the *Grammarians and Rhetoricians*, in which Suetonius reports an affair between Memmius and Pompey's wife Cornelia:

8 Cf. Baldwin 1983, 116 on Memmius. On this episode involving Caesar and Nicomedes, see e.g. D. Braund 1996, 45–7; Osgood 2008. For the reading *et uinum*, see below, Chapter 18.

Curtius Nicia adhaesit Cn. Pompio et C. Memmio, sed cum codicillos Memmi ad Pompei uxorem de stupro pertulisset, proditus ab ea Pompeium offendit domoque ei interdictum est.

Curtius Nicias was associated with Gnaeus Pompey and Gaius Memmius, but since he had brought a note from Memmius to Pompey's wife about a sexual rendezvous, when he was betrayed by her he offended Pompey, being forbidden from his home.

(*Gramm.* 14.1)

Kaster believes that the source of this anecdote is a lost biography of Lucilius by Santra, since Santra is cited at the end of this passage for Nicias' own work on the poet (*Gramm.* 14.4).[9] Santra may indeed have used Nicias in such a work, but it seems unlikely that he would have included biographical details about him that were so far removed from his proper subject. Since Suetonius' other predecessors on Nicias were scant,[10] a better candidate for the source is a composition dealing with Memmius, especially since the story seems characteristic of the latter: given the orator's reputation for amorous activities (Cic. *Att.* 1.18.3; Catull. 28.9–10; Val. Max. 6.1.13), erotic poetry (Ov. *Tr.* 2.433–4; Pliny above; Gell. *NA* 19.9.7), and political scandal due to his impeachment for bribery (Cic. *Q Fr.* 3.2.8, *Fam.* 13.19, *Att.* 5.11, 6.1; App. *B Civ.* 2.24),[11] the anecdote would fit perfectly with source material on Memmius.

What was the source? All of Suetonius' references to Memmius' own works are to his speeches (*oratione*, *Poet.* 36.60; *obicit*, *Iul.* 49.2; *orationibus*, ibid. 73), but it is doubtful that a speech written by him would have contained this embarrassing anecdote. The story may therefore indicate a lost source on Memmius that was found by Suetonius during biographical research conducted specifically on the orator. The only remaining alternative to this would be to argue for the material being pillaged from Suetonius' unused notes in composing an unknown historical work that dealt with Pompey, such as the one posited by Reifferscheid for some of Jerome's entries which do not fit easily into the biographer's corpus (frr. 208–28 Reiff.). Since relating Suetonius' source at *De grammaticis* 14.4 to one of his *known* works is preferable to positing an unknown one, and since Suetonius used the subjects of his literary *Lives* as sources for each other, a source discovered while writing Memmius' biography in the *Illustrious Men* is the best choice.

It is reasonable to conclude that Memmius has been overlooked as one of the probable orators in Suetonius' *Illustrious Men*. The absence of Memmius from Jerome's *Chronicle* has deterred scholars from this conjecture,

---

9 Kaster 1995, 170, 176.
10 Cf. Baldwin 1983, 434.
11 For Memmius' poetry, see Hollis 2007, 90–2. On Memmius' impeachment, see Sumner 1982.

but it cannot be given much weight in this question, because Jerome's entries from Suetonius are by no means exhaustive, and there is enough evidence elsewhere to suggest his Suetonian biography. This conclusion coheres with Suetonius' particular interest in the period surrounding the empire's foundation,[12] and with the fact that no other orator appears as often as a named source in Suetonius who is not also included in his literary *Lives*. Moreover, *De grammaticis* 14.1 may even derive from a source originally consulted by Suetonius for his biography of Memmius. Considering Suetonius' use of the literary writings of the Caesars in the *Illustrious Men* (*Poet.* 43-4.116-21, *Vita Hor.* 5–6, *Vita Luc.* 18–19), we may well wonder whether this lost *Life* contained any quotation from the speeches of Caesar against Memmius, which Suetonius refers to in the dictator's *Life* as written *non minore acerbitate* (*Iul.* 73).[13]

12 For Suetonius' greater focus on this period, see Wallace-Hadrill 1983, 56–7.
13 On these speeches, see *Schol. Bob.* ad Cic. *Sest.* 18, ad Cic. *Vat.* 15, with Gelzer 1968, 97, n. 6. Could Suetonius' *Life* of Memmius be the source of the anecdote in the same scholia about Vatinius' conspirators, who climbed onto the tribunal and seized the ballot-boxes when Memmius as a praetor was appointing a judge for Vatinius' trial (*Schol. Bob.* ad Cic. *Vat.* 34)? Such a story seems characteristic of Suetonius; see e.g. *Gramm.* 9.5, 22.1, 26.2, 30.4–5, *Iul.* 43, 76.2–3, *Aug.* 33, *Calig.* 16, *Claud.* 14–15, *Ner.* 15, *Dom.* 8. There is a precedent in the scholia to Juvenal, which preserve a fragment from Suetonius' *Life* of the orator Passienus Crispus (*Schol. Iuv.* 4.81 = fr. 71 Reiff.). For other possible fragments of Suetonius in the scholia to Juvenal, see Jones 1986.

7   The Sister of Passienus Crispus

The surviving fragments of Suetonius' *Orators*, which was once part of his *Illustrious Men*, are few, and none exist in their full original form. Among the most substantial is the *Life* of Passienus Crispus, which contains the only extant anecdote from this section involving an emperor. The historical identity of the ruler is most likely Gaius Caligula, even though the scant text that has come down to us, a brief summary found in the scholia to Juvenal which hardly represents the whole *Passienus Crispus*, actually mentions Nero:[1]

> omnium principum gratiam adpetiuit, sed praecipue C. Caesaris, quem iter facientem secutus est pedibus. hic nullo audiente ab <u>Nerone</u> [Gaio] interrogatus, *haberetne sicut ipse cum sorore germana consuetudinem*, 'nondum', inquit, quantumuis decenter et caute, ne aut negando eum argueret aut adsentiendo semet mendacio dehonestaret.
>
> Nerone *mss*.: Caesare *Reiff*.

> He tried to gain favour with all the emperors, but especially with Gaius Caesar, whom he attended on foot when the emperor made a journey. When he was asked by <u>Nero</u> [Gaius] in a private conversation *whether he had commerce with his own sister, as the emperor had with his*, he replied 'Not yet'; a very fitting and cautious answer, neither accusing the emperor by denying the allegation, nor dishonouring himself with a lie by admitting it.
>
> (*Schol. Iuv.* 4.81 = Suet. fr. 71 Reiff.)

Passienus was known to have been in the travelling retinue of Caligula, and Nero was still only a young child when Passienus died, so that logically

---

1 As noted by Barrett 2015, 118. Jones 1986, 249 mistakenly refers to Tiberius instead of Nero in his discussion of this scholium. Unless otherwise stated, translations of Suetonius' *Passienus Crispus*, Tacitus' *Annals*, and Cassius Dio in this chapter are taken from the Loeb editions of Rolfe 1913–14; Hutton et al. 1914–37; Cary 1924–5, respectively.

Caligula makes better sense as the emperor in question, especially when one also considers his incestuous relationship with his sister Drusilla.

But why did the scholiast on Juvenal who preserves this fragment confuse him with Nero? This question has never been posed, let alone satisfactorily answered. The solution may in fact be the most important explanation of how Suetonius actually wrote something more general such as 'that emperor', in order to signify Caligula, whether he conveyed it through the word *illo*, *eo*, *imperatore*, or even Reifferscheid's conjecture *Caesare* (which was not accepted by Rolfe), rather than *Nerone*. Such an emendation will turn out to be correct if our aim is to edit the scholium into the best possible fragment of Suetonius' original text, or if we have regard for how the sentence is translated in English. In other words, I wish to defend the manuscript reading *Nerone*, which is what I think the scholiast wrote, but not as a misreading of the original Suetonian word; rather, as a more explicit correction of it, either wittingly or unwittingly, because he was wrongly recalling a part of Suetonius' text that simply meant 'that emperor', following on directly in the biography from the previous mention of C. *Caesaris*, which is more accurately preserved by the scholiast. It will be shown that it is consequently the scholiast, not the biographer, who is in error.

In my estimation, the reason for the scholiast's miscitation is a parallel passage in the *Roman History* of Cassius Dio that involves the emperor Nero in a very similar context, where he brags about having sex with his own mother Agrippina the Younger. It is this tale that the scholiast may have had in mind and have therefore erroneously conflated with the story about Caligula when he recorded his biographical details about Passienus Crispus. The Neronian anecdote comes at the end of Dio's discussion of whether or not the emperor committed incest with his mother:

τούτῳ τὴν Σαβῖναν, ἐξ εὐπατριδῶν οὖσαν, ἀπὸ τοῦ ἀνδρὸς ἀποσπάσας ἔδωκε, καὶ αὐτῇ ἀμφότεροι ἅμα ἐχρῶντο. φοβηθεῖσα οὖν ἡ Ἀγριππῖνα μὴ γήμηται τῷ Νέρωνι ᾽δεινῶς γὰρ ἤδη αὐτῆς ἐρᾶν ἤρξατο, ἔργον ἀνοσιώτατον ἐτόλμησεν· ὥσπερ γὰρ οὐχ ἱκανὸν ὂν ἐς μυθολογίαν ὅτι τὸν θεῖον τὸν Κλαύδιον ἐς ἔρωτα αὐτῆς ταῖς τε γοητείαις ταῖς τε ἀκολασίαις καὶ τῶν βλεμμάτων καὶ τῶν φιλημάτων ὑπηγάγετο, ἐπεχείρησε καὶ τὸν Νέρωνα ὁμοίως καταδουλώσασθαι. ἀλλ᾽ ἐκεῖνο μὲν εἴτ᾽ ἀληθῶς ἐγένετο εἴτε πρὸς τὸν τρόπον αὐτῶν ἐπλάσθη οὐκ οἶδα· ἃ δὲ δὴ πρὸς πάντων ὡμολόγηται λέγω, ὅτι ἑταίραν τινὰ τῇ Ἀγριππίνῃ ὁμοίαν ὁ Νέρων δι᾽ αὐτὸ τοῦτο ἐς τὰ μάλιστα ἠγάπησε, καὶ αὐτῇ τε ἐκείνῃ προσπαίζων καὶ τοῖς ἄλλοις ἐνδεικνύμενος ἔλεγεν ὅτι καὶ τῇ μητρὶ ὁμιλοίη.

It was to him [Otho] that the emperor gave [Poppaea] Sabina, a woman of patrician family, after separating her from her husband, and they both enjoyed her together. Agrippina, therefore, fearing that Nero would marry the woman (for he was now beginning to entertain a mad passion for her), ventured upon a most unholy course, as if it were not notoriety enough for her that she had used her blandishments and immodest looks and kisses to enslave even Nero in similar fashion. Whether this actually occurred, now, or whether it was invented to fit their character, I am not sure; but I state as a fact what is admitted by all, that Nero had a mistress resembling Agrippina of whom he was especially fond because of this very resemblance, and when he toyed with the girl herself or displayed her charms to others, he would say that *he was wont to have intercourse with his mother.*

(Dio Cass. 61.11.2–4)

The two passages are very close in substance and context: both contain sayings by the emperor about incest with a female family member, and both are sort of boasts or recommendations of the practice to others, as implied in Nero's case through his displaying of his mother's lookalike to his associates: 'when he ... displayed her charms to others' (καὶ τοῖς ἄλλοις ἐνδεικνύμενος). Nero is essentially portrayed as flouting Roman decency and morality by bragging about incest and suggesting how good it is to his friends in the exact same manner as Caligula does in the biographical scene with Passienus.

What made matters even more confusing for the scholiast is another incestuous detail, which Suetonius records a few lines earlier in the *Life* of Passienus, at least as it survives in the note to Juvenal: 'He married twice: first Domitia and then Agrippina, respectively the aunt and the mother of the emperor Nero' (*uxores habuit duas, primam Domitiam, deinde Agrippinam, illam amitam, hanc matrem Neronis Caesaris*, Suet. fr. 71 Reiff.). Since Agrippina, one of the people in the above passage from Suetonius' *Passienus Crispus*, was also married at one point to Passienus, the scholiast could plausibly have associated the two historical figures, so that an anecdote about Passienus brought to mind Agrippina, who is even mentioned beforehand in this fragment of the *Life*. Moreover, the reality that the orator had at first been married to Domitia, Agrippina's sister-in-law, whom he divorced in order to marry her, means that his subsequent marriage with Agrippina was technically incestuous too. In other words, Passienus himself had indeed 'not yet' committed incest with his own sister, because he would later actually do so, just as he said to Caligula. This irony in Passienus' reply has been missed by critics, but it was possibly not lost on Suetonius, who may have commented (as is often his manner) in a lost part of the *Life* on the prophetic quality of this statement when one considers the subsequent sisterly incest by Passienus himself. The incestuous connection with Agrippina is at least probably the key to unlocking what went wrong in the transmission of this part of his biography.

Historically speaking, one of Passienus' sisters, albeit not by blood as in Caligula's saying (*sorore germana*), was the very woman referred to in the different emperor's saying related by Dio from a first-century source. If this saying about Nero survived at least as late as the third century when Dio was writing, it stands to reason that it was probably still around at the time of the Juvenalian commentator's composition of his scholium on Passienus in the mid-fifth century. It is important to note that Dio's interpretation of Nero's incestuous relationship with his mother was by no means the only one available to the historian, as he admits by equivocating on whether or not Agrippina dressed in a sexy manner for her son and gave him inappropriate kisses: 'Whether this actually occurred, now, or whether it was invented to fit their character, I am not sure' (ἀλλ' ἐκεῖνο μὲν εἴτ' ἀληθῶς ἐγένετο εἴτε πρὸς τὸν τρόπον αὐτῶν ἐπλάσθη οὐκ οἶδα, Dio Cass. 61.11.4). In fact, the allegation made by Dio is not one of real incest, only flirtation and manipulation, followed by vicarious role play with a prostitute. The historian never goes so far as to claim that Agrippina fully seduced her son by sleeping with him. He stops well short of such a declaration, and does not even accept responsibility for the fact that she sought to arouse Nero. Although Dio offers the taboo anecdote about the emperor's prostitute as clear evidence that her tactic of making him desire her worked, the anecdote also substantiates the view that Nero never really consummated the incest, but rather had to procure a surrogate with whom to live out his forbidden fantasy.

Dio's explicit comparison with Poppaea in his discussion of Agrippina suggests both the similarity and difference between the two women's effect on Nero: Agrippina made her son want her 'in similar fashion' (ὁμοίως), but not the exact same fashion, as Poppaea, whom the emperor actually 'enjoyed' (ἐχρῶντο). Nero is portrayed as having been 'enslaved' (καταδουλώσασθαι) by Agrippina's seductive kisses and alluring attire, just as Poppaea had given him a 'mad passion' (ἐρᾶν) for her charms in bed, which, as Dio tells us, he was sharing with the future emperor Otho. This version of Nero not being truly satisfied by Agrippina, but simply tantalized, is solidified a few chapters later when Dio recounts another story about his surveyance of her dead corpse after ordering her murder:

καὶ διὰ τοῦτο αὐτόπτης ἐπεθύμησε τοῦ πάθους γενέσθαι. καὶ αὐτήν τε πᾶσαν εἶδε γυμνώσας καὶ τὰ τραύματα αὐτῆς ἐπεσκέψατο, καὶ τέλος πολὺ καὶ τοῦ φόνου ἀνοσιώτερον ἔπος ἐφθέγξατο· εἶπε γὰρ ὅτι Οὐκ ᾔδειν ὅτι οὕτω καλὴν μητέρα εἶχον.

He therefore desired to behold the victim of his crime with his own eyes. So he laid bare her body, looked her all over and inspected her wounds, finally uttering a remark far more abominable even than the murder. His words were: 'I did not know I had so beautiful a mother.'
(Dio Cass. 61.14.2)

If indeed Nero 'did not know' that Agrippina had such a lovely body, he must never have fully slept with her. Based on the similar account in Tacitus, who cites his exact sources, it is clear that Dio is here adhering to the version of Nero's relationship with his mother found in the lost first-century historian Fabius Rusticus, which stands in stark contrast to the equally lost work of Rusticus' contemporary Cluvius Rufus.

Tacitus tells us that in Cluvius' historical work, by contrast, Agrippina took the initiative and did completely seduce Nero, because their incest was 'common knowledge' (*peruulgatum*) in the view of the freedwoman Acte, who witnessed Agrippina's own boasting about it; on the other hand, as also emerges from Tacitus, Rusticus wrote that the plan of incest originated with Nero himself, but was 'wrecked' (*disiectum*) by Acte (*Ann.* 14.2). It is thus from Rusticus that Nero's saying in Dio most likely derives. Tacitus also tells us in the same passage that he himself and the other earlier historians concur with Cluvius' interpretation, with which Suetonius too accords, producing the sordid detail of the semen-stained sheets discovered in the litter that Nero shared with his mother after their rides together. As usual, Suetonius contributes a unique fact that was probably recorded by Cluvius, but which only the biographer, of all our parallel authors, found significant enough to hand down to future readers:

> nam matris concubitum appetisse et ab obtrectatoribus eius, ne ferox atque impotens mulier et hoc genere gratiae praeualeret, deterritum nemo dubitauit, utique postquam meretricem, quam fama erat Agrippinae <esse> simillimam inter concubinas recepit. olim etiam quotiens lectica cum matre ueheretur, libidinatum inceste ac maculis uestis proditum affirmant. ... adduntur his atrociora nec incertis auctoribus, ad uisendum interfectae cadauer accurrisse, contrectasse membra, alia uituperasse, alia laudasse, sitique interim oborta bibisse.

> That he even desired illicit relations with his own mother, and was kept from it by her enemies, who feared that such a help might give the reckless and insolent woman too great influence, was notorious, especially after he added to his concubines a courtesan who was said to look very like Agrippina. Even before that, so they say, whenever he rode in a litter with his mother, he had incestuous relations with her, which were betrayed by the stains on his clothing. ... Trustworthy authorities add still more gruesome details: that he hurried off to view the corpse, handled her limbs, criticising some and commending others, and that becoming thirsty meanwhile, he took a drink.

> (*Ner.* 28.2, 34.4)

The necrophilic reaction of Nero getting hot and bothered enough to need a drink when he sees his mother naked more likely suggests that he had in reality been made accustomed to sexual excitement at this sight through sexual intercourse, rather than his arousal from finally gazing upon it for the very first time, which is how it is presented in Dio.

By describing Nero's handling of Agrippina's limbs, and suppressing the remark about her beauty that implied the emperor's innocence of total incest, Suetonius' account of the scene with his mother's nude corpse differs noticeably from that of Dio.[2] By contrast, Tacitus recoils even from discussion of the matter, practically apologizing for having to comment on this part of the story in his sources, even though, as we have shown, he agrees with Cluvius that the incest did happen: 'Whether Nero inspected the corpse of his mother and expressed approval of her figure is a statement which some affirm and some deny' (*aspexeritne matrem exanimem Nero et formam corporis eius laudauerit, sunt qui tradiderint, sunt qui abnuant, Ann.* 14.9). Nonetheless, Tacitus' version of the tale suggests some doubt as to its veracity. Suetonius, however, straightforwardly claims that the story is vouched for 'by rather assured sources' (*nec incertis auctoribus, Ner.* 34.4). It is therefore quite possible that Suetonius has removed that doubt in order to make the event seem more credible than it was, since these details support his overall view of Nero's cruel and lustful character if, when the emperor examined his mother's corpse, he handled her body parts and appraised them, during which he had to take a break for water. Together with the evidence of Nero's soiled private litter, the titbit of his parched mouth, which in Suetonius caps the more affirmatively asserted examination of her limbs, paints a picture of an even unholier debauchery, as it were, than we find in either Dio or Tacitus. If any of these details from Cluvius had been included by Dio, even to refute them, they would have contradicted Rusticus' view that Nero never slept with his mother, which he has chosen to follow. All three authors take material from both earlier variants of the tradition, but Dio is the only one eventually to bolster Rusticus' point that Nero did not sleep with his mother, and he adduces the example of the prostitute acquired by Nero only as evidence for the success of Agrippina's plan to make him sexually attracted to her through her teasing behaviour.

Since the scholiast seems therefore to have in mind Rusticus' more circumspect and reticent version of Nero's incestuous relationship with Agrippina, as preserved best in Dio's account of the reign, rather than the Cluvian one put forth by Tacitus and Suetonius, the parallel with the story involving Passienus is especially strong: neither case is truly incest with Agrippina,

---

2 It is the least favourable account; see Bradley 1978, 201. Meister 2014, 67 thinks that Suetonius 'combines both [versions]' with regard to the attraction: 'Nero was attracted to his mother, but he was dissuaded from incest.' However, if this were an accurate summary of Suetonius, he would simply be following Rusticus. Instead, while the biographer does indeed combine both sources, he sides ultimately with Cluvius: he agrees with Rusticus that Nero initiated the incest (whereas Cluvius had Agrippina as the instigator), yet Suetonius claims not that he was prevented from it *entirely*, but on the contrary only from *continuing* it, since he concedes 'incestuous relations' (*libidinatum inceste*) with Agrippina 'before' (*olim*) Nero resorted to the prostitute, who is portrayed, per this significant temporal marker in the biography – something not always found in Suetonius – as a compensation for the loss of sexual pleasure from his mother. On allusion to Sophocles' *Oedipus Tyrannus* in Suetonius' scene, see below, Chapter 21. For scepticism towards the allegations of incest between Nero and Agrippina, see Drinkwater 2019, 312.

but more of a pretend incest. Nero slept with her lookalike, while Passienus, even though he did sleep with and even marry Agrippina, was not quite her brother, but merely her brother-in-law. Both men were therefore historically connected to Agrippina through a relationship that was both incestuous, and at the same time 'not yet' full incest, so that if the scholiast was thinking of Passienus' wife Agrippina, he could easily have thought that the emperor in this anecdote was Nero. The scholiast's jumbling of events may thus not have been entirely without its own misguided reasoning, with the same themes of Agrippina, sisters, and an emperor's boastful saying about incest all combining to cause the error of 'Nero', rather than 'Gaius'. After all, this particular scholiast was not known for his strong command of Roman history.[3] The comparison with the story of Nero's boast about his maternal prostitute makes it easy to see how the scholiast could have muddled his sources, due to his familiarity with the other saying in Dio's source, who was probably Rusticus, so that he preserves an anecdote about Caligula from Suetonius, but misattributes it to Nero. The confusion is completely understandable, and almost natural, based on the especially similar story that was told about Nero, but no one previously made this connection, which finally offers a good explanation for the scholiast's error. This likely scenario of the misnaming's genesis based on a similar remark in a very close context by Nero at once both gives the manuscript reading *Nerone* credence and undermines its historical accuracy. We may now safely emend our text, if not of the passage in the scholia, then at least of this Suetonian fragment of Passienus' biography, to *illo* – that is, *Gaio*.

---

3 See above, p. 62 on a different confusion of names in this very same fragment from Suetonius' *Life* of Passienus Crispus.

8   Suetonius and the Date of Curtius Rufus*

Curtius Rufus' panegyric of his own emperor in Book 10 of the *History of Alexander* has been the subject of much scholarly debate, since it offers the only internal evidence for the work's date:

> sed iam fatis admouebantur Macedonum genti bella ciuilia; nam et inso-
> ciabile est regnum et a pluribus expetebatur. primum ergo conlisere uires,
> deinde disperserunt; et cum pluribus corpus, quam capiebat, capitibus on-
> erassent, cetera membra deficere coeperunt, quodque imperium sub uno
> stare potuisset, dum a pluribus sustinetur, ruit. proinde iure meritoque
> populus Romanus salutem se principi suo debere profitetur, qui noctis,
> quam paene supremam habuimus, nouum sidus inluxit. huius, hercule,
> non solis ortus lucem caliganti reddidit mundo, cum sine suo capite discor-
> dia membra trepidarent. quot ille tum extinxit faces! quot condidit glad-
> ios! quantam tempestatem subita serenitate discussit! non ergo reuirescit
> solum, sed etiam floret imperium. absit modo inuidia, excipiet huius sae-
> culi tempora eiusdem domus utinam perpetua, certe diuturna posteritas.

> But already fate was bringing civil wars upon the Macedonian race, for
> royal power cannot be shared, and it was desired by many. Thus their
> forces initially clashed, then disbanded, and since they had loaded the body
> with more heads than it could take, the remaining limbs began to fail; and
> the empire that could have stood under one man, fell while it was held up
> by many. Hence justly and deservedly the Roman people proclaim that
> they owe their salvation to their own emperor, who shone forth as a new
> star of the night that was almost our last. It was assuredly not the sun's
> but his rising that returned light to the darkening world, since without
> their head the limbs were in confused disarray. How many torches he then
> extinguished! How many swords he sheathed! How great a storm he dis-
> pelled with immediate clearness! So the empire not only recovers but also
> flourishes. No offence intended, but from the times of this age there will
> follow the same house's continual, I hope, and certainly lasting posterity.
>
> (Curt. 10.9.1–6)

* This chapter was first published in *Hermes* 141 (2013), 117–20.

Many scholars have attempted to identify Curtius' *principi suo*.[1] The best argument has hitherto been for either Claudius or Vespasian.[2] Relevant to this debate is Curtius' praise not merely of the current emperor, but of his whole house (*domus*, Curt. 10.9.6).[3] I should argue that this may be an indication of Vespasian, since ancient writers tend to refer to the whole Flavian family, rather than Vespasian alone (e.g. Plin. *HN praef.* 1, 5, 20; Suet. *Vesp.* 1.1).[4] Moreover, the most obvious Roman parallel with the period following Alexander's death was AD 69, the year of unrest which followed the death of Nero in AD 68, and indeed Plutarch's source for the beginning of his *Galba* made this precise analogy (Plut. *Galb.* 1.1–6),[5] in order to praise the current emperor Vespasian by attributing the cause of that year's wars to the soldiers through the same imagery of Alexander's decapitated army.[6] In the rest of this chapter, I shall add further support for a Vespasianic date for the *History of Alexander* by assessing the meagre external evidence for the life of Curtius Rufus, especially his lost biography by Suetonius.

The possibility that Curtius Rufus wrote under Vespasian would be precluded if we identified him with the soldier and consul of that name who is mentioned by Pliny (*Ep.* 7.27.2–3) and Tacitus (*Ann.* 11.20.4–21.4), since this man appears to have died before the reign of Nero.[7] However, there are inconsistencies between this man's character as described by Tacitus and that of the author of the *History of Alexander*, particularly this Curtius' alleged fondness for flattery and wide military experience, both of which seem contradicted within the work.[8] Sumner argued that this man was the same as another Curtius Rufus who was included in Suetonius' *Grammarians and Rhetoricians* and is known to us only from an ancient index of that

1 For surveys of the debate and bibliography, see e.g. Tarn 1948, 111–14; Korzeniewski 1959, 4–50; Badian 1971, 47–8; Devine 1979, 142–4, 148; Boedefeld 1982; Hamilton 1988, 445–7; Fugmann 1995, 233–4; Atkinson 1998, 3451–5; Baynham 1998, 201–20; Atkinson and Yardley 2009, 2–14. The date of Curtius Rufus' work that is proposed in the present chapter, first published in 2013, is now favoured by Oakley 2020, 199–200. For the *History of Alexander*, I use the text of Lucarini 2009, with my own translation.
2 For Claudius, see Atkinson 1980, 19–57; cf. id. 1994, 26–8; id. and Yardley 2009, 8; Pastor 2018; for Vespasian, Baynham 1998, 213–16. Bosworth 1983, 151–4 makes an appeal for Trajan; furthered in id. 2004.
3 For Curtius' emphasis on *domus*, cf. Baynham 1998, 212 on the possibility that this refers to Augustus and his heirs.
4 For this tendency, see Schwartz 1990, 14–15; Beagon 2005a, 7.
5 See Barzanò 1985, 88.
6 On the presence and purpose of this imagery in Plutarch's source, see, respectively, Godolphin 1935; Powell 1972. Tacitus' imagery for this period is also similar to the Curtian passage; see Grilli 1976, 217–19.
7 See Suerbaum 2004; 2015, 493–511.
8 See Curt. 3.2.10, 3.2.18, 3.6.19, 4.7.31, 6.2.15, 6.6.11, 7.4.9, 8.5.6, 8.8.21–2, 9.4.22, cited by McQueen 1967, 25, 40 nn. 16–17; cf. Kaster 1995, 336; *pace* Atkinson and Yardley 2009, 12, who see military experience as qualifying this Curtius to write history.

work.[9] Since the former Curtius is unlikely to have been the author of the *History of Alexander*, it is less problematic to believe that the author is the latter Curtius, who was a different man. In fact, the Curtius whose *Life* Suetonius wrote may well have lived into the reign of Vespasian, as the index to the *Grammarians and Rhetoricians* shows.

Although it is merely a name without even a corresponding fragment in Jerome, Curtius' entry in the list of Suetonius' lost rhetoricians can tell us a great deal, since Suetonius appears to have written these *Lives* in essentially chronological order,[10] and to have imposed a limit of the Flavian period for the date of the subjects' deaths; only grammarians and rhetoricians who died before AD 96 are treated.[11] The only exceptions to this chronological order are cases where Suetonius was uncertain of the exact date of the subject's rhetorical activity and either presumed the contemporaneity of more than one figure or made inferences from their well-known students' years of age. For example, Suetonius places Valerius Cato before Cornelius Epicadus and Staberius Eros, even though he was younger than both men, because the only temporal marker in his sources for these three grammarians appears to have been 'in the time of Sulla' (*Sullani temporis, Gramm.* 11.1; cf. *temporibus Sullanis*, 13.2); he therefore ordered them freely within this period, putting the most famous writer first.[12] For the rhetorician Otacilius Pitholaus, Suetonius knew only that his pupil was Pompey (*Gramm.* 27.2), who was older than both Antony and Augustus, the pupils of the rhetorician Marcus Epidius (28.1–2); and in this case the biographer appears to have made the correct inferences about the respective ages of Pitholaus and Epidius.[13] Suetonius was therefore trying to keep to the chronological order, even if he sometimes made rough estimations.

When we analyse Curtius' position in Suetonius' index within this context of general chronology, we can see that he appears directly after Porcius Latro, a contemporary of Seneca the Elder's,[14] and before five figures who are best dated to the reign of Claudius. The last of these, Antonius Liberalis, is recorded as flourishing in rhetoric and being a noted enemy of the grammarian Remmius Palaemon during this reign (Jer. *Chron.* Ol. 206.4 = Suet. fr. 5 Kaster), although Palaemon lived to be contemporary also with

---

9 Sumner 1961; cf. Syme 1958, 563 n. 6.
10 On the chronological order of the *Grammarians and Rhetoricians*, see Kaster 1992, 42; 1995, 148, 205–6.
11 For this temporal boundary, see Wallace-Hadrill 1983, 52–6; above, p. 39.
12 Kaster 1995, 162. Suetonius generally ordered these two collections of *Lives* according to political rulers: the above three subjects belong under Sulla (*Gramm.* 11–13); Curtius Nicias and Lenaeus (14–15) under Pompey; and Caecilius Epirota, Verrius Flaccus, Lucius Crassicius, Scribonius Aphrodisius, Iulius Hyginus, and Gaius Melissus (16–21) all under Augustus; see also Viljamaa 1991, 3841.
13 See Kaster 1995, 298.
14 Sen. *Controv.* 1 *praef.* 13–18, 20–4; see Kaster 1995, 329.

Pliny the Elder and Quintilian.[15] The final three names in the index – Iulius Gabinianus, Quintilian, and Iulius Tiro – were all Flavian rhetoricians.[16] This analysis reveals an important point: Suetonius positions these subjects in terms of birthdate and the height of their fame in Rome as grammarians or rhetoricians (their *floruit*) and pays no regard to how long they lived or when they died with regard to the placement of their biographies, aside from ensuring, as we said above, that their deaths preceded Domitian's. Suetonius even records that some of these figures wrote late literary works, but he nonetheless orders their *Lives* according to their practice of grammar or rhetoric. For example, Suetonius tells us that Gaius Melissus, who appears to have gained notice as a grammarian towards the end of the first century BC, did not begin writing his large collection of *ineptiae* until *c.* AD 9 at the age of fifty-nine, and even later added other *libelli* (*Gramm.* 21.4), which probably included several grammatical and historical works.[17]

Our evidence for Suetonius' lost biography of Curtius, then, is compatible with the view that even if Curtius' major fame as a rhetorician was achieved under Tiberius or Claudius, he may have lived to old age and written his *History of Alexander* much later in life. In fact, this plausible conjecture, for which the example of Melissus discussed above provides a fitting parallel, would cohere well with the observation of many scholars that Curtius' history seems the work of someone very familiar with the rhetorical schools.[18] A similar reconstruction of this temporal progression was even advanced by Milns, who argued for a dating of the work under Galba, when Curtius would have been in his seventies.[19] An objection to this theory has been raised by McQueen, who claims that if Suetonius' Curtius had been the author of the *History of Alexander*, Suetonius would not have placed him in the section of his *Illustrious Men* that dealt with rhetoricians, but rather in the section on historians.[20]

However, this objection is easily refuted by comparing Suetonius' seemingly arbitrary categorization of Asinius Pollio as an orator (*Asinius Pollio orator et consularis*, Jer. *Chron.* Ol. 195.4 = Suet. fr. 59 Reiff.), despite his accomplishments as a poet and historian,[21] or that of Asconius Pedianus

---

15 Plin. *HN* 14.49–51; Quint. *Inst.* 1.4.19–20, with *Schol. Iuv.* 6.452; see Kaster 1995, 331–2, cf. 229–30.

16 See Kaster 1995, 332–5 for the first two; and for Iulius Tiro, above, p. 41, n. 76, where I argue that Tiro is unlikely to have been the same man described by Plin. *Ep.* 6.31.7–12 as being alive in the reign of Trajan.

17 Kaster 1995, 215–16; on Melissus' dates, see also id. 1992, 42; cf. id. 1995, 205–6.

18 See e.g. Tarn 1948, 92; McQueen 1967, 32; Kaster 1995, 336; Atkinson and Yardley 2009, 13–14.

19 Milns 1966, 505–6; cf. Baynham 1998, 218, who adds other examples of ancient writers who composed works late in life.

20 McQueen 1967, 25.

21 Contrast, for example, Tacitus' more ambiguous treatment of Pollio at *Dialogus* 12.6, 21.7, with Levene 2004, 165–8, 175 n. 52. On Pollio the historian, see e.g. Morgan 2000.

as a writer of history (*Quintus Asconius Pedianus scribtor historicus clarus*, Jer. *Chron.* Ol. 213.3 = Suet. fr. 79 Reiff.), rather than of grammatical works such as his commentary on Cicero's speeches. Suetonius may also have made a similar decision for C. Calpurnius Piso, who was known for both oratory and poetry;[22] likewise for Licinius Calvus, whom he appears to have categorized as an orator rather than poet.[23] In sum, while a date for the height of Curtius Rufus' rhetorical activities under Tiberius or Claudius fits best with the evidence in Suetonius, this evidence still allows for the possibility that Curtius finished and published his work on Alexander the Great under Vespasian, which seems the best conclusion from the internal evidence of Curtius' panegyric (Curt. 10.9.1–6).

22 See Jones 1986, 248–9.
23 Above, p. 55.

Part II
Poetic Allusions

9 Poetry and Fiction in Suetonius' *Illustrious Men**

Introduction

The historical evidence of ancient literary *Lives* has been almost entirely demolished by scholars, and the charges of invention laid at their door are difficult to refute.[1] For example, Horsfall allows only Virgil's date of birth, his *patria*, and the later reception of his *Bucolics* on the stage as securely known; virtually every other fact in the *Life* of Virgil attributed to Suetonius can be questioned on the grounds of conventionality or possible derivation from the poet's works.[2] However, attempts have been made by Graziosi to rescue ancient literary biographies for their value as the earliest readings of the authors' texts.[3] Irwin has added to these discussions by showing that, in some cases, such readings can even yield inferences about the history of the poet's actual life, since some writers, such as

* This chapter was first published in De Temmerman and Demoen 2016, 217–39.

1 See e.g. Beare 1942; Duckworth 1952, 56–61; Dihle 1956, 105–6; Fraenkel 1957, 1–23; Slater 1971; Fairweather 1974; 1983; Lefkowitz 1976; 1978; 1984; 1987; 2007; 2009; 2012; Saller 1980, 76–7; Garbrah 1981, 189–90 n. 10; Gratwick 1982, 814–16; Arrighetti 1994, 232–4; Horsfall 1994; 1995; 1998; Lindsay 1995a, 77; 2009, 3; Irwin 1998, 178; Jenkyns 1998, 7–8; Bollansée 1999b, 395–6 (on fr. 48), 530–2 (on fr. 76); Gowers 2004, 150; Schorn 2004, 46–9; Geiger 2008, 21, 47–8; Augoustakis and Traill 2013, 1–6; Davis 2014; Fletcher and Hanink 2016.

2 Horsfall 1994, 42; 1995, 5; 2006–7, 4 = 2020, 428; 2016, 32, 80–1. Powell (2017a, 100–1; 2017b) reaches a new level of scepticism by questioning the Suetonian evidence on Virgil's death from an illness that he contracted abroad (*Vita Verg.* 35) to the point of suggesting that Augustus himself may in fact have ordered the poet's murder. More balanced are the discussions of this *Life* by Baldwin 1989a; Smolenaars 2017. On Suetonian bias in the *Illustrious Men*, see Powell 2017b, 178; below, n. 66. Against the same kind of scepticism towards the portrayal of Jesus in the Gospels, see Rosen 1999. We might compare the only two events in Jesus' life that are universally accepted as facts, his baptism and crucifixion; see Levine 2006, 4; also below, Chapter 29, on historical evidence in Suetonius for his flight into Egypt. For the Gospels' similarity to ancient biography, see Burridge 2004; Konstan and Walsh 2016; Praet 2016. On the common ancient practice of deriving material on an author's life from his writings, the flaw in which is often called the 'biographical fallacy', see Williams 1995, 296; Bollansée 1999b, 531 n. 344 (on Hermipp. fr. 76); Bradshaw 2002, 2; Gowers 2003, 55–7; Hanink 2010, 542; Beecroft 2011, 1.

3 Graziosi 2002; 2006; 2009.

Solon, played a large role in shaping how they were viewed within their own lifetimes.[4] Thus, later biographies could at times capture some of this paradoxically authentic material; it was invented *about* the author, but also *by* the author, a fact which gives it a privileged status: there is a kernel of truth in its origin. On the other hand, Kivilo points to the core of authentic facts in the traditions on the early Greek poets, finding that the *Lives* of these figures ultimately spring from historically reliable material formed at the time of their works' first performances, either before or soon after their deaths.[5] Hendrickson has also shown that the process could be even more complicated, when poetry was used in tandem with other primary sources now lost, such as historical works and speeches, to confirm facts in ancient biographical works.[6]

This chapter takes these ideas a step further, with an interest not primarily in contemporary or later views on ancient writers, but in what light ancient *Lives* can cast on their historical subjects themselves, even when they appear to be embracing suspect material, such as their sources' autobiographical readings of the writers' works. My focus will be on the biographer Suetonius' use of literary evidence for a writer's life, particularly some moments when he explicitly quotes or cites as a biographical source poetry which has, by its very genre, a fictional quality or at least a tendency towards invention: in the case of a writer of ancient verse satire, for example, details may well be 'tailored to generic and rhetorical demands'.[7] These moments have been universally regarded as proof of Suetonius' uncritical and over-literal belief in fantastical stories, or of his disregard for the truth in seeking sensationalistic material with which to entertain his reader.[8] It is my intention to show that they do not in fact demonstrate simple gullibility or wilful dishonesty on Suetonius' part, but are included for the purpose of articulating, if only partially, the character of the biography's subject. We shall see that, as often in the analysis of ancient poetry, fiction can still reflect something true about a historical life, but also that, as less often seen in the study of ancient biography, ancient writers were not unconscious of this subtlety.

I shall look at two *Lives* in Suetonius' *Illustrious Men*, a collection of literary biographies which was originally categorized into different groups according to types of profession, but of which only certain parts still exist.

4 Irwin 2005, 132–52; 2006.
5 Kivilo 2010, 5–6, 223–4.
6 Hendrickson 2013.
7 Gowers 2003, 56–7 (quotation at 57) on Horace; cf. Williams 1995, 297. On the complex relationship between truth and fiction in ancient poetry, especially as it pertains to ancient biography, see also Iddeng 2000, 114–15; Osgood 2006, 112–14; Kivilo 2010, 3–4.
8 For Suetonius as allegedly uncritical in this way, see e.g. Munro 1869, 17; Rolfe 1913, 221–2; Carney 1963, 5–6; Goodyear 1982, 663; Horsfall 1994, 53; 1995, 1, 19–20; Williams 1995, 309; Woods 2006, 141, 143 n. 33; 2012, 456 n. 56, 466–7; Landrobe 2008, 434; Lindsay 2009, 3, 7; Champlin 2011, 331; Hägg 2012, 218.

Of the extant portions, the largest and best preserved is the *Grammarians and Rhetoricians*, which mostly survives except for the second half of the *Rhetoricians*, and the individual biographies of poets that have been transmitted along with manuscripts of their works. I shall examine closely one figure from Suetonius' *Poets*, Horace, and another from his *Grammarians*, Valerius Cato.[9] I shall also briefly compare Suetonius' portrait of Cato to his equally scant *Life* of the grammarian Pomponius Porcellus, and contrast it with his better documented biography of Caligula. The paper will conclude with a final comparison between Suetonius' literary biographies and his *Lives of the Caesars*.

The reason for these main selections of Horace and Cato is twofold. First, both figures are well known as poets, and Suetonius is as interested in Cato's poetical output as his grammatical writings (*Gramm.* 11.2, cf. 4.2); in fact, his biography could as easily have been included in the *Poets* as in the *Grammarians*.[10] The second point is related to this focusing by Suetonius on poetical material: both biographies are representative of occasions when the biographer seemingly had few, if any, previous writers on which to build and had to create a *Life* mostly from his own reading and research. On such occasions, Suetonius draws heavily on either the works of the subject himself or on literary works about him by other authors.[11] In the *Horace*, there is only a glimpse of a possible scholarly source for Horace's sexual activities, where the poet 'is reported' and 'is said' (*traditur ... dicitur, Vita Hor.* 10) to have had sex with prostitutes in a bedroom

9 On the transmission of the *Grammarians and Rhetoricians*, see Tibbetts and Winterbottom 1983, 404–5; Kaster 1992, 1–3; 1995, xxiii, liv–lv. For the authenticity of Suetonius' *Horace*, see Porphyrio ad Hor. *Epist.* 2.1 (368 Holder); also Fraenkel 1957, 15; Baldwin 1983, 395, 446–9; Horsfall 1994, 51.

10 See Baldwin 1983, 431–2, with Kaster 1995, 149–51.

11 For how Suetonius' method of research tends to yield facts relevant to different subjects across his biographical collection, see Wallace-Hadrill 1983, 50–9; Viljamaa 1991, 3830–1; Kaster 1995, xxix-xxxix, 43–4, 270; Power 2014b, 12; 2014c, 234. On the paucity of prior biographical sources for the *Grammarians and Rhetoricians*, see *Gramm.* 4.7, 25.6; and for the *Horace*, Kaster 1995, xxx; Lindsay 2009, 2; Thomas 2011, 5. Suetonius had better sources for Terence and Virgil; see, respectively, Horsfall 1994, 48; Bayer 1995, 430–1. It is unlikely that Suetonius' use of sources in the *Horace* has been distorted by the single lacuna on the poet's extant works, on which see Reifferscheid 1860, 390; Fraenkel 1933, 394 = 1964, 202; 1957, 1, 21; Horsfall 1995, 9–10; Paratore 2007, 398. The lacuna is doubted by Baldwin 1983, 394; Lindsay 1995a, 69–70, 76; Johnson 2010, 330. Baldwin notes that readers of the *Horace* would not need a list of the poet's extant works, but Suetonius often provides detailed information on such writings (e.g. *Gramm.* 7.3, 8.3, 9.3, 10.5, 11.2, 12.2, 14.4, 19.2, 21.4, *Aug.* 85.1–2, *Tib.* 70.2, *Claud.* 41.3). The catalogue may have been removed when the biography was prefixed to Horatian manuscripts. The same deletion can be found in Suetonius' *Life* of Terence, which is otherwise complete; see *Poet.* 33–4.36–46, with D'Anna 1956, 36–41; Naumann 1979, 154–5; Brandão 2006, 111. Bibliographies were an integral part of the tradition of literary biography; see Bollansée 1999a, 179–81. Suetonius need not have been a *grammaticus* to have included one; *pace* Martina 1984, 186–8 = 2004, 228–30.

surrounded by mirrors, words which may as easily suggest a written source as a mere rumour.[12] The *Valerius Cato* too contains merely a single variant on the subject's origin, where Suetonius similarly contrasts what 'some have reported' (*nonnulli tradiderunt*) with what the writer himself claims (*ipse ... ait, Gramm.* 11.1).[13]

Suetonius therefore mostly relies in both *Lives* on the authors' own and other literary works, supplementing them at times with original research.[14] They are therefore excellent examples of biographies in which Suetonius was dealing with a great amount of poetical, and thus potentially fictional, material. As Kaster writes of the *Horace*: 'Here Suetonius was essentially on his own; and what is true of the Horatian *vita* is true of *all* the lives of the *professores*.'[15]

Ancestry in the *Horace*

Let us start by taking one piece of information that continues to detain scholars as allegedly spurious attributions to the poet from his, and other, literary writings: his ancestry. The *Life* begins as follows:

> Q. Horatius Flaccus Venusinus, patre, ut ipse tradit, libertino et exactionum coactore, ut uero creditum est, salsamentario, cum illi quidam in altercatione exprobrasset 'quotiens ego uidi patrem tuum bracchio se emungentem.'

> Quintus Horatius Flaccus was from Venusia. His father, according to his own account, was a freedman and collector of money from auctions, or, as has been the common belief, a merchant of salted fish, since someone reproached him in an argument: 'How often I have seen your father wiping his nose on his sleeve!'

> (*Vita Hor.* 1)

According to one view, Suetonius first misconstrues the recurring phrase 'born of a freedman father' (*libertino patre natus*) in *Satires* 1.6 (1.6.6, 45, 46; cf. *Epist.* 1.20.20), taking too literally what may in fact be an embellishment of that particular satire's assumed persona: the phrase was possibly a schoolboy taunt that arose from the father's having been captured during the Social War.[16] However, this theory ignores the fact that Horace would

---

12 See Fairweather 1974, 246 n. 71; cf. Horsfall 1995, 3; *pace* Fraenkel 1957, 21.
13 Kaster 1995, xxx n. 18. On the issue of origin, Suetonius appears less certain of Cato's own authority than of Horace's; see Kaster 1995, 150, with 208–9 (on *Gramm.* 20.1); also below.
14 The date of Horace's birthday (*Vita Hor.* 13) is a good example of Suetonius combining different kinds of primary sources; see Fraenkel 1957, 22–3; Bradshaw 2002.
15 Kaster 1995, xxx.
16 Williams 1995, anticipated by (as he notes at 296) Niebuhr 1848, 133, but also by Fraenkel 1957, 2–3; Highet 1973, 268 = 1983, 165. For acceptance of this view, see e.g. Oliensis 1998, 31; Cels-Saint-Hilaire 1999; Schlegel 2000, 108 n. 19; Nisbet and Rudd 2004,

have been held accountable for this statement by some of his public.[17] If the phrase was meant insincerely, Horace would probably have made its irony stronger within the poem. Since this case for insincerity depends on too subtle a reading of the satire and too speculative a reconstruction of the father's life, as well as a disregard for the detail that prisoners of war were still technically slaves to the Romans, we must revert to taking the poet's word for his father's status as an ex-slave.[18] Horace even alludes through this phrase to a fragment of the historian L. Calpurnius Piso (fr. 27 Peter) on Gnaeus Flavius, the aedile in 304 BC, who had a freedman father and held a similar office as *scriba*.[19] Horace may also play on his reader's awareness of his own background in the same satire (*Sat.* 1.6.58–61, 100–11) when he writes with a pun that he has a *caballus* or *mulus* – words lower than *equus*, which better suit an equestrian (*eques*) with a freedman father.[20]

Suetonius' alternative information on Horace's genealogy, already couched in a phrase that expresses doubt (*ut uero creditum est*), is far more questionable. The anecdote involving the claim that he was the son of a salted-fish merchant (*salsamentarius*) cannot be trusted as a historical fact, since one of Horace's satirical models, Bion of Borysthenes (fr. 1A Kindstrand), reports exactly the same details about himself:[21]

> ἐμοὶ ὁ πατὴρ μὲν ἦν ἀπελεύθερος, τῷ ἀγκῶνι ἀπομυσσόμενος – διεδήλου δὲ τὸν ταριχέμπορον – γένος Βορυσθενίτης ...

> My father was a freedman, who wiped his nose on his sleeve – thus betraying his being a merchant of salted fish – a native of Borysthenes ...
> (Diog. Laert. 4.46)

Furthermore, Horace links the 'dark wit' of Bion's writings – literally his 'black salt' (*sale nigro*) – with his own satirical poetry (*Epist.* 2.2.58–60); in fact, that mention of Bion by Horace is thought to be an allusion in the

---

xix, 188 (on *Carm.* 3.14.18); Freudenburg 2010, 281; Courtney 2013, 102–3; Günther 2013b, 7, 14; and more tentatively, Landrobe 2008, 432; Lowrie 2009, 343 n. 59. The report of Horace's military service by both Suetonius (*Vita Hor.* 2) and Horace himself (*Sat.* 1.6.48, 1.7) has similarly been questioned by Nagy 2003, although unconvincingly. On Suetonius' discussions of *Odes* 4 and *Epist.* 2.1 as possible inventions, see the next section.

17 See Gowers 2009a, 306; Graziosi 2009, 159; Mouritsen 2011, 266–7; Newman 2011, 453–4.

18 Cf. MacLean 2018, 88–91. For the older acceptance that Horace's father was indeed a freedman; see e.g. Nisbet and Hubbard 1970, xxvii; Mayer 1994, 5. The two views are instead oddly melded by Harrison 2014, 10.

19 See Woodman 2009b, 157–60 = 2012, 112–15.

20 Armstrong 1986, 259–61; 2010, 20, 32 n. 19; *pace* Gowers 2012, 234. For wordplay on *eques* in this satire, cf. Brown 1993, 161–2.

21 On this basis, Jahn even considered the anecdote in Suetonius an interpolation; see Reifferscheid 1860, 389–90 on this and another familiar anecdote at *Vita Hor.* 10 ~ Sen. *Q Nat.* 1.16; for a discussion of the latter, see the section below on Horace's prostitutes.

first place to the profession of Bion's father and the well-known phrase 'who wiped his nose on his sleeve' (τῷ ἀγκῶνι ἀπομυσσόμενος), which is both witty and literally about salt.[22] The fact that Horace alludes to this saying of Bion's within his own poetry may make us suspicious of its attribution to Horace's life by Suetonius, although the affinities between the two writers did indeed extend beyond generic similarities to having freedman fathers.[23] The further coincidence that their fathers were also *salsamentarii* seems too convenient and strains our belief, especially since Horace himself never commented on it, and we can clearly see how the attribution may have been derived from Horace's own discussion of Bion's 'salty' words.

While Suetonius' anecdote about Horace's father is unreliable in a literal sense, it does point to something generally true of Horace: his satirical predecessor Bion – and also Lucilius, who was equally admired by Horace for his 'ample salt' (*Lucili ... sale multo*, *Sat.* 1.10.2–3), that is, his abundant wit. In fact, the connection with Lucilius may be greater in the Suetonian passage than has been realized. Horace elsewhere writes that Lucilius had 'a well-wiped nose' (*emunctae naris*, *Sat.* 1.4.8; cf. *Vita Hor.* 1), referring again to his acerbic wit, since the nose could symbolize contempt.[24] The same imagery is used also by Pliny the Elder about Lucilius: 'the first to establish the nose of style' (*primus condidit stili nasum*, *HN praef.* 7).[25] The imagery was therefore associated as much with Lucilius as with Bion.

Moreover, allusion to Bion has been perceived by some scholars not only in *Satires* 1.6 but also implicitly in Horace's references to Lucilius in 1.4.[26] If Suetonius is following a source responsible for the transposition of this detail from Bion's life to Horace's, we might wonder whether Suetonius appreciated the allusion to Horace's generic models and thus the implausibility of the anecdote, considering the biographer's direct reading of Horace's works. If so, or if Suetonius himself found the story and recognized its implications, the decision to include it would be proof not of his gullibility, but rather of the value he placed on a fictional item that was nonetheless fitting and useful in portraying something about the character of Horace. In other words, Suetonius perhaps understood the allusion that the anecdote

---

22 See Fraenkel 1957, 6–7, with earlier bibliography; Kindstrand 1976, 178; Williams 1995, 309. Horsfall 1994, 43 argues that Suetonius himself may have even been inspired to borrow the detail from Bion by this allusion of Horace's in *Epistles* 2.2. For other similarities between Bion and Horace, see Moles 2007, 165–7; Gowers 2012, 13, 240; Nichols 2017, 56–7; for salt as 'wit', Gowers 2012, 312.

23 We need not see the claim of having a freedman father in *Satires* 1.6 as an invention, as Williams 1995, 311 does, in order to admit a possible allusion also to Bion through it.

24 See Brown 1993, 128 (ad loc.), cf. 118 (on *Sat.* 1.3.29–30).

25 Barchiesi and Cucchiarelli 2005, 215.

26 Ibid. 215 n. 16. Horsfall 1998 and Graziosi 2009 add some support to this by arguing that Horace was generally aware of Greek biographical traditions, although they do not discuss Bion. On Horace's discussion of Lucilius in *Satires* 1.4, see also Gowers 2009b, 90–1.

creates when attributed to Horace and preserved it for what it tells us about Horace's *literary* parentage, while at the same time making clear that he does not believe it to be literally true.

This purpose of the anecdote's inclusion ties into the broader aims of Suetonius in writing the *Life* of Horace. Graziosi has pointed to this anecdote's function in advertising the real-life, 'scandalous' kind of stories that the reader will get in reading the biography, that is, its interest and worth in addition to the poet's works themselves.[27] However, entertainment is not the main literary end that this anecdote serves, and we have already undermined the assumption that Suetonius necessarily believed or presents the story as true. It is presented in much the same way as similar stories in the *Caesars*, such as those about Augustus' ancestors – that his great-grandfather was 'a freedman and rope-maker from the outskirts of Thurii' (*libertinum ... restionem e plago Thurino*) and his grandfather 'a money-changer' (*argentarium*) – which are reported by Antony (*Aug.* 2.3); or the tale about Nerva's alleged debauching of Domitian, which Suetonius tells us did not lack supporters (*nec defuerunt qui affirmarent, Dom.* 1.1).[28]

With regard to Augustus, I should argue that Suetonius makes the same kind of clear distinction as he does in the *Horace* between such rumours and the more reliable account of Augustus himself (presumably in his lost autobiography),[29] not only by attributing them to Antony – a clearly biased source – but also in his previous remarks, which recall the contrast in the *Horace* between the poet 'himself' (*ipse*) and the other sources: 'But these things are what others say; Augustus himself says nothing more than ...' (*sed haec alii; ipse Augustus nihil amplius quam ... Aug.* 2.3).[30] Although Suetonius here makes a different distinction between sources of facts about Augustus that are all stated as true and do not contradict each other, he nonetheless draws attention to the separate origins of the information, so that the immediately juxtaposed stories from Antony are not explicitly contrasted, but more subtly discredited through their attribution. As for the anecdote about Domitian, the identity of the source is removed by Suetonius in order to level a more severe charge against the emperor than he could otherwise do.[31] That such things were even said of an emperor, true

---

27 Graziosi 2009, 157.

28 On the allegations about Augustus' ancestors, see Lindsay 1995a, 72; on Domitian and Nerva, Jones 2002. The significance of Suetonius' accounts of Germanicus and Drusus in the *Caesars* is similarly discussed by Penella 2018.

29 For Augustus' autobiography as Suetonius' source here, cf. Carter 1982, 92 (ad loc.); Wiseman 2009, 112–13; Louis 2010, 84 (ad loc.); Wardle 2014, 22.

30 Osgood 2006, 264 n. 72 claims that Suetonius expresses doubt regarding the rumour about Augustus' grandfather at *Augustus* 3.1, but Osgood confuses Augustus' grandfather with his father, who shared the same reputation of being an *argentarius*. However, the point remains that Suetonius disowns that rumour too: 'I am indeed surprised ...' (*equidem mirer ... Aug.* 3.1).

31 For this strategy in Suetonius, see Pauw 1980.

or not, could be taken as revealing by the biographer's Roman audience, as he is well aware. A similar strategy may be observed in our story about Horace (*ut uero creditum est ...*),[32] where Suetonius uses it to remove his own responsibility for the claim, since he makes it clear by the framing of his citation that this is not the version to be preferred.

Like these stories, which are similarly placed at the beginning of the emperors' respective biographies in the *Caesars*, the piece of information about Horace's parentage sets the tone for the biography to come and also establishes the scholarly prowess of Suetonius in weighing conflicting pieces of evidence.[33] As with the Domitian anecdote, it is not that Suetonius records this material because he is interested in early rhetorical attacks on or misconceptions about Horace.[34] The biographer does not so much include these titbits because he wishes to convey contemporary reactions or the political atmosphere of the times, as because, removed in time though they are, they still pack their various punches. To Suetonius, these stories represented at times a middle ground between fact and fiction, since it would make sense to some of his readers that a writer of satire had a background similar to Bion's, which had become almost proverbial for the possession of wit.[35] Suetonius could not have been unaware that disreputable ancestry was a rhetorical *topos*, especially of literary or political figures.[36] But his

---

32 Cf. Kaster 1995, 150: 'clearly a mere slander'.
33 See Fraenkel 1957, 6 n. 2; Baldwin 1983, 394. On the display of scholarship at the beginning of an ancient biography to create interest and establish authority and goodwill in the eyes of the reader, see Duchêne 2016, 274–5 on Suetonius; also Stadter 1988 and Pelling 2002d, 268–70 on Plutarch; cf. Bowie 2008, 154–6; Duff 2008, 187–8. For other examples of research emphasized in the first person at the outset of a Suetonian work, see e.g. *Poet.* 28–32.1–28; *Gramm.* 2.1, 7.1, 25.2, *Aug.* 2.3, *Tib.* 2.1, *Ner.* 1.2, *Vesp.* 1.4. This function of the start of the *Vitellius* (1.1–2.1) has largely been ignored, as has its condemnatory purpose, but the final section (*Vit.* 2.1), which Garrett (2018a, 66–7) oddly sees as being in Vitellius' favour, is extremely negative, despite its non-committal conclusion: by coming at the end, it leaves the reader with a lasting impression of biased claims against the emperor, which are instead tellingly refuted in the more approving *Life* of Augustus, as Garrett herself even observes (ibid. 66). Cf. Jones 2002 on *Dom.* 1.1; and Stadter 2007, 536, who notes how a similarly negative detail two chapters later at *Dom.* 3 also 'sets the tone for the emperor's whole life'. For well-researched details in Suetonius' death scenes, see Ash 2016, 205–9; for Suetonius' use of research more generally, Louis 2010, 50–65. Davis 2014, 391 is incorrect in his claim that the *Terence* contains the only variant in the death scenes of Suetonius' *Illustrious Men*; another may be found in the *Life* of Pliny the Elder (Suet. fr. 80 Reiff.).
34 *Pace* Lindsay 1995a, 72.
35 For this kind of 'creative reconstruction' of a subject's background in Plutarch and Suetonius, see Pelling 1990a, 226–7 = 2002b, 308–9; cf. id. 1988, 33–6. On the tendency of an ancient literary figure's biographical tradition to create a proverbial expression, see Kivilo 2010, 218–19.
36 On this *topos*, see Fraenkel 1957, 6; Lindsay 1995a, 72; Graziosi 2009, 157. See Kivilo 2010, 208 on the formulaic theme of 'significant origin' in ancient literary biography. For Suetonius' familiarity with rhetorical *topoi* generally, see e.g. Barton 1994. For fish merchants in particular as disreputable in the ancient world, see Kindstrand 1976, 178–9.

inclusion of it in this case may have more to do with the story's relevance to what *was* true about Horace than with anything else: Suetonius is able to suggest – without taking responsibility for the claim – that Horace possessed a wit worthy of the writers whom the poet admired.[37] Suetonius simply records that this connection with Bion and Lucilius 'has been the common belief' (*creditum est*) about Horace, a belief which alludes to the heritage of his poetry.

Suetonius on Horace, *Odes* 4

Another passage in Suetonius' *Horace* that has attracted criticism as possible fiction is his account of how the poet was forced to write *Odes* 4 by the emperor Augustus, which scholars think the biographer could have derived from reading other interactions with the emperor in Horace's works:[38]

> scripta quidem eius usque adeo probauit mansuraque perpetua opinatus est, ut non modo saeculare carmen componendum iniunxerit, sed et Vindelicam uictoriam Tiberii Drusique priuignorum suorum, eumque coegerit propter hoc tribus carminum libris ex longo interuallo quartum addere, post sermones uero quosdam lectos nullam sui mentionem habitam ita sit questus: 'irasci me tibi scito, quod non in plerisque eiusmodi scriptis mecum potissimum loquaris. an uereris ne apud posteros infame tibi sit, quod uidearis familiaris nobis esse?', expressitque eclogam ad se, cuius initium est:

> > cum tot sustineas et tanta negotia solus,
> > res Italas armis tuteris, moribus ornes,
> > legibus emendes: in publica commoda peccem,
> > si longo sermone morer tua tempora, Caesar.

> He so approved of his writings and thought they would endure for all time, that he not only required him to compose the *Carmen Saeculare* but also the Vindelician victory of his stepsons Tiberius and Drusus, and he urged him based on this to add to his three books of *Odes* a fourth after a long hiatus. However, after reading certain conversations

---

37 The anecdote might also fit with the theme of poetry as a body, which, according to Graziosi (2009, 156–8), Suetonius develops in the *Horace* from Greek biography. However, this view may overstate the importance of Greek biography for Suetonius; cf. Power 2014c, 235–6. Its influence on the *Horace* is more likely a general one; see Lindsay 1995a, 71, 75, 77.

38 See e.g. Bowditch 2001, 59; Tarrant 2007, 65; Ingleheart 2009, 125; Scott 2010, 264–5; Thomas 2011, 4–5. Hills 2001, 615–16 thinks that Suetonius alludes in this passage to the Caecilii Teucri (Plin. *HN* 7.101 = Enn. *Ann.* 16 fr. 6 Skutsch; the Caecilii Teucri are possibly to be identified with T. and C. Aelius: Bauman 1983, 125; Briscoe 2012, 35), but the similarities are too general, and fraternal *pietas* in war is a common Roman *topos*; see e.g. Bannon 1997, 136–73; Armstrong 2013.

of his, he complained that they had no mention of him as follows: 'You should know that I am angry with you, because in several such writings you do not speak with me in particular. Are you afraid that in posterity you will have notoriety because you seem to be our friend?', eliciting the poem to him that begins:

> Since so many great affairs depend on you alone, the Italian world defended by you with arms, provided with customs, improved by laws: I would sin at public cost if I should take up your time with a tedious discussion, Caesar.

(Vita Hor. 8)

Suetonius indirectly supports his claim about *Odes* 4 through analogy with another request by Augustus for new *Epistles*, quoting the first four lines of *Epist.* 2.1 together with a letter from the emperor (fr. 39 Malcovati), which is genuine and known to us from this biography alone.[39] If Suetonius had been uncertain about the origin of *Odes* 4, he probably would not have stated it so factually. For example, when Suetonius has to surmise why Augustus appointed Tiberius as his successor, he tells us so and weighs other letters by the first emperor in more circumspect light (*Tib.* 21.2–7), and in his discussion of Caligula's birthplace, he shows characteristic caution and interest in biographical controversy (*Calig.* 8.1–5).[40] Suetonius also displays a thorough examination of Terence's birthplace (*Vita Ter.* 1–10). Although Suetonius appears to have had fewer secondary resources for Horace than for Terence,[41] it is nonetheless doubtful that he would have made the statement about Augustus' request for *Odes* 4 if he had no foundation for it; he might even have said nothing, or else made it explicitly clear that no further information could be found (e.g. *Aug.* 2.2; cf. *Vesp.* 1.3; *Gramm.* 4.7, 25.6).[42]

Despite Suetonius' diligence on matters of origin and aetiology, the vagueness of the phrase *quosdam sermones* has suggested the possibility that Suetonius did not even know which poems were meant by Augustus in his complaint about not being an addressee.[43] However, this phrase was probably not Suetonius' at all, but rather reflects the original language of Augustus' letter.[44] The phrase 'speak with me' (*mecum ... loquaris*) used by Augustus suggests that the emperor may indeed have described the *Epistles*

---

39 Although it may not have been 'archival' material, since some of Augustus' letters were clearly in circulation; see above, pp. 42–4. On the certain authenticity of this letter, see Giordano 2000, 26–7.

40 Cf. *Tib.* 5. See Hurley 1993, 19 for further examples; also above, pp. 44–5 on the later imperial *Lives*. On Suetonius' careful research (*satis curiose inquirerem, Vit.* 1.4), cf. above, n. 33, and my discussion of the *Caligula* below.

41 Cf. above, n. 11.

42 For Suetonius' exhaustiveness also on other matters such as omens, see e.g. Gascou 1984, 444–50.

43 Scott 2010, 265, anticipated to some extent by Rudd 1989, 1; Kilpatrick 1990, 3.

44 Brink 1963–82, 3.548; cf. White 1993, 114–15.

as conversations. If the biographer had wished to use a broad term that encompassed both the *Satires* and the *Epistles*, he would have used *satura* (e.g. *Vita Hor.* 9; *Vita Pers.* 10; *Gramm.* 2.2, 5.1, 15.2);[45] and *quidam* can be shown usually not to indicate uncertainty in Suetonius, but rather the opposite. Suetonius refers to *honores ... quosdam noui generis* in the *Augustus* (26.1), but it is evident from a later chapter (27.5) that he knows exactly which ones they were.[46] Similarly, in the same *Life* Suetonius mentions Augustus' respect for *dies quosdam*, and then immediately names them (92.2). We might also compare Suetonius' citation *ut quidam tradiderunt* for the detail of Otho's adoption of the name Nero (*Otho* 7.1), which he clearly derived from Cluvius Rufus (cf. Plut. *Otho* 3.2), or *quidam* for the other conspirators who killed Caligula (*Calig.* 58.3), for he probably had these names too from his source,[47] but removed them to maintain focus on the emperor.[48] Suetonius, and Augustus, must therefore be referring to *Epistles* Book 1,[49] and this allusion makes a smooth transition to the next rubric in which Suetonius describes Horace's physical appearance using evidence from that book (*Vita Hor.* 9; *Epist.* 1.4.15, 1.20.24), which Suetonius again confirms with another letter of Augustus (fr. 40 Malcovati).[50] He was not simply making blind inferences: he was closely following particular texts.

Although we have only the biographer's word for how *Odes* 4 came to be, it is a word based on familiarity with whole letters of Augustus from which he merely excerpts. Suetonius may indeed have put the exchange between Augustus and Horace in phraseology better suited to his own day (*iniunxerit ... coegerit*), when imperial wishes were more pressing,[51] but there is no reason to think that he did not accurately convey the facts as he found them in Augustus' letters. Chronological difficulties in assigning the inception of *Odes* Book 4 as late as the Vindelician victory of Tiberius and Drusus, which is celebrated in *Odes* 4.4 and 4.14, can be explained by the composition of some of the poems in the book prior to Augustus' request.[52] Horace's renewed interest in lyric poetry may have had nothing to

---

45 For *satura* as in fact the more general term in Suetonius with regard to poetry, see Rolfe 1913–14, 2.487; Kaster 1992, 90. In Horace, by contrast, *sermo* is broader; see Rudd 1989, 11, n. 9. As Rudd points out, Horace himself even likens the word *sermo* to the *Epistles* in the lines quoted above (*longo sermone*, *Epist.* 2.1.4); cf. Tarrant 2007, 65 n. 8.
46 Carter 1982, 8.
47 See Joseph. *AJ* 19.17, 91–2, 125, 159; Tac. *Ann.* 11.1; Dio Cass. 59.29–30; with Kavanagh 2010, 1007–8, 1017.
48 For this tendency in Suetonius, see e.g. Baldwin 1983, 513, 534.
49 Cf. Osgood 2011, 100.
50 On this letter, see Giordano 2000, 27–8.
51 See Fraenkel 1957, 15–16, 364–5, 383; J. Griffin 1984, 203; Fantham 2013c, 102, 299 n. 59. Cf. Günther 2013b, 44 on *expressit* in the same passage, although I do not agree that the anachronism was committed by Suetonius 'mindlessly' (Günther 2013c, 494).
52 Cf. Nisbet 2007, 16. The period of the composition of Odes 4 is reconstructed by Thomas (2011, 5–7) as being from 23 BC to its publication in 13 BC. The victory over the Vindelici which Suetonius claims spurred Augustus to ask for *Odes* 4 did not take place until 15 BC; see Gruen 1996, 170.

do with Augustus, whose request may have been conventional, with little or
no force to it;[53] yet, the decision to release a fourth book may still have arisen
in the way that Suetonius says, without the poems added to the Vindelician
ones being mere filler.[54] As Suetonius tells us, Horace was entirely capable of
refusing Augustus, such as when he declined his offer of the post *ab epistulis*
(*Vita Hor.* 5–6), so his agreement to *Odes* 4 must ultimately be read as an
indication of his enthusiasm for the task.[55] In this way, the views that Suetonius' story is correct and that Horace, *Odes* 4 is still carefully crafted are not
incompatible.[56] Horace's less successful fourth book is almost as much of an
independent creation as *Odes* 1–3, even if the artistic result is somewhat viti-
ated by its publication having been prompted by the emperor, and by some of
the poems having been composed before the idea of their collection.

Prostitutes in the *Horace*

A much better case for fictional material in Suetonius' biography of Horace
may be found in his discussion of the poet's sexual interests:

> ad res ueneras intemperantior traditur; nam speculato cubiculo scorta
> dicitur habuisse disposita, ut quocumque respexisset ibi ei imago coitus
> referretur.
>
> referretur *mss.*: obuiaret ç

> In matters of venery, he was reportedly unrestrained; it is even said
> that he would position and use prostitutes in a mirror-lined bedroom,
> so wherever he looked, a sexual image would be reflected there at him.
> (*Vita Hor.* 10)

The most recent editor of this passage has a misleading note on Suetonius' *intemperantior*: 'the sentence that follows was obelized (i.e., marked
as spurious) by prior editors, including Roth, but for no reason other than

---

53 White 1993, 113–15.
54 For this more balanced view, see e.g. Belmont 1980, 4; Thom 2001, 44 n. 6; Lowrie
    2010b, 211; Mitchell 2010, 45, *passim* (arguing that Tiberius and Drusus are made a
    recurring theme of the book); Rees 2012b, 10; Fantham 2013a; Günther 2013b, 46–7.
    For bibliography on *Odes* 4 as still unsatisfactory, see Scott 2010, 258–9, 261; Thomas
    2011, 9–10.
55 I am not convinced by McNeill (2001, 163–4 n. 18) that this request by Augustus would
    have been taken any less seriously by Horace than the emperor's wish for *Odes* 4. The
    emperor may plausibly have urged Horace (in a letter that is not quoted, but which was
    used as a source by Suetonius) to write his fourth book in the same witty manner as his
    playful request for an address in the *Epistles* above (*irasci me tibi scito ...*) and his joking
    threats to Virgil for a preview of the *Aeneid* (*Vita Verg.* 31–2); on the latter, see above,
    pp. 33–4.
56 *Pace* Babcock 1981, 1599. Cf. above, n. 54.

modern prudery!'[57] Some scholars have indeed rejected the sentence about Horace's bedroom, but not due to 'modern prudery'; it has been considered suspect in light of the similar anecdote reported by Seneca about Hostius Quadra, a contemporary of Horace:[58]

> non erat ille ab uno tantummodo sexu impurus, sed tam uirorum quam feminarum auidus fuit, fecitque specula huius notae, cuius modo rettuli, imagines longe maiores reddentia, in quibus digitus brachii mensuram et crassitudinem excederet. haec autem ita disponebat, ut cum uirum ipse pateretur, auersus omnes admissarii sui motus in speculo uideret ac deinde falsa magnitudine ipsius membri tamquam uera gaudebat.

> He had not only been defiled by one sex, but coveted men as much as women; and he created mirrors of the sort I mentioned above, rendering images much larger, in which a finger exceeded the length and width of an arm. What is more, he used to position them so that, when he was submitting to a man and facing away from him, he could see all of his partner's movements in the mirror, and then enjoy the false magnitude of that man's member as though it were real.

(Sen. Q Nat. 1.16.2)

It is thought by some that the similar Latin names of the two men may have been confused (*Hostius* ~ *Horatius*), and thus these details have sometimes been considered spurious with regard to the later Suetonian passage, with the fault allegedly belonging to the biographer's source.[59] This explanation is especially likely if we accept the different reading of *obuiaret* in place of Suetonius' *referretur*, suggesting that the image 'would appear in reverse' to Horace,[60] which is closer to Seneca's emphasis on the distortion in the mirrors of Hostius. Others contend that the notion of Horace's excesses with prostitutes may have been derived by Suetonius directly from his poems,

---

57 Osgood 2011, 101. Such a motive can only be found in Vollmer's (1908) *editio minor* of Horace's *Odes*, from which the entire passage from *ad res uenereas* was removed. It had been included, however, in his *editio maior* (Vollmer 1907). Roth had other reasons; see the next note. In fact, the actual prior editors of this *Life* (Rolfe 1913–14; Rostagni 1944; de Gubernatis 1945; Klingner 1959; Steffen 1960, 24–5; Brugnoli 1968b; Borzsák 1984) do *not* obelize it.

58 The original questioning of this passage by Lessing (1754, 28–9 = 1890, 281–2), who was followed by both Roth (1858, lxxxiv–lxxxv, 298) and Reifferscheid (1860, 47, 389–90), was based on this Senecan passage; see Berthold 2008, 25–7; also Brugnoli 1968b, 33–5. Fraenkel 1957, 21 has been taken to task for obelizing the Suetonian passage in his book on Horace, and for giving short shrift to the conjecture of Lessing; see Baldwin 1983, 452 n. 27; 1989a, 478; Calder 1988, 134; Williams 1995, 311. For the meaning of Seneca's *admissarii*, see Leitão 1998, 136 n. 15.

59 Cf. Wilkinson 1949, 47; Herrmann 1955, 28; also above, n. 16. Accusations of lechery were conventional in literary biography; see e.g. Bollansée 1999b, 531–2.

60 *OLD* s.v. *obuio*: 'act contrary to, go against'.

such as the one in which he points to rumours about his own licentiousness (*Sat.* 2.3.325).[61]

What is less often noted is that there is another story of relevance. In the Senecan passage, Hostius seems to imitate Cratinus, a fifth-century Greek poet of comedy, about whose love of wine Pseudo-Acro says (2.492 Hauthal):

> hic per hanc uinolentiam tantae libidinis fuit, ut cubiculum suum spe-
> culis adornaret, quatenus et coitum suum spectare posset.

> This man became so lustful from his drunkenness that he decorated his
> bedroom with mirrors, so that he could also watch his own sexual acts.
>
> (Ps.-Acro ad Hor. *Epist.* 1.19.1)

It may be no coincidence that Pseudo-Acro tells the story about Cratinus' mirrored bedroom in reference to a comment on the poet's drinking made by Horace (*Epist.* 1.19.1–3, cf. *Sat.* 1.4.1–2).[62] Cratinus was clearly one of Horace's literary models, even if he did not follow that model completely as a writer.[63] If Suetonius can be believed, Horace also followed Cratinus through his fondness for orgiastic sex, and for multiplying its effect by way of mirrors. As an expert on Horace's writings, Suetonius would hardly have been unaware of the poet's interest in Cratinus, and is therefore possibly fashioning his discussion of Horace's lust to recall his poetic predecessor, just as we have seen with Bion and Lucilius. The error had probably been committed by an earlier source because of the similar story about Hostius, but it may have been preserved by Suetonius in his *Life* of Horace due to this connection with Cratinus.

The confusion with Hostius may even have been apparent to Suetonius, who wrote a *Life* of Seneca (frr. 86–9 Reiff.), and whose method of research for any biography included reading all of his subject's writings.[64] Seneca

---

61 Nisbet 2007, 21; cf. Horsfall 1998, 48; Gowers 2012, 25; Günther 2013b, 355 n. 515: 'perhaps the notorious story of the mirrors ... is almost too well invented to be true'; id. 2013c, 51. A different passage, *Satires* 1.2.116–18, is adduced in a similar vein by Baldwin 1989a, 478. Less sceptical is Newman 2011, 34–5, but I am not convinced by him (6–7) that Horace's mirrors evoke the purity of glass, or for that matter the apt metaphor of life reflected in art (Graziosi (2009, 158–60; Lowrie 2010a, 30). Nor do I find them signifying the themes of secrecy, spectacle, or a general 'artificiality' in this biography (Hulls 2014, esp. 188–90).

62 Cratinus' famous line 'Drinking water, you will create nothing wise' (ὕδωρ δὲ πίνων οὐδὲν ἂν τέκοις σοφόν, fr. 203 = *PCG* 4.226), had become proverbial and made its author famous as a great drinker of wine; see Mayer 1994, 259; Bakola 2010, 17, 56–7.

63 On Cratinus and Horace, see the balanced remarks of Morgan 1999, 34–5.

64 See Wallace-Hadrill 1983, 62–3; Kaster 1995, xxxii–xxxiii; above, pp. 43–4. It is thought by Hulls (2014, 187–8) that Suetonius consciously models his scene in the *Horace* on the Senecan passage, but his discussion relies on too sceptical a view of Suetonian biography (cf. 192, 196); see also above, n. 61.

even tells us of the notable comment by Augustus that Hostius' murder seemed justified (*iure caesum uideri, Q Nat.* 1.16.1), which would probably not have escaped the notice of someone as familiar with that emperor as Suetonius, even if Hostius does not warrant an appearance in his biography of Augustus.[65] The context of the mirror anecdote in Suetonius is far less hostile than in Seneca, and the biographer is careful to avoid his usual heading *libido* ('lust'), categorizing this detail instead under the more discreet rubric *res uenereas*.[66] The reason for this somewhat favourable bias may lie in his admiration for Horace, a writer who, like himself, rose from humble origins.[67] Suetonius was adept at negotiating the line between fact and fiction without compromising his honesty, and he is often beholden to a scholarly or historical source, whether he himself vouches for it or assigns it, as here, to rumour through the word *dicitur*, which probably hides a real source – however suspect that source may be.[68] In his portrait of Horace's bedroom, Suetonius may have decided to include a mistaken detail about Hostius because it suited the character of Horace known from his poetry.

Fiction and Valerius Cato

Let us continue to look at this middle ground for Suetonius between fact and fiction in his brief *Life* of the grammarian Valerius Cato. Suetonius

---

65 For Suetonius' expertise in the Augustan age, see Wallace-Hadrill 1983, 56–7.
66 Cf. Baldwin 1983, 506. For the subtler *uenereus*, see *Tib.* 43.2. On the moral category of *libido* in Suetonius, see Wallace-Hadrill 1983, 171–4; Morgan 2004, 322–3; Wardle 2015, 1007–8; below, p. 135. Suetonius also avoids telling us the gender of Horace's prostitutes, although we know from his poetry that he was bisexual. The biographer usually makes his subject's sexual preference clear (e.g. *Gramm.* 23.7, *Iul.* 50–2, *Tib.* 43–4, *Claud.* 33.2, *Dom.* 22). For similar acquittals by Suetonius, see *Vita Verg.* 11 (cf. 9), *Aug.* 69.1, and 72.1 (cf. 71.1), with Powell 2017b, 178 (*pace* Baldwin 1983, 390, 503; 1989a, 478); Charles and Anagnostou-Laoutides 2010a, 180; and Baldwin 1983, 504; Wardle 2015, 1008, respectively. However, I do not agree with Charles and Anagnostou-Laoutides (2012a, 1081–2) that Galba's homosexual activities (*Galb.* 22) are quite as sympathetically portrayed, since they contain the morally condemning word *libido*, which is neither excused as with Virgil, nor simply withdrawn as it is elsewhere (*Tit.* 7.1, *Vesp.* 11). It is similarly believed by Charles and Anagnostou-Laoutides (2013–14, 206–8) that Otho is portrayed as essentially heterosexual in Suetonius, but the phrase *mutui stupri* used of his debaucheries with Nero (*Otho* 2.2) recalls the wanton bisexuality of Caligula; see *Calig.* 36.1, with Langlands 2006, 355. On Suetonius' disapproval of homosexuality, see also Baldwin 1983, 221–2, 286, 302.
67 Newman 2011. For Suetonius' interest in the upward social mobility of writers, see esp. Baldwin 1983, 395–6 (on Horace); also e.g. 439–42; id. 1989, 472; Viljamaa 1991, 3829 n. 9; Kaster 1995, xliii, xlvii; Gibson 2014, 217–29. On Suetonius' bias generally, see e.g. Jones 2002; Power 2013b, 342.
68 See above, n. 12.

quotes two epigrams by the Republican poet Furius Bibaculus (frr. 84–5 Hollis) in support of the final details in the biography that Cato lived a long life but died poor in a paltry house:[69]

uixit ad extremam senectam, sed in summa pauperie et paene inopia, abditus modice gurgustio postquam Tusculana uilla creditoribus cesserat, ut auctor est Bibaculus:

> si quis forte mei domum Catonis,
> depictas minio assulas, et illos
> custodis uidet hortulos Priapi:
> miratur quibus ille disciplinis,
> tantam sit sapientiam assecutus,
> quem tres cauliculi, selibra farris,
> racemi duo tegula sub una
> ad summam prope nutriant senectam.

et rursus:

> Catonis modo, Galle, Tusculanum
> tota creditor urbe uenditabat.
> mirati sumus unicum magistrum,
> summum grammaticum, optimum poetam,
> omnes soluere posse quaestiones,
> unum deficere expedire nomen.
> en cor Zenodoti, en iecur Cratetis!

modice X: modico Y | deficere *Toup*: difficile ω

He lived to extreme old age, but in the greatest poverty and almost destitution, hidden meagrely in a hut after he had forfeited his Tuscan villa to creditors, as Bibaculus tells us:

> If by chance anyone sees my Cato's house, mere splinters painted red, and those little gardens of the guard Priapus: he will wonder by what teachings he has progressed to such wisdom that three cabbages, a half-pound of grain, and a couple of bunches of grapes feed him under a single roof almost until extreme old age.

---

69 For the readings of *modice* and *deficere*, see Kaster 1995, 158, 160 (ad locc.), respectively. Brugnoli 1996, 203–4 retains *difficile* with different punctuation, but see Kaster 1992, 80 on 'the obvious care that Bibaculus took in crafting these lines', which supports my argument below. On the formulaic themes of old age and an unusual death in ancient literary biography, see Kivilo 2010, 216–18; on that of poverty, ibid. 221–2. For Suetonius' interest in locations associated with his subject, see e.g. Allen 1958; Baldwin 1983, 14, 127, 182, 187; Gibson and Morello 2012, 227.

And again:

> Cato's Tusculan estate, Gallus, was just now being offered for sale by a creditor through the whole city. We were amazed that this unique teacher, greatest grammarian, and best poet could solve all literary questions, but failed to put in order one name. Behold the mind of Zenodotus, behold the energy of Crates!
>
> (*Gramm.* 11.3)

A criticism is made of Suetonius' use of evidence here by Kaster that is not uncommon in the biographer's scholarship, namely, that he is being naïve: '[Suetonius] plainly took the poems to be literal and earnest reports of actual events ... simple reportage.'[70] This allegation is unwarranted: we should not be so quick to believe that Suetonius considered these poems entirely factual. On the contrary, I have elsewhere shown that there may be more to the poems than suspect facts; there is a possible two-letter variation of the 'gamma-acrostic' in the first two lines of the second poem, which spell 'Cato':[71]

> **CA**tonis modo, Galle, Tusculanum
> **TO**ta creditor urbe uenditabat.

This acrostic is made more likely by the poem's phrase *expedire nomen*, which seems to pun on the removal of a debtor's name from the ledgers, in order to suggest both the grammarian's art of supplying names to literary puzzles and the poem's own arrangement of Cato's name through its initial letters.[72] Suetonius may have used these poems to lodge the impression of Cato's troubles with his reader, but he did not himself perhaps take them, as Kaster claims, to be straightforwardly factual, but rather saw how they illustrated the grammarian's final days in a way that also captured something authentic about him, such as the philological wordplay involved in his profession. Although placed as evidence after the poem about Cato's dire straits, according to Suetonius' orderly rubric method (*summa pauperie ... Tusculana uilla*), this poem about his estate has an emphatic beginning that has a different sort of relevance to the biographer's portrait.

Other examples can be adduced of this usefulness that Suetonius often sees in such poetical quotations. For instance, Suetonius quotes an epigram

---

70 Kaster 1995, 157–8. For Suetonius' alleged naïveté or over-literalness in trusting spurious sources, see bibliography above, n. 8.

71 Above, pp. 48–52; for the term 'gamma-acrostic', see Morgan 1993a, 143. In light of Bibaculus' interplay in these two poems with Catullus, as shown by Loomis 1969, the acrostic's double 'Cato' possibly corresponds to Catullus 56, where this same grammarian's name is written twice (56.1, 56.3).

72 For the former pun, see Hollis 2007, 141–2; cf. Kaster 1992, 78–80; Vacher 1993, 124; for the latter, above, p. 51.

by Asinius Gallus (*FLP* 342) for the background of the grammarian Pomponius Porcellus:

> pugilem olim fuisse Asinius Gallus hoc in eum epigrammate ostendit:
>
>> qui 'caput ad laeuam!' didicit, glossemata nobis
>> praecipit. os nullum – uel potius, pugilis.

> That he was once a boxer, Asinius Gallus shows in this epigram against him:
>
>> The one who learned 'head to the left!' instructs us on glosses. He has no expression – or rather, that of a boxer.
>>
>> (*Gramm.* 22.3)

This evidence has similarly been questioned by Kaster as possible invention, which may have been taken too literally by Suetonius: 'it is not clear how literally Gallus' insult should be taken … it would require no more than the appropriate physiognomy on [Porcellus'] part … combined with his evidently aggressive character, to inspire the scurrilous conceit.'[73] Yet, this criticism points to the reality that satirical verses can at least have their origin in truth and, however conventional their attacks, be important evidence for a historical life. There was something pertinent about the description of Porcellus as a boxer, and Suetonius valued the authority of Gallus, who was a contemporary of Porcellus. It is certainly conceivable that Porcellus had indeed been a boxer, but at any rate there was relevance to Suetonius in his being labelled one, which suggested a certain physiognomy or type of character.[74]

It is instructive to view Suetonius' willingness to accept this fact from Gallus' epigram in light of his inclusion of other questionable poetry even when better evidence is available. An example from the *Caligula* should suffice. Suetonius quotes some 'doggerel verses'[75] on the birthplace of the emperor:

> uersiculi imperante mox eo diuulgati apud hibernas legiones procreatum indicant:
>
>> in castris natus, patriis nutritus in armis,
>> iam designati principis omen erat.

---

73 Kaster 1995, 227.
74 On physiognomy as revelatory of character in Suetonius, see e.g. Evans 1950, 279–81; 1969, 51–6; Rohrbacher 2010, 94–103; Power 2014c, 231; Trimble 2014, 126–7; Chiai 2019.
75 Goodyear 1972, 286.

Some little verses that were circulated soon after he became emperor suggest he was born within the winter legions:

> Born in the camps, reared among the arms of his forefathers – already it was an omen of a destined emperor.
>
> > (*Calig.* 8.1)

Suetonius provides the couplet in full, only to disprove it immediately by appealing to 'those who committed Augustus' deeds to the record' (*qui res Augusti memoriae mandarunt, Calig.* 8.3), and an actual letter written by that emperor (8.4). The biographer concludes: 'Credence in the little verses too is lessened by this, and all the more easily because they are author-less' (*uersiculorum quoque fidem eadem haec eleuant et eo facilius quod ii sine auctore sunt*, 8.5). So, why then report them at all? True, the dispute evinces Suetonius' scholarly prowess, which, in turn, establishes further authority towards his audience.[76]

But again, we should not assume that Suetonius cares only for the task at hand;[77] the second line of the couplet may be no less important than the first. There seems an additional purpose in the fact that by annulling this omen, the biographer implicitly contradicts Caligula's suitability to rule. As often in the *Caesars*, comparison and contrast are left to the reader, who must infer the context as either eulogy or blame from other *Lives* in the collection.[78] Here, it is noteworthy that for emperors such as Augustus and Vespasian, omens foretelling their rule are recorded as a separate category (*Aug.* 94–7, *Vesp.* 5), whereas in condemnatory biographies such as the *Caligula*, *Nero*, and *Domitian*, omens of demise are the order of the day (*Calig.* 57, *Ner.* 46, *Dom.* 15–16). By introducing an omen of the former type and then swiftly disproving it, Suetonius emphasizes the negative tenor of the biography, which will even end with the claim that all members of the Caesar household who bore the name 'Gaius' met violent deaths (*Calig.* 60).[79] The couplet therefore subtly denies the success of Caligula's reign, just as later Suetonius' famous statement that he was a 'monster' rather than an 'emperor' (22.1) will do more explicitly.

In a way similar to these examples, Suetonius' lines from Bibaculus may (or may not) take liberty in inventing what Cato ate and where he lived before he died, but they at least espouse something of the literary games that were the grammarian's stock in trade by forming an acrostic, since acrostics were no less indicative of Alexandrian learning than Bibaculus' reference to Zenodotus. Since Suetonius likes to comment elsewhere in the same collection on these kinds of linguistic flourishes (*Gramm.* 6.3, 9.6), it is probable that the biographer would have noticed this one and been influenced by it in his pragmatic decision to include the poems. It is even possible

---

76 Duchêne 2016, 284–5.
77 As thought by Woods 2011, 160; cf. Hurley 2003, 113.
78 See Hägg 2012, 222–3; Power 2014a, esp. 70–2; 2014b, 13–14; below, p. 118.
79 For a discussion of the final passages of each biography in the *Caesars*, see Power 2014a.

that Bibaculus' use of an acrostic not only signals Cato's profession as a *grammaticus* but also offers a glimpse of the character of Cato's poetry, for he was no less famous as a poet than as a grammarian (*poetam simul grammaticumque notissimum*, *Gramm.* 4.2; cf. 11.2). Furthermore, these verses by Bibaculus may merely exaggerate history: their humour would have had a greater impact if the alleged financial difficulty at the end of Cato's life had been true. One way or the other, the point to note is that these poems about Cato were not simply part of a mythology of rumour that surrounded the figure during his life: they also engaged with, and were partially born out of, the substance of that life. Baldwin writes on this biography: 'The notice contains several standard items ... The only solid fact given is that [Cato] lost his patrimony as a young orphan *licentia Sullani temporis.*'[80] As I have shown, there may also be some truth preserved about his later misfortunes and the character of his grammatical endeavours in the poems by Bibaculus. From this discussion, and from that of the *Horace*, we may thus redeem Suetonius as a more credible biographer in the *Illustrious Men* than he has generally been thought.

Conclusion

I shall conclude by drawing from these studies some broader implications for Suetonius' biographical approach in general and for the relationship between fact and fiction in ancient biography. The nature of Suetonius' use of poetry in the *Illustrious Men* differs to a great extent from that in the *Caesars*, where emperors are by contrast often shown quoting poetry in *ipsissima uerba*, especially Homer, as direct illustrations of their character;[81] and where discussions of the subject's own literary writings have the same purpose, being placed under the category of imperial *studia*.[82] In the *Illustrious Men*, on the other hand, poetry is used more as a direct source for the history of the subject's life, a practice which was common in ancient literary biography and often led to the inclusion of fantastical stories.[83]

However, as we have seen, sometimes when Suetonius explicitly cites or quotes material that has a potentially fictional origin, such as the story of the salted-fish merchant in the *Horace*, he is cautious in the same way as in the *Caesars* about bringing it into the service of his portrait, and clarifies his stance towards its factuality, just as he does in the *Augustus* and *Domitian*. We might also compare Suetonius' *praeteritio* when reporting the notorious verses by Calvus and others about Caesar's alleged sexual

---

80 Baldwin 1983, 431.
81 On Suetonius' verbatim quotations, see e.g. Damon 2014; Slater 2014; Mitchell 2015; below, Chapters 12, 16, 19, 23. On fictional material in the *Caesars*, see also Mouchová 1968, 55–7; Sansone 1993; Barton 1994; Hurley 2014a; Ash 2016; below, Chapters 28, 32.
82 See Bradley 1991, 3727–8; Power 2014b, 12; below, pp. 118, 193.
83 For such stories in Suetonius' *Terence* and *Virgil*, see e.g. Horsfall 1994, 45–7.

relationship with the Bithynian king Nicomedes, which Suetonius reproduces in full, but with explicit reservations (*Iul.* 49.1–4). Like the passages we examined in the *Illustrious Men*, these verses about Caesar reflect some historical truth in bearing witness to a real visit to Nicomedes in the dictator's life around 80 BC, even if the episode was very different,[84] while at the same time they achieve for the biographer a literary purpose of denigrating Caesar's character.[85] Suetonius likewise conveys in this example, through his eschewing of credence in the source, that he possessed a critical awareness of the tendency of such poetry to distort reality;[86] we should therefore always ask ourselves whether there is not some purpose to his use of questionable details, especially when he denies their truth in order to maintain his authority to the reader. Suetonius is careful not to lose his credibility as a factual source, but as a biographer he also uses available material to emphasize important points about the character of his subject.

These comparisons with the *Caesars* may also have some bearing on the distinction between Suetonius' literary and political biographies, which Wallace-Hadrill has shown cannot be explained as simply the result of Suetonius' applying to both collections, as once proposed by Leo, the generic model of Alexandrian or 'literary' biography, rather than that of Peripatetic or 'philosophical' biography.[87] Although Suetonius' two sets of *Lives* display a similar handling of poetical sources when used as direct evidence for the subject's life, this kind of source is much more central in the *Illustrious Men*, frequently because of the lack of other documentation. Yet, the use to which poetry and fiction are put in each collection probably depends less on generic models than on the overall presentation for which Suetonius is aiming in each biography.[88] In the case of Caesar, negative verses are reported because Suetonius wishes to condemn his subject. In the case of Horace, a fictional story about his ancestry contrasts with a realer account of it, but also suggests an important part of Horace's poetical works, just as the *Odes* and *Epistles* are adduced as much for his winning of Augustus' favour (*Augusto insinuatus*, *Vita Hor.* 3) as for their own biographical details; and a probably mistaken detail about his use of prostitutes is nonetheless retained for its relevance to the poet. In the case of Valerius Cato, poems are

---

84 See Osgood 2008; Pelling 2011, 137–8; Beneker 2012, 141–4, 222.
85 On Calvus in Suetonius, see above, Chapter 3. For the similar purpose to Suetonius' quotation of the orator Memmius in this section of the *Julius*, see above, Chapter 6.
86 Cf. generally Lindsay 1995a, 70–1, contrasting Suetonius' methods in his literary *Lives* with Satyrus' greater acceptance of poetry as historical evidence; also Hägg 2012, 217 on Suetonius' disinclination to imagine for the reader the scene reported indirectly at *Vita Verg.* 27–30.
87 Leo 1901; *contra*, see Wallace-Hadrill 1983, 66–72.
88 The inclusion of fiction thus speaks to an ancient author's programme rather than genre, *pace* Momigliano 1993, 56–7, who argues that fiction was more acceptable in biography; cf. also Reichel 2007, 41. For criticism of Momigliano's view, see Pelling 1990b = 2002b, 143–70.

included as proof that he lost money before his death,[89] but also as a taste of the flavour of his scholarly life and writings; so too verses are included on Porcellus and Caligula for what they say about the subject's character.

Suetonius' reasons are narrower reasons than those for which we value his evidence today, such as the light it casts on the climate of a particular reign or on the jesting relationship between particular writers, but they were the biographer's reasons, dictated by his aim in each *Life*. Histories and commentaries might find in the scandalous verses about Caesar that circulated in the camps important testimony about the political atmosphere among his troops,[90] but this is not the point of their use in the *Julius*. If Suetonius preserves fictional elements that entered the tradition before him, it is not that he wishes to preserve later reactions to his subject, or that he 'fell victim' to his sources;[91] the value of his material for portraying the subject as he sees him simply outweighed its dubiousness. Nevertheless, Suetonius often clarifies his stance towards the veracity of this material, and he certainly refrains in both collections from making the kinds of leaps and inventions found in earlier literary biography.

Suetonius' use of fiction in all of his *Lives*, then, is not very different from that of the biographer Plutarch, who was also willing occasionally to be flexible with the facts if it served a higher truth, as he saw it, about his subject.[92] As Lindsay writes with respect to the *Horace*: 'the strength of Suetonius' characterization lies in the fact that every episode treated contributes in an important way to the image he is presenting.'[93] If Suetonius at times bends the truth, it cannot be used in any simple way to impugn his judgement or honesty as a biographer. Suetonius had to work with the existing evidence, and in the *Illustrious Men* he often chose to preserve an array of first-hand material, from poetical testimonia to letters by the emperor Augustus. This material is often historically valuable despite its rhetorical aims or generic conventions not only because it was created during or shortly after the subject's life, but also because it succeeds in portraying what Suetonius felt must have been true about literary figures whose characters he believed he knew already from their writings – 'the important reality', as Pelling puts it about Plutarch,[94] that the biographer wants his reader to grasp – even if he did not read these writings as strictly autobiographical. It is this reality that Suetonius strives to represent, even if he must sometimes do so through half-truths.

89 We might also compare the lines quoted by Suetonius on Sevius Nicanor at *Gramm.* 5.1, which are used to confirm his freedman status and double name; on the aim of that quotation, cf. Kaster 1992, 56.

90 Cf. Pelling 2010, 375–6 (on Tac. *Ann.* 4.37–8).

91 Thus e.g. Lindsay 2009, 3, 7 on Suetonius' use of Nisus at *Vita Verg.* 42.

92 See Pelling 1990b, 35–43 = 2002b, 152–6. On Plutarch's inclusion of material to suit his literary ends despite its unreliability, see e.g. *Them.* 2.8, *Solon* 27.1, *Alc.* 3.1–2, *Cam.* 5.5–6, 6.1–6, with Duff 2003b, 92–3; 2008, 201–2; *Alex.* 2–3, with Stadter 1996, 293; *Brut.* 53.5–7, with Moles 1997, 144–5, 161.

93 Lindsay 1995a, 77; cf. id. 2009, 3.

94 Pelling 1990b, 43 = 2002b, 156.

10 Caesar and Sophocles' *Electra*

In his biography of Julius Caesar, Suetonius reports two scenes from lost plays that were read by a mime at the dictator's funeral. The first belongs to Pacuvius' *Trial of the Arms* (fr. 31 Schierl), and Suetonius quotes the same verse as Appian (*B Civ.* 2.146). The line probably came from a speech shortly before the suicide of Ajax, who had saved the Greeks in the Trojan War, only to see them award the arms of Achilles to Odysseus.[1] The context of the second scene, however, is more difficult to infer, even after we accept Kaster's new reading *Atili*:[2]

> inter ludos cantata sunt quaedam ad miserationem et inuidiam caedis eius accommodata ex Pacuui Armorum iudicio:
>
> > men seruasse ut essent qui me perderent?
>
> et ex Electra Atili ad similem sententiam.
>
> Atili ç: Acili ω, Ihm

> Among the performances, certain verses were recited that aroused pity and anger at his death from Pacuvius' *Trial of the Arms*:
>
> > Did I save them so that they could destroy me?
>
> and from Atilius' *Electra* expressing a similar sentiment.
>
> > (*Iul.* 84.2)

It has been argued that these verses may have been selected by Mark Antony, or else by the mime himself ex tempore.[3] Whoever chose them, Tilg has shown that they represent some of our earliest evidence for how Caesar's death was portrayed in terms of the myth of Orestes, which Augustus

---

1 See Butler and Cary 1927, 152; Schierl 2006, 136, 153–4; Scantamburlo 2011, 244.
2 Kaster 2016a, anticipated by Rolfe 1913–14. Ihm 1907 had printed *Acili*.
3 Sumi 2002, 570–1. As Sumi points out (566–70), by *inter ludos* Suetonius almost certainly refers to mime performances, rather than funerary games; *pace* Osgood 2006, 13 n. 5; Hurley 2011, 46; Scantamburlo 2011, 244.

was later to exploit politically in presenting himself as an avenger of his adoptive father's murder.[4] This theme of revenge is one of the few things that can fairly be said of Atilius' work, since it is now lost, and even if it was a 'translation' (*conuersio*) of Sophocles' *Electra*, as Cicero claims (*Fin.* 1.5), we cannot know how much was changed in the Latin version. Nevertheless, there is still some point to a search for the specific passage in Sophocles' play that formed the direct basis for the unquoted verse in Suetonius. Butler and Cary, for example, ventured the lament by Electra (*Elec.* 86–120),[5] but Tilg himself makes no conjecture, pointing instead to the possible relevance of the play's ending (*Elec.* 1508–10).[6]

In my view, Butler and Cary were correct. However, Electra's speech can be narrowed down even further to the exact original verses containing the 'same sentiment' as that of Pacuvius, and there is even good reason to think that this sentiment is among the elements of the tradition inherited from Sophocles that would have been preserved by Atilius. The lines of the extant *Electra* that fit best with Suetonius' description are 97–9:

μήτηρ δ' ἡμὴ χὠ κοινολεχὴς
Αἴγισθος ὅπως δρῦν ὑλοτόμοι
σχίζουσι πελέκει.

My mother and her lover Aegisthus, as if cutting down an oak tree, split his head with a deadly axe.

This vivid simile, or one similar to it, would certainly have aroused *miseratio* and *inuidia* at Caesar's death.[7] Sophocles' scene is itself based in the first place on a well-known simile in Homer, where Agamemnon in the underworld compares his own murder by his adulterous wife and her companion not to the felling of an oak tree that has been split open, but to the slaying of an ox in a stable (ὥς τίς τε κατέκτανε βοῦν ἐπὶ φάτνῃ, *Od.* 11.409–11).[8] It was therefore an integral part of the story's tradition that Atilius would hardly have omitted. Indeed, he would probably have felt the need to try his hand at its reinvention in Latin, just as Sophocles had done before him in Greek tragic metre. Whatever new form it took, Atilius' own simile would no doubt have been descriptive and memorable in its own right, and Suetonius' simple reference to it thus all the more obvious and dramatic.[9]

---

4 Tilg 2008, 369–70: 'the drama must have conveyed a clear exhortative message of revenge.'
5 Butler and Cary 1927, 152.
6 Tilg 2008, 369 n. 6.
7 For the vividness of this simile, underscored by its metre, see Finglass 2007, 121.
8 See ibid. 127.
9 On Suetonius' dramatic purpose in this passage, see Dueck 2009, 181.

In focusing on his subject, the biographer tends to leave out only what can be easily discovered.[10]

Just as the sentiment of this Homeric simile about Agamemnon's death does not substantially change in its transition from the *Odyssey* to Sophocles' *Electra*, despite its revised imagery, so too the basic sense of these lines is unlikely to have been altered by the time they found a new form in Atilius' lost Roman play. The common thread is that Agamemnon's betrayal was tragic because of its violent nature and unforeseen perpetrators. This point explains the parallel with Caesar, who met an equally violent end because he too was betrayed by those whom he most trusted. It is not that Agamemnon was killed by people who were literally in his debt, as in the quote from Pacuvius, but rather by someone who should likewise have been loyal to him, that is, his wife. This is the way in which these lines contain a 'similar sentiment'. As a pair of lovers, the murderers Clytemnestra and Aegisthus anticipate Augustus' campaign against Antony and Cleopatra (*RG* 2), and these recitations at Caesar's funeral would have invited comparisons with Orestes' justified vengeance. Through Atilius' version of these Sophoclean lines, Caesar was likened to a powerful force surprisingly and unnaturally cut down – whether a strong ox, a mighty oak, or something else – and this description was probably so moving as to inspire Augustus' political presentation of himself as a second Orestes. The recitation of Atilius' simile was especially appropriate for a ruler such as Julius Caesar, who according to Suetonius was known to allude often to characters from Greek tragedy in an arrogant manner, drawing comparisons with tyrannical kings such as Agamemnon (*Iul.* 30.5).[11]

---

10 See Power 2014b, 4–8; below, p. 212. Cf. also p. 117 with bibliography on *Claud.* 15.3–4, where Suetonius seems to refer to, or at least to assume the reader's knowledge of, a specific line of Homer (*Il.* 1.26), but without quoting it.

11 See Morgan 1997b, 39–40; Pelling 1997b, 218.

11 Pyrrhus and Priam in Suetonius' *Tiberius*[*]

In a brief note, Turner recognized the similarity of an anecdote reported by both Suetonius (*Tib.* 57.2) and Cassius Dio (57.14.1–2) on the emperor Tiberius' treatment of a jester, who was complaining that Augustus' legacies had not yet been paid, to the final moments of Priam's slaughter at the hands of Pyrrhus in the *Aeneid* (2.535–50). However, she commented merely on the contextual parallel of Tiberius' command that the jester personally carry his message to Augustus. Her conclusion reads as follows: 'It is impossible (I think) to say whether Suetonius or Dio or some earlier source consciously reproduced Vergil's story.'[1]

There is, in fact, more to this possible allusion in Suetonius, where a unique variation contains a strong verbal and contextual similarity to Virgil's passage that has previously gone unnoticed:

> scurram qui praetereunte funere clare mortuo mandarat ut nuntiaret Augusto nondum reddi legata quae plebei reliquisset adtractum ad se *recipere debitum* ducique ad supplicium imperauit et patri suo uerum referre.

> When a jester during a funeral procession loudly advised the corpse to report to Augustus that the legacies he had left the people had not yet been rendered, he [Tiberius] ordered that he be brought to him to *receive his due* and be executed, and that he report the truth to his father.
> (*Tib.* 57.2)

Of these two joking remarks of Tiberius' recorded by Suetonius, Dio contains only the second, that the jester himself should carry the message

---

[*] This chapter was first published in CQ 62 (2012), 430–3.

1 Turner 1943, anticipated by de la Cerda 1612, 237 (on *Aen.* 2.547–50), who noted the Suetonian parallel to Virgil's scene: 'similem huic historiam & atrocitatem Suetonius narrat de Tiberio in illius vita cap. 57.' Austin 1964, 211 (on *Aen.* 2.550) adds the parallel of Odysseus, who is also a messenger to Achilles about Neoptolemus (Hom. *Od.* 11.505–37); cf. Horsfall 2008, 413–14.

to Augustus (ἵνα αὐτάγγελος αὐτῷ, ὥς που καὶ ἐπισκώπτων εἶπε, γένηται, 57.14.2).[2] The first remark has a parallel in Dio, but it is rather different: the historian states that Tiberius not long afterwards 'discharged his debt' to the rest of the people (τοὺς δ' ἄλλους οὐκ ἐς μακρὰν ἀπήλλαξε, 57.14.2), and this may have been the language contained in the original source shared by Suetonius and Dio for this anecdote about the jester.[3]

However, in Suetonius, this language of reciprocity is turned into a command by Tiberius, which takes on a very different sense. In Dio, the word ἀπήλλαξε is written straightforwardly, but in Suetonius, the phrase *recipere debitum* is written with great irony, since there is a pun on 'receive his due' to mean 'receive death'.[4] The same ironic pun may be witnessed in Virgil's scene, where Priam calls on the gods to kill Pyrrhus for killing his sons: 'May they pay worthy thanks and render *due rewards*' (*persoluant grates dignas et* praemia *reddant* / debita, *Aen.* 2.537–8).[5] Suetonius' Tiberius therefore echoes not only the words of Pyrrhus, but also those of Priam, and by uttering these words of Priam's from the position of Pyrrhus, implicitly suggests that in the Virgilian scene, it is Priam who in fact gets his just desserts.

As this part of Dio's *Roman History* is complete, not abridged, the uniqueness of Suetonius' variation cannot be explained as simply an omission by Dio's epitomator: it was probably not in the common source. One possibility is that Suetonius found it in a supplementary source unknown to Dio.[6] Another is that Suetonius' *recipere debitum* is a clever reworking of the detail in the common source that Tiberius later 'discharged his debt' (ἀπήλλαξε, Dio Cass. 57.14.2) to suit an analogy with Priam. There is some support for the latter possibility in Suetonius' verb *imperauit*, which begins an indirect command that frees him from the responsibility of quoting the emperor verbatim. It seems likely that Suetonius alone noticed the similarity of this scene to Virgil's *Aeneid* and fashioned his words to create the

---

2 Cf. Pyrrhus' words at *Aen.* 2.547–50: 'Report these things, then, and go as a messenger to my father, the son of Peleus. You must remember to tell him of my harsh deeds and the degenerate Neoptolemus. Now die!' (*referes ergo haec et nuntius ibis / Pelidae genitori. illi mea tristia facta / degeneremque Neoptolemum narrare memento. / nunc morere!*).

3 See LSJ s.v. ἀπαλλάσσω A4. Dio does not appear to have used Suetonius, but to have drawn independently on the first-century sources, and similarities between the two authors are therefore best attributed to a common source; see below, pp. 111, 199. For the Tiberian period, this source appears to have been a Latin annalist; see e.g. Swan 2004, 23. The original phrase was therefore possibly *debitum soluit*. On Suetonius and Dio, see also id. 1987, 286–8 with bibliography. Another textual correspondence between these two passages is *mortuo mandarat* (*Tib.* 57.2) ~ νεκρόν ... ἐντετάλθαι (Dio Cass. 57.14.1). However, Dio's fact in this section that the body was being carried 'through the Forum' (διὰ τῆς ἀγορᾶς), which is not included in Suetonius, demonstrates that he used this source independently; cf. Swan 2004, 301 on a similarly unique detail at 56.29.4.

4 For this pun in Suetonius, see Pike 1903, 187 (ad loc.).

5 For this pun in Virgil, see Coffee 2009, 46–7.

6 Suetonius' use of supplementary sources should not be underestimated; see below, p. 124.

allusion, perhaps believing that Tiberius intended it in the first place and strengthening the connection by extending the emperor's wit further than in his source.[7]

That Suetonius was well attuned to such inversions of epic, and particularly of Priam, can be demonstrated elsewhere in his *Lives* where he preserves similar references. For example, a little earlier in the same biography, Tiberius offers ironic condolences to the Trojans on the death of Hector, in exchange for theirs on his son Drusus (*Tib.* 52.1–2). The biographer's explicit point is that the emperor cared as little about Drusus as the Trojans did about a hero who had died many centuries before; both deaths are equally remote and irrelevant. A more implicit example of such irony is Suetonius' preservation of a Homeric quotation by Claudius: 'Defend against any man who attacks you first' (ἄνδρ' ἀπαμύνασθαι, ὅτε τις πρότερος χαλεπήνῃ, *Claud.* 42.1). Here, Suetonius expects the reader to recall not merely a character from poetry, but a specific Homeric scene (*Il.* 24.369, cf. *Od.* 16.72, 21.133), where this line is about *not* being able to ward off enemies due to the physical incapacity of old age, a fact which renders Claudius' use of it comical. This irony is lost without an understanding of the line's original context. However, Suetonius does not point this irony out to the reader, but rather leaves it as an added layer of meaning, enhancing his portrait of Claudius as a fool.[8]

Moreover, there is evidence that Suetonius was not opposed to manipulating his source material for the purpose of allusion. His account of the death of Galba can be usefully compared to the parallel versions in Plutarch, Tacitus, and Dio, and Suetonius' unique variations strongly recall Priam's words in *Aeneid* 2; Suetonius has probably altered the language of the common source to suit an allusion to the words of Priam in a specific Virgilian passage (*Galb.* 19.2–20.1 ~ *Aen.* 2.148–51).[9] In another case, Suetonius may have even transferred an anecdote to the *Tiberius* from source material on Nero: Suetonius has Tiberius state that Priam's living to see his sons' deaths is his great fortune, rather than misfortune (*Tib.* 62.3). This saying is found also in Dio (61.16.1), but there it is attributed to Nero. Suetonius may have decided to appropriate this item to the *Tiberius* as more fitting to that emperor's character. It is therefore believable that Suetonius also made the present change to the description of Tiberius' punishment of the jester, in order to facilitate the reader's recognition of the allusion to Priam.

The strong allusion to Virgil in Suetonius' scene about the jester further confirms the biographer's awareness of parallels in poetry and the importance of literary analysis to the interpretation of his *Lives*. This particular scene is placed in a prominent position in the biography (*Tib.* 57.2), at the

---

7 On Tiberius' knowledge of literature generally, see e.g. Goodyear 1984, 605–6.

8 See the next chapter below; *pace* Eaton 2011, 61. For other examples of Suetonius' expectation of the reader's knowledge of Homer, see below, Chapters 16 and 23.

9 On these unique echoes, which are not present in the other accounts, see Chapter 14.

culmination of the section on the emperor's vices. The anecdote comes just after the rubric *saeua*, and represents Suetonius' first example of Tiberius' 'cruelty' as an emperor:

> **saeua** ac lenta natura ne in puero quidem latuit ... sed aliquanto magis in principe eluxit, etiam inter initia cum adhuc fauorem hominum moderationis simulatione captaret.

> His **cruel** and unrelenting character was not even hidden in the boy ... But it shone through a little more in the emperor, even at the beginning, when he was still seeking the favour of the people by feigning restraint.
>
> (*Tib.* 57.1)

It may be no coincidence that the slaughter of Priam and the words of Pyrrhus to which Suetonius' first anecdote alludes constitute a highpoint of cruelty in the *Aeneid*, forcing Aeneas to break off his narrative: 'But then for the first time I was confronted by the *cruel* horror!' (*at me tum primum* saeuus *circumstetit horror! Aen.* 2.559). Suetonius' rubric has a similar prominence in his biography to this part of Virgil's Book 2, and his passage draws an important distinction between the reigns of Augustus and Tiberius, just as Virgil's scene contrasts Achilles with Pyrrhus, and the world of the *Iliad* with the much darker one of the *Aeneid*.[10]

10 On these contrasts in the Virgilian passage, see e.g. O'Sullivan 2009, 459–62.

12 Claudius' Homeric Quotation[*]

In his *Life* of Claudius, Suetonius uses a Homeric quotation to demonstrate the emperor's propensity for using Greek (*Claud.* 42.1).[1] Scholars have generally viewed this part of the biography as favourable towards the emperor.[2] However, the quotation only serves to reveal Claudius' obliviousness to its meaning; although he can quote the line verbatim, the unsuitability of its context escapes him:

> multum uero pro tribunali etiam Homericis locutus est uersibus. quotiens quidem hostem uel insidiatorem ultus esset, excubitori tribuno signum de more poscenti non temere aliud dedit quam,
>
> ἄνδρ' ἐπαμύνασθαι, ὅτε τις πρότερος χαλεπήνῃ.

> But often on the tribunal he even spoke in Homeric verses. In fact, whenever he took revenge on an enemy or conspirator, and the tribune of the guard asked as usual for the watchword, he never gave him anything besides,
>
> Defend against any man who attacks you first.
>
> (*Claud.* 42.1)

This line appears three times in Homer: once in reference to Priam on his journey to Achilles towards the end of the *Iliad* (24.369), and twice in reference to Telemachus in the *Odyssey* (16.72, 21.133). Some scholars favour the first appearance over the other two,[3] and no doubt rightly, due to Claudius' similarity to Priam in age (see below). However, a similar sense

---

[*] This chapter was first published in *Latomus* 70 (2011), 727–31.

1 This is the only preserved Homeric quotation by Claudius of historical provenance, and is also quoted at Dio Cass. 60.16.7–8. It has been suggested by Levick 1989, 113–14 that another lies behind *Claud.* 15.3–4, but it requires guesswork. Claudius' quotation at Sen. *Apocol.* 5.4 is possibly an invention of satire. Both passages will be discussed below. On the emperors' general fondness for Greek sayings, especially Homer, see e.g. Horváth 1996; Adams 2003, 336.

2 See e.g. Wardle 1992, 470; Hurley 2001, 226–7, 231–2. A partial exception is Townend 1960, 103, who recognizes the hostile context surrounding Claudius' quotation.

3 Berthet 1978, 330; Hurley 2001, 232.

is conveyed in each passage, where the point is the lack of ability to defend oneself due to age: Priam is too old, Telemachus too young. The tragic old age and helplessness of Priam in particular is a memorable theme in the *Iliad*,[4] and in that poem shortly before the above quotation, Homer signals this theme through the contrast with Priam's escort Hermes, the speaker of the verse, who is disguised as a youthful prince πρῶτον ὑπηνήτῃ ('with his first beard', *Il.* 24.348) and who warns Priam that he is too weak to travel alone through the enemy camp. Yet, Telemachus' two utterances of the quotation in the *Odyssey* are comparable: he himself laments that he is not yet strong enough to fight the suitors (*Od.* 16.72) or to string Odysseus' bow (*Od.* 21.133).

In its new context in Suetonius' *Caesars*, however, Claudius uses the line instead in a positive sense, rather than in the original sense as something he *cannot* do.[5] As with Galba's similarly ill-chosen quotation of Homer later in the *Caesars* (*Galb.* 20.2 = *Il.* 5.254 = *Od.* 21.426), the joke here is on the emperor, although the contrast between the two passages is instructive: in Galba's case, he understands the original meaning but is unaware of its possible connotations in the new context, and it is the military servants who twist his meaning;[6] Claudius, on the other hand, unwittingly produces the irony in his own quotation, since he understands the present context but does not comprehend its dissimilarity to the Homeric one. If the audience is aware of their Homer, the line in fact implies to them that the emperor is *not* able to defend himself, which is the quotation's original meaning. The line furthermore draws attention to the idea of weakness from age, which is not very tactful, given that Claudius is fifty-two years old when he utters this quotation, and lame from a physical impairment.[7] The point to note is that in all three Homeric passages, the speaker of this verse is especially youthful, and in the case of the *Iliad* is speaking to someone especially old: the irony of Claudius' quotation results from his being better suited to the role of its recipient Priam than its speakers Hermes and Telemachus.

The interpretation that in quoting this verse Claudius left himself open to ridicule can be supported by comparing the parallel account in Cassius Dio:

Κλαύδιος δὲ οὕτω που πρὸς τὴν τιμωρίαν τήν τε ἐκείνων καὶ τὴν τῶν ἄλλων ἔσχεν ὥστε καὶ σύνθημα τοῖς στρατιώταις τὸ ἔπος τοῦτο συνεχῶς

4 See *Il.* 22.66–76, with Falkner 1989, 37–8; Vernant 1991, 64–6.
5 This irony has gone unnoticed by scholars. Berthet 1978, 326–7 sees the line as adapted in a sense similar to the original passage: 'Claude a peur d'être attaqué dans son palais? Il invoque la protection d'Hermès sur Priam'; cf. Aparicio 2008, 449–50. But it is not precisely Priam's protection by Hermes that is the subject matter, but rather his need for protection. Hurley 2001, 232 similarly thinks that the quotation is fitting, and ironic only in view of Suetonius' recent discussion of Claudius' anger (*Claud.* 38.1–2). Dueck 2009, 181 believes that the direct quotation simply adds to the drama of the scene.
6 On Galba's Homeric quotation, see below, Chapter 16.
7 From its contextual placement in Dio, the quotation can be dated to the conspiracy of AD 42; see Hurley 2001, 231. On Claudius' physical affliction, see e.g. Levick 1990, 13–16; Eden 1984, 172 ('Addenda et corrigenda', in the 2002 repr.).

διδόναι, τὸ ὅτι χρὴ Ἄνδρα ἀπαμύνασθαι ὅτε τις πρότερος χαλεπήνῃ. καὶ ἄλλα δὲ πολλὰ καὶ πρὸς ἐκείνους καὶ πρὸς τὴν βουλὴν τοιουτότροπα ἑλληνιστὶ παρεφθέγγετο, ὥστε καὶ γέλωτα παρὰ τοῖς δυναμένοις ἔστιν ἃ αὐτῶν συνεῖναι ὀφλισκάνειν.

But Claudius was so engaged with revenge against those men and others that he even continually gave as the watchword to the soldiers that saying that one must 'defend against any man who attacks you first'. And he even interjected many other sayings of this kind in Greek both to them and the senate, so that he was laughed at by those able to understand any of them.

(Dio Cass. 60.16.7–8)

According to Dio, Claudius provoked laughter (γέλωτα) through his use of Greek, particularly quotations such as this one from Homer, which the historian provides as an example. The fact that Dio emphasizes how only those who understood the quotations laughed at Claudius is significant: it is not merely the general contrast with the line's grandiose tone of epic that was funny, which would have been discernable from its metre, but more specifically its contrast with the original Homeric context.

Additional support for our reading of the quotation as humorous at Claudius' expense may be found in two other passages. The first is in Seneca's *Apocolocyntosis*:

itaque et ipse Homerico uersu Caesarem se esse significans ait:

Ἰλιόθεν με φέρων ἄνεμος Κικόνεσσι πέλασσεν

(erat autem sequens uersus uerior, aeque Homericus:

ἔνθα δ' ἐγὼ πόλιν ἔπραθον, ὤλεσα δ' αὐτούς).

And so he too implied that he was Caesar with a Homeric verse, saying:

The wind took me from Ilium to the Cicones.

(but the verse that followed was more accurate, also from Homer:

And there I sacked the city, and killed the men).

(Sen. *Apocol.* 5.4)

In this scene, Seneca has Claudius quoting a line from Homer to identify himself as the emperor, since the Julio-Claudians claimed descent from Ilium.[8] Even though the original speaker of the first line (*Od.* 9.39) is Odysseus, a Greek, it may have seemed to Claudius to serve his purpose when spoken proverbially, that is, taken out of context. However, the line that follows it (*Od.* 9.40) ironically undermines Claudius, suggesting his

8 See Eden 1984, 86–7 (ad loc.).

bloodlust and the tyrannical aspects of his reign; Seneca quotes this second line in a parenthetical aside to bring out the irony, and hence foolishness, of the first. The scene therefore satirizes Claudius as quoting ill-chosen Greek verses, suggesting that this is something he was accustomed to do.

The second passage which may provide further evidence for this kind of tactless quotation by Claudius is found earlier in his Suetonian biography:

> illud quoque a maioribus natu audiebam, adeo causidicos patientia eius solitos abuti ut discedentem e tribunali non solum uoce reuocarent sed et lacinia togae retenta, interdum pede apprehenso detinerent. ac ne cui haec mira sint, litigatori Graeculo uox in altercatione excidit, καὶ σὺ γέρων εἶ καὶ μωρός.

> I also used to hear from my elders that advocates were accustomed to abuse his patience so much that they would not only call him back from the tribunal with their voice as he was exiting but also detain him by grabbing the hem of his toga, occasionally by holding his foot. And so that this is not amazing to anyone, a Greek litigant let slip these words during a lawsuit: 'You too are an old man, and a fool!'
>
> (*Claud.* 15.3–4)

It is possible that this remark from the Greek lawyer was in fact a reply to a quotation of Homer by Claudius that contained the address γέρον, most likely the line of Agamemnon in Book 1 of the *Iliad* to the priest of Apollo, who had sought the return of his daughter Chriseis: μή σε, γέρον, κοίλῃσιν ἐγὼ παρὰ νηυσὶ κιχείω ('Do not let me find you, old man, by the hollow ships!' *Il.* 1.26).[9] By drawing attention to age, and by likening himself to the Agamemnon of Book 1, Claudius was vulnerable to the lawyer's reply that the emperor was not only himself old, but like Agamemnon also a fool, since by sending away the priest with these very words, the Greek king causes the plague on his own Achaeans.[10]

In conclusion, the Homeric quotation uttered by the emperor in Suetonius' *Divine Claudius* should not be read as simply illustrating his learning, but rather as undermining him as an emperor. There appears to have been a tradition, represented by passages in Seneca, Suetonius, and Dio, in which Claudius was well known for quoting passages of Homer that could easily be turned against him to humorous effect. In reality, Homeric quotations such as this one may have become proverbial sayings detached from their original contexts, and Claudius may have seen nothing wrong in his use of this line for the punishment of the conspirators of AD 42. However, for

---

9 As proposed by Levick 1989, 113–14. The line fits well, and the setting of the tribunal makes it more plausible that Claudius has quoted Homer, since this is where he is said to have frequently done so in our passage of Suetonius above (*Claud.* 42.1).

10 See Levick 1989, 113.

writers such as Suetonius, and probably for the source he shared with Dio, the line was not straightforward, and said a great deal about the emperor's character. Claudius' inability to foresee the consequences of this quotation adds to Suetonius' general portrait of him as a fool, but it is noteworthy that the biographer does not make it explicit for the reader that Claudius is here the object of ridicule, as Dio does in his narrative of the same event. Instead, it is left to the reader to draw the connection between the original Homeric context and its misapplication in the new passage, and to observe this passage's pointing of an ironic contrast, which is made explicit earlier in the biography (*Claud.* 3.1–2), between the emperor's literary pursuits and his natural stupidity. The quotation undercuts its own section on Claudius' literary achievements (*Claud.* 41–2),[11] just as the previous section, building on a discussion of Claudius' stupidity (*Claud.* 38.3), is an inversion of Suetonius' typical category on an emperor's literary studies, since it describes Claudius' negative qualities of *inconsiderantia, obliuio*, and *neglegantia* (*Claud.* 39–40).[12] The thematic thread of Claudius' foolishness therefore does not stop at the section on literary achievements, but continues through it, culminating in perhaps the emperor's greatest blunder, his marriage to Agrippina (*Claud.* 43), and finally his death (*Claud.* 44), probably at her hands.

---

11 Notice also in this section Suetonius' description of Claudius' autobiography, which was written *magis* inepte *quam ineleganter* ('more *unsuitably* than inelegantly', *Claud.* 41.3).
12 See Hurley 2001, 221, contrasting e.g. *Iul.* 55, *Aug.* 84.

13 Galba, Onesimus, and Servitude[*]

The allusion to comedy with which the people of Rome greeted the emperor Galba after he had acquired a reputation for cruelty and greed during his long absence from the city remains mysterious:[1]

> quare aduentus eius non perinde gratus fuit idque proximo spectaculo apparuit, siquidem Atellanis notissimum canticum exorsis,
>
> > uenit Onesimus a uilla,
>
> cuncti simul spectatores consentiente uoce reliquam partem rettulerunt ac saepius uersu repetito egerunt.

> uenit Onesimus *Paris, BnF lat. 5804*: uenitione simus *Ω*: uenitione simul G: uenit io simus *Basil. 1533*: uenit ohe Simus *Gronovius*: uenit Dorsennus *Ribbeck*

> This is why he was not so welcomed on his arrival, and that became apparent at the next public show, for when the Atellan actors began that most famous chorus:
>
> > Onesimus arrived from his summer estate
>
> the entire audience together in a unified voice completed the remaining part, and acted it out many times, starting again with this verse.
>
> (*Galb.* 13)

The public show at which this Atellan verse was repeated probably formed part of the Plebeian games that took place from 4 to 12 November AD 68.[2]

---

* This chapter was first published in *Eranos* 107 (2012–13), 38–40.

1 On the tendency of Roman audiences to see contemporary political allusions in literary works, see e.g. Verg. *Aen.* 2.557–8; Cic. *Att.* 2.19.3, *Sest.* 118–23; Tac. *Dial.* 2.1, 3.3, *Ann.* 4.14.3, 4.35.1–5, 6.29.3; Suet. *Iul.* 84.2, *Aug.* 53.1, 68, *Tib.* 45, 61.3, *Ner.* 39.2–3, *Dom.* 10.4; Macrob. *Sat.* 2.7.2–5; with Reynolds 1943; Bartsch 1994; Wardle 1998a, 439–47; Groot 2008, 251–3, 320–4.

2 Murison 1992, 65 (ad loc.).

Although the manuscript readings differ, and other conjectures have been proposed, *Onesimus* is by far the most convincing,[3] and may even be confirmed by the name's use as a spurious source of information in the *Historia Augusta* (*Quad. tyr.* 13.1, 14.4; *Carus* 4.2, 7.3, 16.1, 17.6), which was most likely inspired by this passage in Suetonius.[4]

Since the original passage of the farce is lost, we shall never know the ensuing lines that the audience quoted, but in the latest translation of Suetonius, the note to the name Onesimus reads: 'Evidently a parsimonious old man from the countryside.'[5] This conclusion takes its lead from the name's derivation from the Greek ὀνίνημι ('have profit or advantage', *LSJ* II), which carries the implication of someone miserly.[6] It is also suggested by the preceding passage, in which the emperor's cruelty and greed are described (*Galb.* 12.1–3).[7] No one has yet noticed a possible secondary meaning of the quotation, which could equally have been the point of the verse. Onesimus was among the seven most popular slave names at Rome, and was the third most popular Greek name for a slave, after Hermes and Eros.[8] It was also one of the most common names for a slave or freedman in the imperial household.[9]

Could this verse's ironic repetition have painted Galba not only as the harsh and avaricious master, but also as the master who is really a slave? Although Suetonius' *quare* points back to the prior discussion of Galba's fame for cruelty and greed (*Galb.* 12.1), the next section contains the arresting opening *regebatur* ('He was ruled'), which signals the emperor's subservience towards his 'tutors':[10]

> regabatur trium arbitrio quos una et intra Palatium habitantis nec umquam non adhaerentis paedagogos uulgo uocabant. ii erant T. Vinius, legatus eius in Hispania, cupiditatis immensae, Cornelius Laco, ex assessore praefectus praetorii, arrogantia socordiaque intolerabilis, libertus Icelus, paulo ante anulis aureis et Marciani cognomine ornatus ac iam summae equestris gradus candidatus.

---

3 See Mooney 1930, 229 (ad loc.); Reynolds 1943, 41; *pace* Venini 1977, 47 (ad loc.).

4 Another influence of the *Galba* on the *Historia Augusta* can be seen at *Alex.* 20.3 ~ *Galb.* 3.4. For the borrowing of 'Onesimus' from Suetonius, see Bird 1971, 134, who is sceptical about identification with the historian Onasimos (*Suda* o 327; *FGrH* 216); cf. Baldwin 1979c, 21 = 1984, 47.

5 Hurley 2011, 275 n. 32; cf. Rolfe 1913–14, 2.212.

6 Hofstee 1898, 35 (ad loc.); cf. Shotter 1993, 123 (ad loc.).

7 Bartsch 1994, 240 n. 36; cf. Brandão 2009, 309.

8 See e.g. Solin 1996, 465–8. On the Romans' sensitivity to such names, see e.g. *Gramm.* 5.1, 18.1, with Kaster 1995, 107, 109–10, 198–9 (ad locc.); Cheesman 2009, 513 n. 17, 528–9.

9 See Weaver and Wilkins 1993, 244.

10 The atypical use of the passive is emphatic: cf. *Ner.* 16.2–17, with Townend 1982b, 1058; Wallace-Hadrill 1983, 122–3.

He was ruled by the opinion of three who, since they lived together at the palace and were always clinging to him, were commonly called his 'tutors'. These were Titus Vinius, his general in Spain who had unlimited lust; Cornelius Laco, the praetorian prefect and a former judge who was insufferable in arrogance and stupidity; and his freedman Icelus, who was newly decorated with the gold ring and the surname Marcianus, and already a candidate for the highest equestrian rank.

(*Galb.* 14.2)

Suetonius makes this same kind of negative comment in his *Vitellius* about that emperor's habit of being manipulated by 'the opinion and fancy of every most vile actor and chariot driver ... and mostly of his freedman Asiaticus' (*consilio et arbitrio uilissimi cuiusque histrionum et aurigarum ... et maxime Asiatici liberti*, *Vit.* 12). The biographer is clearly likening Vitellius to Claudius, who, as he reminds us earlier in the *Life*, was 'bound to his wives and freedmen' (*uxoribus libertisque addictum*, *Vit.* 2.5). A parallel with Claudius is also at work in the passage about Galba's tutors, especially the line that 'being bound to these [freedmen] ... and to his wives, he played the role not of emperor, but of slave' (*his [libertis] ... uxoribusque addictus non principem {se} sed ministrum egit*, *Claud.* 29.1, cf. 25.5).[11]

This same theme is brought to the fore in our preceding passage of the *Galba* through the metaphor of the stage: the emperor plays the role of Onesimus, or slave, which anticipates the following section on his pliability by his tutors. The ironic name Onesimus in the Atellan verse thus begins the biography's transition from cruelty and avarice to the more condemning vice of imperial passivity, which for Suetonius is tantamount to servitude.[12] By being swayed by his tutors, literally his 'child-minders' (*paedagogi*), the emperor is soon shown to be even lower than a slave, since *paedagogi* were themselves slaves at Rome. The division Suetonius makes between Galba's reputation and his actual rule (*Galb.* 14.1) may be no less characteristically stark than his bifurcation of the *Caligula* into 'emperor' and 'monster' (*principe ... monstro*, *Calig.* 22.1), but it is likewise enhanced by the subtle touch of the next section, a new beginning similar to that which follows the *diuisio* of the *Caligula*: 'After assuming a number of titles ...' (*compluribus cognominibus adsumptis ... Calig.* 22.1). Suetonius paints Caligula as the opposite of Augustus, who refused divine honours (*Aug.* 52–3),[13] just as he reveals Galba to be even worse than Claudius.

11 See Morgan 2004, 317 n. 59.
12 For other crescendos in Suetonius, see e.g. *Iul.* 68–75, *Aug.* 57–60, and *Ner.* 33–8, with Steidle 1951, 56–8; Carter 1982, 178–81 (ad loc.); Gascou 1984, 697–700. On this technique in Tacitus, see Morgan 1993c, 576–7.
13 See Mouchová 1968, 103 n. 21; also Wardle 2012, 308–9.

14 Priam and Pompey in Suetonius' *Galba*[*]

The criteria for determining the significance of allusion or intertextuality have often been discussed and can be difficult to evaluate. For example, Wills has provided two general criteria that are useful for the task: (i) context and (ii) content, that is, echoes of the text – whether verbal, positional, or rhythmical.[1] (i) may be insufficient on its own, but when combined with (ii), it can make for a very strong case. (ii) is by far the most important, provided the uniqueness cannot be accounted for by an earlier source or *topos*.[2] However, a cumulative case of weak allusions, however many they are, simply will not stand unless a solid allusion to the text in question already exists, or else the author's knowledge of that work is demonstrable in some other way.[3] In the present chapter, I want to look at some possible allusions to Priam and Pompey at the end of Suetonius' *Galba* with regard to these two factors. I will then show what significance the allusion has for the wider interpretation of the text.

Let us begin by looking at a case that to some extent anticipates my argument, yet does not convince because it is less cogent on our two conditions for significance, particularly (ii). Benario argues that Tacitus alludes to Priam through the death of Galba in his *Histories*.[4] His case rests largely on four parallels of context: both are elderly rulers; they arm themselves in vain, are killed near a sacred spot, and then decapitated. To these, Benario adds two parallels of content. First, he claims that Tacitus' description of Galba as 'the emperor, a defenseless old man' (*imperatorem ... inermem et senem*, *Hist.* 1.40.2) recalls Virgil's epithet for Priam: 'the old man' (*senior*, *Aen.* 2.509, 544). Second, he compares Priam's 'shoulders trembling from age' (*trementibus aeuo / ... umeris*, *Aen.* 2.509–10) to Tacitus' line 'he

* This chapter was first published in *CQ* 57 (2007), 792–6.

1 Wills 1996, 18.
2 Hinds 1998, 19, 25–6.
3 On the importance of a clear and specific echo (either of context or content) in establishing an allusion with certainty, see Power 2014a, 75; below, pp. 128, 184 with bibliography.
4 Benario 1972; cf. id. 1975, 109. For acceptance of Benario's argument, see e.g. Ash 1999, 79–80; Damon 2010, 383 n. 13; Keitel 2010, 346–7. On Tacitus' use of epic poetry generally, see e.g. Ash 2007, 24–5; 2010b; Manolaraki and Augoustakis 2012.

had neither the youth nor strength to stand' (*neque aetate neque corpore sistens, Hist.* 1.35.1), suggesting that neither ruler can bear the weight of his armour. However, Benario fails to compare all the accounts of Galba's death. His four contextual parallels are all present in the other three versions of Plutarch, Suetonius, and Dio. Therefore, if these similarities were shaped with Priam in mind, it was probably done by an earlier source, not by Tacitus.[5] The content cited by Benario is also too general. The description of Galba as 'the emperor, a defenseless old man' is found in the same place in two of the other accounts, and is therefore not unique.[6] Benario's other parallel of content is based on a misunderstanding of both passages, since Priam trembles simply 'from age' (*aeuo*),[7] and Tacitus' line refers to the force of the mob.[8]

Let us now turn to Suetonius' account, where there is more concrete evidence for allusion to Priam. Besides the same contextual parallels that we have already discussed, there are two striking echoes of Virgil's text in Suetonius' death scene. Both are in direct speech and thus thrown into sharp relief:

> iis ut occurreret prodiit tanta fiducia ut militi cuidam occisum a se Othonem glorianti '*quo auctore?*' responderit ... sunt qui tradant ad primum tumultum proclamasse eum, '*quid agitis commilitones? ego uester sum et uos mei*', donatiuum etiam pollicitum.

> He went up to meet them with such confidence that to a certain soldier boasting that he had killed Otho, he replied: '*On whose authority?*' ... According to some, at the first upheaval he cried out: '*What are you doing, fellow-soldiers? I am yours, and you are mine*', and even promised the donative.

> (*Galb.* 19.2–20.1)

Galba's words are reminiscent of Priam's speech to Sinon:

> quisquis es, amissos hinc iam obliuiscere Graios;
> *noster eris*, mihique haec edissere uera roganti:

---

5 It is generally held that all four accounts independently derive in large part from a single source now lost, although this does not preclude the additional use of supplementary sources. For full discussion and bibliography, see Murison 1999, 12–17.

6 πρεσβύτου ... ἄρχοντός τε κοσμίου καὶ ἀρχιερέως καὶ ὑπάτου (Plut. *Galb.* 27.4); γέροντος ἀνόπλου (Plut. *Otho* 6.2); τὸν γέροντα τὸν ὕπατον τὸν ἀρχιερέα τὸν Καίσαρα τὸν αὐτοκράτορα (Dio Cass. 64.6.3).

7 Cf. *trementem* again at *Aen.* 2.550, with Austin 1964, 211. Trembling is a stock characteristic of the elderly; see Parkin 2003, 82.

8 Galba had to be carried in a litter because he could not withstand the *inruenti turbae* ('onrushing crowd', *Hist.* 1.35.1), not because he was unable to rise in his armour; see Morgan 1993b, 374; also Chilver 1979, 95–6.

quo molem hanc immanis equi statuere? *quis auctor?*
quidue petunt? quae religio, aut quae machina belli?

Whoever you are, forget now the Greeks who have been lost; *you will be ours*, and tell me these things truly: why did they erect this giant construction of a horse? *Who had the authority?* What were they trying to do? What sacred object is it, or what instrument of war?

(*Aen.* 2.148–51)

Comparison with the other accounts reveals that these echoes are unique. For the first echo (*quo auctore?*), the other sources have a similar version, but it is differently phrased: 'Who ordered it?' (*quis iussit?*/τίς ἐκέλευσε;).[9] Given the consistency of this phrasing in the other three accounts, Suetonius' *auctor* was probably not in the common source.[10] The second echo is no less unique and was even noticed by Ruhnken.[11] Suetonius' *uester sum* ironically recalls Virgil's *noster eris*. For this too, the other accounts have something different: 'What was my crime?' (*quid mali?*/τί κακόν;).[12] Interestingly, the variation serves the same purpose of degrading Galba, and in Tacitus' case even includes the same detail about paying the donative (*exoluendo donatiuo*).[13] This suggests that if Suetonius changed Galba's words, it was not in such a way as to distort the earlier tradition completely. Plutarch omits this version of Galba's last words in keeping with his generally more favourable account,[14] but considering that the other two authors agree, it is again probable that they are the ones following the common source and Suetonius has deviated from it, perhaps supplementing it with a different writer.[15]

Suetonius' death scene also evokes the text to which Virgil's Priam alludes in the first place, which further confirms the allusion in Suetonius.[16] It has long been recognized that Virgil's model for Priam's death was almost certainly the account of Pompey's death in the *Histories* of Asinius

---

9 *quis iussit?* (Tac. *Hist.* 1.35.2); τίς σε ... ἐκέλευσε; (Plut. *Galb.* 26.3); καὶ τίς σοι τοῦτο ποιῆσαι ἐκέλευσεν; (Dio Cass. 64.6.2).

10 The biographer may also be annotating his allusion through this word; cf. Wills 1996, 31 on *Aen.* 10.510–12. Virgil's *auctor* at *Aen.* 2.150 may itself be an annotation of Euripides' *Philoctetes*; see Jones 1965. For echoes of that play in Priam's words, see Austin 1964, 78–9.

11 Ruhnken 1828, 340–1.

12 *alii suppliciter interrogasse quid mali meruisset, paucos dies exoluendo donatiuo deprecatum* (Tac. *Hist.* 1.41.2); καὶ τί κακὸν ἐποίησα; (Dio Cass. 64.6.4).

13 Gorringe 1993, 337; cf. previous note. However, Tacitus' depiction of Galba's last words is generally more dignified; see van Wassenhove 2008, 631–2.

14 Keitel 1995, 281.

15 Cf. Townend 1964, 360. See also above, n. 5.

16 In general on a 'window allusion' to an earlier writer and that writer's source, see Thomas 1986, 188–9; McKeown 1987–98, 1.37–45; Hinds 1998, 8–10; above, p. 5.

Pollio.[17] While this narrative is now lost, it seems to have been the canonical version upon which all later versions were based.[18] Whatever changes may have been made, Pompey's last words at least were an important detail that would have probably survived the transmission. Let us look at our two fullest accounts to see if they accord:

ἀποβλέψας εἰς τὸν Σεπτίμιον, Οὐ δή πού σε, εἶπεν, ἐγὼ γεγονότα συστρατιώτην ἐμὸν ἀμφιγνοῶ; κἀκεῖνος ἐπένευσε τῇ κεφαλῇ μόνον ...

Turning his eyes to Septimius, he said: 'Am I not mistaken that you are a *fellow-soldier* of mine?' And that man merely nodded his head ...

(Plut. *Pomp.* 79.1)

ἐπιστραφεὶς ἐς αὐτὸν εἶπεν· Ἆρά σε γινώσκω, *συστρατιῶτα;* καὶ ὃς αὐτίκα μὲν ἐπένευσεν ...

Turning to him, he said: 'Do I not recognize you, *fellow-soldier?*' And that man nodded at once ...

(App. *B Civ.* 2.85)

From this comparison, it appears likely that, unless Plutarch and Appian are both following the same supplementary source,[19] Pompey's word συστρατιώτης comes from Pollio and is a translation of *commilito*.[20] If this is true, not only Virgil but also Asinius Pollio may be echoed in Galba's *quid agitis commilitones? ego uester sum et uos mei*, since it is very likely that Suetonius knew Pollio's work and made use of it for the *Divine Julius*.[21] The word *commilito* has an ingratiating sense,[22] and thus not only the content but also the dramatic context of the scene is mirrored in Suetonius: both Pompey and Galba use the word in futile attempts to regain the allegiance of their former soldiers, who assassinate them nonetheless. While the word itself is not rare, its use in both scenes in unusual, since the point is not to recognize, but to *be recognized*.

17 Moles 1983b; Morgan 2000, 52–5; Horsfall 2010.
18 See Moles 1983b; 2017, 292; also Pelling 1979, 84–5 = 2002b, 12–13.
19 It is improbable that Appian follows Plutarch's *Pompey* here, although a case could be made for Appian's occasionally direct use of his *Caesar*; see Pelling 1979, 84–5 and n. 75 = 2002b, 12–13, 35–6, n. 75; 2011, 43–4; cf. Duff 1999, 254 n. 43; and of his *Brutus*; see Moles 2017, 15, 18, 24, 30, 35, 133–4, 138, 306, 339, 360, 374.
20 Conceivably, Pompey could have spoken in Greek, but Plutarch usually marks Greek utterances in his Roman *Lives*; see Moles 1983a, 775. On Plutarch and Appian's use of Pollio, see Pelling 2011, 40, 43–7; Moles 2017, esp. 34–5 with bibliography; also 37, 39–40, 108, 134, 196, 208, 210, 229, 293, 302, 334, 339, 373, 377.
21 See Pelling 1979, 84 and n. 74 = 2002b, 12, 35 n. 74.
22 See Oakley 1997–2005, 1.520.

We have shown that there is evidence of both (i) context and (ii) content for allusions to Priam and Pompey in Suetonius' *Galba*. It therefore remains to ask whether the allusions have any meaning for the biography as a whole. Suetonius leaves no doubt about the condemnatory verdict of his *Galba*:

> maiore adeo et fauore et *auctoritate* adeptus est quam gessit imperium, quamquam multa documenta egregii principis daret. sed nequaquam tam grata erant quam inuisa quae secus fierent.

> He won the empire with greater favour and *authority* than he ran it, although he gave many signs of an excellent emperor. But they were in no way as celebrated as the contrary result was despised.
>
> (*Galb.* 14.1)

This sentence is epigrammatic and a counterpart to Tacitus' famous line that Galba was thought by all capable of ruling, until he did.[23] The sentiment must have been in the common source, but only Suetonius interprets it as an absence of *auctoritas*. Tacitus too has Otho pointing out Galba's *auctoritas fluxa* ('fleeting authority', *Hist.* 1.21.2), and a few chapters later use the word with considerable irony in his own narration:

> igitur consultantibus placuit pertemptari animum cohortis, quae in Palatio stationem agebat, nec per ipsum Galbam, cuius integra *auctoritas* maioribus remediis seruabatur.

> After discussion it was agreed that the feeling of the cohort on guard in the palace should be tested, but not by Galba himself, whose *authority* was being kept intact for greater emergencies.
>
> (*Hist.* 1.29.1)

In the death scene, this theme is especially prominent, underscoring the above statement that it was the reason for Galba's fall. Only Suetonius mentions the emperor's 'authority' in the advice given to him before his death: auctoritate *et praesentia praeualere* ('prevail by his *authority* and presence', *Galb.* 19.1).[24] The theme is picked up again in the following section by the rioters' promise of total obedience (*omne obsequium*) and of course by Galba's question *quo* auctore? (*Galb.* 19.2). Suetonius even announces the theme in the first line of the biography by reminding the reader that Galba had no claim to the Empire: *progenies Caesarum in Nerone defecit* ('The descendents of the Caesars ended with Nero', *Galb.* 1). The double allusion

---

23 *omnium consensu capax imperii, nisi imperasset* ('deemed by all to be capable of rule, had he not ruled', *Hist.* 1.49.4).

24 Contrast Tac. *Hist.* 1.32–3; Plut. *Galb.* 26.1.

to Priam and Pompey fits in with this theme, occurring at the moment when Galba is shown no longer able to wield any authority in the eyes of fellow-soldiers, just as Priam before Pyrrhus,[25] or Pompey before his slayers.

To conclude, there is a strong case for an allusion to Priam in Suetonius' death of Galba. There are two verbal echoes of Virgil's *Aeneid* that do not appear in the other versions. The uniqueness of these evocations combined with an abundance of contextual similarities suggests the allusion's certainty. It is further supported by a possible reminiscence of Virgil's model, the death of Pompey, if we accept that the word *commilito* was uttered by Pompey in the account of Asinius Pollio. The allusion is also especially compelling because it reinforces the central theme of *auctoritas* within the *Life*. It is undeniable that the *peripeteia* of Galba lent itself to a comparison with Priam and Pompey. However, no writer seems to have developed this connection before Suetonius. The deaths of Priam and Pompey were the final nails in the coffin of Troy and the Republic, respectively,[26] both phases of the Roman past whose end brought great instability and strife. In the same way, Suetonius' account of Galba's death symbolically punctuates the end of the Julio-Claudian regime with which the biography begins, and the *Life* ends by mentioning the future dynast Vespasian (*Galb.* 23). Thus, Suetonius' allusion makes the same point as Tacitus' remark that Galba's last year was nearly that of the Roman Empire (*Hist.* 1.11.3).

25 See Mills 1978, 162–3.
26 See Morgan 2000, 53–4; on Priam and Troy, cf. Heinze 1993, 23–4.

15 Galba and Priam in Tacitus' *Histories**

This chapter concerns the use (or non-use) of poetry in Roman historiography. In recent years, some attention has been devoted to Tacitus' allusions to epic.[1] One monograph by Joseph in particular has tried to strengthen Benario's unconvincing argument for an allusion in the historian's account of the death of Galba (*Hist.* 1.35–41) to Priam in Book 2 of Virgil's *Aeneid*.[2] This same allusion has also been unconvincingly proposed by previous Tacitean scholars, who cited tenuous parallels such as the extreme old age of the rulers and the abandonment of their decapitated corpses.[3] However, two main contextual resemblances between these writers are newly offered in its support by Joseph, and the uniqueness of these similarities is distinguished through contrast with the different version of Suetonius, although ultimately to no avail. Firstly, the emperor's arming himself and meeting the soldiers (*Hist.* 1.35.1–2) are said to be portrayed as nobler actions in Tacitus than in the account of Suetonius (*Galb.* 19.1–2), where Galba, unlike Priam, is allegedly 'resigned' to believing that all hope is lost, especially in the description of his arming: 'Suetonius, we see, has Galba pointedly anticipate the *futility* of his defense, whereas Tacitus' Galba equips himself in earnest' (original italics).[4] Secondly, emphasis on the theme of blasphemy in the setting of the assassination near a sacred spot, the *lacus Curtius*, is thought to be placed by Tacitus alone (*Hist.* 1.40.2): 'only Tacitus develops this theme'.[5]

---

* This chapter was first published in *RhM* 157 (2014), 216–20.
1 See e.g. Ash 2007, 24–5; 2010b; Manolaraki and Augoustakis 2012; Ginsberg 2020.
2 Joseph 2012, 79–85 with bibliography, building on Benario 1972. Joseph clearly makes much of Benario's alleged allusion, which even becomes the basis for the whole rest of his chapter (85–112).
3 See Ash 1999, 79–80; Keitel 2010, 346–7. On the importance of a clear and specific echo (either of context or content) in establishing an allusion with certainty, see e.g. Kelly 2008, 166–9.
4 Joseph 2012, 80–1.
5 Ibid. 81 n. 7; see also 82 (cf. 87–8, 111–12), where he attempts to revive the suggestion of Miller 1986, 100 that a verbal echo may possibly be found in Tacitus' phrase *foedare ... sanguine* (*Hist.* 1.26.1 ~ *Aen.* 2.501–2), but as Joseph himself concedes (82 n. 8, citing

Both points may be seriously questioned. The description of Galba as 'resigned' in Suetonius is not only selective, but misleading. In the biographer's account, Galba merely intimates his recognition that the feeble armour itself would not withstand a military confrontation by a number of armed men (*loricam tamen induit linteam, quamquam haud dissimulans parum aduersus tot mucrones profuturam*, *Galb.* 19.1), not that he expects to die. In fact, it is in this *Life*, not Tacitus' *Histories*, where reference is even made to the emperor's 'confidence' (*fiducia*, *Galb.* 19.2) in meeting the soldiers, after he hears of an incorrect report that the rebels have been crushed. Galba's reaction to this news even serves to portray him as *overconfident* in Suetonius, where the emperor's arrogant question to the soldier claiming to have killed Otho, 'Who told you to do that?' (*quo auctore?* ibid.), also suggests how out of touch he has been in his brief rule of the Roman people – the way his old-world *seueritas* has bordered on cruelty.[6] If Galba accepts that his chances are slim in Suetonius, he is quickly made oblivious again with false hope, ironically recalling at his death the high expectations that preceded his doomed reign (Plut. *Galb.* 29.2; Suet. *Galb.* 14.1; Tac. *Hist.* 1.49.4). To say that Galba is resigned in Suetonius is not the full story.

Moreover, in depicting Galba's view of his armour, Suetonius is simply developing the theme of Galba as a 'defenceless old man' (*inermem et senem*, Tac. *Hist.* 1.40.2) that was already present in his source (cf. Plut. *Galb.* 15.4, 16.4, 27.4; Plut. *Otho* 6.2; Dio 64.3.4[2], 64.6.3), an emphasis which is also placed by Virgil himself through his references to Priam as 'the old man' (*senior*, *Aen.* 2.509, 2.544), and to his 'shoulders trembling from age' (*trementibus aeuo / ... umeris*, *Aen.* 2.509–10) as he dons his armour, as we have just shown.[7] Mention, too, should be made of the fact that Tacitus' portrayal of Galba wishing to wade through the crowd, were it not for his lacking the youthful strength, depends partly on Gabriele Faerno's sixteenth-century conjecture of *resistens* for the manuscript tradition's *sistens* (*Hist.* 1.35.1); otherwise, it is at least possible – albeit hardly preferable – to understand the word less valiantly in the sense simply of

---

e.g. Ov. *Met.* 3.522), such language is common for bloodshed, and does not necessarily carry associations of 'gory sacrilege' (82). The observation that the religious buildings surrounding Galba are more prominent in Tacitus is hardly new; cf. Frangoulidis 1990, 3 n. 7 with bibliography.

6 See e.g. Tac. *Hist.* 1.18.3, discussed below, Chapter 16. Cf. *Iul.* 81.4, with Toher 2017, 338–9 on Caesar's 'fatal confidence' (339) before his death. For the weighty force of *auctor* in Suetonius, see e.g. *Vita Verg.* 37, *Tib.* 27.

7 See above, Chapter 14, refuting the alleged allusion by Tacitus, although the original article is oddly cited in its support by Damon 2010, 383 n. 13. Turpilianus is described as a 'defenceless and unarmed old man' (γέροντα γυμνὸν καὶ ἄνοπλον) by Plutarch (*Galb.* 15.4), seemingly to foreshadow Galba's death; see Keitel 1995, 280; *pace* Morgan 1994, 242, who thinks that Tacitus' phrase *inermem et senem* about Galba derives from a reference to Turpilianus in the original source material.

standing.[8] At any rate, Tacitus' greater focus on the noble dignity of Galba may be attributed to his concern for the tragic representation of the emperor's final hours, since it lends drama and pathos to the opening book of his *Histories*.[9] It therefore could equally not have its origin in Virgil.

The privileging of the *religio* of the emperor's death solely in Tacitus can also be discounted. Being killed near a sacred spot is not the same as actually being killed before the altar like Priam. However, the latter image is strongly evoked in Suetonius' description of Galba, who offers himself to the soldiers as a victim in religious language. The command *hoc age* uttered by Galba (*Galb.* 20.1) was the same one used by a priest during a Roman sacrifice when he was prepared for the assistant to hit the animal with an axe: these ceremonial words and the image of the outstretched neck (*optulisse ultro iugulum*, *Galb.* 20.1) signal the metaphor of a Roman execution staged as a sacrifice (cf. Sen. *Controv.* 2.3.19), and Galba thus frames his own assassination as an execution that is no less a perverse violation of Roman ritual, a sacrifice gone wrong.[10] This language is not unique to Suetonius, but can be found also in Plutarch (ὁ δὲ τὴν σφαγὴν προτείνας, Δρᾶτε, εἶπεν, *Galb.* 27.1) and Tacitus (*plures obtulisse ultro percussoribus iugulum: agerent ac ferirent, si ita e re publica uideretur*, *Hist.* 1.41.2). It was therefore almost certainly shaped by a common source, much like the image of Galba as *inermem et senem*. If the emphasis on the impiety of the soldier's crime was already present in an earlier source, then Tacitus' description of the nearby sacred buildings is more likely to stem from that source than from Virgil.[11]

This latest argument from Joseph in favour of Tacitus' supposedly nobler and more religious account of Galba's fall is simply special pleading. There is nothing in the historian's death scene even as tangible as, for example, his earlier words 'almost the last year of the empire' (*annum ... rei publicae prope supremum*, *Hist.* 1.11.3), which possibly liken at least the year AD 69 more generally to the fall of Troy in Virgil (*sorte suprema*, *Aen.* 5.190; *suprema / nocte*, *Aen.* 6.502–3; *supremam ... noctem*, *Aen.* 6.513). However, even in that line, Tacitus could also have had different precedents in mind, such as the Capitol's attack by Gauls in 385 BC (*noctis illius quae paene ultima atque aeterna nomini Romano fuerit*, Livy 6.17.4), the death of Alexander the Great (*noctis, quam paene supremam*, Curt. 10.9.3), or

---

8 See Damon 2003, 173.

9 See Frangoulidis 1990, 7 n. 17 with bibliography. On this aspect of Tacitus' work generally, see e.g. Woodman 1993 = 1998b, 190–217; L'Hoir 2006; Galtier 2011; Schulz 2020, 307–8.

10 Cf. *Calig.* 32.3, 58.2, with Brandão 2009, 285–6; Hurley 2014a, 148–9; below, p. 208; also Ash 2016, 213 on this phrase in the death of Caligula (*Calig.* 58.2).

11 A possibility admitted by Joseph 2012, 92–3 n. 38; see also 90 on Tacitus' general fondness for topography; cf. 98–103 with bibliography, to which add Poignault 2001.

the more contemporary eruption of Mount Vesuvius (*aeternam ... illam et nouissimam noctem mundo*, Plin. *Ep.* 6.20.15).[12] The case for Tacitus' 'Priam-like' death of Galba, like the case for his Trojan *annum supremum*, remains weak.

Priam was by no means the only literary model for Galba that was available to Tacitus, or indeed to the emperor's biographers. Plutarch demonstrates as much when he writes that the soldiers impaled the emperor's head on a spear and ran around with it 'in the manner of bacchanals' (ὥσπερ αἱ βάκχαι, *Galb.* 27.4), clearly alluding to Pentheus in Euripides' *Bacchae* – an allusion which suits Plutarch's invocation of the tragic genre in the *Life*'s preface.[13] Suetonius' version lays even greater focus on the abuse to Galba's head, but no connection with Pentheus is ever firmly drawn, and Suetonius instead alludes to Homer (*Galb.* 20.2 = *Il.* 5.254 = *Od.* 21.426).[14] Indeed, Suetonius' portrait of Galba's end also alludes to Virgil's model, Asinius Pollio's famous historical account of the death of Pompey (as partially preserved in Plutarch and Appian), through the emperor's last words to his murderers: 'What are you doing, fellow-soldiers?' (*quid agitis, commilitones? Galb.* 20.1; cf. Plut. *Pomp.* 79.1; App. *B Civ.* 2.85).[15] Virgil was not necessarily the only, or even the most obvious, choice of precursor for Tacitus in writing the death of Galba. In light of the sacrilegious context we have discussed, when Tacitus has the emperor beg his assassins for a few days to pay the donative, and they care little for his words (*non interfuit occidentium quid diceret, Hist.* 1.41.2), one might also be tempted to recall Odysseus' abrupt beheading of the suppliant priest Leiodes, who is killed in mid-speech (*Od.* 22.310–29). But Homer's passage is never specifically evoked by the historian.[16]

Although Virgil's general influence on Tacitus was underestimated by Goodyear,[17] allusions must be pinpointed securely by a concrete reminiscence that cannot otherwise be explained as coincidental; cumulative cases such as those of Benario and Joseph do not pass muster, if their instances are individually weak.[18] No matter how much the *Histories* of Tacitus may draw on Virgil in several other passages, such as the death of Vitellius (*Hist.* 3.84.4–85),[19] its account of Galba's end need not be a direct allusion to

---

12 See Kraus 1994, 194 (ad loc.); Oakley 1997–2005, 1.540 (ad loc.); Bosworth 2004, 554.
13 Ash 1997a, 200–1; Brandão 2010, 33, 83 n. 93.
14 See below, Chapter 16; *pace* Brandão 2009, 286.
15 See above, Chapter 14, esp. 123–5. On Virgil's allusion to Pompey, see also Horsfall 2010.
16 For a Homeric allusion elsewhere by Tacitus, see Mayer 2003a.
17 Goodyear 1972, 325; 1981, 86, 117, 200, 243–4; *contra*, see Pelling 1993, 73 n. 31; Woodman 1998a, 232–3; 2009c, 6–7.
18 See den Hengst 2009, 96–7; above, p. 122, with further bibliography.
19 Keitel 2008; Oakley 2009b, 210; cf. 196 n. 9.

Priam. We should not be so quick to assume that Tacitus always has Virgil in mind, even in passages where we might expect an allusion to the *Aeneid*, without assessing the individual merits of the evidence in each case. What we find is that, with regard to the portrait of Galba's death in Tacitus, there is simply no foundation of solid evidence on which to base that interpretation, such as we do in fact have in Suetonius.[20]

20 See the previous chapter on *Galb.* 19.1–20.1 ~ *Aen.* 2.149–50. For other clear allusions and references to Priam in Suetonius, see *Tib.* 52.1–2, 57.2, 62.3, with above, Chapter 11; *Claud.* 42.1 (= *Il.* 24.369 = *Od.* 16.72 = 21.133), with above, Chapter 12.

16 The Servants' Taunt
Homer and Suetonius' *Galba**

In his biography of the emperor Galba, Suetonius ends his death scene with seemingly insignificant details about the mistreatment of the dead emperor's head, which are not found in any other source:[1]

> ille [sc. Otho] lixis calonibusque donauit, qui hasta suffixum non sine ludibrio circum castra portarunt adclamantes identidem, 'Galba Cupido, fruaris aetate tua', maxime irritati ad talem iocorum petulantiam quod ante paucos dies exierat in uulgus laudanti cuidam formam suam ut adhuc floridam et uegetam respondisse eum,

> ἔτι μοι μένος ἔμπεδόν ἐστιν.

> He [Otho] gave it to the personal and military servants, who impaled it on a spear and carried it around the camp with great ridicule, shouting at it repeatedly: 'Lover-boy Galba, enjoy your youth!', greatly provoked to such insolent humour by the report a few days earlier that when someone complimented his appearance as still lively and energetic, he replied,

> My strength is still intact.

> (*Galb.* 20.2)

The meaning of the servants' taunt, and of the Greek quotation that explains it, has not yet been understood. In this chapter, I shall argue for a new interpretation of this incident and its lost historical significance. It will be shown that Suetonius is here illustrating Galba's vice of cruelty, which contributed to his failure as an emperor and forms a major theme in the biography.

Scholarly disagreement about the meaning of the above passage has centred on the question of Galba's sincerity. Some contend that the Greek

---

* This chapter was first published in *Historia* 58 (2009), 242–5.
1 Contrast Plut. *Galb.* 28.2–3; Tac. *Hist.* 1.49.1; Dio Cass. 64.6.3–4. The *lixae* in this passage appear to be the soldiers' personal servants, rather than sutlers: cf. Tac. *Hist.* 1.49 and its discussion by Roth 1998, 94. The *lixae* and *calones* were non-combatant attendants (*apparitores*); on their status and roles generally, see ibid. 91–116.

quotation must be sarcastic, since the emperor was seventy-two years old and well-known for not accepting flattery.[2] However, this view has more recently been challenged, and a different possibility suggested: Galba may have been earnestly accepting the flattery through the quotation, prompting the servants to deride his vanity through the epithet *Cupido*, which evokes the stock character of the *senex amator* ('elderly lover') in Roman comedy.[3] While it is true that a sarcastic interpretation of the quotation would attribute to Galba an ironic sense of humour for which there is no evidence,[4] it does not necessarily follow that the quotation was meant to agree with the flattery.

The true purpose of Galba's quotation is clear from an examination of its original Homeric context. The line appears in the same sense at two climactic moments: it is said by Diomedes in his ἀριστεία (*Iliad*, Book 5) when he refuses to yield ground in the midst of battle (*Il.* 5.254), and even more notably by Odysseus after he is able to string the bow and prove his rightful position as the king of Ithaca to close the *Odyssey*'s Book 21 (*Od.* 21.426).[5] In both scenes, the point is not vanity, but rather an affirmation of the speaker's strength as a soldier and hero. I should argue, therefore, that Galba must have instead been trying to curb the flattery by drawing attention to his competence to rule as the only important matter. This reading would resolve any inconsistency in Galba's character and render the servants' anger more intelligible, especially when one considers the emperor's *incapacity* to rule, as well as his blindness to that incapacity.[6]

2 E.g. Tac. *Hist.* 1.35.2: 'He had a noted zeal for curbing military licence, unassailable by threats, immune to flattery' (*insigni animo ad coercendam militarem licentiam, minantibus intrepidus, aduersus blandientis incorruptus*). Nutting 1933 first argued for a sarcastic reading of the Greek quotation in Suetonius. This interpretation was later followed by Venini (1977, 67), who added in his note that the sarcasm must have been simply lost on the servants; and also by Berthet (1978, 326), who found the quotation 'hors-contexte'. Adams 2003, 336 n. 77 similarly thinks that Galba's use of the line is 'jesting' in the first place.

3 Morgan 2004, 322. Cf. also Aparicio 2008, 450–1, who notices the sexual aspect that the new context brings to the quotation. On the *senex amator* generally, see Ryder 1984.

4 Cf. Morgan 2004, 322 n. 84. I am not convinced by Ash 1997a, 190, that Galba's remark about the crucified man (Suet. *Galb.* 9.1) is an example of 'dark humour'; it is not included in the examples of 'intentional misunderstanding' collected by Reekmans 1992, 211–12. Suetonius' introduction to this section reveals the point of the anecdote to be Galba's immoderate cruelty in deciding punishments (*in coercendis quidem delictis uel immodicus, Galb.* 9.1); compare, for example, the similar story of the Roman knight in Suetonius (*Calig.* 27.4), which is categorized under the rubric *saeuitiam* (27.1).

5 Nutting 1933, 45 n. 3 thinks that the intended reference is to the passage in the *Odyssey*; Berthet 1978, 326 ignores that passage and discusses only the *Iliad*. Although the same proverbial sentiment is conveyed by each passage, the quotation was most famously from the climactic scene of the *Odyssey*, which signifies the hero's return and the fulfilment of the poem's main theme.

6 See Tacitus' remark about the soldiers at *Hist.* 1.18.3: 'It is agreed that their hearts could have been won over by the smallest generosity from the miserly old man: fatal was his

This new reading of Galba's quotation reveals an unnoticed aspect of the servants' 'insolent humour' (*iocorum petulantiam*). Although Galba recites a verse from a Homeric context that has distinctly military associations, he does so in response to flattery that, since it is of his physical appearance, has an inevitably sexual dimension. The servants through their taunt thus imply an understanding of the quotation not as contrasting with the flattery (as Galba intended it to do), but rather according with it. Ruhnken's note on their words confirms this implication:

> *Galba Cupido, fruaris aetate tua*, i.e. cape uoluptatem, quae conuenit aetati tuae. *frui* proprium uerbum est in re amorum.[7]

> *Galba, you Cupid, enjoy your age*, that is, take the pleasure that belongs to your age. *Enjoy* is an appropriate word in a sexual context.

The servants do not play merely on the *topos* of the *senex amator* in Roman comedy but also on the elegiac *topos* of *militia amoris*, which is evoked through their combining of a clichéd elegiac sentiment about the fleeting nature of time with a Homeric quotation about warfare.[8] When the servants shout *Galba Cupido, fruaris aetate tua*, they are punning on the emperor's words μένος ἔμπεδόν ('intact strength'), as if he had been referring to his sexual prowess. Furthermore, the servants' intention to construe Galba's quotation in a sexual way is supported by the fact that Suetonius' very next section describes the emperor's excessive lust (*Galb.* 22).[9]

This kind of inference that someone's 'strength' is sexual has precedents in elegiac poetry describing *militia amoris*. For example, Ovid employs the same euphemism for another elderly figure, Tithonos: 'At the touch of that

---

old-world sternness, and excessive strictness which is now more than we can bear' (*constat potuisse conciliari animos quantulacumque parci senis liberalitate: nocuit antiquus rigor et nimia seueritas, cui iam pares non sumus*); also 1.49.4: 'in everyone's opinion he was capable of rule, if only he had not ruled' (*omnium consensu capax imperii, nisi imperasset*); cf. Suet. *Galb.* 14.1. On Galba's blindness to his loss of authority, see above pp. 126–7.

7 Ruhnken 1828, 341 (on *Galb.* 20.2).

8 Nutting 1928, 287–8 suggests the generally elegiac connotation of the servants' *aetate frui* by comparing Ovid's use of the phrase *aetate uti* at *Ars am.* 3.65; on that line, which has its roots in elegy, see Gibson 2003, 109–10, 113–14 (ad loc.). Ovid goes on in the same passage to make Horace's *carpe diem* sexual through the phrase *carpite florem*, which implies the flower not only of youth but of virginity; see ibid. 118 (on *Ars Am.* 3.79). A phrase similar to that of the servants is also used in the context of lovers by Livy (*frui ... ludo aetatis*, 26.50.5); see Nutting 1928, 288. On the topos of *militia amoris*, see e.g. Murgatroyd 1975; Lyne 1980, 71–8; McKeown 1987–98, 2.258–9 (on *Am.* 1.9).

9 On Galba's excessive lust, see Morgan 2004, 320–3; Wardle 2015, 1007–9; also 1010–13 for its transgressive nature. The moral rubric *libido* (*Galb.* 22) is ironically missed in a study of Suetonian structure by Garrett (2018b, 207–8), who appeals less convincingly to the proximity of the preceding negative section announced by *cibi* in the same chapter of the *Life*.

girl Nestor would grow young, and Tithonos be *stronger* than his years' (*illius ad tactum Pylius iuuenescere posit / Tithonosque annis* fortior *esse suis*, *Am.* 3.7.41–2). Another good example is Ovid himself: 'I have often spent the hours of night wantonly, being of use and *strong* in body at dawn' (*saepe ego lasciue consumpsi tempora noctis, / utilis et forti corpore mane fui, Am.* 2.10.27–8). Moreover, a sexual pun on war can also be witnessed elsewhere in Suetonius, who reports a similar anecdote about the emperor Vespasian:

> utebatur et uersibus Graecis tempestiue satis, et de quodam procerae staturae improbiusque quatiente,
>
> μακρὰ βιβάς, κραδάων δολιχόσκιον ἔγχος.

quatiente *scripsi*: nato *mss.*, *Ihm*: uenato *Mooney, Kaster*

> He also used Greek verses aptly enough, and of someone of large stature and thrusting rather obscenely,
>
> Far-striding, waving a spear that casts a long shadow.
>
> (*Vesp.* 23.1)

Like Galba's quotation, this Greek line from Vespasian derives its humour from contrast, not comparison (see the next chapter on my conjecture *quatiente*). In fact, the two Homeric quotations balance each other by occurring in roughly the same position within their respective *Lives* and books of the *Caesars* (Books 7 and 8), and by achieving opposite effects of blame and praise, since Vespasian's quotation illustrates his amiability (*comissimus*, *Vesp.* 22), while Galba's suggests the lack of it.[10]

In conclusion, while the amatory sense of the servants' taunt in Suetonius' *Galba* has previously been noted, scholars have related it either to the emperor's alleged vanity or sarcasm about vanity. No one has yet recognized the pun on 'strength' in this passage, or that Galba originally intended to draw attention to his valour (μένος) as a leader, rather than his appearance. The twisted chronology of the passages adds to the confusion, since the servants' taunt acts as a setup to Galba's quotation, which is thus read ironically, rather than as intended; the quotation is told in retrospect as a punch line to the passage, just as Suetonius' remark about a man waving his genitals (*improbiusque quatiente*) in the next book of the *Caesars* becomes ironic only after the last two words of Vespasian's Homeric quotation (δολιχόσκιον ἔγχος).[11] Since Galba was elderly and hated by many at the time, his literary quip would have lent itself to a double entendre, and had obviously been the popular subject of ridicule for a few days (*ante paucos dies exierat in uulgus* ...). In light of the fact

---

10 Vespasian also makes the pun in his line himself, whereas the pun in Galba's line is made by others, who reverse his meaning. For balance and structure in the eight books of Suetonius' collection, see Power 2014a.

11 See below, Chapter 23.

that military valour was a known metaphor for sexual prowess in ancient literature, the choice of lines was unfortunate, but only reemphasizes Galba's general blindness to possible interpretations of his actions. In this way, our elucidation of this passage recaptures an important historical moment told exclusively by Suetonius following the emperor's death that epitomizes both the anger against Galba (*maxime irritati ...*) and the vices of the emperor that caused it.

This last point may be taken a step further, since the anecdote performs an important function within the *Life* by illustrating its major theme of cruelty (*saeuitia*). In the tradition on Galba, there existed the sentiment that the emperor's strictness (*seueritas*) stemmed from a cruel character. This is expressed most succinctly in Tacitus' *Histories* by Otho: 'With false names he calls his cruelty "strictness"' (*falsis nominibus seueritatem pro saeuitia ... appellat*, *Hist.* 1.37.4). However, Tacitus as a historian ultimately endorses the more nuanced view that historical circumstances made Galba's strictness *seem* worse than it really was:[12]

> laudata olim et militari fama celebrata *seueritas* eius angebat aspernantis ueterem disciplinam atque ita quattuordecim annis a Nerone adsuefactos ...

> His *strictness*, once praised and honoured due to his military reputation, troubled those who were disdainful of the old discipline and had been made accustomed in this way by Nero over fourteen years ...
>
> (*Hist.* 1.5.2)

In Suetonius, no such view is put forward, and in fact the opposite view is implied by the biographer's change in vocabulary from *seueritas*, which is used at the beginning of the *Life* (*Galb.* 6.3, 7.1), to his later word *saeuitia* (*Galb.* 12.1).[13] The theme of strictness as cruelty is developed by Suetonius through Galba's comments leading up to his death. For example, when Galba refuses to pay the soldiers' donative, he says that he is 'used to levying troops, not buying them' (*legere se militem, non emere consuesse*, *Galb.* 16.1). And in Suetonius' death scene itself, the emperor is shown reprimanding a soldier, who claims to have killed Otho, with the question, 'On whose authority?' (*quo auctore? Galb.* 19.2). The final details about the Homeric quotation (*Galb.* 20.2) thus connect with this theme, since as we have shown, the line was meant to curb flattery. The passage therefore exemplifies the cruel *seueritas* that led to Galba's demise, and acts as a fitting 'summarizing vignette' at the end of Suetonius' death scene.[14]

---

12 Cf. also above, n. 6.

13 See Ferrero 1997, 319; van Wassenhove 2008, 626–7, 629–30. Tacitus' judgement on Galba is generally more moderate than that of Suetonius; see e.g. Shochat 1981.

14 For the 'summarizing vignette' as a literary device at the end of ancient historical narratives, see Pelling 1997a, 232–4 = 2002b, 368–9; cf. Marincola 2005, 298–9, on the end of Herodotus' *Histories*.

Part III

Textual Conjectures

17 Suetonius, *De grammaticis* 13.1[*]

L. Staberius Eros, †<u>nametra</u>† emptus de catasta et propter litterarum studium manumissus, docuit inter ceteros Brutum et Cassium.

nametra X: nametra *et* (h)ero suo Metre Y: suomet aere *Roth*: nam erat *Vahlen*: <libertinus> – nam erat *Robinson*: natione Trax *Funaioli*: nomine, Trax *Brugnoli*: natus in Syria *Della Corte*: Ναμέρτης *aut* Νημερτὴς *Verdière*: natione Syrus *Viljamaa*: a Metra *Murgia*

Lucius Staberius Eros ... bought at auction and set free on account of his study of literature, taught among others Brutus and Cassius.

(*Gramm.* 13.1)

So prints Kaster in his 1995 text of this beginning to one of the short-est biographies in Suetonius' *Grammarians*, that of Staberius Eros.[1] The corruption *nametra* in the manuscripts is puzzling, and has attracted sev-eral conjectures from the mid-nineteenth century onwards.[2] Funaioli's *natione Trax* (GRF 1.106) is the most tempting to Kaster, who supports it by comparing Suetonius' typical practice of beginning with the subject's origin.[3] Funaioli's conjecture has been influential. For example, Wallace-Hadrill seems at least partly to accept it: 'one point which Suetonius' biog-raphies illustrate is the parallel movement in the first century BC by which

---

* This chapter was first published in CQ 62 (2012), 886–8.

1 Kaster 1995 with his sigla, but my own expansion of the apparatus criticus. In his up-dated edition of the *Grammarians*, Kaster (2016a) now accepts the conjecture *nam erat* for which the present chapter argues.

2 Canvassed in Kaster 1992, 80–7. See also Vacher 1993, 128–9.

3 See Kaster 1992, 84, citing e.g. *Gramm.* 8.1: *M. Pompilius Andronicus, natione Syrus*; 20.1: *C. Iulius Hyginus, Augusti libertus, natione Hispanus*. On Brugnoli's (1960, 353–6 = 1968a, 117–21) implausible alteration of Funaioli, see Kaster 1992, 83–4. Against the conjectures of Roth (1858) and Murgia (2002, 71–2), the former accepted in Rolfe's (1913–14) Loeb edition, see Kaster 1992, 83 and 86, respectively; for Verdière's unconvincing conjecture of a Greek cognomen *Namertes* or *Nemertes*, see Vacher 1993, 129. Some scholars have found Della Corte's *natus in Syria* appealing; see e.g. Quinn 1982, 133–4; Viljamaa 1991, 3836. However, Della Corte's conjecture is unfounded; see Kaster 1992, 85–6 and below, n. 15.

Latin-speaking slaves were trained up as teachers ... Slaves of eastern origin indeed could learn Latin if caught early enough. Staberius Eros was a Thracian bought as a boy from the slaver's stand.'[4] However, Kaster could not at last bring himself to adopt *natione Trax*, and is not alone in leaving the corrupt text exactly as it is.[5] I propose that we should instead read Vahlen's conjecture *nam erat*, which was accepted by Robinson – although he did so only with an alleged omission of *libertinus* in order to maintain the logic of the *nam*-clause.[6] It is for this reason that Kaster rejects the reading: 'I would be reluctant to posit the omission that *nam erat* entails.'[7]

However, an omitted *libertinus* may be unnecessary to Vahlen's conjecture, if a new logic in the sentence is understood. Kaster points out that 'Eros' was one of the most common names for a slave at Rome, and was probably imposed on Staberius when he was a slave.[8] If Suetonius believed this name implied that Staberius was a slave, he may have felt compelled to explain how the grammarian *docuit inter ceteros Brutum et Cassium*, for only as a public teacher could he have gained such important students as Brutus and Cassius; he was therefore already a freedman by the mid-70s BC.[9] Brugnoli points out several examples of Suetonius' omission of any indication of social class where the grammarian's or rhetorician's freeborn status is clear from his name (*Gramm.* 9.1, 14.1, 22.1, 24.1, 28.1, 29.1, 30.1);[10] the reverse may be the case here, where the grammarian's status as an ex-slave is already pronounced in the same way.[11] To the restored text 'Lucius Staberius Eros – for he was bought at auction and set free on account of his study of literature – taught among others Brutus and Cassius' (*L. Staberius Eros – nam erat emptus de catasta et propter litterarum studium manumissus – docuit inter ceteros Brutum et Cassium*), a passage in Suetonius' *Vita Vergili* offers a fitting parallel, where *nam* anticipates the main clause to follow: 'Augustus in fact, for he happened to be away on a Cantabrian expedition, demanded with entreaties and even threats jokingly in letters ...' (*Augustus uero, nam forte expeditione Cantabrica aberat,*

4 Wallace-Hadrill 1983, 34; cf. also Bradley 1987, 103.
5 Cf. the Budé edition of Vacher 1993.
6 Vahlen's conjecture was discovered written below *nametra* in a copy of Reifferscheid's (1860) edition of Suetonius' fragmentary works; see Robinson 1920, 85. On Suetonius' use of *nam* in its explanatory sense, see Kaster 1992, 48–9.
7 Kaster 1992, 83.
8 Kaster 1995, 165, citing Solin 1982, 328–37 (s.v. Eros) and 1361 (s.v. Erotianus). See now also id. 2001, 312, 316.
9 For this last point, see Kaster 1995, 166.
10 Brugnoli 1960, 355–6 = 1968a, 119–20; cf. Kaster 1995, 222.
11 Cf. Laelius Herma at *Gramm.* 10.3 and 10.5, with Kaster 1995, 142.

supplicibus atque etiam minacibus per iocum litteris efflagitaret ... Vita Verg. 31).[12] Such brevity is a regular feature of Suetonius' style.[13]

In conclusion, we should reject the conjectures of Funaioli and Della Corte and accept Vahlen's *nam erat,* where the whole *nam*-clause functions as a gloss on the name *Eros,* which otherwise would imply that Staberius was a slave. This is the reading closest to the manuscripts and also suits Suetonius' general stylistic practice as much as beginning with an explicit statement of the subject's *patria,* which was occasionally unknown for his grammarians and rhetoricians.[14] A Thracian or Syrian origin is therefore no likelier for Staberius than any other. Pliny the Elder also appears not to have known the grammarian's origin, since he records only that of his shipmates, Publilius and Manilius, who were Syrians (*HN* 35.199);[15] Suetonius knew this at least about Publilius, of whom he wrote a lost *Life* that has been scantily preserved in a fragment of Jerome (*Publilius mimographus natione Syrus Romae scenam tenet, Chron.* Ol. 184.2 = Suet. fr. 26 Reiff.). Suetonius does not seem to have had any such information on Staberius.

12 To this explanatory, yet anticipatory, use of *nam,* we might equally compare Suetonius on the rhetorician Plotius Gallus: 'This same man – for he lived a very long time – Marcus Caelius indicates in the speech that he gave defending himself on the charge of violence, dictated the action for his prosecutor Atratinus' (*hunc eundem – nam diutissime uixit – M. Caelius in oratione quam pro se de ui habuit significat dictasse Atratino accusatori suo actionem, Gramm.* 26.2). Cf. also *Tib.* 1.1, using the postpositive *enim* to clarify social status in the opening of a *Life* in a similar way: 'The patrician branch of the Claudii – for there was also another plebeian one of no less power or prestige – arose from the Sabines' town of Regilli' (*patricia gens Claudia – fuit enim et alia plebeia nec potentia minor nec dignitate – orta est ex Regillis oppido Sabinorum*); with *Gramm.* 22.1, *Iul.* 24.2, *Aug.* 35.1, 76.1, 99.2, *Tib.* 13.1, *Calig.* 4, 8.4, 26.1, *Galb.* 3.3, 19.1, *Vit.* 17.1, *Dom.* 11.3.
13 On the brevity of Suetonius' style, see Mooney 1930, 634–6.
14 Baldwin 1983, 434 points to Curtius Nicias (*Gramm.* 14.1–4) as odd in this regard, but see also Sevius Nicanor (5.1–2), Lenaeus (15.1–3), Verrius Flaccus (17.1–3), Scribonius Aphrodisius (19.1–2), and Pomponius Porcellus (22.1–3); cf. also subjects whose origins are not explicitly stated, but may be suggested already by their names: Aurelius Opillus (*Gramm.* 6.1), Cornelius Epicadus (12.1), Plotius Gallus (26.1), and Otacilius Pitholaus (27.1–2), with Kaster 1995, 111–12, 162, 292, and 299, respectively.
15 Baldwin 1983, 433–4 argued for the dependence of *Gramm.* 13.1 on Plin. *HN* 35.199–200, but a common source may be more probable; see Kaster 1995, 344–5. For the interpretation of Pliny's passage, which does not imply that Staberius too was Syrian, see ibid. 167; cf. above, n. 3. On Publilius Syrus, see Bradley 2019.

18 Suetonius, *Iul.* 49.2 and *Galb.* 20.1

sed C. Memmius etiam ad cyathum <u>eum</u> Nicomedi stetisse obicit cum reliquis exoletis pleno conuiuio accubantibus nonnullis urbicis negotiatoribus, quorum refert nomina.

eum *Salmasius*: et uinum Y´O²: et ui *MVL²δ*: et uina G

But Gaius Memmius even charges that <u>he</u> bore the drinking-cup of Nicomedes together with the rest of his boys at a full banquet attended by many of the town-merchants, whose names he reports.

(*Iul.* 49.2)

Suetonius hands down for posterity this salacious accusation by the orator Gaius Memmius that Julius Caesar sexually submitted to the Bithynian king Nicomedes around 80 BC.[1] Kaster's acceptance of the grammatically unnecessary correction *eum* by Salmasius in this fragment of Memmius for his OCT of Suetonius,[2] which goes undefended in his companion volume of textual studies,[3] instead of Rolfe's *et uinum* from the Loeb edition that at least has a basis in the manuscript tradition,[4] is needless. Besides cleaning up a dirty passage of Suetonius in which it is stated that Caesar 'bore the drinking-cup *and wine* of Nicomedes', this over-editing makes the orator's reference a less coherent allusion to Ganymede, who infamously '*poured wine* for Zeus' (Διὶ οἰνοχοεύειν, Hom. *Il.* 20.234), through Caesar's role as a cup-bearer to Nicomedes. It is a sympotic cliché that Roman wine servers were slave boys, so that without the word 'wine', which is a strong aphrodisiac, the sexual insinuation becomes faint, if not entirely obscured. We should thus return to *et uinum*, because it is doubtful that Suetonius would have recorded Memmius' allegation as evidence of the

---

1 On this story, see Osgood 2008. For Suetonius' probable lost biography of Memmius, see above, Chapter 6.
2 Kaster 2016a.
3 Id. 2016c.
4 Rolfe 1913–14.

sexual relationship between Caesar and Nicomedes unless it contained this homoerotic innuendo.

As further support for retaining Memmius' *et uinum*, comparison can be made with another passage where Kaster has again edited Suetonius too drastically, following Lipsius in arguing for the radical deletion of *ac ferirent* from the emperor Galba's emphatic last words before his death:

> plures autem prodiderunt optulisse ultro iugulum et ut hoc agerent {ac ferirent}, quando ita uideretur, hortatum.
>
> ac ferirent *del. Lipsius*

> However, most have reported that he presented his neck voluntarily and urged them, if it seemed correct, to do this <u>and strike</u>.
>
> (*Galb.* 20.1)

To justify the suggestion of this draconian omission, which would steal the dramatic pathos from the statement, Kaster quotes Plutarch's simpler Greek version of the emperor's final words in his own version of the death scene: 'Do it!' (Δρᾶτε, Plut. *Galb.* 27.1).[5] However, no reference is made to Tacitus' *agerent ac ferirent* ('Do it *and strike!*' *Hist.* 1.41.2), which contains the same elaboration *ac ferirent*, clearly indicating that this whole Latin phrase was originally in both Suetonius and their common source, and should consequently be accepted, despite the religious saying *hoc age*, since the presence of this phrase is hardly incompatible with a brief gloss.[6] Therefore, more restraint seems warranted in editing these paraphrased utterances of Memmius and Galba.

5 Kaster 2016c, 230.
6 On the shared diction between the parallel sources on Galba, including *ac ferirent*, see Hardy 1890, xl, lviii = 1906, 319, 333. For the saying *hoc age*, see above, p. 130.

19 Augustus' Mime of Life (Suetonius, *Aug.* 99.1)[*]

The last words of Augustus, as reported by his biographer Suetonius (*Aug.* 99.1–2) and the historian Cassius Dio (56.30.3–4), have received much attention from scholars, especially Augustus' reference to the 'mime of life' (*mimum uitae*) in Suetonius' recording of the emperor's preamble to some Greek verses:[1]

> supremo die identidem exquirens an iam de se tumultus foris esset, petito speculo capillum sibi comi ac malas labantes corrigi praecepit et admissos amicos percontatus ecquid iis uideretur <u>mimum</u> uitae commode transegisse adiecit et clausulam,
>
> > ἐπεὶ δὲ †ΤΙΑΧΟΙ† καλῶς τὸ παίγνιον,
> > δότε κρότον καὶ πάντες ἡμᾶς μετὰ χαρᾶς προπέμψατε.
>
> mimum *corr.* P² *(Beroaldo):* minimum Ω: nimium *edd. pleraeque uet.*

On his last day, as he repeatedly inquired whether there was already a commotion outside over him, after asking for a mirror, he ordered his hair to be combed and his drooping jaw corrected, and when he had received friends posed the question, whether it seemed to them that he had completed the <u>mime</u> of life fittingly, even adding this closing verse:

> If it is going well, give your applause to the play and send us all off with joy.
>
> (*Aug.* 99.1)

[*] This chapter was first published in *CW* 107 (2013), 99–103.

[1] See e.g. Davis 1999; Sumi 2002, 572; van Hooff 2003, 101; Swan 2004, 303–4; Beagon 2005b, 91–2, 128–9; Edwards 2007, 145; Wardle 2007; 2008; Brandão 2009, 95, 174, 271–3, 323, n. 46; Louis 2010, 566–7 (ad loc.); Toher 2012. Both Wardle (2014, 550) and Kaster (2016a) have now accepted the word *mimum*, based on the earlier version of the present chapter that was published in 2013. On the Greek textual crux in this passage, which does not affect my argument, see Rollo 2015–16, 55–6, 66; 2018, 618–20; Kaster 2016c, 129–31.

This passage contains the penultimate words of the emperor in his life according to this biography (in his very last words reported by Suetonius, he urges his wife Livia to remember their marriage: *Aug. 99.1*). We have a rather close parallel to Augustus' introductory words above in Dio's account of his death:

> κρότον δὲ δή τινα παρ' αὐτῶν [ἑταίρων] ὁμοίως τοῖς γελωτοποιοῖς, ὡς καὶ ἐπὶ μίμου τινὸς τελευτῇ, αἰτήσας καὶ πάμπανυ πάντα τὸν τῶν ἀνθρώπων βίον διέσκωψε.

> After asking for some applause from them [his companions] in a manner similar to comic actors, as if at the end of some mime, he thoroughly mocked the whole life of men.
>
> (Dio Cass. 56.30.4)

Dio is very close to Suetonius' language, and for this reason, the humanist scholar Beroaldo's emendation *mimum*, where the manuscripts of Suetonius had *minimum*, has been almost universally accepted;[2] Ihm alone is uncertain, printing *mi[ni]mum* rather than simply *mimum*, which amounts to the same thing, but is nonetheless cautious. Toher has recently offered an argument in favour of doubting the emendation and restoring *minimum*, but it ultimately fails to convince.

First of all, Toher claims that 'there is no support in the manuscript tradition of Suetonius for the reading *mimum vitae*' and that '*mimum vitae* was hardly likely to have been corrupted into *minimum vitae* of the MS tradition.'[3] Both statements can be challenged. As noted in the *criticus apparatus* above, *mimum uitae* can be found as a correction (P[2]) to the twelfth-century codex of Suetonius designated P (Parisinus = Paris, BnF lat. 5801).[4] Since all of the manuscripts of Suetonius depend on a lost archetype from the Carolingian monastery at Tours, as represented by our oldest existing manuscript M (Memmianus = Paris, BnF lat. 6115), which is a contemporary ninth-century copy,[5] and since all other manuscripts have *minimum*, this therefore must have been the reading in the archetype. However, it remains significant that Beroaldo in the fifteenth century was not alone in his conjecture *mimum*: a hand contemporary with the scribe who copied the twelfth-century manuscript P also corrected what he found into this same word. It is certainly possible that the ninth-century original

2 In addition to Kaster's text printed above, see also e.g. Roth 1858; Ailloud 1931–2; de Climent 1964–70; Carter 1982.

3 Toher 2012, 41, 44, respectively.

4 On the manuscripts of Suetonius' *Caesars* generally, see Preud'homme 1904; Ihm 1907, viii–xxiv; Rolfe 1913–14, 1.xxi–xxv; Boman 2011, 369–73; Kaster 2014; 2016a, v–xlviii; 2016c, 3–45, 265–94.

5 See Innes 1997 with bibliography. The manuscripts P and M are both available online via Gallica (the digital library of the Bibliothèque nationale de France).

from which M and the later manuscripts derive was flawed on this occasion, and that the error was preserved by the copiers of this archetype and its descendants. To the hurried eye, the words look alike and are easily confused.[6]

Other occurrences of *mimum* in the *Caesars*, where *minimum* has been found incorrectly in some manuscripts from the Biblioteca Apostolica Vaticana, militate against Toher's second point that the latter is an unlikely mistake for the former. We may point, for example, to another introduction to a verse at *Augustus* 53.1: 'When during his watching of the games it was pronounced in a mime' (*cum spectante eo ludos pronuntiatum esset in mimo*). One of our most valuable codices, the eleventh-century V (Vaticanus = Vat. lat. 1904),[7] has instead *minimo*, but it has been universally rejected by editors without comment. A far less trustworthy twelfth-century manuscript, the Codex Reginae Latinus 833 (Reg. lat. 833), which was ignored as useless by Ihm,[8] offers two other instances of this same divergence from our present text of Suetonius. Let us look at the passages as they stand today. When Suetonius comments on the charade of one of Caligula's military actions, he writes: 'in this mime too he was extreme beyond measure' (*in hoc quoque mimo praeter modum intemperans, Calig.* 45.2);[9] and regarding the sham rivalry over Poppaea, the biographer says that Nero exiled Otho 'to prevent a harsher punishment from making the whole mime public' (*ne poena acrior mimum omnem diuulgaret, Otho* 3.2). In both cases, this variant manuscript reads *minimo/minimum*, but no responsible editor would accept the texts as such. It is plain to see from these identical errors, which appear in rather unambiguous references to mimes,[10] how Augustus' *mimum* was probably misread at some point before its Carolingian transmission.

Moreover, the reading *mimum* was supported by Beroaldo with reference to a similar passage about life as a comedy in Cicero's treatise *On Old Age* (*De senectute*),[11] which Toher does not discuss:

6 For a similar confusion, see e.g. Vell. Pat. 2.59.1, with Wiseman 2009, 113. Other examples are listed in Brown 1972, 37–8.

7 On the codex Vat. lat. 1904, which ends halfway through *Calig.* 3.3, see Nogara 1912, 346–8. A microfilm is available in the Knights of Columbus Vatican Film Library at Saint Louis University.

8 Ihm 1907, xvi. This codex belonged to Queen Christina's collection of almost 2,000 manuscripts, which so far has only been partly catalogued (Reg. lat. 1–500): Wilmart 1937–45. Reproductions of this manuscript may be requested directly from the Biblioteca Apostolica Vaticana.

9 Saddington 2004, 26 suggests that these were in fact 'training manœuvres'.

10 Especially the passage about Nero and Otho, which recalls the theme of adultery that was common in mimes; see Osgood 2011, 78 (ad loc.).

11 Beroaldo 1493, 120. On the commonplace metaphor of life as a mime, cf. e.g. Apul. *Flor.* 16.16–18, with Prauscello 2004; Hunink 2006, 37–8; Wardle 2007, 450–2.

neque enim histrioni, ut placeat, peragenda fabula est, modo, in quocumque fuerit actu, probetur, neque sapientibus usque ad 'plaudite' ueniendum est. breue enim tempus aetatis satis longum est ad bene honesteque uiuendum.

For indeed the actor need not, to please his audience, act out the entire play, but only be successful in whichever scene he appears, nor need wise men live all the way to the final 'applaud!' For a short lifetime is long enough to live well and honourably.

(Cic. *Sen.* 70)

This passage reveals that the plural command to 'applaud' (*plaudite*/δότε κρότον) was sufficient to recall the conclusion of a comedy and, in the common metaphor for life that is usually found there, the extremity of old age.[12] Comparison of Cicero's phrase *peragenda fabula* with our Suetonian passage would seem to suggest the same rendering of Augustus' construction *mimum ... transegisse* ('completed the mime'), since the two verbs are related, and in light of this passage, the reading of *mimum* seems especially likely. Toher himself even mentions Cicero's more metaphorical use of the phrase *fabulam aetatis peregisse* in the same work (*Sen.* 64), a parallel to Suetonius first noticed by van Broekhuizen,[13] and Seneca's *humanae uitae mimus* (*Ep.* 80.7), which was adduced by Shuckburgh.[14]

By contrast, the use of *transigo* with the phrase *minimum uitae* would lack sense, since this verb usually applies to things done over some duration (*OLD* 2, 5b).[15] Augustus lived to be almost eighty years old, and even if he had made, as Toher suggests, some ironic reference to his 'very short life', we should expect it to have been followed by a philosophical quotation on the brevity of human existence, not a *clausula* from the end of a mime. Such an unexplained reference is too obscure to have been uttered by Augustus. As a parallel to this reading, Toher finds only a single example from Pliny the Elder: 'Doves and turtle-doves live eight years. The sparrow, on the other hand, has *a very short life*, even though he is equally lustful' (*columbae et turtures octonis annis uiuunt. contra passeri minimum uitae, cui salacitas par*, *HN* 10.107).[16] But as Pliny's construction does not support the

---

12 Cf. Brink 1963–82, 2.231. For the formula *ualete et plaudite*, see Plaut. *Men.* 1162, *Pers.* 858, *Truc.* 968; Ter. *Haut.* 1067, *Phorm.* 1055, *Eun.* 1094, *Ad.* 997; Hor. *Ars P.* 155; also Davis 1999, 13 n. 1; Louis 2010, 567.

13 See Burman 1736, 469 (ad loc.).

14 Shuckburgh 1896, 171 (ad loc.); Toher 2012, 44 n. 20, also citing Suetonius' discussion of the emperor's fondness for the theatre at *Aug.* 53.1, on which see Kessissoglu 1988, 386. On public shows in the Augustus generally, see Groot 2008, 142–6.

15 Cf. Wardle 2007, 452 n. 40, comparing Plaut. *Pseud.* 564 (*hanc fabulam dum transigam*) and *Truc.* 11 (*dum transigimus hanc comoediam*).

16 Toher 2012, 42.

use of *transigo* (or a related verb) with this phrase, it does not offer much help with regard to the Suetonian passage.

Finally, if we were to accept Toher's proposition *minimum*, we should also have to allow for the possibility that Dio's version is a coincidental invention, owing to the conflicting versions of Augustus' death.[17] However, while Dio is unlikely to have read Suetonius' version, he nonetheless probably draws on a common source.[18] If the two writers rely on the same source for this scene, there can be no doubt about Suetonius' *mimum* in light of Dio's μίμου. While the use of *mimus* as a metaphor for a charade in general, as in our examples from the *Caligula* and *Otho*, seems to have been post-Augustan,[19] the Ciceronian phrases above suggest that a similar reference at least to the comedy of life was indeed common in Augustus' lifetime.

In sum, the standard text *mimum* in the death scene of Suetonius' *Life* of Augustus, which is a medieval alteration adopted by most modern editions, should not be questioned. The ninth-century archetype's *minimum* is a common mistake for this word, as shown by the manuscript tradition of Suetonius. Moreover, this sensible correction favoured since Beroaldo in 1493 – a correction which was in fact first made to one of Suetonius' manuscripts three centuries earlier – is also supported by the overall context of the passage, the syntax of the sentence, and an unambiguous passage in the later Greek writer Dio, who is probably drawing independently on the same first-century account. Suetonius' source may be suspected of embellishing a fitting ending for an emperor fond of the theatre and of Greek quotations,[20] but either way, that historian clearly wrote *mimum*.

---

17 Ibid. 43.
18 See Swan 2004, 23, 301; above, p. 111; below, p. 199.
19 Shotter 1993, 144 (on *Otho* 3.2).
20 For the recitation of dramatic verses before one's death, we might compare e.g. Brutus' quotation of *Eur. Med.* 332 (Plut. *Brut.* 51.1–2; App. *B Civ.* 4.130). Brutus was similarly fond of Greek verses: e.g. Hom. *Il.* 16.849 (Val. Max. 1.5.7; Plut. *Brut.* 24.6; App. *B Civ.* 4.134); see Wardle 1998b, 177–8.

20 Nero in Furs (Suet. *Ner.* 29)[*]

suam quidem pudicitiam usque adeo prostituit ut contaminatis paene omnibus membris nouissime quasi genus lusus excogitaret quo ferae pelle contectus emitteretur e cauea uirorumque ac feminarum ad stipitem deligatorum inguina <u>inuaderet</u> et, cum affatim desaeuisset, conficeretur a Doryphoro liberto, cui etiam, sicut ipsi Sporus, ita ipse denupsit, uoces quoque et heiulatus uim patientium uirginum imitatus.

inuaderet *edd.*: euaderet M

He so prostituted his own chastity that after defiling almost every part of his body, he at last devised a kind of game, in which, covered with the skin of some wild animal, he was let loose from a cage and <u>attacked</u> the private parts of men and women, who were bound to stakes, and when he had sated his mad lust, was dispatched by his freedman Doryphorus; for he was even married to this man in the same way that he himself had married Sporus, going so far as to imitate the cries and lamentations of a maiden being deflowered.

(*Ner.* 29)

In the 332 pages of Kaster's *Studies on the Text of Suetonius' De uita Caesarum*,[1] which he published in tandem with his OCT of the author,[2] the above passage is not explained or even discussed, even though it is one of the most textually problematic in the *Caesars*. Editors universally accept, without justification, the emendation *inuaderet* ('attack') for the actual act that Nero performs on these victims' genitals, but our earliest manuscript M has *euaderet* ('avoid'). Historical considerations complicate both options: comparison with parallel sources suggests that neither verb can support the interpretation of this scene by Champlin, which has remained

---

[*] This chapter was first published in *MD* 73 (2014), 205–9.
[1] Kaster 2016c. Unless otherwise stated, translations of Suetonius and Cassius Dio in this chapter are taken from the Loeb editions of Rolfe 1913–14 and Cary 1924–5, respectively.
[2] Kaster 2016a.

the most sensible, despite not finding general acceptance. Champlin showed the different ways in which the emperor plays here with role reversal.[3] As he pointed out, the historian Cassius Dio's version of this tale is more reticent, even if he changes the men and women to 'boys and girls': 'Nero would fasten naked boys and girls to stakes, and then putting on the hide of a wild beast would attack them and satisfy his brutal lust under the appearance of devouring parts of their bodies' (καὶ μειράκια καὶ κόρας σταυροῖς γυμνὰς προσδέων θηρίου τέ τινος δορὰν ἀνελάμβανε καὶ προσπίπτων. σφίσιν ἠσέλγαινεν ὥσπερ τι ἐσθίων, 63.13.2).[4] Champlin offered a reading of the exact misdeed preserved by both authors that has been ignored by all subsequent scholars, who have instead viewed Nero's action as either senseless violence or a doublet for the emperor's punishment of the Christians (Tac. *Ann.* 15.44.5–6).[5] However, Champlin's interpretation is worthy of serious consideration: 'Nero's bestial act was surely meant to imply oral sex.'[6]

Although I think that Champlin is almost certainly correct, he presumably bases his claim likewise on an acceptance of *inuaderet*, offering no linguistic evidence to support such a use of the verb. Therefore, Suetonius' text, at least as it stands, cannot possibly sustain Champlin's meaning. In this chapter, I shall propose a new textual conjecture that finally substantiates the view that Nero does indeed perform oral sex on these men and women. Nero's game is in fact a play on *damnatio ad bestias*, the form of punishment in which prisoners were fed to the wild beasts.[7] In such executions, the victims were often raped by the animals and killed in the process.[8] As Champlin observes, Suetonius adopts Nero's parody already in at least one example of sexual language, when he writes that the emperor *conficeretur a Doryphoro liberto*, using the verb in the sense of both 'kill' and 'finish off sexually', and referring to the freedman who dispatched the wild beast as Doryphorus ('spear-carrier'), even though we know from other sources that his name was really Pythagoras (Mart. 11.6.10; Tac. *Ann.* 15.37.4; Dio Cass. 62.28.3, 63.13.2, 63.22.4).[9] Although Suetonius

---

3 Champlin 2003, 160–1, 165–71. For a similar portrayal of Nero at Tac. *Ann.* 15.37.4, see Woodman 1992, 180–1 = 1998b, 178–9.

4 Champlin 2003, 169–70, 315 n. 66.

5 See, respectively, Langlands 2006, 356–7; Starbatty 2010, 226; and Woods 2006–7; Brandão 2009, 78, 163 n. 18, 197–8. The doublet was first suggested by Bradley 1978, 164, and more recently by Drinkwater 2019, 313. *Contra*, see Bessone 1979, 107.

6 Champlin 2003, 169. Cf. Williams 2010, 399–400, where the translation of *inuaderet* is now provided as 'devoured' in the book's second edition, and Charles and Anagnostou-Laoutides 2012b, 541 n. 48. See also Champlin's translation of Dio's προσπίπτων and σφίσιν ἠσέλγαινεν in the passage above: '*falling upon them he would act licentiously*, as if he were devouring [them]' (169, my italics).

7 Habinek 1990, 58 n. 15; cf. Brandão 2009, 385.

8 Coleman 1990, 64–5.

9 For this identification, see Bessone 1979, 105–7. On the double meaning of *conficere*, see Adams 1982, 159; Baldwin 1983, 506, 513, 524 n. 63; and on that of *Doryphoro*, Pipitone 2015.

possibly confuses this man with Nero's actual freedman 'Doryphorus' in charge of petitions (*a libellis*), who had died two years earlier than the wedding between the man in question and Nero occurred,[10] it is no less likely that this was simply a nickname of Pythagoras, since the word δορυφόρος in Greek was heavily associated with the bodyguards of tyrants (e.g. Hdt. 1.59.5; Thuc. 6.57.4; Isoc. 10.37).[11] Aristophanes may even use the word as a sexual pun in the claim that Cleon's grandfather was δορυφόρος to Hippias' wife (*Eq.* 447–9). If Pythagoras was already known as 'Doryphorus' – whether suggesting Nero's tyranny, his own role as the emperor's ἀνήρ ('husband', Dio Cass. 63.13.2), or both – Suetonius takes advantage of this fact to produce the phallic pun in this context. The biographer suggests that at the end of the game, Doryphorus pretends to kill the animal played by Nero, but is actually satisfying him sexually.[12] It follows that there was an erotic reality also to the game's first part.

As the text stands, there is no basis for inferring any suggestion of dining such as we find in Dio's ἐσθίων ('devouring'). The word *inuaderet* in its Suetonian context must mean 'attack', which is how it is usually taken by translators, but *inuaderet* may not be what the biographer wrote. As it turns out, it is merely a conjecture long favoured by editors due to the lack of sense given by *euaderet* ('he avoided'), the verb found in the oldest manuscript M, representing the archetype from which all later manuscripts of Suetonius' *Caesars* descend. The conjecture *inuaderet* can already be found, for example, in the twelfth-century manuscript P, and it has not since been questioned.[13] Some scribal error in the transmission of the work must therefore have produced *euaderet* before M was copied in the ninth century. One writer who possibly saw a version of the original text before the error was committed is Aurelius Victor, who drew on Suetonius in the fourth century, either directly or indirectly through the epitome known as the *Kaisergeschichte*,[14] as his source for the same story about Nero: 'For, in fact, while decked out in the skin of a wild beast he would nuzzle the genitals of people of either sex who had been chained up like criminals' (*quippe noxiorum uinctis modo pelle tectus ferae utrique sexui genitalia uultu contrectabat, Caes.* 5.7).[15] While it is possible that Victor is simply inferring oral sex from *inuaderet* in the manner of Champlin, which as we have said is linguistically unfounded, or making the leap of altering his source based

---

10 Champlin 2003, 161, 313 n. 39. However, Suetonius was more likely aware of this other freedman, since he refers to him elsewhere through a vague plural (*Ner.* 35.5); see Warmington 1999, 55, 67.

11 See e.g. Lavelle 2005, 95–6.

12 For games as sexual metaphors, cf. *Dom.* 22, with Adams 1982, 157–9, 161–3.

13 On the manuscripts of Suetonius' *Caesars*, see Kaster 2016a, v–xlviii; also above, p. 137 with bibliography.

14 For this lost work, see Rohrbacher 2009 with bibliography.

15 The translation is that of Bird 1994, 7. On Suetonius as the ultimate source for Victor, see id. 1984, 20–3; Charles and Anagnostou-Laoutides 2010b, 127–8.

on comparison with Dio, it seems more likely that he is simply following the Suetonian material, as he was accustomed to do, and modelling his sentence on a more explicit verb than *inuaderet*, before that verb became corrupted into *euaderet*, which, at least one way or the other, according to the scholarly consensus, must be incorrect.

Based on this passage of Victor, in which Nero literally embraces the prisoners' genitals with his face (*genitalia uultu contrectabat*),[16] as well as the similarly gastronomic language in Dio, who independently relies on the same source as Suetonius,[17] a more probable conjecture is *deuoraret* (in the *sensu obsceno*), which could easily have been corrupted into *euaderet* through metathesis. I therefore propose that Suetonius records how Nero 'feasted on their private parts' (*inguina deuoraret*). The word *uorare* and its cognates were often used in this way, and we might compare especially the inscription *Caliste, deuora!* ('Caliste, swallow it!' *CIL* IV.1854) referring to fellatio, or the more euphemistic *medias uorat puellas* ('she devours the middle of girls', Mart. 7.67.15) for lesbian cunnilingus; *inguina* too can be found with the sexual metaphor of eating, as in Martial's *rodas inguina* ('you eat his penis', 14.70.2).[18] It would be neither the only, nor the most exotic example of this kind of metaphor in Suetonius. In the famous poem about Augustus' 'banquet of the twelve gods' recorded by the biographer, there is even the phrase †*cenat*† *adulteria* (*Aug.* 70.1), which describes how the emperor 'dined on adulteries'.[19]

Our new reading thus makes the passage about Nero's dressing in furs less horrific, and suggests that Suetonius' feral language about him having 'taken his fill of savagery' (*affatim desaeuisset*) is simply in keeping with the metaphorical scenario of *damnatio ad bestias*, just like *deuoraret* and *conficeretur*. Through unwanted oral sex, the captives were essentially raped – the detail of their being 'tied to stakes' (*ad stipitem deligatorum*) proves that they were not willing participants or 'actors', as postulated by Champlin[20] – but Nero did not otherwise violate their groins (contrast *Calig.* 58.3). As Suetonius makes clear in his ordering of categories (*Ner.* 26.1), this section is on *libido* (*Ner.* 28–9), not *crudelitas* (*Ner.* 33–8). The emendation

---

16 *OLD* s.v. *contrecto* I.B.2. Cf. *Dom.* 1.3: *contrectatis multorum uxoribus*. For Victor's use of this word here with *uultus* as a euphemism for oral sex, see Adams 1982, 212 n. 1.

17 Cf. Champlin 2003, 161. The identity of this source remains mysterious; for possibilities, see Devillers 2003, 12–27. For the independence of Dio from Suetonius, see below, p. 199.

18 For these and other examples, see Adams 1982, 139; cf. Richlin 1992, 27, 115.

19 See *FLP* 474: 'A remarkable construction of *cenare*'. Kaster 2016a simply obelizes *cenat*, hesitantly suggesting the conjecture *cantat* by Lucarini; see Kaster 2016c, 114–15. But for the sense of this poem, see Marrone 2002; Wardle 2014, 445 (ad loc.). Cf. also the metaphorical phrase *pascere oculos* ('feast his eyes') at *Vit.* 14.2, although in that case eating is instead combined with cruelty (*saeuitia*), as announced by the heading to the section (*Vit.* 13.1); on that phrase, see below, p. 233.

20 Champlin 2003, 170; cf. Curry 2014, 211–12; Drinkwater 2019, 313.

deuoraret also allows for a smoother crescendo from the emperor's indiscriminate performance of oral sex on both men and women, to his being married as a bride to a freedman, and even 'going so far as to imitate the cries and lamentations of a maiden being deflowered' (*uoces quoque et heiulatus uim patientium uirginum imitatus*).[21] As usual in his negative portraits, Suetonius saves the most condemning details for last.

21 On this line, see Vout 2007, 152–3, 163 n. 48. What follows after this is merely a generalization on the emperor's high regard for lust in others, which rounds off the section with a wider perspective (*Ner.* 29). Suetonius' crescendo technique within the category of Nero's lust is noted by Verdière 1975, 15–17; Champlin 2003, 161; Brandão 2009, 86, 227; and more generally in the *Life* by Meulder 2002, 375. For this technique elsewhere in the *Caesars*, see e.g. Henderson 2014, 99, n. 37; above, p. 121. On the category of sexuality in Suetonius, particularly the vice of lust, see above, p. 99; also Chapter 16; cf. below, Chapter 31.

21 Oedipal Nero
The Farewell Kiss

As Nero savours the final moments with his mother Agrippina before she goes off to the eventual death that he will arrange for her, the text of the ninth-century manuscript M (BnF lat. 6115) of Suetonius' *Nero* – our best guide to the lost archtype that is the ultimate origin of all other copies of the biography in existence – includes a further salacious detail about a goodbye kiss that diverges from the other surviving ancient accounts of this event:[1]

> atque ita reconciliatione simulata iucundissimis litteris Baias euocauit ad sollemnia Quinquatruum simul celebranda. datoque negotio trier-archis qui liburnicam qua aduecta erat uelut fortuito concursu con-fringerent, protraxit conuiuium repetentique Baulos in locum corrupti nauigii machinosum illud optulit, hilare prosecutus atque in digressu <u>papillas</u> quoque exosculatus.

> Then he pretended a reconciliation and invited her in a most cordial letter to come to Baiae and celebrate the feast of Minerva with him. On her arrival, instructing his captains to wreck the galley in which she had come, by running into it as if by accident, he detained her at a ban-quet, and when she would return to Bauli, offered her his contrivance in place of the craft which had been damaged, escorting her to it in high spirits and even kissing her <u>breasts</u> as they parted.

> *(Ner.* 34.2)

Each of the two independent versions of this kiss in Tacitus and Cassius Dio is slightly different from that of Suetonius, at least according to their Loeb translations. In Tacitus, when Agrippina leaves, Nero is instead described as having 'escorted her on her way, clinging more closely than usual to her breast and *kissing her eyes*' (*prosequitur abeuntem, artius* oculis *et pectori*

---

1 In this chapter, I use or adapt the Loeb translations of Sophocles, Suetonius, Tacitus, and Dio by Lloyd-Jones 1994; Rolfe 1913–14; Hutton et al. 1914–37; Cary 1924–5, respectively. Translations of all other authors are my own.

haerens, *Ann.* 14.4). The epitome of Dio's Book 62 contains a similar contradiction of Suetonius, claiming not that Nero kissed her breasts, but that he kissed her eyes: 'he embraced her at the close of dinner about midnight, and straining her to his breast, *even kissed her eyes* and hands' (οὕτω δὴ ἀπὸ τοῦ δείπνου περὶ μέσας νύκτας περιλαμβάνει τε αὐτήν, καὶ πρὸς τὸ στέρνον προσαγαγών, καὶ φιλήσας καὶ τὰ ὄμματα καὶ τὰς χεῖρας, Dio Cass. 62.13.2).

Because of the similarities not only of diction but also of syntax between Suetonius and the other two accounts (e.g. *prosecutus/prosequitur, digressu/abeuntem, quoque exosculatus*/φιλήσας καί), all three authors must here be following a common first-century source, most likely Cluvius Rufus,[2] so that Suetonius' word 'breasts' is oddly incoherent with the other two parallel nouns (*papillas* ~ *oculis*/τὰ ὄμματα). For this reason, Questa long ago attempted to resolve the divergence by emending Suetonius' *papillas* ('breasts') to *pupillas* ('eyes'),[3] but he has since met with refutations by D'Anna and Benediktson, who are both cited in Kaster's apparatus criticus to his OCT.[4] Kaster eschews any discussion of the Suetonian passage in his companion volume of textual studies,[5] presumably opting simply to retain the manuscript's *papillas* in agreement with these scholars. However, their arguments against the proposed conjecture *pupillas* are misguided, and a strong defence of it may still be offered.

First of all, it certainly seems true that Dio, or at least his epitomator Xiphilinus, has misleadingly condensed the arrival and exit scenes of Agrippina, transposing the two details of her son's embrace and kissing of her hands: 'he embraced her at the close of dinner about midnight, and straining her to his breast ... kissed her ... hands' (περιλαμβάνει τε αὐτήν, καὶ πρὸς τὸ στέρνον προσαγαγών, καὶ φιλήσας ... τὰς χεῖρας). This more properly must have belonged with her earlier greeting by Nero in the common source, since this is where it appears in the account of Tacitus: 'He went down to the beach to meet her (she was arriving from Antium), *took her hand, embraced her,* and escorted her to Bauli' (*obuius in litora, nam Antio aduentabat,* excepit manu et complexu *ducitque Baulos, Ann.* 14.4).[6] As Benediktson observes, Suetonius' account shows a similar compression to Dio's, with Agrippina coming and leaving in the same sentence, but he omits the hand-holding and hug upon their initial meeting, focusing exclusively on the later details of their goodbye. Second, as we have said, Tacitus' word *oculis* corresponds without question at least to Dio's τὰ ὄμματα.

---

2 See Benediktson 1992, 161–2.

3 Questa apud Paratore 1959, 335; also Questa 1963, 188–93; cf. Verdière 1960; 1975, 13–14.

4 D'Anna 1963; Benediktson 1992.

5 Kaster 2016c.

6 See Benediktson 1992, 162. This explanation seems preferable by far to the different possibility, which he leaves open (cf. 163), that Dio simply misread the Latin word *mammas* ('breasts'), which was allegedly in his source, as *manus* ('hands').

However, the verb *haerens* used by Tacitus does not correlate with Dio's φιλήσας, as Benediktson, among others, would like to make it: 'It seems most logical to interpret *oculis et pectori haerens* as "kissing" and parallel to φιλήσας ... τὰ ὄμματα and *papillas ... exosculatus* respectively.'[7] But this translation cannot be extracted from the participle *haerens*, since the specific entry 'to kiss' is not found among its definitions in the Oxford Latin Dictionary. The fact that he offers no parallel passage for this use of the verb is significant, because none in fact exists in classical Latin. Verdière points out that one key to understanding Tacitus' meaning comes in the ensuing reasons that he provides for the fact that Nero drew out this final moment: in the speculation of the Roman historian, it was done 'possibly as a final touch of hypocrisy, or possibly the *last look* upon his doomed mother gave pause even to that brutal spirit' (*explenda simulatione, seu periturae matris* supremus aspectus *quamuis ferum animum retinebat, Ann.* 14.4).[8]

The phrase *oculis ... haerens* therefore refers to a 'look' (*aspectus*) shared between Nero and his mother, and must literally mean 'keeping eye contact'. This poetic sense of the verb has the advantage of being supported by one of its actual definitions: 'To fasten (on) with the senses' (*OLD* s.v *haereo* 6a). We might compare Ovid's description of Myrrha in the similar tale about incest with her father from the *Metamorphoses*: 'and on her father's face her gaze was fixed' (*patriisque in uultibus haerens, Met.* 10.359).[9] It is also corroborated by Yardley's more recent translation of the Tacitean phrase, which rightly improves on the incorrect Loeb translation that was quoted above: 'hanging on her gaze and clinging closely to her'.[10] Tacitus has cleaned up the farewell scene by recording Nero's last act of kissing his mother's eyes in slightly more general terms, as a kind of staring and cuddling, while Suetonius and Dio were happy to leave the gesture exactly as they found it in the common source. This meaning of *haereo* becomes even clearer when we understand the particular lines of poetry evoked by Tacitus, who is the only one of the three authors to allude here to the beginning of the *Aeneid*.

In Book 1 of Virgil's *Aeneid*, Venus makes the boy Cupid disguise himself as Aeneas' son Ascanius, in order to cause the hero and Dido to fall in love with each other. Tacitus uniquely underscores how Agrippina is deceived by her own boy Nero through the same vocabulary as Virgil's passage on Cupid's trickery:[11]

---

7   Ibid. 162; cf. D'Anna 1954, 200; 1963, 117.
8   See Verdière 1960, 775: '*oculis haerens* est, en quelque manière, commenté par *matris supremus aspectus* que nous lisons quelques mots plus loin.'
9   For this use of *haereo*, see also e.g. Prop. 1.3.19; Val. Max. 9.9.2; Petron. *Sat.* 89.1; with Verdière 1960, 775 n. 2, who provides further references.
10 Yardley 2008, 305.
11 Verdière 1960, 775 n. 2 compares *Aen.* 1.717–19; cf. Benediktson 1992, 163: 'Tacitus has stylized the passage ... artistically modelling the passage on Vergil.' However, they

ille ubi *complexu* Aeneae colloque pependit
et magnum falsi impleuit genitoris amorem,
reginam petit. haec *oculis*, haec *pectore* toto
haeret et interdum gremio fouet, inscia Dido,
insidat quantus miserae deus.

As soon as he has *embraced* Aeneas, holding on to his neck, and has
produced great passion in his pretend father, he seeks the queen. With
her *gaze*, with her whole *chest*, Dido *clings to* him, now and then caressing him in her lap, unaware of how powerful a god has settled on
the unhappy woman.

(Verg. *Aen.* 1.715–19)

The context of Nero's late running banquet recalls the night of feasting
that Dido is compelled by Cupid to extend with Aeneas. Indeed, Tacitus'
Nero even similarly comes in the guise of a child, acting 'boyishly familiar'
(*familiaritate iuuenili*) with Agrippina.

By having the emperor hug his mother when she arrives, and not only
stare lingeringly but also snuggle against her as she leaves, Tacitus brings to
mind the clinging not only of Cupid to Aeneas, but also of Dido to Cupid.
The verbal echoes follow Virgil's order for these two affectionate embraces
(*complexu … oculis et pectori haerens*). Moreover, in containing datives
instead of ablatives with *haerens*, Tacitus' new scene ironically reverses the
agency of Virgil's second action, so that rather than being looked at and
touched himself, Nero hangs on to Agrippina's eyes and body: the mother
of the *Annals* does not willingly cling to her boy; rather, it is he who affixes
her eyes and chest to himself by distracting her attention, which makes the
scene even more malicious and manipulative. Tacitus' reminiscent phrase
should no doubt be construed in the same way as Virgil's in my above translation. We might also compare, for example, the translation of Fagles: 'Her
gaze, her whole heart / is riveted on him now.'[12] Agrippina is seduced, as if
by a spell sent from Venus herself.

This allusion is in keeping with Tacitus' fondness for poetic language,
as well as his reserved and selective style, which often leads him to con-
tribute his own expressions in place of what was in his source.[13] Dio must
therefore reflect the common source more accurately than Tacitus, whose
entire phrase *oculis et pectori haerens*, including *pectori*, is probably simply
his own rhetorical embellishment of the source's original version of Dio's
φιλήσας … τὰ ὄμματα, so that the Virgilian word *pectori* cannot in any

---

both miss the further similarity of *complexu* (*Aen.* 1.715). For Virgil's great influence on
Tacitus, see above, pp. 122, n. 4, 131.

12 Fagles 2006, 71.

13 On Tacitus' dignified approach to historiography through his omissions and imprecision,
see e.g. Syme 1958, 189; Oakley 1991, 344; 2009b, 209; Woodman 2018, 174. On the
pretentions of ancient historians more generally, see Power 2014b, 13 with bibliography.

way be used to support *papillas* in Suetonius, since it is demonstrably part of Tacitus' own stylized improvement upon the inherited tradition about the tale. The same kind of Tacitean sanitization may be witnessed in the historian's later treatment of the inspection of Agrippina's corpse by Nero (on which, more in a moment). In that case, Tacitus disavows an obviously sordid picture that he finds unworthy of the grandeur of his work, which Dio and Suetonius nonetheless both report in their accounts.

Why does Tacitus feel the need to do the same thing here as he does in the scene between Nero and his dead mother? The answer is that kissing someone's eyes was a gesture of great affection in the Roman world, since the eyes were seen as an especially intimate part of a person's body; hence, both Suetonius and Dio (and probably the common source) write that Nero 'even' (*quoque*/καί) did this: *pupillas quoque exosculatus*/φιλήσας καὶ τὰ ὄμματα. As Pliny the Elder puts it in his *Natural History*: 'The soul lives in the eyes ... when we kiss them we seem to touch the soul itself' (*profecto in oculis animus habitat ... hos cum exosculamur animum ipsum uidemur attingere*, HN 11.145–6). For Nero to perform this act upon his own mother seemed inappropriate by Tacitus' standards, and thus he turns something sordid into a poetic passage more fitting for his own kind of historiography. Tacitus portrays Nero as instead hanging on to a final shared look and clinging to his mother's chest. This echoes the emperor's greeting a few sentences earlier, where, as we have seen, Tacitus had likewise expressed their embrace with two parallel words accompanying a single verb (*excepit manu et complexu*). This closural circling back by Tacitus suggests invention: the word *pectori* is his own contribution as a final artistic touch to his narration, which fills out the line with an allusion to his opening of the scene through this formal chiastic symmetry with the earlier phrase (*excepit manu et complexu ... oculis et pectori haerens*). To sum up, Tacitus' whole phrase *oculis et pectori haerens* is parallel to Dio's φιλήσας καὶ τὰ ὄμματα, and reflects only an original reference to Nero's kissing of his mother's eyes as he left.

Although Tacitus reinvents Nero's sexually suggestive last act of kissing Agrippina's eyes into a more romantic stare and longing embrace, he nonetheless preserves at least the object of the emperor's action: Agrippina's eyes. He therefore maintains the earlier source's basic theme of sight, conveying that this was the last time the two would see each other – their *supremus aspectus*, as he puts it. This theme also seems to have been present in the common source followed by all three writers during the later episode after Agrippina's death, when Nero wishes to look upon her dead body. Let us begin with Tacitus' abbreviated version, where he again refuses to admit material that, in his view, is simply out of bounds with respect to its salacious nature, almost apologizing even for its very mention:

> aspexeritne matrem exanimem Nero et formam corporis eius laudauerit, sunt qui tradiderint, sunt qui abnuant.

Whether Nero inspected the corpse of his mother and expressed approval of her figure is a statement which some affirm and some deny.

(*Ann.* 14.9)

Neither Dio nor Suetonius passes over this event. In fact, Dio is the fullest source of the three, even though he selected unique parts from the story. For a direct comparison, here are two depictions of the scene by the later authors Suetonius and Dio, one after the other:

adduntur his atrociora nec incertis auctoribus, ad uisendum interfectae cadauer accurrisse, contrectasse membra, alia uituperasse, alia laudasse, sitique interim oborta bibisse.

Trustworthy authorities add still more gruesome details: that he hurried off to view the corpse, handled her limbs, criticising some and commending others, and that becoming thirsty meanwhile, he took a drink.

(*Ner.* 34.4)

καὶ διὰ τοῦτο αὐτόπτης ἐπεθύμησε τοῦ πάθους γενέσθαι. καὶ αὐτήν τε πᾶσαν εἶδε γυμνώσας καὶ τὰ τραύματα αὐτῆς ἐπεσκέψατο, καὶ τέλος πολὺ καὶ τοῦ φόνου ἀνοσιώτερον ἔπος ἐφθέγξατο: εἶπε γὰρ ὅτι Οὐκ ᾔδειν ὅτι οὕτω καλὴν μητέρα εἶχον.

He therefore desired to behold the victim of his crime with his own eyes. So he laid bare her body, looked her all over and inspected her wounds, finally uttering a remark far more abominable even than the murder. His words were: 'I did not know I had so beautiful a mother.'

(Dio Cass. 61.14.2)

Despite Suetonius' customarily terser style, neither of these writers declines to tell the story, unlike Tacitus. Baldwin has argued that the further detail of touching the body ironically recalls the handling of Pentheus' limbs by his mother, who had unintentionally killed him, at the end of Euripides' *Bacchae*, since Nero may have performed a work on this theme soon after Agrippina's death (Dio Cass. 61.20.2).[14] However, even more relevant, due to the thematic connections with incest and sight, is the emphasis on Nero's need to see the body for himself, and on his very personal gaze, which is one fact that is preserved by all three authors, and probably comes from their common source. It of course points to the most immediately obvious literary model for this scene, namely, Oedipus, who has already been brought to mind in Suetonius' biography by his earlier report that one of the tragic works performed by Nero was entitled 'The Blinding of Oedipus' (*Ner.* 21.3, cf. 46.3).

14 Baldwin 1979b = 1985, 280–1.

This compulsion by Nero to find his mother and leer at her dead body clearly resembles that of Oedipus in the climactic scene of Sophocles' *Oedipus Tyrannus*, even though no one to my mind has previously compared the two passages. When Oedipus impetuously breaks into the room where his mother Jocasta has hanged herself, he then blinds himself with her brooches:

δεινὸν δ᾽ ἀΰσας ὡς ὑφ᾽ ἡγητοῦ τινος
πύλαις διπλαῖς ἐνήλατ᾽, ἐκ δὲ πυθμένων
ἔκλινε κοῖλα κλῇθρα κἀμπίπτει στέγῃ.
οὗ δὴ κρεμαστὴν τὴν γυναῖκ᾽ ἐσείδομεν,
πλεκταῖσιν αἰώραισιν ἐμπεπλεγμένην.
ὃ δ᾽ ὡς ὁρᾷ νιν, δεινὰ βρυχηθεὶς τάλας
χαλᾷ κρεμαστὴν ἀρτάνην. ἐπεὶ δὲ γῇ
ἔκειτο τλήμων, δεινά γ᾽ ἦν τἀνθένδ᾽ ὁρᾶν.
ἀποσπάσας γὰρ εἱμάτων χρυσηλάτους
περόνας ἀπ᾽ αὐτῆς, αἷσιν ἐξεστέλλετο,
ἄρας ἔπαισεν ἄρθρα τῶν αὑτοῦ κύκλων.

And with a dreadful cry, as though someone were guiding him he rushed at the double doors, forced the bolts inwards from their sockets and fell into the room. There he saw the woman hanging, her neck tied in a twisted noose. And when he saw her, with a fearful roar, poor man, he untied the knot from which she hung; and when the unhappy woman lay upon the ground, what we saw next was terrible. For he broke off the golden pins from her raiment, with which she was adorned, and lifting up his eyes struck them.

(Soph. *OT* 1260–70)

The original scene in Sophocles' play is latently sexualized, suggesting Oedipus' incestuous relationship with Jocasta even beyond death in the way that he treats her corpse. The Greek king blinds himself with the pins from her clothing, an unwittingly sexual gesture of technically undressing his mother. This act thus ironically brings to mind the very sin of sleeping with her for which he seeks to punish himself, as Verhoeff has discussed:

The dual, two-sided significance of the final encounter between mother and son expresses itself in the very specific instrument for Oedipus' self-blinding. The clasps of Jocasta's dress are taken off by the son who has – a further transparent symbol – forced his way in by opening the doors Jocasta had closed behind her. Yet, the clasps really belong to the mother and, as a result, it is possible to regard Oedipus' self-blinding as both a repetition and a punishment of the incest.[15]

15 Verhoeff 1984, 279.

In ancient Greece, the use of female dress-pins (περόναι) for violence is usually the practice of women (Hdt. 5.87.2–3; Eur. *Hec.* 1169–71), for whom they obviously made convenient makeshift weapons.[16] The use of them by a man in this scene is a unique reversal, and brings attention to the implications of the act within the play itself. Oedipus' breach of the room underscores the transgressive nature of this episode, but his violation of his mother's privacy really comes in the rough act of ripping off her dress-pins, which especially accentuates the idea of invading her person in a manner similar to Nero. By removing the clasps that hold his own mother's dress together, Oedipus is effectively undressing her once again, unbeknownst to him, as Nero does more literally, and thereby violating the norms of appropriate behaviour.

According to this interpretation, the unwittingly salacious detail of Oedipus' posthumously undressing Jocasta fits with the general atmosphere of dramatic irony within the play, and with its other sexual imagery, such as the more explicit metaphors of the filled port and ploughed field, which are directly used not long before this passage to describe their incestuous relations (*OT* 1207–12). Although Suetonius and Dio both preserve different elements of their common source on Nero, an allusion to Oedipus in that source is probably based on specific echoes of Sophocles' text. Indeed, it cannot even be dismissed that Nero himself acted out an ironic reversal of the blinding scene in the first place as a matter of historical fact, when one considers his flair for theatricality. What can at least be determined for certain is that one of the contemporary historical sources appears to have developed this literary parallel. All three of our accounts make a point of Nero's viewing the corpse for himself (*aspexeritne*, Tac. *Ann.* 14.9; *ad uisendum*, Suet. *Ner.* 34.4; αὐτόπτης ... ἐπεσκέψατο, Dio Cass. 61.14.2), which recalls the similar emphasis on the theme of sight in the above passage of *Oedipus Tyrannus* (ἐσείδομεν ... ὁρᾷ ... ὁρᾶν ... ἄρθρα τῶν αὑτοῦ κύκλων, 1263–70), where Oedipus' mother becomes the last image that he will ever see. Moreover, in Suetonius' version of Nero's scene, the emperor 'hurried off' (*accurrisse*) to view Agrippina, which is reminiscent of how Oedipus hastily 'rushed' (ἐνήλατ', *OT* 1261) to find Jocasta. Furthermore, Dio tells us that Nero personally 'laid bare' (γυμνώσας) his mother, which most closely recalls the Greek king's implied undressing of Jocasta by removing her dress-pins. Although Suetonius does not record that the emperor stripped her naked, he does report that he actually 'handled her limbs' (*contrectasse membra*), whereas in Tacitus and Dio, Nero only looks at and comments on her body.

When taken together, these various evocations of Oedipus are undeniable, and the earlier detail that Nero kissed Agrippina's eyes during their last farewell must be interpreted as part of this Sophoclean allusion from the

---

16 See Finglass 2018, 556.

same lost source that was used by our three extant accounts for the later scene with her dead body. This source, or perhaps Nero himself, appears to have alluded originally to the blinding scene in *Oedipus Tyrannus* both shortly before and after the death of his mother. Nero's excitement from Agrippina's corpse, replete with a beverage, is the very opposite of Oedipus' sorrow in his final moments with the lifeless Jocasta, and rather than putting out his own eyes after his mother dies, he kisses her eyes before her death, and once she is deceased, gazes not only extra-long at her but also at much more of her than usual. The emperor feasts his own eyes upon her nude corpse, violating her beyond the grave by leering at the woman he murdered, as opposed to the tragic hero of Sophocles' drama, who laments over a mother who took her own life. Instead of merely unfastening the clothing of his mother's dead body like Oedipus, Nero goes one step further, rendering her fully nude and feeling her limbs. These intimate details were deemed by Tacitus too inappropriate to report, much like the especially intimate kissing of her eyes in the farewell scene, and thus he ignored his source's allusion to Sophocles. As it turns out, Nero's kissing of his mother's eyes is even more Oedipal than either caressing or kissing her breasts, due to its thematic resonance of the Sophoclean play. The word *pupillas* now completes Suetonius' ironic retelling of the *Oedipus Tyrannus*.

22 Suetonius, *Galba* 1
Beginning or Ending?[*]

progenies Caesarum in Nerone defecit, quod futurum compluribus quidem signis sed uel euidentissimis duobus apparuit. Liuiae olim post Augusti statim nuptias Veientanum suum reuisenti praeteruolans aquila gallinam albam ramulum lauri rostro tenentem ita ut rapuerat demisit in gremium, cumque nutriri alitem, pangi ramulum placuisset, tanta pullorum suboles prouenit ut hodieque ea uilla 'ad Gallinas' uocetur, tale uero lauretum ut triumphaturi Caesares inde laureas decerperent, fuitque mos triumphantibus alias confestim eodem loco pangere, et obseruatum est sub cuiusque obitum arborem ab ipso institutam el- anguisse. ergo nouissimo Neronis anno et silua omnis exaruit radic- itus et quidquid ibi gallinarum erat interiit, ac subinde tacta de caelo Caesarum aede capita omnibus simul statuis deciderunt, Augusti etiam sceptrum e manibus excussum est.

The descendants of the Caesars ended with Nero, which was foretold as going to happen by several omens, but two were especially clear. Once when Livia was staying at her Veientine estate shortly after her marriage to Augustus an eagle flying past dropped into her lap a white hen that was holding a laurel twig in its beak just as it was snatched, and when she chose to raise the chicken and plant the twig, the result was an offspring of chicks so great that the villa is now called 'The Henhouse', and such a laurel grove that the Caesars used to pick laurels there for triumphs, usually planting others quickly in the same place without delay, and it was observed that before the death of each, the tree that he had planted wilted. Accordingly, in Nero's last year not only did the whole grove dry up by the root but the last of the hens died too, and then immediately afterwards the temple of the Caesars was struck by lightning, the heads toppled from all the statues at once, and even Augustus' sceptre was knocked out of his hands.

(*Galb.* 1)

In his *Tacitus*, Syme suggested the possibility that the last six biographies of Suetonius' *Caesars* (*Galba* through *Domitian*), which are thought to form the final two of eight books, may not have been part of the author's original

* This chapter was first published in *CP* 104 (2009), 216–20.

design, but were written later as a sequel.[1] In Syme's opinion, the first six *Lives* seemed a self-contained hexad: 'Six books, one for each ruler, embraced the Caesars in their dynastic sequence from the Dictator to Nero: a fitting term and climax, rounded off with a brief epilogue about a spurious Nero.'[2] In two later papers, Syme slightly modified his theory, albeit with no less reservation or characteristic brevity.[3] In both, he conjectured (hesitantly) that what now stands as the beginning of the *Galba* may have originally been at the end of the account of Nero, where the same material is found in Cassius Dio (63.29.3), and later transferred. Despite the caution with which Syme offered these ideas, his later proposal that *Galba* 1 may have once belonged to the *Nero* has seemed compelling, since Suetonius' chapter is about Nero and not Galba or his ancestors, and no other biography in the *Caesars* begins with a focus so removed from the subject. Even the opening of the *Vespasian*, which begins, 'After the overthrow and death of three emperors' (*rebellione trium principum et caede*, *Vesp.* 1.1), maintains its focus on the Flavian family.

Moreover, conjectures by Syme are often influential. For these reasons, the proposal has not met with much opposition from scholars. Wallace-Hadrill in his book on Suetonius and Murison in his commentary on the *Galba* both cite Syme's opinion and appear to leave open the possibility that *Galba* 1 was written as an ending to the *Nero*.[4] Furthermore, Syme is not the only scholar to have found the passage curious. The background information that it supplies must have seemed odd also to Bowersock, who suggested that the last six *Lives* had been written first, which assumes a reading of *Galba* 1 as inceptive rather than continuative.[5] Bowersock's theory was refuted by Bradley, whose comparison with *Vespasian* 1 as a similar 'bridge-passage' – that is, one which presupposes knowledge of the preceding *Life* – indicated that the *Galba* was written after the *Nero*.[6] Nevertheless, even if the *Vespasian* provides a parallel to *Galba* 1 in this

---

1 The eight book-divisions of Kaster's (2016a) OCT are based on the evidence of the Suda (τ 895), for which see Roth 1858, xi–xii, 283. Casaubon conjectured in 1595 that since the last six *Lives* are much shorter than the first six, Books 7 and 8 must have contained three *Lives* each; see Ihm 1907, vii. This results in eight books of relatively comparable length. Garrett 2015, 110–11 n. 2 tries to distinguish her own argument from the original version of this chapter, first published in 2009, which demonstrated the programmatic function of the ancestry section of the *Tiberius* (1–4), but I hardly claimed that its prologue is not also 'tailored to that Caesar', or that it is merely 'a generic Claudian introduction', as she puts it.
2 Syme 1958, 501; see also 779–80. The idea that the last six *Lives* were not part of Suetonius' original design has been accepted by e.g. Townend 1982b, 1053.
3 Syme 1980a, 117–18 = *RP* 3.1264–5; 1981, 117 = *RP* 1348–9.
4 Wallace-Hadrill 1983, 62 n. 14 without discussion; Murison 1992, 24: 'This chapter could equally well have served as a postscript to the *Life* of Nero.' Bradley 1998, 16–17, however, rejects the notion in passing in his introduction to the revised Loeb. Yet, Bradley's mention of it at all is a testament to the influence of Syme's opinion.
5 Bowersock 1969, anticipated by Paratore 1950, 743; cf. id. 2007, 207 n. 83.
6 Bradley 1973; *pace* Pausch 2004, 252–8. On Bowersock's theory, see also the discussion of Baldwin 1983, 468–91.

way, any presumed knowledge in the latter could equally be accounted for if it were the last chapter of the *Nero*. In light of the seemingly anomalous nature of *Galba* 1 and the conflicting theories on its composition, a re-evaluation is justified. In this paper, I shall argue that the passage was written specifically as the beginning of the *Galba* by examining the structural unity that it creates within the triad of biographies (*Galba, Otho,* and *Vitellius*) that probably comprises Suetonius' seventh book, to which it functions as a prologue.

The way in which *Galba* 1 may be read as a prologue to the *Galba, Otho,* and *Vitellius* emerges from a comparison of how Suetonius begins his other *Lives*. The biographer customarily begins with the section on ancestry, introducing each new genealogical tree or branch with the word *gens* ('family'), which is his standard first heading: *gentem Octauiam* (*Aug.* 1.1); *patricia gens Claudia* (*Tib.* 1.1); *ex gente Domitia* (*Ner.* 1.1); *gens Flauia* (*Vesp.* 1.1). In some cases, this account of ancestry frames the following three *Lives*: for example, *Tib.* 1–4, on which Suetonius also builds his *Caligula* and *Divine Claudius*; and *Vesp.* 1, which provides the most convenient parallel to our passage, since it contains the section on ancestry for the three short biographies of Book 8 (*Divine Vespasian, Divine Titus,* and *Domitian*) and also begins with a reference to the preceding book.[7] However, in comparing these other beginnings, we can immediately notice that the *Galba* is unique, commencing not with a family's origin, but with one's demise. Furthermore, the family whose extinction it marks is not that of the biography's subject, but rather an entirely different one: the emperor's own ancestry is postponed until the next two chapters (*Galb.* 2–3), hence Syme's desire to read *Galba* 1 as an ending to the *Nero*. How then does the beginning of the *Galba* unify the entire book?

For the emperors of Book 7, Suetonius had no common family background on which to build and therefore unified the book through contrast rather than similarity. The *Galba* begins with a family that has already died out, which then calls for three accounts of new ancestries (*Galb.* 2–3, *Otho* 1, and *Vit.* 1–3.1). The predication of these sections concerned with ancestry on the prologue of the *Galba* is made clear from the transition that directly follows it: 'Galba succeeded Nero and was *related in no degree* to the household of the Caesars, but was undoubtedly of the highest birth and from great ancient *stock*' (*Neroni Galba successit,* nullo gradu contingens *Caesarum domum sed haud dubie nobilissimus magnaque et uetere* prosapia, *Galb.* 2). Flory brings out well the consistency of theme in these two chapters:

> Suetonius tells us about the omen of the hen and laurel at the beginning of the life of Galba, emphasizing the ... impact of the end of Augustus' line on the Romans. Then he goes on to describe how Galba 'nullo

---

7 For *Vespasian* 1 as a prologue to Book 8, see Braithwaite 1927, 19; for its similarity to *Galba* 1 in alluding to the previous *Life*, Bradley 1973, 257–8.

gradu contingens Caesarum domum' – set up his own family stemma in the atrium of the palace and claimed he was the descendent of Jupiter and Pasiphaë, daughter of the Sun (*Gal.* 2). He created, in other words, a divine family line to rival that of his predecessors.[8]

This thematic link of a break in hereditary succession is underscored in the second chapter not only by the detail of Galba setting up a new *stemma* ('family tree') in the palace atrium but also by the absence of the word *gens*: Suetonius refers instead to the emperor's *prosapia*.[9] The first words of the *Otho* and *Vitellius* similarly deny the standard Suetonian heading and therefore also presuppose *Galba* 1: 'The *ancestors* of Otho' (maiores *Othonis, Otho* 1.1); 'The *origin* of the Vitellii' (*Vitelliorum* originem, *Vit.* 1.1). The use of these other words implies the same connection to the prologue as in *Galb.* 2, since Otho and Vitellius were also *nullo gradu contingens Caesarum domum*. The sections on ancestry in all three *Lives* therefore spring from *Galba* 1.[10]

Unity can be seen also in the correspondence of *Galba* 1 to the ending of Book 7.[11] The *Vitellius* (and thus the whole of Book 7) ends with an image that recalls the prologue of the *Galba*:

> periit cum fratre et filio anno uitae septimo quinquagesimo, nec fefellit coniectura eorum qui augurio quod factum ei Viennae ostendimus non aliud portendi praedixerant quam uenturum in alicuius Gallicani hominis potestatem, siquidem ab Antonio Primo aduersarum partium duce oppressus est, cui Tolosae nato cognomen in pueritia Becco fuerat: id ualet gallinacei rostrum.

> He died, along with his brother and son, in his fifty-seventh year of life, nor was the interpretation proved false of those who predicted from the portent that we have said befell him at Vienna simply that he was destined to come under the control of a Gaul. For he was slain by Antonius Primus, a general of the opposing party who was born at Tolosa and in childhood had the surname Becco, meaning rooster's beak.

(*Vit.* 18)

---

8 Flory 1989, 347.

9 Other words such as *prosapia*, *stirps*, *domus*, and especially *genus* (e.g. at *Galb.* 3.1) should not be construed as mere *uariatio* or as synonymous with *gens*; the latter is used exclusively to designate a Roman clan: see Rolfe 1915.

10 It has also been suggested by Baldwin 1983, 528, 541 that commencing with Livia may be a 'touch of subtle artistry', since Galba owed his rise to her *gratia* (*Galb.* 5.2), as did the grandfather of Otho (*Otho* 1.1). I should note too that the latter even grew up in her house.

11 Benediktson 1996–7, 170 sees a general correlation with the final chapter of the *Galba* (23): 'the Galba opens and closes with references to destruction of statues as symbolic of death.' However, Galba's statue was vetoed, not destroyed, and *damnatio memoriae* is symbolically different from an omen. References to the emperors' statues are also naturally common in the *Lives*; see Wardman 1967, 419.

Suetonius clarifies the significance of a portent as having foretold the manner of the emperor's death, since Vitellius' killer was from Tolosa, which was in Gaul, and moreover he used to be called 'Becco', which means *gallinacei rostrum*. The portent occurred earlier in the *Life*, and here Suetonius directs the reader with a rare first-person verb (*ostendimus*) to that section (*Vit.* 9), where the same three details appear as in the prologue of the *Galba* except in reverse order: the emperor's statues (*statuae*) crumbled with broken legs, his laurel (*laurea*) fell off, and a fowl (*gallinaceus*) landed on him. Now Suetonius adds the interpretation (punning on *gallus* as 'rooster' or 'Gaul')[12] of the last of these portents, which recalls the first of the prologue (gallinam ... *ramulum lauri* rostro *tenentem, Galb.* 1). The correlation is especially pronounced since these are the only two instances in Suetonius of the singular *rostrum* to mean literally a bird's 'beak'.[13] Suetonius' focus on the word *Becco* is therefore not simply an idiosyncratic interest of the author in etymology.[14] By drawing attention to a fowl's *rostrum* as the last word of the *Vitellius*, Suetonius gives closure to Book 7 by echoing its beginning.

In addition, the fact that Suetonius withholds this interpretation for nine chapters suggests not only its relevance to Vitellius' death but also a possible manipulation of sources to achieve unity with the prologue of the book. In framing the whole of Book 7 through the Caesars' laurel grove – a symbol of the divine power of the *gens Iulia*[15] – Suetonius emphasizes the lack of divine right of the three brief emperors of AD 69. We may draw a fitting comparison between our passage and *Vespasian* 1, which not only frames Book 8 by providing the section on ancestry for all three of its *Lives* but is also mirrored by the book's final passage (*Dom.* 23.2).[16] Another parallel is the beginning of Plutarch's *Galba* (1–2), which serves in a more formal way as a prologue not only to that *Life* but also to his *Otho* and probably his lost *Vitellius*, suggesting a similar book-division for these three biographies in Plutarch's *Lives of the Caesars*.[17] But perhaps the closest analogy is Plutarch's tendency in some of his *Lives* to fashion the first section, which often includes an account of ancestry, into what has been described by Stadter as an 'informal prologue' or by Duff as a 'proemial opening', which announces themes that are important in the rest of the *Life*.[18]

---

12 See Murison 1992, 152.
13 Howard and Jackson 1922, s.v. *rostrum*.
14 *Contra* Shotter 1993, 12.
15 Flory 1989, 355.
16 The two vices at the beginning of Book 8 (*cupiditatis ac saeuitiae, Vesp.* 1.1) contrast with the two virtues at the end (*abstinentia et moderatione, Dom.* 23.2); see Gorringe 1993, 502–4; cf. Baldwin 1983, 491 on *Dom.* 23.2 as 'an obvious pendant to the exordium of the Vespasian'. I should add that the beginning also mentions earlier emperors (*trium principum*), and the end later ones (*insequentium principum*).
17 Cf. Georgiadou 1988, 354–5; Duff 1999, 19–20; *pace* Stadter 2005, 420 = 2014, 56–7.
18 Stadter 1988. For a critique of Stadter's concept of informal prologues, see Duff 2008.

In conclusion, *Galba* 1 unifies both its own *Life* and the book that it begins by connecting the three emperors' lack of hereditary succession through the missing heading *gens*, which does not reappear until the 'seemingly drifting empire' (*quasi uagum imperium*) is finally stabilized by the *gens Flauia* (*Vesp.* 1.1). The prologue of Suetonius' *Galba* further unifies Book 7 through the recurrence of some of its details at the end of the *Vitellius* (18), which taken together with an earlier chapter to which it alludes (9) strongly echoes *Galba* 1. My conclusion lends credence to the view that Suetonius carefully structured his *Galba*, *Otho*, and *Vitellius* as a single book, and that the opening section is not out of place, since it conforms to the structure by which Suetonius unifies the rest of his *Caesars*. Although the biographies were probably written in order, it is unlikely that the passage was transferred from the end of the *Nero*, due to the structural unities that we have discussed. Moreover, *Galba* 1 is an appropriate beginning, establishing a theme that runs throughout the whole of Book 7 by announcing the single greatest cause of the civil wars of that year: 'The descendants of the Caesars ended with Nero.' The innovation of the passage can therefore be explained by its unique subject matter: the end of the Caesars' bloodline was the starting-point of a new era, as Tacitus has Galba himself declared in the first book of the *Histories* (1.16.1–2).

23 Vespasian's Sexual *Iliad*

utebatur et uersibus Graecis tempestiue satis, et de quodam procerae staturae improbiusque <u>uenato</u>:

μακρὰ βιβάς, κραδάων δολιχόσκιον ἔγχος.

uenato *Mooney*: nato *mss.*: irato *Torrentius*: uasato *Rutgers*: mutoniato *Heinsius*: nasato *Bernegger*: pedato *Perizonius*

He also used Greek verses aptly enough, and of someone of large stature and with an obscenely large <u>penis</u>:

Far-striding, waving a spear that casts a long shadow.

(*Vesp.* 23.1)

This line in Homer refers literally to the spear of Ajax (*Il.* 7.213). However, in its new context, the line provides a direct Suetonian parallel to the same kind of sexual pun on Homer as we find earlier in the *Caesars* in the biography of Galba; like the servants in that scene, Vespasian plays on the *topos* of *militia amoris*.[1] Editors of this passage almost universally agree on two points. Firstly, because of the context of physicality suggested by 'large stature' (*procerae staturae*) and the comparison not only with mighty Ajax – who in Homer's *Iliad* has an incredibly huge body (*Il.* 3.226–7), and is the most impressive Greek in the strength of his appearance and capabilities after Achilles (*Il.* 17.279–80) – but also with that hero's long-shadowing spear (δολιχόσκιον ἔγχος) in particular, the quotation must be some kind of euphemistic joke about the male member, especially since weapons in the ancient world were often seen as symbolically phallic.[2] Secondly, the text as we have it does not support this double entendre, since the manuscripts'

---

1 See above, Chapter 16.
2 On the use of military weapons as phallic imagery, see Adams 1982, 19–22. An exception is Torrentius, who instead conjectured *irato* ('angered'). Perizonius' suggestion of *pedato* ('footed'), which is a word found in the *Otho* (12.1), might be taken as having a sexual implication within the context of the present passage. For a few tenuous defences of the manuscript reading *nato* as non-sexual, see the scholars cited by Mooney 1930, 457.

word *nato* ('born') cannot quite be made to mean 'endowed', even if *impro-bius* might seem to mean 'gigantically'. Hence, Kaster has emended *nato*, which had been retained by Ihm, into Mooney's awkward hapax *uenato* ('penisèd') in his OCT of Suetonius.[3]

But either way, whether Suetonius meant 'well-endowed' or 'having a huge penis', it ruins the joke, because to make explicit what the pun in the Homeric quotation to come will be, before it is quoted, would be to steal the joke's humour. Suetonius does not usually undermine his own punch-lines. On the contrary, he can occasionally even be somewhat subtle in his sexual references, as when he writes that Nero was 'dispatched by his spear-carrier' (*conficeretur a Doryphoro*, *Ner.* 29),[4] or evokes the idea of an erection by stating that Galba wanted Icelus to 'arouse himself at once' (*sine mora ... oratum*, *Galb.* 22). Moreover, when he does directly refer to male private parts, he prefers the word *inguen* in either the singular (*Tib.* 44.1) or the plural (*Ner.* 29, *Dom.* 17.1), which was generally used in Latin literature,[5] or else *obscena* (*Calig.* 58.3, *Dom.* 10.5). We should also expect a present active participle, rather than a perfect passive participle such as *uenato*, in parallel with Homer's κραδάων. In place of our paradosis *impro-biusque nato*, let us therefore read *improbiusque quatiente* ('and thrusting rather obscenely'). A huge man performing a lewd gesture through a repet-itive motion, implying a pantomime of the sexual act, would more sensibly have suggested Vespasian's Homeric tag. When taken this way, *improbus* does not signify the meaning that has long been presumed: 'Immoderate in size' (*OLD* 6a). Instead, it must be construed as 'shameless in one's sexual desires or behaviour, immodest, wanton' (*OLD* 7). The word is often used in the latter sense by love poets, so that Vespasian's Homeric quotation, like Galba's, is given an amatory context, whereby Suetonius once again sexualizes Homer.[6] The verb *quatio* literally means to 'move vigorously to and fro' (*OLD* 1a), and significantly, it can also sometimes mean to 'shake threateningly (a weapon or sim.); brandish' (*OLD* 1c), much like the verb κραδαίνω in the Greek quotation.

Paleographically, the *quatie-* in <*quatie*>*nte* was absorbed into the ending *-que* of *improbiusque*, by a similar logic to the haplography of *ue-* in the conjecture *uenato* for *nato* that was proposed by Mooney. This leaves us with the unintelligible remnant *nte*, which could easily be mistaken for, or corrected to, *nato* by a later scribe. The conjecture *uenato* for *nato* ren-ders Vespasian's joke too crude and obvious within the scene; on the other hand, when *quatiente* is accepted, one perhaps needs a little more thought to comprehend the humour, yet it is wittier and more pleasing, with the sexual innuendo saved for the punchline of the Greek quotation. According

3 See his discussion in Kaster 2016c, 247–8.
4 For the sexual interpretation of this line, see above, pp. 152–3.
5 Adams 1982, 47.
6 On the elegiac use of this meaning of *improbus*, see Fantuzzi 2013, 164.

to this better interpretation, the man was waving his penis, just as Ajax waves his spear, and some verb of 'waving' is therefore clearly demanded. My conjecture is also more consistent with the subtly ironic way in which emperors tend to quote Homer and poetry more generally in the *Caesars*.[7] Although *quatio* is not attested elsewhere in Suetonius' works, he does use the related verb *quasso* (*Aug.* 81.2), and *quatiente* is at any rate more common Latin than the oddity *uenato*, which does not fully fix the sentence with the meaning that seems required. Ergo, *quatiente* is at least preferable to both *nato* and *uenato*.

Once accepted, my emendation renders Vespasian's quotation a much closer parallel to the Homeric quotation in the *Galba*, according to my interpretation of the latter as similarly ironic. It is not that the man whom Vespasian mocked was 'monstrously endowed' and thus depravedly complimented by the emperor.[8] Rather, it is quite the opposite: the emperor is portrayed by Suetonius as ridiculing the gesture, morally censuring the conduct as unacceptable like a good Roman leader. The comparative adverb *improbius* with regard to the man's action, as opposed to his penis, does not simply denote inordinate size but inordinate behaviour, which poorly matches the nobility of Ajax. The emperor is shown to be in fact paradoxically curbing such licentious behaviour through this vulgar witticism, and thus the anecdote contributes to Suetonius' generally favourable portrait of Vespasian. This jesting analogy with a Homeric hero is in no way contradicted by Suetonius' prefatory words *tempestiue satis* ('aptly enough'), since the Homeric line's ironic relation to the new context does not detract from its suitability, but is precisely what gives Vespasian's allusion its perfect timing.

---

7 For this tendency, see e.g. Aparicio 2008, 451; Mitchell 2015, 353; above, pp. 115, 118, 136–7.

8 *Pace* Milns 2010, 120, who thinks that such a compliment by the emperor would be 'brilliantly appropriate'. Berthet 1978, 326 oddly considers Vespasian's quotation to be 'hors-contexte', having no strong connection of either contrast or similarity to the Homeric passage.

24 Helvidius Priscus in Suetonius, *Domitian* 10.3*

complures senatores, in iis aliquot consulares, interemit, ex quibus Ciuicam Cerealem in ipso Asiae proconsulatu, Saluidienum Orfitum, Acilium Glabrionem <in> exilio, quasi molitores rerum nouarum, ceteros leuissima quemque de causa: Aelium Lamiam ob suspiciosos quidem uerum et ueteres et innoxios iocos, quod post abductam uxorem laudanti uocem suam 'eutacto' dixerat quodque Tito hortanti se ad alterum matrimonium responderat, μὴ καὶ σὺ γαμῆσαι θέλεις; Saluium Cocceianum quod Othonis imperatoris patrui sui diem natalem celebrauerat, Mettium Pompusianum quod habere imperatoriam genesim uulgo ferebatur et quod depictum orbem terrae in membrana contionesque regum ac ducum ex Tito Liuio circumferret quodque seruis nomina Magonis et Hannibalis indidisset, Sallustium Lucullum Britanniae legatum quod lanceas nouae formae appellari Luculleas passus esset, Iunium Rusticum quod Paeti Thraseae <u>et Heluidi Prisci laudes edidisset appellassetque</u> eos sanctissimos uiros, cuius criminis occasione philosophos omnis urbe Italiaque summouit.

et Heluidi Prisci laudes edidisset appellassetque *mss.*: et <Herennium Senecionem quod> Heluidi Prisci laudes edidisse<n>t appellasse<n>tque *Macé*

A number of senators, among them several ex-consuls, were slain by him, including Civica Cerealis while he was still proconsul of Asia, Salvidienus Orfitus, and the exiled Acilius Glabrio as conspirators for revolution; each of the rest on a most trivial charge: Aelius Lamia on account of jokes that were admittedly suspicious, but both made long ago and harmless, because after his wife was stolen from him, he had said to someone complimenting his voice, 'I practice abstinence', and because when Titus suggested he marry another woman, he had replied: 'You do not want a wife too, do you?'; Salvius Cocceianus on the grounds that he had celebrated the birthday of his paternal uncle, the emperor Otho; Mettius Pompusianus on the grounds that it was widely said that his horoscope predicted he would rule, and on the grounds that he carried around a map of the world on parchment and speeches of kings and generals from Titus Livius, and on the grounds that he

* This chapter was first published in *CP* 109 (2014), 79–82.

gave his servants the names Mago and Hannibal; Sallustius Lucullus, the governor of Britain, on the grounds that he had allowed lances of a new kind to be called 'Lucullean'; Junius Rusticus on the grounds that <u>he had published eulogies</u> of Paetus Thrasea <u>and Helvidius Priscus, and had called</u> them moral paragons; he took the opportunity of this accusation to banish all the philosophers from the city and Italy.

(Dom. 10.2–3)

It is usually thought that Suetonius nodded in this passage, attributing to Junius Rusticus a biographical work on the death of Helvidius Priscus that was in fact written by Herennius Senecio (cf. Plin. *Ep.* 7.19.5; Tac. *Agr.* 2.1; Dio 67.13.2).[1] A conjecture was long ago made by Macé that resolves the inconsistency, supplying the missing words *Herennium Senecionem quod,* which probably dropped out through homoearchon before *Heluidi.* He furthermore suggested that after this omission another scribe then 'corrected' the verbs from plural to singular.[2] Both errors would have occurred before our oldest existing manuscript was copied in the ninth century. The proposal was briefly cited by Ihm in his apparatus criticus and mentioned by both Rolfe and Kaster, but adopted by none of them, and the *Domitian*'s other editors (Ailloud, de Climent, Galli, and Jones) have also ignored it.[3] Macé's second proposed error seems unnecessary, since the single verbs could be construed elliptically, but the first part of his conjecture has much to speak for it. The text would be restored to mean that Domitian ordered the executions of, among many others, 'Junius Rusticus on the grounds that he had published a eulogy of Paetus Thrasea and had called him a moral paragon, and Herennius Senecio on the grounds that he had done so of Helvidius Priscus.'[4]

Two points can be made in favour of accepting this emendation. First, Suetonius' literary research was rigorous, and he was especially strong on bibliographical inventories, having already held the posts of *a bibliothecis* and *a studiis* by the time he was writing the *Caesars.*[5] It is from Suetonius alone that we learn, for example, of Aurelius Opillus' *Pinax (Gramm.* 6.3) and Augustus' *Sicilia (Aug.* 85.2). He is also the only one to tell us about Augustus' biography of Drusus *(Claud.* 1.5). Moreover, he is elsewhere knowledgeable about Priscus in particular, recording details about

1 See e.g. Wallace-Hadrill 1983, 58; Syme 1991, 583: 'The hasty and careless biographer'; Jones 1992, 187; id. and Milns 2002, 5; Haaland 2005, 303 n. 26. Suetonius was certainly not infallible on historical points; see Butler and Cary 1927, xii–xiii. Less plausible is the interpretation of Rudich (1993, 295) that these *laudes* were mere references in a single book by Rusticus. On Rusticus' work, see also Plin. *Ep.* 1.5.2–3.

2 Macé 1900, 413 n. 14.

3 Ihm 1907; Rolfe 1913–14; Kaster 2016a, citing an earlier version of the present chapter. See also Ailloud 1931–2; de Climent 1964–70; Galli 1991; Jones 1996.

4 On the meaning of *sanctissimos uiros,* see Ruhnken 1828, 368 (ad loc.).

5 Wallace-Hadrill 1983, 79–88. For some rare works known only to Suetonius, see above, pp. 43–4.

his death (*Vesp.* 15).[6] Is not a likely source for these details the well-known biographical work on Priscus' death by Senecio? Such *exitus* literature had become rather popular at Rome by Suetonius' day.[7] Second, the conjecture can be defended on stylistic grounds in light of the author's typically condensed style. This kind of correlative construction inside a subordinate clause, with parallel ideas being framed by a single verb, is characteristic of Suetonius. Take, for instance, the following sentence:

> sed et Vergili ac Titi Liui scripta et imagines paulum afuit quin ex omnibus bibliothecis amoueret, quorum *alterum ut nullius ingenii minimaeque doctrinae, alterum ut uerbosum in historia neglegentemque* carpebat.

> But he came close to removing from all libraries both the writings and statues of Virgil and Titus Livius, of whom he criticized *the one as being of no talent and the least erudition, the other as wordy and careless about history.*

> (*Calig.* 34.2)

Here, the repeated use of *alter* is similar to that of *quod* in Macé's conjecture, and the elliptical verb *carpebat* is omitted the first time in the same way as *edidisset appellassetque*, albeit with a single subject.[8] Thus, Suetonius withholds the verb until the end in his typical manner, achieving his usual compact brevity.[9] Rusticus and Senecio would have been categorized together in the list of Domitian's victims because they were both condemned for the same reason – the single accusation of both eulogies to which Suetonius' following *cuius criminis* refers; only the topics of their writing differed. Based on the sense called for in the passage, and Suetonius' tendency to merge similar items grammatically in his sentences, the conjecture *Herennium Senecionem quod* should be accepted, and Suetonius' alleged ignorance of *exitus* literature rejected.

---

6 It has been suggested by Jones (1986, 251 n. 24) that *Schol. Iuv.* 5.36 may even preserve a fragment of a lost biography of Priscus from Suetonius' *Illustrious Men*.

7 See e.g. Wallace-Hadrill 1983, 11; Edwards 2007, 131–6, 248–50. Suetonius often records the victims of emperors; see *Aug.* 13, *Tib.* 61, *Ner.* 37, *Dom.* 10–11, 15, with Jones 1992, 43, 187; 1996, 86–7; cf. id. and Milns 2002, 145. For an inversion of this category, see *Aug.* 51, where the emperor's small number of victims instead illustrates his mercy. On victims of the emperors, see also Lendon 1997, 118–19.

8 Cf. also e.g. *Gramm.* 3.2, *Aug.* 13.3, 51.1, *Tib.* 24.1, 61.3, *Calig.* 57.2, *Claud.* 13.1, 16.4, 20.1, 38.1, 42.2, *Ner.* 37.1. For other verbal ellipses in Suetonius, see e.g. *Claud.* 12.3, 15.1, with Hurley 2001, 110, 120 (ad locc.), respectively.

9 On the brevity of Suetonius' prose style, cf. e.g. above, p. 143.

Part IV
Suetonius and History

25 Suetonius' Tacitus*

One of the misconceptions that continue to haunt Suetonian scholarship is the notion that the biographer's *Lives of the Caesars* must in some way have been inspired by Tacitus, or have used the historian as a source. Naturally, Suetonius is often compared with Tacitus, usually to bring out their unique perspectives on the Roman emperors, and occasionally differences in the two writers' styles.[1] However, scholars have also long speculated on Suetonius' possible influence by Tacitus, whose last work, the *Annals*, seems to have been published at least in part by AD 118,[2] probably in time to have been consulted by Suetonius in advance of the publication of his *Caesars*, which occurred sometime between AD 119 and 122.[3] Yet, more space has been devoted to discussion of Tacitus in books and commentaries on Suetonius than is warranted by the evidence, and he should perhaps not be mentioned at all except as a representative of the historiographical genre and a parallel author who drew on the same sources.[4] The problem is that our estimation of Tacitus is increased by the loss of so much other ancient literature on the early imperial period, and the history of the Caesars has become indistinguishable to us from Tacitus, much like the Peloponnesian War was to the ancients from Thucydides.[5]

* This chapter was first published in *JRS* 104 (2014), 205–25.

1 For stylistic comparisons, see e.g. Ektor 1980, 317–26; Mouchová 1986–7; 1991, 95–6, 99; Bayer 2002, 43–5; Oakley 2009b, 206–11; Damon 2014, 44–6, 49–50. Translations of the *Caesars* and *Annals* in this chapter are taken from the Loeb editions of Rolfe 1913–14 and Hutton et al. 1914–37, respectively.

2 For this date, see Goodyear 1981, 393, but the matter is controversial; cf. Birley 2000, 242–7.

3 On the publication date of Suetonius' *Caesars*, see Power 2014a, 76–7; above, p. 17.

4 For Tacitus as a parallel author who used common sources, see e.g. Syme 1958, 674–6; Shotter 1993, 33–5; Murison 1999, 12–17; Damon 2003, 22–30; Champlin 2008, 418–19; Potter 2012, 131–4.

5 On distinguishing whether an allusion is to an historical event or its literary treatment, see Levene 2010, 85; Pelling 2013b, 3–4 with bibliography. For the little difference at times between allusion and mere stylistic imitation in the case of ancient historical writers, see Oakley 2020, 203.

We must be careful when assessing Suetonius' broad and programmatic contrast with historiography, which he states as writing *neque per tempora sed per species* ('not in chronological order, but by classes', *Aug.* 9), to use Tacitus only as an example, among others, of that genre's conventions, rather than taking Suetonius to be engaging directly with Tacitus. However, this error of exaggerating the importance of Tacitus in studies of Suetonius has unfortunately been committed by scholars to the point where the biographer's entire project has been recast in terms of Tacitus. This recasting has compelled scholars such as Lindsay to muse on whether Suetonius included Julius Caesar in his collection to fill a gap left by Tacitus,[6] or Hurley to ponder the possibility that the biographer's account of the death of Nero is so lengthy because it completes, as it were, a last part of the *Annals*, which Tacitus may have died writing.[7] It has even been proposed by one of Suetonius' translators that his *per species* method may be due to competition with Tacitus, and one recent commentator suggests that the same reason may possibly lie behind Suetonius' greater research for the period of the foundation of the Principate.[8] This is not to mention the arguments for allusions to lost books of Tacitus, where the reconstruction of the original text is suspect,[9] or those *ex silentio*, such as Baldwin's suggestion that Agricola and Verginius Rufus are avoided by Suetonius because they are particularly Tacitean themes.[10]

Suetonius is frequently held to be 'supplementing' Tacitus in this way, that is, subtly correcting or one-upping him.[11] In this chapter, I shall first trace the origin of this viewpoint, which may be found in a 1967 argument

---

6 Lindsay 1993, 4–5. For more profitable discussions of Suetonius' decision to include Julius Caesar, see e.g. Pelling 2009, 253–4; Rohrbacher 2009, 712; Henderson 2014; Wardle 2014, 8–9.

7 Hurley 2013, 40–1. This argument is weak least of all because there is no way to know that Tacitus did not finish and publish the *Annals* in its entirety, including the death of Nero.

8 See, respectively, Edwards 2000, xv; Osgood 2011, xxiii-xxiv. With the latter, cf. Hurley 2011, xix-xx. For a better explanation of Suetonius' biographical form, see Power 2014b, 4–14; and of the biographer's concentration on this period, including his naming of sources, above, pp. 43–4; cf. Fantham 2013c, 189.

9 Luck 1964, 75; Townend 1967, 89; Gascou 1984, 690; Hurley 2001, 9, n. 33, 74, 189, cf. 102.

10 Baldwin 1979a, 104–5 = 1983, 72 = 1989b, 15–16; cf. Syme 1980a, 123 = *RP* 3.1270, pointing also to Corbulo's absence. However, Baldwin is elsewhere more circumspect; see references below, n. 15. Suetonius generally marginalizes or excludes secondary figures; cf. SHA, *Quad. Tyr.* 1.1–2, with e.g. Townend 1964, 351.

11 See also e.g. Bird 1973; Cizek 1977, 46 n. 80; Wallace-Hadrill 1983, 1–2, 8–10, 111–12 n. 15; Birley 1984, 249; 1997, 96; Gascou 1984, 284, 292, 345, 542, 776; Momigliano 1984, 1147 = 1987, 394; Hurley 1989, 325–7; 1993, 26; Lindsay 1993, 54; Mellor 1993, 138; 2011, 196; Barrett 1996, 204–5; Whittaker 2000; Baltussen 2002, 33, 39; Sharrock and Ash 2002, 365; Damon 2003, 24 n. 21; Devillers 2003, 221–2; Longrée 2003, 315; Ash 2009, xxx; Martin 2009, 83–4; O'Gorman 2011, 293; Fantham 2013b, 160; Curry 2014, 212.

by Townend for three subtle allusions to the *Annals*, as well as in the earlier description by Syme of Suetonius' relationship to the historian as that of a 'supplement'. Identifying this origin is especially necessary because there is often an unstated acceptance of the theory of Tacitean corrections in Suetonius, which is thought to have been proven viable long ago, and few scholars take the time to investigate, or even cite, its basis. The effects of Townend's argument in particular continue to be felt because it has never been systematically refuted. As groundwork for this refutation, appeal will be made to more current models for the practice of allusion in ancient texts. I shall then go through the allusions proposed by Townend one by one in the second part of this chapter, to show how they do not in fact constitute a sufficient basis for the probability that Suetonius alludes to Tacitus. In the third part, conclusions will be drawn that suggest a new understanding of Suetonius' task as a biographer.

Previous Scholarship

More than fifty years ago, Townend put forth an interpretation of Suetonius that continues to influence the way that the biographer's works are read by scholars. On the one hand, Townend, like Syme, had earlier conceded that there was no solid support for Suetonius' direct borrowing from Tacitus:

> Syme is surely right in his conclusions that there is no positive evidence that Suetonius used either the *Annals* or the *Histories* ... Suetonius recognized the double unsuitability of employing Tacitus for his own work. In the first place, borrowings from the *Annals* would require much more thorough assimilation than he normally allowed his material, if they were not to stand out from the non-descript style of the *Caesars*; and secondly he was well aware of the cavalier use Tacitus had made of sources which might more safely be used at first hand.[12]

On the other hand, both scholars still believe that Suetonius must have been acquainted with Tacitus' historical works. Take the rather different tack of Townend in his most famous paper, in which he offered what is still the most forceful argument to date for implicit criticisms of Tacitus by Suetonius:

> if Suetonius irritates modern readers ... it is because they are hoping to use him as an historical source, to provide a factual account of the events of such-and-such an emperor's reign. This is not, of course, how Suetonius intended his *Lives* to be read. He could hardly have dreamed that an age would come when readers lacked even certain books of

---

12 Townend 1959, 285.

Tacitus' *Annals* and *Histories*, not to mention the less-brilliant historical works of Aufidius Bassus and the elder Pliny.[13]

To some extent, Townend's argument is in the right spirit, but there is no doubt that it goes too far by claiming Suetonius' familiarity with Tacitus' *Annals*. Compare the provocative comments by Syme, in which the word 'supplement' first appears in a prominent discussion of Suetonius:

> Suetonius estimated correctly the taste and market of the times. Readers were drawn to the personal items that formal history disdained. There was room for a rival or supplement to the *Annales* – and the chronicle of ancient folly and depravity, compiled by a government official, carried no political danger.[14]

Syme and Townend are certainly correct to assume that Suetonius was familiar with the history of the period that he covered, and expected his readers to be, especially since he regularly omits so much historical material that could be considered commonly known by educated Romans. However, the idea that he relied specifically on Tacitus in any way has never been proven, and until it can be proven it is a dangerous proposition, relegating Suetonius' *Caesars* to the less important office of being a mere 'supplement' to Tacitus, rather than a work that stands on its own. The implications of this view for the study and interpretation of Suetonius are considerable, and so this point should not be taken lightly. Prudence on the matter of Suetonius and Tacitus could always be found among sober-minded scholars,[15] but these voices of scepticism have not been the most heeded.

For example, Wallace-Hadrill's book on Suetonius, which has long been considered the standard introduction to the author among Anglophone readers, makes much of this notion that Suetonius was a follower, rather than equal, of Tacitus:

> Rather than let biography become history, he would write not-history ... history for him was what Tacitus wrote. He had no reason not to admire it. Written by one who understood public life as it was traditionally defined, devastating in its exposé of the springs of human action

---

13 Id. 1967, 84. This paper's influence is wider than its acknowledged use, but for citations by adherents still in the present century, see e.g. Edwards 2000, xxviii n. 32; Whittaker 2000, 103 n. 20; Baltussen 2002, 33 n. 14. For precursors of Townend's theory, see e.g. Lehmann 1858, 40–7; Macé 1900, 179; Haverfield 1916, 198; Harrer 1918, 342–3; Braithwaite 1927, xiv; Della Corte 1958, 118–39; Questa 1963, 109–23.

14 Syme 1958, 502, cf. 689. However, Syme is elsewhere more sceptical on the matter; see ibid. 689–91, 781–2.

15 E.g. Heeren 1820, 189; Goodyear 1972, 135–6, 167–8; 1982, 663; Bradley 1978, 287; Baldwin 1983, 151–2, 178, 191–2; von Albrecht 1997, 1393; Pettinger 2012, 177–8 n. 28, 217; Cornell 2013a, 127–8; Duchêne 2016, 281, 283.

and stylistically a self-conscious masterpiece, it could hardly be rivalled on its own terms. Suetonius was too modest or honest to challenge Tacitus. But there was still room for a supplement. As a man of learning and a servant of Caesars, he had something to add.[16]

Townend's argument for occasional corrections of Tacitus in the *Caesars* and Syme's passing denunciation of the work as a less austere version of the *Annals* have here melded into the more developed view that Suetonian biography was actually modelled as an inversion of Tacitus. For Wallace-Hadrill, 'not-history' means 'not-Tacitus', but the argument would otherwise lack controversy: ancient historians and biographers used sources in some of the same ways, at times sharing much of the same material and being somewhat close in purpose, so that distinctions often had to be made through mutual contrast.[17] There is certainly validity in comparing Suetonius with Tacitus, the major extant example of the historiographical tradition from the same era, but the danger is in eliding that tradition with Tacitus' unique writing, a fine line which has certainly been crossed in these discussions. This is the difference that I mentioned above between using Tacitus as a source for Suetonius and using him simply as a representative annalist or a parallel author with sources in common, that is, between allusion and source-criticism. The latter remains a useful way to contrast the two writers' styles, as well as to draw wider conclusions about the unique natures of ancient historiography and biography.

Another distinction should here be made between two different kinds of intertextuality. While some scholars have certainly argued for direct borrowings by Suetonius from Tacitus for particular phrases and details,[18] there is another layer of criticism, inaugurated by Townend and followed by Wallace-Hadrill, which supports a belief that Suetonius was merely double-checking with Tacitus or 'supplementing' him, while still relying on earlier first-century material, as we have already discussed. In other words,

16 Wallace-Hadrill 1983, 9–10; cf. Goodyear 1982, 663: 'he never attempted to vie with writers of major history'; also Hurley 1989, 325; 2001, 8–9; Edwards 2000, xiii–xv; Pausch 2004, 271–3; Ash 2007, 30 n. 84; Konstan and Walsh 2016, 32. A similar contrast with biography too in Suetonius is implied by Konstan 2009, 459, who draws partly on Wallace-Hadrill's argument, which concludes that Suetonius is ultimately '*sui generis*'; see esp. Wallace-Hadrill 1983, 66–72 (quotation at 72). Cf. the next note.

17 See esp. Gascou 1984, with Wallace-Hadrill 1986. On Wallace-Hadrill's phrase as meaning 'not-Tacitus', cf. Tatum 2014, 164. For defining Suetonius by contrast, see also Henderson 1989, 168: 'imperial hagiography and its bend sinister, the Suetonian *Vita*'. Against the view of Suetonius as a 'tabloid Tacitus', see Sharrock and Ash 2002, 365. On biography's proximity to, and distinctions from, history in antiquity, see Power 2014b, 1–3, 13.

18 E.g. Gascou 1984, 254 n. 2; Brugnoli 1985, 330, 334; Delarue 1995, 299–300; Lindsay 1995b, 10–11; Woodman 2009d, 36 = 2012, 248; Levick 2012, 276; Ash 2016, 210–11; cf. De Temmerman 2016, 25.

according to Townend's view, a less obvious competition with the historian may exist on top of their shared use of common sources. The weakness of this argument lies in its lack of tangible evidence, since more recent models for allusion would reduce this case to being pointless speculation without at least one solid allusion (or external testimony for one author's acquaintance with the other's text). While it would be astonishing if Suetonius was not aware of Tacitus the man, especially when one considers their shared friendship with Pliny the Younger,[19] whether he actually read his historical works is another, unattested matter – especially since authors of the same time whom we might expect to have been familiar with each other sometimes wrote independently, despite mutual acquaintances. Even Townend's delicate argument for more implicit engagement with Tacitus must have a basis on which to build; otherwise, the belief that Suetonius read him would be nothing more than *a priori* assumption: 'he simply *must have* read Tacitus', '*surely* he read Tacitus', '*of course* he did, if Pliny did', and so on.

Before subtler Tacitean allusions can be cogently detected in Suetonius, a connection between the two authors must first be established to anchor the argument. Since there is no explicit mention of Tacitus' *Annals* by Suetonius (or other external testimony), this connection must come in the form of a clear allusion. Recent scholarship on allusion shows that the criteria for establishing such an anchoring allusion may be stated as follows: there must be (i) a contextual similarity or (ii) a textual echo – be it verbal, positional, or rhythmical; and the certainty of the allusion is determined by the uniqueness and extent of these connections, so long as they cannot be explained by a common source or *topos*.[20] The presence of (i) alone can occasionally be sufficient,[21] but clear evidence of (ii) removes practically all doubt. Cumulative cases can only stand if the author's familiarity with the text alluded to is already somehow certain, or if a solid allusion has already been established.[22] As Momigliano put it, when he argued

---

19 Mackail 1895, 230; Syme 1958, 502; 1980a, 111–12 = 1984, 1258–9; Warmington 1999, xi; Wardle 1994, 44. Pliny's statements that the *Histories* was an 'eternal' (*aeternitas*, *Ep.* 6.16.2) and 'immortal' (*immortales*, *Ep.* 7.33.1) work are made in letters to Tacitus himself, where effusiveness could be expected, and Tacitus' influence on later antiquity was at any rate minimal; cf. Whitton 2012, 347; Rutledge 2014, xiii; *pace* Benario 2012, 103, whose view that Pliny's opinion echoes 'the response of the reading public to the work' is unconvincing. Suetonius' estimation of literature differed from Pliny's on several points, not the least important of which was the biographer's favouring of earlier eras; see Gibson 2014.

20 Wills 1996, 18. Cf. Syme 1958, 690; Hinds 1998, 25–6; Bosworth 2004, 551 n. 1; Kelly 2008, 166–9; Gibson 2011, 189–93; also above, pp. 20, 122; below, n. 23.

21 See e.g. Trinacty 2009, 271–2; Baldwin 2010, 459–60.

22 Cf. Ash 1997b, 46; Kelly 2008, 170. For the fallacious view that the quantity of alleged allusions is in itself significant, see e.g. Whitton 2019a, 85, discussing various uncertain reminiscences of Quintilian in Pliny the Younger: 'these are just two of *seven or eight* close similarities in short space. Coincidence? Surely not'; 248: 'even the most recalcitrant

against Syme's fanciful attempt to prove the *Augustan History*'s use of Ammianus, many bad allusions do not add up to one good one.[23] As I shall argue, the argument of Townend is weak even as a cumulative case, and would remain so, however many even subtler allusions we combined with it.

Alleged Allusions

Scrutiny of Townend's three allusions reveals how the perception that Suetonius is doing very uncharacteristic things in these passages is misguided, and even the *semblance* of polemic with Tacitus is more convincingly explained in other ways. Although these three allusions may seem few, they are the strongest and most compelling passages that have been put forth for allusion to Tacitus in Suetonius. Not only have they found the widest acceptance, but they have also inspired countless other lesser arguments. According to our model for allusion above, one clear case of allusion must be independently established for others to be in any way valid. Our best bet for such a case, therefore, is among these three originally proposed allusions. If we cannot establish one of Townend's allusions as distinct in its own right, then all subsequent arguments fall.

Let us take the alleged allusions in order of appearance. The first occurs when the biographer refutes the belief that Augustus chose Tiberius to succeed him merely to throw his own good deeds into sharp relief:[24]

---

recusant will struggle to explain them *all* away as accident'; 266 n. 72: 'the little echoes cannot *all* be accident'; cf. 57 n. 197 in a different context of allusion: 'surely not *all* inadvertent' (my emphases). In fact, Whitton's (2019a; cf. id. 2013, 111; 2018a, 153–5; 2018b, 49–57) entire book seems an undisciplined and over-subtle exercise in just such a cumulative case, since as he himself admits (2019a, 32–3), most readers presume that Pliny in his *Letters* had been influenced by discussions with his former teacher – a sort of common source, in this case – which explains much shared material between them, but scholars have not averred his direct knowledge of Quintilian's published work, the *Institutio oratoria*, due to a lack of proof. I count a total of eighty-five uses of the word 'surely' in Whitton's book, which is to say nothing of the phrase 'to be sure', which appears another thirty times, but an allusive relationship between these two classical texts is by no means assured. For a similarly unfruitful comparison between Apollonius of Rhodes and Herodotus, see Morrison 2020, although he at least concedes (2–5, 17–22) that the poet may actually be engaging with historiography more broadly, rather than with Herodotus in particular. Indeed, there is no strong evidence for Apollonius' direct acquaintance with this historian, despite some general parallels between their works; see e.g. Clauss 1983, 83; *pace* Priestley 2014, 147–55.

23 Syme 1968, 69–71, 94–103; *contra*, Momigliano 1968–9, 429 = 1975, 98; cf. den Hengst 2009, 96–7; above, pp. 131–2.

24 An allusion to Tacitus is perceived here by Townend 1967, 89; 1982b, 1054; Edwards 2000, xxviii; Hurley 2001, 74; Shotter 2008, 9.

ne Tiberium quidem caritate aut rei publicae cura successorem adsci-
tum, sed quoniam adrogantiam saeuitiamque eius introspexerit, comparatione deterrima sibi gloriam quaesiuisse. etenim Augustus paucis
ante annis, cum Tiberio tribuniciam potestatem a patribus rursum pos-
tularet, quamquam honora oratione quaedam de habitu cultuque et
institutis eius iecerat, quae uelut excusando exprobraret.

Even in the adoption of Tiberius to succeed him, his motive had been
neither personal affection nor regard for the state: he had read the pride
and cruelty of his heart, and had sought to heighten his own glory by
the vilest of contrasts. For Augustus, a few years earlier, when requesting the Fathers to renew the grant of the tribunician power to Tiberius,
had in the course of the speech, complimentary as it was, let fall a few
remarks on his demeanor, dress, and habits which were offered as an
apology and designed for reproaches.

(*Ann.* 1.10.7)

scio uulgo persuasum quasi egresso post secretum sermonem Tiberio
uox Augusti per cubicularios excepta sit, 'miserum populum R., qui
sub tam lentis maxillis erit.' ne illud quidem ignoro *aliquos tradidisse*
Augustum palam nec dissimulanter morum eius diritatem adeo im-
probasse ut nonnumquam remissiores hilarioresque sermones superu-
eniente eo abrumperet, sed expugnatum precibus uxoris adoptionem
non abnuisse uel etiam ambitione tractum ut tali successore desiderabilior ipse quandoque fieret. adduci tamen nequeo quin existimem
circumspectissimum et prudentissimum principem in tanto praesertim
negotio nihil temere fecisse, sed uitiis Tiberi uirtutibusque perpensis
potiores duxisse uirtutes, praesertim cum et rei p. causa adoptare se
eum pro contione iurauerit et epistulis aliquot ut peritissimum rei mil-
itaris utque unicum p. R. praesidium prosequatur. ex quibus in exemplum pauca hinc inde subieci ...

I know that it is commonly believed, that when Tiberius left the room
after this confidential talk, Augustus was overheard by his chamber-
lains to say: 'Alas for the Roman people, to be ground by jaws that
crunch so slowly!' I also am aware that *some have written* that Augustus so openly and unreservedly disapproved of his austere manners, that
he sometimes broke off his freer and lighter conversation when Tiberius
appeared; but that overcome by his wife's entreaties he did not reject his
adoption, or perhaps was even led by selfish considerations, that with
such a successor he himself might one day be more regretted. But after
all I cannot be led to believe that an emperor of the utmost prudence
and foresight acted without consideration, especially in a matter of so
great moment. It is my opinion that after weighing the faults and the
merits of Tiberius, he decided that the latter preponderated, especially

since he took oath before the people that he was adopting Tiberius for the good of the country, and alludes to him in several letters as a most able general and the sole defence of the Roman people. In illustration of both these points, I append a few extracts from these letters ...

(*Tib.* 21.2–3)

Although Suetonius sometimes likes to generalize from specific instances, turning singulars into plurals and characterizing events in such a way as possibly to suggest that they occurred more than once,[25] there is reason to think that *aliquos tradidisse* does not refer to Tacitus, even if it masks a single source. For one thing, Suetonius reports details that were unknown to Tacitus about Augustus' opinion of Tiberius, such as the exclamation that he quotes, which no doubt would have been found in the same source as the theory about Augustus' more self-serving motive.[26]

For another thing, where the two writers do overlap, Suetonius seems clearly not to echo Tacitus, but to have rephrased whatever lost historical writer he is following in his usual matter-of-fact style (*ut tali successore desiderabilior ipse quandoque fieret*), just as Tacitus does in his more flamboyant language (*comparatione deterrima sibi gloriam quaesiuisse*). It is usually assumed that when Suetonius and a parallel author diverge, despite his uniform prose style, the biographer is generally closer to the common source and preserves its diction,[27] but it is equally possible that

---

25 Although this ambiguous use of the plural renders history less precise, it is by no means dishonest, but arises from the genre of biography itself, where the author is more likely to use events to discuss topics or types of characterizing behaviour: instead of stating, for example, that an emperor once killed a prisoner, a biographer might list 'killing prisoners' as one of the things that he did, which is merely another way of putting what is still factually true. See e.g. *Tib.* 30 (cf. Tac. *Ann.* 1.52.2), *Tib.* 51.2 (*Ann.* 6.10.1), *Tib.* 61.4 (*Ann.* 6.40.1), *Tib.* 61.5 (*Ann.* 5.9.3), with Wiseman 1979, 57–8; Woodman 2017, 74, 254; *Tib.* 36 (Joseph. *AJ* 18.84; *Ann.* 2.85.5), with Williams 1989, 772–3 = 2013, 69–70; Woods 2019, 236 n. 4; *Tib.* 39–40 (*Ann.* 4.57–59.2), with Woodman 2018, 269; *Tib.* 61.2 (*Ann.* 4.70.1–3), with Damon 2020, 127; *Calig.* 52 (Dio 59.17.3; Aur. Vict. *Caes.* 3.11–12), with Woods 2018b, 427–8; *Claud.* 24.3 (*Ann.* 11.20.3), with Malloch 2013, 299–300; *Ner.* 30.2 (Tac. *Ann.* 11.20.2; Dio 60.30.5), with Bradley 1978, 166–7 (ad loc.); Suet. *Otho* 7.1 (Plut. *Otho* 3.2), with *FRHist* 3.619 (on Cluvius Rufus fr. 4b = Suet. loc. cit.; cf. Levick 2013, 556 n. 38); cf. below, p. 226. See also Townend 1959, 289; Pauw 1980, 91–3; Syme 1981, 115 = 1984, 1347; Baldwin 1983, 256–7; Kaster 1995, 354, 359; Westall 2016, 60–1.

26 Cf. Goodyear 1972, 167; Lindsay 1995b, 103.

27 For the tendency to presume that Suetonius is closer to the common source, see e.g. Harrer 1918, 343; D'Anna 1954, 208; Grant 1954, 118–19; 1970, 338; Carney 1963, 5; Wardman 1967, 418; Goodyear 1970, 27–8; Ektor 1980, 325; Townend 1982a, xv; Hurley 2001, vii, 17; Bellandi 2006, 637 n. 11; Ripat 2006, 167–8; Ash 2007, 303; Shotter 2008, 10; Woods 2009, 73 n. 1; 2018, 874 n. 4, 877–9; Rodeghiero 2012, 113 n. 1; Damon 2018, 125. Cf. also Duff 1960, 508: 'Compared with Tacitus, he is as a photograph to a picture or a finished engraving'; Goodyear 1982, 663: 'pillage rather than innovation'; Garrett 2018a, 65: 'careful curation of material'.

this Suetonian line constitutes no less an independent and unique revision than Tacitus' does. Suetonius was certainly capable of drawing a sentiment from the earlier first-century material and moulding it to suit his own ends. In fact, he occasionally chose as his raw material the same verdict on an emperor in his source as Plutarch and Tacitus, which took on a different form in each of their hands.[28] It seems that here Suetonius did something similar, responding with a critical view to the same originally hostile passage that Tacitus more approvingly included. Suetonius' version in fact seems to be closer to the truth, with Tacitus' sensationalistic claim finding no support in the historical realities of the time.[29]

Moreover, it is important to remember that, despite these tangents between them, both authors also creatively assimilated material from additional sources, which can be especially instructive with regard to their distinctive emphases.[30] Here the letters of Augustus on this matter, appended at length after the above quoted passage (*Tib.* 21.4–6), serve a higher agenda for the biographer. Those believing that Suetonius goes out of his way in an uncharacteristic manner to refute this theory about the Tiberian accession in large part because it is an opportunity to one-up Tacitus do not take into account the necessity of excusing Augustus' adoption of Tiberius if Suetonius is to maintain the positive portrayal of the previous biography.[31] The same mandate had necessitated the biographer's dismissal of the evil deeds of Octavian the triumvir (*Aug.* 27),[32] as well as his vices of sexual debauchery and gambling (*Aug.* 71.1). For Augustus to remain a programmatically good emperor in the *Caesars*, Suetonius must take pains to disprove the adoption as an object of criticism. Augustus' exemplary role in Suetonius' biographical collection therefore stands as a much more convincing reason for this digression than a polemical dialogue with Tacitus. Suetonius, after all, ultimately viewed the Principate created by Augustus as a blessing, while Tacitus viewed it more sceptically[33] – an

---

28 Cf. esp. Suet. *Galb.* 14.1 (~ Plut. *Galb.* 29.2; Tac. *Hist.* 1.49.4), with Damon 2003, 200–1; above, p. 126; Suet. *Otho* 12.1 (~ Plut. *Galb.* 25.2; Tac., *Hist.* 1.22.1), with Perkins 1993, 851; Morgan 2005, 581; Suet. *Otho* 12.2 (~ Plut. *Otho* 18.3; Tac. *Hist.* 2.50.1; Dio 64.15.22), with Potter 2012, 132; Power 2014a, 63 n. 8. See also more generally id. 2014b, 13.

29 See Stevenson 2013, 136–7.

30 Flach 1972, 289; Wilkes 1972, 180–1; Bradley 1978, 17–18; Gascou 1984, 317–26; Murison 1992, xii-xiii; Lewis 1993, 631–2; von Albrecht 1997, 1109.

31 This necessity is brought out by Osgood 2013, 20–3, 35–8.

32 See also McDermott 1972b, 496–7 on the suppression of his most notable victim Cicero.

33 Baldwin 1980, 58; Wallace-Hadrill 1983, 111. On Suetonius' very positive view of the Principate, see also e.g. Devillers 2003, 224; Duff 2003a, 106; Tuori 2016, 228; for Tacitus as anti-imperialist, Syme 1958, 408; Davies 2004, 145. However, the characterization of Tacitus' works themselves by Strunk (2017, 181) as 'a testament to resistance against tyranny' is overstated; see esp. Oakley 2009a, 192–3 on the historian's admiration for the discretion of his father-in-law Agricola. Nevertheless, it is indeed telling that the Empire's founder Augustus, who in Suetonius is an exemplary emperor, is instead portrayed by Tacitus like a tyrant and rapist; see Strunk 2014, 134–5. For these reasons, it

ideological reason which can also better explain the discrepancy between their interpretations of this event. Literary imperatives trump scholarly squabbles.

The second passage typically adduced by adherents to the allusion theory concerns the birthplace of Caligula, and once again the Suetonian version is at odds with Tacitus:[34]

> iam infans in castris genitus, in contubernio legionum eductus, quem militari uocabulo Caligulam appellabant, quia plerumque ad concilianda uulgi studia eo tegmine pedum induebatur.

> There was also her little son, born in the camp and bred the playmate of the legions; whom soldier-like they had dubbed 'Bootikins' – Caligula – because, as an appeal to the fancy of the rank and file, he generally wore the footgear of that name.
>
> (*Ann.* 1.41.2)

> ubi natus sit incertum *diuersitas tradentium* facit. Cn. Lentulus Gaetulicus Tiburi genitum scribit, Plinius Secundus in Treueris uico Ambitaruio supra Confluentes, addit etiam pro argumento aras ibi ostendi inscriptas OB AGRIPPINAE PVERPERIVM. uersiculi imperante mox eo diuulgati apud hibernas legiones procreatum indicant:

> > in castris natus, patriis nutritus in armis,
> >   iam designati principis omen erat.

> ego in actis Anti editum inuenio. Gaetulicum refellit Plinius quasi mentitum per adulationem, ut ad laudes iuuenis gloriosique principis aliquid etiam ex urbe Herculi sacra sumeret, abusumque audentius mendacio, quod ante annum fere natus Germanico filius Tiburi fuerat appellatus et ipse C. Caesar, de cuius amabili pueritia immaturoque obitu supra diximus. Plinium arguit ratio temporum, nam qui res Augusti memoriae mandarunt Germanicum exacto consulatu in Galliam

---

is misleading to suggest that the equestrian Suetonius necessarily represents the same 'senatorial', 'aristocratic', or 'elite' positions as Tacitus or other upper-class Romans, contrary to e.g. Jones 1992, 196; Bittarello 2011, 94; Howley 2014, 186; 2018, 82; Kemezis 2016, 115; Hulls 2019, 268, 270 (cf. id. 2014, 193–4); Szoke 2019, 430; Whitton 2019a, 103; Lavan 2020, 45; Slootjes 2020, 282–3. I doubt that Suetonius would have joined the aristocratic Pliny and Tacitus, for example, on their hunting trips (Plin. *Ep.* 1.6.3). Furthermore, Suetonius' middle-class concern for *all* social groups in his works belies any alleged 'elite' perspective; see Simcox 1883, 211, 218; Wallace-Hadrill 1983, 157, 162; Stadter 2007, 535. For how the senatorial biases of Tacitus and Dio, on the other hand, inform their audiences, see Schulz 2016, 277–8, 295–6; 2019a, 172–5; 2019b; on the difference between Pliny and Suetonius with regard to social status, see Gibson 2014; Power 2014b, 17–18.

34 This alleged allusion is believed by Townend 1967, 89; 1982b, 1054–5; Hurley 1989, 325–7; 1993, 19, 22; 2001, 74; Lindsay 1993, 64; Edwards 2000, xxviii; Shotter 2008, 9; cf. Barrett 1989, 7; 2015, 22.

missum consentiunt iam nato Gaio. nec Plini opinionem inscriptio arae
quicquam adiuuerit, cum Agrippina bis in ea regione filias enixa sit et
qualiscumque partus sine ullo sexus discrimine puerperium uocetur,
quod antiqui etiam puellas pueras, sicut et pueros puellos dictitarent.
extat et Augusti epistula ...

Conflicting testimony makes his birthplace uncertain. Gnaeus Lentulus Gaetulicus writes that he was born at Tibur, Plinius Secundus
among the Treveri, in a village called Ambitarvium above the Confluence. Pliny adds as proof that altars are shown there, inscribed 'For the
Delivery of Agrippina'. Verses which were in circulation soon after he
became emperor indicate that he was begotten in the winter-quarters
of the legions:

> He who was born in the camp and reared 'mid the arms of his
>   country,
> Gave at the outset a sign that he was fated to rule.

I myself find in the gazette that he first saw the light at Antium. Gaetulicus is shown to be wrong by Pliny, who says that he told a flattering lie,
to add some luster to the fame of a young and vainglorious prince from
the city sacred to Hercules; and that he lied with the more assurance
because Germanicus really did have a son born to him at Tibur, also
called Gaius Caesar, of whose lovable disposition and untimely death I
have already spoken. Pliny has erred in his chronology; for the historians of Augustus agree that Germanicus was not sent to Germany until
the close of his consulship, when Gaius was already born. Moreover,
the inscription on the altar adds no strength to Pliny's view, for Agrippina twice gave birth to daughters in that region, and any childbirth,
regardless of sex, is called *puerperium*, since the men of old called girls
puerae, just as they called boys *puelli*. Furthermore, we have a letter
written by Augustus ...

(Calig. 8.1–5)

In this case, there is even less reason to suspect a correction of Tacitus,
since the birthplace receives only the briefest mention in the *Annals*, unlike
the historian's more fully delineated opinion on Tiberius' adoption, which
as we saw is forcefully argued with evidence. Would Suetonius really have
gone out of his way to debate such a fleeting reference about Caligula?
The same criticism could be made of Suetonius' alleged allusion to Tacitus' quick aside about Drusus (*Ann.* 2.82.2) in his sizeable justification for
believing in Augustus' fondness for that stepson (*Claud.* 1.4–5),[35] which

---

35 For this alleged allusion, which to my mind is unconvincing, see Questa 1963, 109;
   Townend 1982b, 1055; Gascou 1984, 776; Hurley 2001, 64.

again seems to have been included by the biographer to redeem the emperor, rather than anything else. More importantly, just as in that passage – 'some have made bold to write' (*nonnullos tradere ausos*) – the biographer here shows that there was indeed a pre-existing controversy in the sources (*diuersitas tradentium*), which he even names outright: Gaetulicus, Pliny the Elder, anonymous verses, *acta*, the 'historians of Augustus', and Augustus himself.[36]

Since there was disagreement in the earlier sources about Caligula's birthplace, this would have been reason enough to detain Suetonius, and the more likely motive than responding to a passing reference in Tacitus. In fact, further considerations preclude a possible swipe at Tacitus from being taken seriously even as a secondary aim. Scholars have noted that such scholarly excursuses as we find at *Tiberius* 21 and *Caligula* 8 are rare in Suetonius,[37] although their scarcity has certainly been overstated.[38] We have already accounted for the former passage; on the latter, appeal can now be made to the simple explanation that the category of birthplace is more germane to biography than historiography,[39] and sometimes involves a display of research by Suetonius (e.g. *Poet.* 28–9.1–10). Such passages of explicated erudition increase the biographer's authority with the reader and demonstrate his ability to weigh conflicting pieces of evidence, often in the first person.[40] These ultimate biographical aims are what really lie behind Suetonius' lengthy comments on Caligula's origin, which are hardly a historiographical tangent by the biographer; rather, the parallel passage in the *Annals* is a biographical moment by Tacitus.[41] Suetonius is shown judiciously getting the facts right even about a bad emperor such as Caligula, gaining himself credibility as a supposedly fair and impartial biographer for when he later denounces the same ruler as a 'monster' (*monstro*, *Calig.* 22.1).

The third passage often thought to be an allusion to Tacitus is Suetonius' discussion of Nero's poems:[42]

---

36 On the same grounds, one might also suspect the similarly weak case of Gascou 1984, 284 and Hurley 2001, 237–8 for allusion to Tac. *Ann.* 12.66–7 at *Claud.* 44.2, where the Tacitean passage is more substantial, yet the alleged corrections are presented by Suetonius as variants, and are not only negligibly slight, but independently supported in part by Dio Cass. 60.34.2–3. Hurley herself even brings out the advantageous literary effect of the differences in Suetonius' and Dio's respective versions.

37 Syme 1958, 690; Hurley 1989, 326; Wardle 1998, 428.

38 See e.g. *Aug.* 5–6, *Tib.* 5; also Baldwin 1983, 362–5.

39 Cf. Malloch 2004, 206–7. On birthplaces in Suetonius, see Steidle 1951, 68–70; Allen 1958, 2–3; Questa 1963, 109–10; Baldwin 1979c, 21 = 1984, 47; 1983, 128–9; 1989a, 471–2; de Coninck 1983, 110–20; Wardle 1994, 127; 2007, 444; Hurley 2003; above, pp. 94, 143; below, pp. 230–1.

40 See e.g. *Gramm.* 2.1, 7.1, 25.2, *Aug.* 2.3, *Tib.* 2.1, *Ner.* 1.2, *Vesp.* 1.4, with above, p. 92.

41 On biographical moments in historiography generally, see Power 2014b, 2 n. 5.

42 For this proposed allusion, see Townend 1967, 89; 1982b, 1055; anticipated by Harrer 1918, 343. It has since found other supporters: e.g. M. Griffin 1984, 235; Baldwin 1989a, 486; Shotter 2005, 106; 2008, 9; Fantham 2013b, 160 (cf. ead. 2013a, 25–6); Hurley 2013, 41; cf. Pausch 2013, 63 n. 73.

ne tamen ludicrae tantum imperatoris artes notescerent, carminum quoque studium adfectauit, contractis quibus aliqua pangendi facultas necdum insignis aestimatio. hi considere simul, et adlatos uel ibidem repertos uersus conectere atque ipsius uerba quoquo modo prolata supplere. quod species ipsa carminum docet, non impetu et instinctu nec ore uno fluens. etiam sapientiae doctoribus tempus impertiebat post epulas, utque contraria adseuerantium discordia frueretur.

And yet, lest it should be only the histrionic skill of the emperor which won publicity, he affected also a zeal for poetry and gathered a group of associates with some faculty for versification but not such as to have yet attracted remark. These, after dining, sat with him, devising a connection for the lines they had brought from home or invented on the spot, and eking out the phrases suggested, for better or worse, by their master; the method being obvious even from the general cast of the poems, which run without energy or inspiration and lack unity of style. Even to the teachers of philosophy he accorded a little time – but after dinner, and in order to amuse himself by the wrangling which attended the exposition of their conflicting dogmas.

(Ann. 14.16.1–2)

liberalis disciplinas omnnis fere puer attigit, sed a philosophia eum mater auertit, monens imperaturo contrariam esse, a cognitione ueterum oratorum Seneca praeceptor, quo diutius in admiratione sui detineret. itaque ad poeticam pronus carmina libenter ac sine labore composuit nec, *ut quidam putant*, aliena pro suis edidit. uenere in manus meas pugillares libellique cum quibusdam notissimis uersibus ipsius chirographo scriptis, ut facile appareret non tralatos aut dictante aliquo exceptos sed plane quasi a cogitante atque generante exaratos: ita multa et deleta et inducta et superscripta inerant. habuit et pingendi fingendique {maxime} non mediocre studium.

When a boy he took up almost all the liberal arts; but his mother turned him from philosophy, warning him that it was a drawback to one who was going to rule, while Seneca kept him from reading the early orators, to make his admiration for his teacher endure the longer. Turning therefore to poetry, he wrote verses with eagerness and without labour, and did not, *as some think*, publish the work of others as his own. I have had in my possession note-books and papers with some well-known verses of his, written with his own hand and in such wise that it was perfectly evident that they were not copied or taken down from dictation, but worked out exactly as one writes when thinking and creating; so many instances were there of words erased or struck through and written above the lines. He likewise had no slight interest in painting and sculpture.

(Ner. 52)

Both passages are obviously informed by a single common source that criticized Nero's interests in poetry and philosophy together. However, as with the historian's ultimately groundless claim about Augustus' adoption of Tiberius, Tacitus does not appear to show any of the scepticism here towards his source's bias that he elsewhere exhibits (e.g. *Ann.* 14.9.1, 15.38.1).[43] In this case it is Tacitus who seems to be following the source more closely than Suetonius, who instead enriches the tradition with his own unique research and even turns up the emperor's actual drafts, although not necessarily from the palace's secret archives.[44] The biographer also appears to have gleaned the detail about Nero's oratory from a different source that was hostile to Seneca, which is likewise used elsewhere by Dio, but notably not by Tacitus.[45] It cannot easily be guessed whether Suetonius' last sentence on Nero's other artistic abilities was in the source that he shared with Tacitus, but if so, it was unlikely to have been as positive towards the emperor as we find it in the *Caesars*, where it bolsters the point that the emperor did indeed show signs of artistic creativity.

The most probable interpretation of this comparison is that Tacitus and Suetonius have both read the same lost source, which was likely one of the main annalistic accounts of the reign – possibly the historian Cluvius Rufus, who was a palace insider and thus in a better position than other sources such as Pliny the Elder to know personal information.[46] Whoever it was, this source was obviously hostile to Nero, and discussed his interests in both philosophy and poetry in the same place. Why else would these two subjects pop up together so prominently in Tacitus, who only rarely discusses the emperors' literary output, and then only briefly?[47] Suetonius, on the other hand, habitually gathers literary material together in the same rubric as indications of the imperial virtue of *studia*; hence his inclusion of other material too on Nero's oratory, painting, and sculpting.[48] It is the common source (*ut quidam putant*) that Suetonius refutes by defending

---

43 M. Griffin 1984, 236–7.
44 See Baldwin 2005, 309; above, pp. 42–4; *pace* Bradley 1978, 287; Duchêne 2016, 278.
45 Warmington 1999, 86 (ad loc.).
46 For Cluvius Rufus, who at least wrote on Nero and may have begun with Caligula, see *Ner.* 21.2; also Plut. *Quaest. Rom.* 107; Tac. *Ann.* 13.20, 14.2; Dio Cass. 63.14.3; with Murison 1993, 75–80; Wardle 1994, 48–54; Devillers 2003, 24–7; Wiseman 2013, 109–16. Cf. references above, nn. 4, 25.
47 Although see *Ann.* 13.3.2 on Nero as the first Caesar whose speeches were written for him (cf. *Dom.* 20). Literary endeavours are mentioned by Tacitus at *Hist.* 4.86.2, *Ann.* 11.13–14, 15.39.3, and a speech is quoted at *Ann.* 6.6.1, but titles of writings are never catalogued in the manner of Suetonius; on Tacitus' evidence for the emperor's works, see Dilke 1957, 81, 93–4.
48 On Nero's interest in painting and sculpting, see Pausch 2013, 64. For *studia* as a moral category in Suetonius, see Wallace-Hadrill 1983, 83–6; Coleman 1986, 3088–9, 3093; Billerbeck 1990, 198; Bradley 1991, 3727–8; Hurley 2014b, 27, 29–30, 33–4; Power 2014b, 12; Tatum 2014, 167–9; Buongiovanni 2016, 363 n. 4; above, p. 118.

Nero as a poet, and by portraying his mother's clichéd intervention during his dangerous philosophical dabbling, an intervention which was a familiar *topos* in the context of a young ruler preparing for a career in public life, he points for a brief instant to the semblance of Nero as a virtuous leader (cf. Tac. *Agr.* 4.3; SHA, *Alex. Sev.* 14.5).[49]

Suetonius therefore draws on the same tradition as Tacitus, but reshapes it for his own purposes. What is more, the two versions are not as incompatible as they might at first appear. Nero certainly did pursue philosophy, for however little time,[50] and the erratic corrections to the writing tablets described by Suetonius do not disprove that he pieced together the verses of others; on the contrary, they suggest that he may indeed have done so.[51] The version of Suetonius even leaves room for a merely cursory focus on liberal arts by the emperor through its verb *attigit*, which could imply only a brief interest.[52] If we had lacked Tacitus' account, which explains the poems' revisions in a plausibly sinister way as a patchwork of other poets, we might instead take the biographer's word, which could now serve ironically to confirm the common source's scathing report that Nero's poems were not his own. Suetonius apparently decided to diminish this source's bias for being too overt. In adducing the new evidence of Nero's drafts of poetry, and excusing his errant forays into philosophy as signs of the typical good ruler, Suetonius questions these charges and emerges all the more ostensibly even-handed in his presentation of Nero. As in our previous passages, Suetonius again demonstrates how he can carefully interpret contradictory pieces of evidence; his trustworthiness as a seemingly objective source is thus bolstered, and by extension the reader's credence in his overall considered verdict on this emperor.

The context of this literary rubric within the *Life* may cast further light on Suetonius' generally uncharacteristic defence here of Nero, which has prompted some to feel that he must have had some alternative reason, such as a wish to attack Tacitus, due to this supposed goodwill towards the emperor. The rubric falls in an extensive addendum of personal characteristics that follows the death and funeral of Nero, which has been fittingly compared to that at the end of the *Domitian* in its disproportionate length.[53]

---

49 See Morgan 1998, 420–3; Levick 2002, 137. For the conflict between philosophy and politics more generally, see e.g. Cic. *Tusc.* 2.1, with Baraz 2012b, 15–22; and for suspiciousness towards the former, e.g. Cic. *Off.* 2.1.2; Tac. *Hist.* 4.5; with Bradley 1978, 286. On Nero's poetry generally, see ibid. 288 with bibliography; also Morford 1985, 2015–18; Baldwin 2005.

50 For further evidence of Nero's interest in philosophy, see Bradley 1978, 286.

51 Warmington 1999, 86–7; *pace* Bradley 1978, 287. That Suetonius and Tacitus might instead refer to two entirely different, yet both seemingly amalgamated, works of Nero's poetry would seem a coincidence beyond belief; *pace* Morford 1985, 2017–18 n. 73.

52 Bradley 1978, 285 (ad loc.).

53 See e.g. Hägg 2012, 227–9, erring in the claim that the emperor's physical description directly follows his death only in those two *Lives*; *contra*, see *Galb.* 21, *Otho* 12.1 (and

Many of the categories found in this final part of the biography (*Ner.* 51–7) are more often witnessed preceding an emperor's death in Suetonius. In the *Nero*, however, these indications of character, some of which appear positive, are removed to a sort of appendix, as though these attributes can now be seen to reveal the truth of his character and how it led to his death through a sort of post mortem explanation. Nero's literary pursuits are part of this condemning crescendo, and supply a transition to his arrogant desire for immortal glory.[54] They are the one exception to this list of bad traits, and noticeably come towards the front, so that the final rubrics are entirely negative and pack more of a punch by contrast, being left as the reader's last, and lasting, impression. By redeeming Nero's writing, Suetonius therefore paradoxically reinforces his point about the emperor's ultimately evil character all the more through chiaroscuro.[55] Even the rubrics of Suetonius that may appear trivial have a higher purpose; they need not simply be attacks on a contemporary writer.

Finally, a more recent case for allusion to Tacitus in Suetonius is worth considering for good measure, since it takes its lead from the general belief in Townend's theory by subsequent scholars. Whittaker has tried to revive the neglected suggestion of Wallace-Hadrill that the statement in the *Augustus* about the emperor's disallowance of temples being dedicated in his honour may be a similar kind of implicit correction of Tacitus:[56]

nihil deorum honoribus relictum, cum se templis et effigie numinum per flamines et sacerdotes coli uellet.

He had left small room for the worship of heaven, when he claimed to be himself adored in temples and in the image of godhead by flamens and by priests!

(*Ann.* 1.10.6)

templa quamuis sciret etiam proconsulibus decerni solere in nulla tamen prouincia nisi communi suo Romaeque nomine recepit. nam in urbe quidem pertinacissime abstinuit hoc honore atque etiam argenteas statuas olim sibi positas conflauit omnis exque iis aureas cortinas Apollini Palatino dedicauit.

Although well aware that it was usual to vote temples even to proconsuls, he would not accept one even in a province save jointly in his own

---

cf. *Vit.* 17.1–2), with Lewis 1991, 3661–2, who compares Tac. *Agr.* 44.2 and the ancient death-mask (*imago*). Cf. also *Aug.* 99.1 and *Vesp.* 24 on the emperor's concern for his appearance at his death.

54 Cf. Hurley 2014b, 30. For other crescendos in this *Life*, see *Ner.* 28–9 and 33–8, with above, pp. 154–5, and Gascou 1984, 697–700, respectively.

55 For Suetonius' chiaroscuro technique, see Power 2014b, 11.

56 Whittaker 2000, 103, making a more forceful argument for this allusion, which had been tentatively proposed in the first place by Wallace-Hadrill 1983, 111–12 n. 5.

name and that of Rome. In the city itself he refused this honour most emphatically, even melting down the silver statues which had been set up in his honour in former times and with the money coined from them dedicating golden tripods to Apollo of the Palatine.

(Aug. 52)

As has been noted, Dio too says that Augustus received unprecedented divine honours (51.20.7),[57] so that it appears to have been a claim in the first-century source material used by both historians for the emperor. If anything, therefore, Suetonius probably refutes a report in a common source shared with Tacitus. Against her own case, Whittaker even adduces two passages of Cicero (*QFr.* 1.1.26, *Att.* 5.21.7) on which Suetonius may plausibly rely for the existence of temples dedicated to magistrates.[58] The argument for direct use of Tacitus is less than thin, with no clear verbal echoes and only a loose contextual resemblance that could well have been expected, since the subject of divine honours was an important gauge of an emperor for both historian and biographer alike. Moreover, this chapter is an integral part of an important discussion in Suetonius' biography (*Aug.* 52–6) that establishes Augustus' virtue of *ciuilitas* in part through the refusal of the sort of divine honours adopted by Caesar in the previous *Life* (*Iul.* 76–9, cf. *Aug.* 52–3).[59] Once again, contrast with other parts of the *Caesars*, not with Tacitus, is at issue, and Suetonius' chiaroscuro technique is further underscored by another implied comparison with Caesar in the *Caligula*, where Suetonius alludes to the same topic of divine honours, only this time to suggest similarity, rather than difference (*Calig.* 22.1).[60]

Tacitus or Historiography?

Important conclusions may be drawn from this study about the nature of Suetonius' political *Lives*. The idea that Tacitus had been read by Suetonius has lingered for too long in the biographer's scholarship, and has fostered the misconception of his task in the *Caesars* as merely supplemental, rather than a unique form of biography that distinguishes its independence from a broader tradition of history- and biography-writing. As a consequence, Suetonius' own literary reasons for adapting his material in the way that he

57 Whittaker 2000, 99–100.
58 Ibid. 101.
59 Wallace-Hadrill 1983, 162–3. For an emperor's *recusatio* upon accession, see also id. 1982, 36–7; Yakobson and Cotton 1985, 497.
60 See above, p. 121 with bibliography. For other implicit comparisons with Caesar in the *Caligula* and elsewhere in Suetonius, see Power 2014a, 64, 70; also Henderson 2014, esp. 93–9; Hurley 2014a, 154, 156–8; 2014b, 28.

does have been ignored.[61] Wallace-Hadrill begins his book on Suetonius by speaking of the biographer's 'temerity' in writing so soon after the historian, claiming that he was 'undoubtedly looking over his shoulder at Tacitus'.[62] But this alleged awareness of Tacitus and avoidance of his themes can no longer be held to explain Suetonius' selection of details and subject matter. The famous methodological statement that he will articulate his text *neque per tempora* can now be said to refer to the eschewal of a convention of historiography in the larger sense (true 'not-history').

Tacitus survives as merely one of our best examples of the annalistic framework, and, aside from his use of common sources, it is in this that his value for comparison with Suetonius lies. The full-scale roundedness of the *Caesars* with regard to biographical matters implies a readership that was interested in the character of these men in and of itself. Suetonius did not mean for his work to be interpreted as history, even if that is what eventually happened.[63] At the same time, biography need not be interpreted alongside it either; it may still be considered an alternative to history, even if it cannot fully substitute for it. In other words, neither is it the case that Suetonius' *Lives* themselves need to be supplemented by historiography, for they rewrite and supplant the first-century sources on this period in the same way as the *Annals*. Suetonius only assumes that his readers are already familiar with the history of the time-period in question and with historiography in general, not necessarily with any of those particular predecessors. If anything, Suetonius' political biographies are better conceived of more

---

61 Equally distracting from appreciation of Suetonius' choices are alleged contemporary reminiscences of Trajan and Hadrian, whether through the same kind of subtle criticism or *ex silentio* by avoidance of particular themes, since these too have yet to be substantiated by a solid allusion other than the explicit references to these emperors (*Aug.* 7.1 and *Dom.* 23.2; cf. Nerva at *Dom.* 1.1), which cannot be used to support the kind of oblique dialogue suggested by scholars: Syme 1958, 490; 1980a, 128 = *RP* 3.1274; 1981, 117 = *RP* 3.1348; Townend 1959, 290–3; 1967, 90; 1982b, 1055–6; Carney 1968; Bowersock 1969; Cizek 1977, 181–92; Abramenko 1994; Pausch 2004, 258 n. 142; Vout 2007, 138–40; Charles and Anagnostou-Laoutides 2010a, 184–6; Rowland 2010; Uden 2015, 139, 143; and more tentatively, Wallace-Hadrill 1983, 6, 198–200; *contra*, see Bradley 1976; 1991, 3723; Baldwin 1983, 13–14, 278; Gascou 1984, 758–73; Lindsay 1993, 18; Wardle 1994, 338; 1998, 434–6; Chong-Gossard 2010, 304–6, 315–21; Tuori 2016, 226. We might compare Syme's (1958, 481–5, 517–9) speculative case for allusions to Hadrian in Tacitus, which was demolished by Goodyear 1970, 20–1; 1972, 127–8, 183–4. For a similar argument about Plutarch and Trajan, see Pelling 2002c = 2002b, 253–66. Langlands 2018a, 249 (cf. 245, 252 n. 75; ead. 2018b, 331, 343) points to the soldier's suicide at Suet. *Otho* 10.1 as alleged evidence for 'the immediacy of exempla, and the need for present, living role models, standing right in front of one', which she considers 'a new emphasis in the exemplary ethics that is characteristic of literature from this post-Domitianic era', but the story's appearance also in our parallel historical accounts means that it actually comes from a *pre-Domitianic* common source.

62 Wallace-Hadrill 1983, 1–2.

63 Ibid. 13, 25; cf. Martin 1981, 37–8.

positively as their own version of 'anti-history', the term used by Clarke of Tacitus, who himself opposed some of the expectations of historiography.[64]

Although Pliny the Younger may try to better Tacitus through some of his more historiographical letters, Suetonius' implicit contrast in the *Caesars* appears to be with historiography in general, as represented by the earlier historians whose biographies he had written in the *Illustrious Men*, such as Sallust (Suet. frr. 73–4, 177, *Gramm.* 10.6, 15.2, *Aug.* 86.3) or Livy (Suet. frr. 76–7, *Calig.* 34.2, *Claud.* 41.1, *Dom.* 10.3).[65] Pliny could conceivably have had Tacitus in mind when he coyly professed, *neque enim historiam componebam* ('I was not composing history', *Ep.* 1.1),[66] but the same cannot be said of Suetonius, who seems entirely ignorant of Tacitus' writing. Whether he knew the man personally through Pliny, he does not appear to have read his work even once. With regard to Tacitus' *Histories*, Suetonius wrote 'as though that masterpiece did not exist'.[67] Perhaps to the biographer, it did not. There were certainly other, more valuable historians for Suetonius to consult on this period – those containing first-hand information. In addition to his own individual research from other sources, Suetonius was working from the same main accounts from the first century as Tacitus, which were relatively dependable and rich in detail. As Townend rightly asked, why would Suetonius have used Tacitus as a source if he had these earlier ones? The argument that Suetonius merely double-checked with Tacitus is also unconvincing. The twice removed version of Tacitus was superfluous, derivative, and, given the rhetorical nature of Roman historiography, doubly tainted. It would have been deemed a poor source in contrast to the earlier, more direct evidence by any responsible biographer or historian, and rightly shunned.[68]

Comparison with the later historian Cassius Dio is likewise instructive. About a century after Suetonius, when Tacitus was certainly available, the same pattern can be seen in Dio's similar neglect of the historian.[69] Dio too

64 See Clarke 2002. On Tacitus' ironic contrast with historiography, cf. Martin and Woodman 1989, 170–2 on the digression at *Ann.* 4.32–3.

65 On Suetonius' *Lives* of historians, see Wallace-Hadrill 1983, 54–9; Gibson 2014, 213.

66 Cf. Pliny's insincere claim that 'writing a letter is indeed one thing, history another' (*aliud est enim epistulam aliud historiam ... scribere*, *Ep.* 6.16.22), which, although a generalization, may have referred to Tacitus, the letter's addressee. For Pliny's rivalry with Tacitus in that letter, see Ash 2003; Berry 2008, 301, 308; above, p. 26; and more generally, Griffin 1999, 142–4 = 2018, 250–2; Edwards 2018.

67 Syme 1980a, 111 = *RP* 3.1258.

68 My point here is not, as argued by Pomeroy (2017, 585), that Tacitus was 'a mere compiler of earlier written accounts', but rather the opposite: the historian rhetorically embellished his sources to such a great extent that he did not preserve them very precisely. If he *had* simply compiled his sources, he *would* have been useful to Suetonius.

69 *Pace* e.g. Pigoń 1993, 189; Baltussen 2002, 34. Against the brittle arguments of Syme (1958, 690–2; 1980a, 112 = *RP* 3.1258) that Dio used Tacitus for the reign of Tiberius, see Townend 1959, 290–1. Dio's use of Tacitus is unconvincingly suggested for Tiberius' accession (Dio Cass. 56.45.3 ~ Tac. *Ann.* 1.10.7) by Lindsay 1995b, 103; and for the campaigns of Nero's general Suetonius Paulinus (Dio Cass. 62.1–12 ~ Tac. *Ann.* 14.29–39) by Peter, *HRRel.* 2.cxxxviii-cxxxviiii (*contra*, see Martin 1981, 210).

understood the valuable quality of the original first-century sources in preference to later ones for the early imperial period. To write history or biography is to decide for oneself on an interpretation of events and characters, and Tacitus' already polished vision would thus have precluded Dio's new opinion of the facts. This is why Suetonius himself was, in turn, avoided by Dio, despite some *a priori* assumptions to the contrary.[70] It is also for this reason that Plutarch would have been disregarded by Suetonius,[71] or for that matter by Tacitus and Dio – if they had at least heard of him (an uncertainty at best).[72] If their respective chronologies had been reversed, Tacitus would neither have used Suetonius. By the same token, what use to

[70] That Dio drew on Suetonius is held by Hardy 1890, lx = 1906, 334; Fabia 1898, 166–8; Questa 1957, 42–6; Millar 1964, 85–6, 105; Hurley 1989, 326; 2003, 114 n. 43; Gowing 1992, 258; del Castillo 2002, 455; Brunet 2004, 150–1; Freyburger-Galland 2009; Davenport 2014, 97–8 n. 10, 100, 108, 112; Ziogas 2016, 136; Burden-Strevens 2020, 251–3; cf. Woods 2006–7, 52; 2019, 239, entertaining the possibility. It has even been believed that Dio may have used an allegedly lost work of Suetonius' for the triumviral wars; see Reifferscheid 1860, 470; *contra*, Macé 1900, 346–54. For Dio as almost certainly independent of Suetonius, see Syme 1958, 690–1; Gascou 1984, 10–87; Baar 1990, 234; Barrett 1996, 205; Murison 1999, 17; Power 2011, 486; Carlsen 2016, 318; above, pp. 111, 150.

[71] Suetonius' use of Plutarch is tenuously proposed by Krause 1831, 6; Della Corte 1958, 139–48; Jones 1971, 61–2; Baldwin 1979a, 115–18 = 1983, 86–90 = 1989b, 26–9; 1983, 49, 117–18, 181, 294, 509, 526, 544–6; *contra*, see Bowersock 1998, 195, 205; Hägg 2012, 240–1; Fantham 2013b, 189; Geiger 2014, 302; Georgiadou 2014, 259–60; cf. Wardle 1998, 430–1; 2014, 7; Schropp 2017; Gibson 2018, 404. Suetonius possibly did not even know who Plutarch was (*pace* Pelling 2009, 252). Conversely, it has been argued that Plutarch for his *Cicero* used Suetonius' earlier work the *Illustrious Men* (Plut. *Cic.* 1.1–2 ~ Suet. fr. 50 Reiff.; *Cic.* 3.4–6 ~ fr. 52 Reiff.); see Gudeman 1889, 150–8; 1902, 48–63, esp. 49–52; cf. Macé 1900, 244, 411; Wright 2001, 444–5 n. 30. Although Plutarch's *Cicero* could have been written as late as AD 115 (Jones 1966, 69), and Suetonius' *Illustrious Men* probably appeared by AD 110 (above, pp. 38–41), the more likely source is M. Tullius Tiro's lost biography of Cicero, which is not only cited by Tacitus (*Dial.* 17.2) but also by Plutarch himself (*Cic.* 41.4, 49.4); see McDermott 1972a, 282–4; 1980, 486. As Gudeman (1889, 151–2) points out, the common material can also be found in the *De uiris illustribus* attributed to Aurelius Victor (81). The error that Cicero's assassins were Herennius and Popillius (Plut. *Cic.* 48.1 ~ Suet. fr. 54 Reiff.), which was by no means unique (Sen. *Controv.* 7.2.8), simply suggests the use of another common source that was post-Augustan; cf. *FRHist* 3.507 (on Tiro fr. 3). Nor is Suetonius a likely source for the dream at Plut. *Cic.* 44.2–6 (as thought by Gudeman 1902, 60); see Wardle 2005, 40 n. 49.

[72] *Pace* Hardy 1890, lx = 1906, 334; Pigoń 1993, 188 n. 18; Pade 2007, 45–8; Ash 2016, 205 n. 13; whose proposals that Dio had read Plutarch are unconvincing. The same goes for the presumption of Momigliano 1931, 171–87 = 1992, 170–81 that Tacitus' *Histories* may have been a source for Plutarch's *Caesars*, which seems impossible for chronological reasons, since the latter work was probably published first; see Bowersock 1998, 203–4. Against Plutarch and Tacitus' use of each other, see Syme 1980a, 110 = *RP* 3.1257; Martin 1981, 190; Levick 2013, 555 n. 36 with further references. We might also compare Langlands' (2018b, 335, 345) contemplation of whether Tacitus may have drawn on Suetonius' *Otho* in his *Histories*; on the earlier date of the *Histories*, see e.g. Woodman 2009d, 31 = 2012, 243.

Suetonius was Tacitus' filtered and elevated language, devoid of the spar-
kling minutia that would make his biographies so vivid and lively?

Suetonius availed himself of far more than Tacitus' leavings: he drew
from the original reservoir of first-century sources, appropriating some of
the same items, but probably without consciousness of the substance of his
older contemporary's work. While Tacitus is relevant to discussions of Suetonius' sources, and of his contrast with the historiographical framework
more generally, further tangents between the two authors cannot be accepted. Their few moments of close overlap are simply a tribute to the occasionally similar focus of two Roman imperial minds, which was inevitable
in their sifting through the same earlier writers. In acquitting Suetonius of
such pedantic allusion, most telling of all is the fact that these moments are
more precisely when Tacitus' history leans towards biography, rather than
when Suetonian biography approximates annals. It is Tacitus who crosses
paths with Suetonius, not vice versa, and it is mostly when he follows the
more hostile traditions, which naturally included personal details. Since
no solid evidence for the biographer's specific use of Tacitus has yet been
offered, the source material that they are known to have shared is the only
cogent explanation for correspondences between them. The *Caesars* does
not seem indebted to the *Annals*, and the author of the latter cannot be
said to have inspired the former. As Plutarch demonstrates, Tacitus did not
invent the Caesars as a literary theme.[73] Without Tacitus, there would still
have been Suetonius.

---

73 Syme 1980a = *RP* 3.1251–75; Georgiadou 1988; 2014; Bowersock 1998.

26 The Disgrace of Suetonius

The alleged scandal from Suetonius' own life in the *Augustan History* is supposed to have been an indiscretion with the emperor Hadrian's wife Sabina that resulted in his dismissal from the Roman court, after an illustrious climb through the official ranks to reach a position in charge of government correspondence (*ab epistulis*). This rumour about a mysterious intrigue behind Suetonius' downfall is widely accepted, but probably never actually happened. Our anecdotal evidence for the incident is worth reviewing, so that we can see not only how the gossip written *by* Suetonius is sometimes too easily believed, but also the stories written *about* him. Nothing is known of Suetonius after AD 122, when his imperial career came to an abrupt end around the age of fifty-two, as he was surveying the location for Hadrian's Wall with the emperor on his trip to Britain.[1] It was as unexpected as the death of Julius Caesar, which Suetonius himself had described as intervening *talia agentem atque meditantem* ('in the midst of so many endeavours and plans', *Iul.* 44.4).

The only evidence for this fall from grace is found in the *Life* of Hadrian from late antiquity, which was among the few early biographies in the *Augustan History* to draw on generally credible sources.[2] The 1976 Penguin translation of this passage by Birley has contributed to the lack of understanding about this historical event, which remains hindered by an unsolved crux in the text:[3]

> Septicio Claro praefecto praetorii et Suetonio Tranquillo epistularum magistro multisque aliis, quod apud Sabinam uxorem †uniussu eius† familiarius se tunc egerant, quam reuerentia domus aulicae postulabat,

---

1 Syme 1958, 779–80; 1971, 114–15; 1980a, 113–14 = *RP* 3.1260–1; 1980b, 68–9 = *RP* 3.1283–5. The dismissal gives us an endpoint for the window of publication for Suetonius' *Lives of the Caesars*, which occurred sometime during Septicius Clarus' tenure as praetorian prefect (AD 119–22); see above, p. 17. See also Brennan 2018, 84–5, 251 nn. 31–2.
2 Rohrbacher 2013, 153, 175. On Suetonius and the *HA*, see e.g. Fry 2010; Arbo 2010.
3 Birley 1976, 69.

202 Suetonius and History

successores dedit, uxorem etiam ut morosam et asperam dimissurus, ut ipse dicebat, si priuatus fuisset.

uniussu eius *P*: iniussu eius *P corr.*: nimio usu *Petschenig*: in usu eius *Peter*: in uisu eius *Bennett*: in eius usu *Callu*: inusitatius et *aut* inusitatius familiari-us<que> *Pelling*

Septicius Clarus, prefect of the guard, and Suetonius Tranquillus, director of his correspondence, he [Hadrian] replaced, because they had at that time behaved in the company of his wife Sabina, <u>in their association with her</u>, in a more informal fashion than respect for the court household demanded. He would have dismissed his wife too, for being moody and difficult – if he had been a private citizen, as he himself used to say.

(SHA, *Hadr.* 11.3)

Birley renders the corrupt phrase to mean 'in their association with her', accepting Peter's conjecture *in usu eius*,[4] and thus differs from the version by the Loeb edition's translator Magie, who had much earlier favoured the reading *iniussu eius*, taking it as 'without his [Hadrian's] consent':

He removed from office Septicius Clarus, the prefect of the guard, and Suetonius Tranquillus, the imperial secretary, and many others besides, because without his consent they had been conducting themselves toward his wife, Sabina, in a more informal fashion than the etiquette of the court demanded. And, as he was himself wont to say, he would have sent away his wife too, on the ground of ill-temper and irritability, had he been merely a private citizen.[5]

This was by far, in my view, the better translation. The correction *iniussu eius* is written in another hand on the earliest ninth-century manuscript P, and is certainly preferable to all of the modern proposals for the unintelligible paradosis *uniussu eius*.[6] However, the most recent editor of the Latin text, Callu, instead follows Birley in accepting, with a minor variation, the different conjecture *in eius usu* in his Budé edition.[7]

The ninth-century correction to P is rejected in this manner for two reasons that have been offered by scholars since Magie. The first is that it has been construed as more likely describing the wishes of Sabina ('without

---

4 Peter 1884, 13, anticipated to some extent by Petschenig 1879, 390–1, who had suggested *nimio usu*. Peter's conjecture is also supported by the Teubner edition of Hohl 1927, 13, who prints *in [i]us[s]u eius*.
5 Magie 1921, 35, followed by Hemelrijk 1999, 113.
6 On the various conjectures, see Fündling 2006, 2.584–5 with further bibliography. My sigla for manuscripts of the *Augustan History* are taken from Hohl 1927.
7 Callu 1992, 30.

her permission'), for if Hadrian himself had been the one to take offence, we should rather have expected *iniussu suo*, and consequently the words *iniussu eius* seem somewhat redundant when applied to the empress after the clause *apud Sabina uxorem* ('in the presence of his wife Sabina').[8] This objection is easily discounted, because the *Augustan History* regularly has *eius* for *suus*, a stylistic tendency which had even been noted long before Magie's translation.[9] However, the second reason is more difficult to refute. As Baldwin observes, the emperor's wish that he could have dismissed Sabina too on the grounds of being *morosam et asperam* seems incompatible with the complaint being Hadrian's, and points us in the direction of taking *eius* as 'her'.[10] In fact, Syme believed the two notions so incongruous that he even suggested a change of source at the end of this passage.[11]

This belief in an apparent contradiction is unnecessary. Hadrian was perfectly capable of both dismay at having to dismiss these men because of his troublesome wife and resoluteness in the punishment of impropriety at his court, which, after all, reflected on his authority as an emperor. Not being pleased with your wife is one thing; ignoring violations of court etiquette quite another. Hadrian would probably have wished that this incident of disrespect never came to his attention, but if it did, he would have been left with no choice but to take the appropriate action. One possible implication to my mind seems to be that this was not the first time that these men behaved badly, at least in his wife's view, and that Hadrian had to order them specially never to do it again, whatever it is that they had once done, which is a better explanation for why the emperor also considered her 'moody and difficult'. Once this alleged inconsistency is resolved, we may accept *iniussu eius* as a plausible conjecture and 'against his [Hadrian's] instruction' as the more likely translation; it is not that Clarus and Suetonius lacked his order to offend the empress (which logically no emperor would be likely to give), but rather defied his explicit order not to do so in a particular manner. This would make better sense of the word *iniussu*, which is most naturally used of commands by the princeps himself.[12] Sabina, after all, did not give the orders. The mysteriousness of the nature of this charge has caused wild speculations about the exact liberty that the biographer may have taken in his speech or conduct around the empress – from Hadrian's uncovering

---

8 See e.g. D'Anna 1988, 64; Rowland 2010, 23, 27. The same may be said of the conjecture *in uisu eius* ('in her sight') by Bennett 1891. It is on account of this perceived redundancy that Christopher Pelling has also suggested to me *inusitatius et* ('more unusually and') or *inusitatius familiarius<que>*.

9 Bitschofsky 1888, 4–5, cf. 10–11 (on SHA, *Ant. Phil.* 25.6).

10 Baldwin 1975a, 67–9 = 1975b, 22–3 = 1983, 42–4 = 1989b, 37–8 = 1997, 254–5, with appeal to Hadrian's irascible character known from Book 69 of Dio's *Roman History*.

11 Syme 1981, 112 = *RP* 3.1344.

12 Cf. Brugnoli 1993, 52 on *iniusso eius* as a military formula at SHA, *Hadr.* 5.6. The Σ manuscripts even have *iniussu eius*, which is preferred by Callu 1992, 98: '*iniusso est à corriger, faute de parallèle.*' See also Fündling 2006, 1.423.

of a conspiracy between Suetonius and Sabina,[13] to Sabina's refusal to be recruited against the emperor,[14] to some kind of a romantic liaison between Suetonius and Sabina.[15]

An important detail has not yet been considered, which is even oddly omitted from the translation of Birley.[16] Hadrian's biographer reports that Clarus and Suetonius were not the only ones to be dismissed for this misdeed: there were also *multisque aliis* ('many others'). Did they all commit the indiscretion, or simply pay the same penalty for it? A final conjecture may be offered that will bring even greater coherence to the situation. The corruption *uniussu eius* might be lacunose, and could originally have been *iniu<rii>s sue<t>ius <et>* ('in a manner more accustomed to insults and'), or possibly even *unice Sue<ton>ius* ('especially Suetonius'), perhaps later suffering from some damage to the papyrus or subsequent codices that rendered certain letters illegible, despite the plural subject of the verb *egerant*, since the *Augustan History* typically uses the adverb *unice* in this sense of distinguishing a particular person or persons within a larger group (*Maxim. duo* 4.4, *Gord.* 6.3). The ancient biographer of Hadrian would no doubt have been aware of Suetonius as the author of the work that he was effectively continuating, and may have thus been inclined to mention a prominent role played by his famous literary predecessor in the incident with Sabina, whether or not the source that he was following had singled out Suetonius. The latter conjecture would explain why Clarus was also dismissed, because he was the biographer's patron and dedicatee of the *Caesars*, according to John Lydus (*Mag.* 2.6). If this second reading is accepted, it would mean that Suetonius was foremost among those who did not show the requisite respect towards Sabina, and that the others were simply held no less accountable as his associates. It is not, therefore, that 'Suetonius fell with Septicius', as is generally presumed,[17] but the other way around. Whatever act of disrespect was stated as the reason, the significant point is that the others fell along with Suetonius, who was the main person whom Sabina, or perhaps Hadrian, wished to dismiss.

In light of this focus on Suetonius as the main cause of these dismissals, their vague and trivial grounds suggest a probable interpretation that was

---

13 Paratore 1970, 224; D'Anna 1988, 64–5; Hemelrijk 1999, 114.

14 Cizek 1977, 189–92.

15 Freisenbruch 2010, 166–7; Williams 2010, 66. For the even more remote possibility that Suetonius gave offence by publishing his *Famous Courtesans*, see Birley 1997, 139; cf. Speller 2003, 144. But on this work as less scandalous than it has long seemed, see Power 2014c. The exact slight is considered 'impenetrable' by Bradley 2016, 148; see also 150–1. Uden 2020, 596–7 similarly considers the story a *topos* in Suetonius' works and thus a complete fabrication. For the far-fetched idea that Hadrian himself contrived the whole incident, instructing the pair to slight his wife in order to have an excuse to fire them, see Brennan 2018, 201, 267 n. 6 with earlier references.

16 He has since corrected the error; see Birley 2005, 223–4.

17 Wallace-Hadrill 1983, 6.

first put forth by Brugnoli: the supposed indiscretion was not the real reason, but the pretence for a hidden agenda, such as the division of the post of *ab epistulis* into two positions, one for letters in Latin and another for those in Greek.[18] In fact, the version of this story that we have was merely one sensational rumour about what had happened, which the author of the *Augustan History* – or the information's likely source, Marius Maximus – simply preferred over others, since these later biographers were less honest than Suetonius in their reporting of variant traditions. The actual transgression of decorum turns out to be historically irrelevant, since it was probably no real mistake at all, and would certainly have been unworthy of the consequence that Suetonius incurred. Rather, it was a convenient excuse for what Hadrian wanted to do anyway. As Baldwin writes, 'it is quite feasible that he had to wait and cast around for an excuse to get rid of a praetorian prefect and an imperial secretary.'[19] One could argue that Hadrian did not need a reason to fire his secretary, because he had absolute authority to do so, but at least politically some reason would have been required, especially if he wished to divide his secretaries' duties, making them less individually powerful.

Suetonius seems, on the contrary, to have been a married man who was romantically devoted to his wife, according to Pliny the Younger, who writes in AD 110 that the biographer at the age of about forty had 'experienced little fortune in his marriage' (*parum felix matriomonium expertus est*, *Ep.* 10.94.2), which is a misleading euphemism that does not imply an unhappy marriage, but rather simply that he had not been blessed with children, so that the emperor Trajan might grant him the tax exemptions of the *ius trium liberorum*.[20] The real implication is that the couple's lack of success had not been for lack of trying, which suggests that they were otherwise committed to one another, and after a long period of time together, had not had any children despite the great length of their marriage. The basis for speculations on Suetonius' infidelity is uncertain, and we must not rely on the bad reputation that he has long had to interpret his life. Suetonius' life, like his writings, is often thought to have been more controversial than it actually was.

18 See Brugnoli 1964, 65; 1968a, 27. For this division of *ab epistulis* as probably occurring under Hadrian, see Lindsay 1994, 458–9.
19 Baldwin 1975a, 68 = 1975b, 23 = 1983, 43 = 1989b, 37 = 1997, 255.
20 Cf. Mart. 9a.5, with Watson and Watson 2003, 3, 107 (ad loc.); Zeiner 2005, 176. On this letter to Trajan, see above, pp. 12, 40–1.

27 Caligula and the Bludgeoned Priest*

In a much discussed passage, Suetonius tells the story of when the emperor Caligula was pretending to perform the job of a minister's assistant (*popa*), who during a religious ceremony would normally bludgeon the animal on the head with his sacrificial axe, so that the higher minister (*cultrarius*) may then slit its throat; in this case, however, the emperor felled the minister instead (*Calig.* 32.3).[1] In order to appreciate the anecdote in its full context within the biography, more of the passage should be quoted:

> animum quoque remittenti *ludoque et epulis* dedito eadem factorum dictorumque saeuitia aderat ... murmillonem e ludo rudibus secum battuentem et sponte prostratum confodit ferrea sica ac more uictorum cum palma discucurrit. admota altaribus uictima succinctus poparum habitu elato alte malleo cultrarium mactauit. lautiore conuiuio effusus subito in cachinnos consulibus, qui iuxta cubabant, quidnam rideret blande quaerentibus, 'quid', inquit, 'nisi uno meo nutu iugulari utrumque uestrum statim posse?'

> In diversions too, when engaged in *play and banquets*, he displayed the same cruel deeds and words ... When a gladiator who was still in training was sparring with him using wooden swords, and had deliberately fallen, he stabbed him with an iron dagger, and ran around in the manner of winners with a trophy. When a sacrificial animal had been led to the altars, he dressed himself in the attire of a minister's assistant and, raising his axe in the air, slew the minister. In a glorious feast, when he suddenly burst into laughter, and the consuls sitting next to him obsequiously enquired why he was smiling, he said: 'What, if not the fact that, with one nod from me, each of your throats can be instantly cut?'
> (*Calig.* 32.1–3)

---

* This chapter was first published in *Mnemosyne* 68 (2015), 131–5.
1 Due to an earlier version of this chapter, the standard biography of Caligula has now been emended to include this story about the emperor, which had long been dismissed as mere fiction; see Barrett 2015, 187 n. 42.

The biographer here demonstrates his customary ability to group the items of his rubric *ludoque et epulis* in ascending order of effect, moving from gladiator to religious minister to consuls, and culminating in a pithy saying.[2] Woods has speculated that the story about the minister never happened, and that Suetonius' source merely invented it based on a misunderstanding of a different episode, which is reported by Cassius Dio:[3]

κυβεύων δέ ποτε, καὶ μαθὼν ὅτι οὐκ εἴη οἱ ἀργύριον, ἤτησέ τε τὰς τῶν Γαλατῶν ἀπογραφάς, καὶ ἐξ αὐτῶν τοὺς πλουσιωτάτους θανατωθῆναι κελεύσας ἐπανῆλθέ τε πρὸς τοὺς συγκυβευτὰς καὶ ἔφη ὅτι Ὑμεῖς περὶ ὀλίγων δραχμῶν ἀγωνίζεσθε, ἐγὼ δὲ ἐς μυρίας καὶ πεντακισχιλίας μυριάδας ἤθροισα. καὶ οὗτοι μὲν ἐν οὐδενὶ λόγῳ ἀπώλοντο· ἀμέλει εἷς τις αὐτῶν Ἰούλιος Σακερδὼς ἄλλως μὲν εὖ χρημάτων ἥκων, οὐ μέντοι καὶ ὑπερπλουτῶν ὥστε καὶ ἐπιβουλευθῆναι δι' αὐτά, ὅμως ἐξ ἐπωνυμίας ἀπεσφάγη· οὕτως ἀκρίτως πάντα ἐγίγνετο.

When he was playing dice once, and realized that he had no money, he demanded the census-list of Gauls, and, after ordering the wealthiest of them to be executed, returned to his fellow players, saying: 'You compete for a few drachmas, while I have taken in a hundred and fifty million.' And these men died unnoticed; indeed, one of them, Julius Sacerdos, who had generally decent funds, but not so abundant as to draw the attention of plotters for it, had his throat cut due to his similar name. This was how senselessly everything happened.

(Dio Cass. 59.22.3–4)

According to Woods, the source followed by Suetonius mistook the victim's name Sacerdos, which means 'priest', for an actual priest, and embellished the entire anecdote to fit the bill. Woods does not find the story in Suetonius well-suited to the rubrics of *ludus* and *epulae*, and 'the realization that the story originates in a description of his behaviour while playing at dice solves this problem.'[4]

---

2 See Hurley 1993, 128 (ad loc.); cf. Brandão 2009, 223 for this section as part of a larger crescendo (*gradatio*) in the *Life*. On this technique in Suetonius, see e.g. Steidle 1951, 56–8; Mouchová 1968, 79–104; Cizek 1977, 118–34; Gascou 1984, 697–700; Pausch 2004, 294–301; for the biographer's use of characterizing sayings, Damon 2014; Mitchell 2015.

3 Woods 2012, 452–4. For scepticism about the historical reliability of Suetonius' story, cf. Plass 1988, 68, 82; Guastella 1992, 212 (ad loc.): 'Di questo episodio, raccontato nella consueta forma generica, e così privo di un qualsiasi inquadramento da sembrare francamente incredibile, ancora una volta Svetonio è l'unico testimone'; also Brandão 2009, 184, 322. It was notably absent from two previous major biographies of Caligula (Barrett 1989; Winterling 2011), but my argument in its favour has now been accepted; see above, n. 1.

4 Woods 2012, 454. Nor is he the only scholar to feel the need to explain, or apologize for, the story's placement; see Hurley 1993, 128: 'Suetonius classifies religious ritual among leisure activities (*animum ... remittenti*, 32.1)'; Wardle 1994, 26: 'within examples of

First of all, Woods' explanation ignores the problem that a *sacerdos* is not the same as a *cultrarius*, who was merely one of the priest's ministers, rather than the priest himself, who would never actually slay the animal during a sacrifice: Suetonius' story is not that of a bludgeoned priest, but of a bludgeoned minister. More importantly, his explanation is needless if we observe the humorous and playful context of Suetonius' scene and of the other examples surrounding it in the same section. Caligula is simply playing the role of *popa* for fun, and the murder is therefore categorized as an 'amusement' in the same way as the emperor's preceding diversion (the more literal *ludus*, OLD 3) with the gladiator, as well as his following threat to the consuls.[5] This amusement is underscored by the verbal wit of Suetonius' sentence, which is an excellent example of an unforeseen twist (Cic. *De or.* 2.284; Quint. *Inst.* 6.3.84), since the punch line ironically defies expectation: *elato alte malleo | cultrarium mactauit.*[6] The careful order of Suetonius' heading also suggests that 'play' will be illustrated before 'banquets', and, just as the final anecdote provides a cruel example of the latter, the story about the minister speaks to the former.[7] Hence, Suetonius is able to make a smooth transition in the very next section (*Calig.* 33) from the emperor's playful relaxations to his 'jokes' (*ioci*). This interpretation is the most sensible way to reconcile the story's position in this part of the biography, and renews credence in its possible factuality, allaying the doubts of some that the emperor, as *pontifex maximus*, would ever really discharge such menial duties.[8]

Since there is nothing in the passage of Dio quoted above to support a connection with Suetonius' rather dissimilar anecdote, aside from the loose resemblance of a man named Sacerdos, which at any rate does mean *cultrarius*, it is better taken as describing different deaths, which Suetonius himself also records to illustrate other points about Caligula in the

---

saeuitia at times of relaxation, at play or banquets, Caligula's murder of the *cultrarius* at a sacrifice seems ill chosen ... However, compared to the occasions where Suetonius orders and classifies his material consistently and appropriately, his failures, or apparent failures, are a small problem.'

5 See OLD s.v. *ludus* 5: 'Light-hearted or idle conduct or talk, fun, merriment, frivolity, etc.' We might compare the word's use at *Claud.* 8, where the sleeping Claudius is whipped as a joke; see Hurley 2001, 89 (ad loc.). It is also used of mime performances at *Iul.* 84.2; see Sumi 2002, 566–70; *pace* Osgood 2006, 13 n. 5; Hurley 2011, 46; Scantamburlo 2011, 244 (ad loc.). Cf. *Aug.* 53.1, *Tib.* 45. Suetonius' phrasing may imply something of this sense, since he says that Caligula was merely 'dressed' as a minister's assistant (*succinctus poparum habitu*); cf. Lindsay 1993, 124 (ad loc.).

6 Reekmans 1992, 230; Brandão 2009, 80; cf. Plass 1988, 35.

7 On the similar precision of other headings in Suetonius, see e.g. Carter 1982, 8; Townend 1982a, xii; Wardle 2001, 65.

8 See e.g. Hurley 1993, 128; also Wardle 1994, 262 with bibliography. This perceived inconsistency has no doubt led to the story's widespread dismissal.

biography (*Calig.* 30.1, 41.2).[9] Taken together, the latter passages do not so much form a doublet, as the separate and careful distribution by Suetonius of details from the same historical event for different purposes;[10] the biographer has removed the confusion over Sacerdos' name that is reported by Dio to an earlier section (*Calig.* 30.1), just as he often returns to familiar terrain with further information. In fact, it is admirable how little he repeats himself, and his points of overlap are usually distinctive for providing only new material.[11] There is thus no concrete basis for equating the passage about the bludgeoned minister with the murder of Sacerdos, just as there is no reason to find it unsuitably classified by Suetonius.

9 See Edmondson 1992, 173 (on Dio 59.22.3–4); *pace* Saller (1980, 75) and Wardle (1994, 64–5), who question whether Suetonius reports the same event as Dio at *Calig.* 41.2, but fail to observe the evidence of 30.1.
10 Cf. Hurley 1993, 122 on *Calig.* 30.1; and generally, Bradley 1978, 263.
11 See e.g. *Aug.* 101 ~ *Tib.* 21.3; *Tib.* 52 ~ *Calig.* 6.2; *Claud.* 44.1–2 ~ *Ner.* 33.1; *Galb.* 19.1 ~ *Otho* 6.2; *Vit.* 9 ~ 18; *Tit.* 10 ~ *Dom.* 2.3.

28 The Conspirator against Caligula

Towards the end of his *Life* of Caligula, Suetonius recounts with customary brevity an omen that portended the emperor's death:

sacrificans respersus est phoenicopteri sanguine.

As he was sacrificing, he [Caligula] was sprayed with the blood of a flamingo.

(*Calig.* 57.4)

The historian Josephus, who appears to have drawn on the same first-century source as Suetonius, provides a partly contradictory version of this event, in which he states that it was not Caligula himself who was sprayed with blood, but one of the senators involved in his assassination named Asprenas. In Josephus, the omen therefore predicted – or *also* predicted (Asprenas was subsequently killed too, as Josephus later reports at *AJ* 19.98), or was at least *misunderstood* to predict – the conspirator's demise instead:

πίπτοντος τῶν ἱερείων τινὸς συνέβη αἵματι τὴν Ἀσπρῆνα στολὴν ἑνὸς τῶν συγκλητικῶν ἀνάπλεων γενέσθαι.

As one of the sacrificial animals fell, it happened that the clothes of Asprenas, one of the senators, were sprayed with blood.

(*AJ* 19.87)

This is a small, but significant, historical discrepancy, and Woods interprets the Suetonian passage as follows: 'It is clear that Suetonius understood that Caligula had accidentally splattered himself with the blood of the sacrifice.'[1]

---

1 Woods 2018a, 874. The question of whether Suetonius was confused by his source here is simply side-stepped by Köster 2021. For other arguments that the biographer has misread an earlier writer, see e.g. Bowersock 1990, 387, who is discredited by Courtney 2009, 42 n. 4; Woods 2004 and 2006, 138–47, who is again refuted below, Chapters 30 and 31, respectively; Cook 2020, 253, whose conclusion is also overturned below, Chapter 29. Another case made by Woods (2019) for the detail of Caligula's constant invitations

Is it? Woods' ultimate conclusion is that Asprenas must have been the one who was sprayed in historical reality, but Suetonius simply misread the story as referring to Caligula, possibly misled by the original source's discussion of the later confusion over the omen's double meaning, since both men eventually died.[2] In other words, according to Woods, both versions were essentially in the common tradition, and Suetonius' error or reduction of the tale's richness was due either to haste or to carelessness. But such anecdotes were often in flux, and able to be fitted to any new rhetorical context by creative writers.[3] It is a disservice to Suetonius not to afford him the same capability of doing what other historical writers regularly did in antiquity, that is, change a detail to conform better with what they viewed as the gist of its significance.[4] For scholars such as Woods, Suetonius is never being clever in his ingenuity, so much as obtuse in his selectivity: his process is one of distillation alone, since he is not considered sly enough to have deftly made the story his own.

Making such assumptions about the biographer is a common practice, and Suetonian invention is almost always dismissed as the most unlikely scenario, if it is conceived of at all.[5] In this regard, he is unique among his peers, being routinely underestimated more than any of our parallel authors on the early Roman Empire. But note the cautious way in which Suetonius segues to this anecdote: 'omens of the event [Caligula's death] were even perceived in things that transpired by chance a little earlier that very day' (*prodigiorum loco habita sunt etiam quae forte illo ipso die paulo prius acciderant, Calig.* 57.3). Josephus, by contrast, is far more assured about the omen's genuineness: 'it soon proved an obvious omen' (ἦν δ᾽ ἄρα εἰς οἰωνὸν … φανερόν, *AJ* 19.87). In a footnote, Woods admits to being perplexed by Suetonius' noticeable contextualization just before the biographer presents his evidence, which suggests that it may be untrue in some respect:

It is not clear why Suetonius should seem to distance himself from accepting the divinatory reality of the alleged omens occurring in the final hours before the assassination, as revealed by his impersonal

---

of the moon to his bed (*Calig.* 22.4) as the result of a misunderstanding by Suetonius or his earlier source is no less speculative, based on the presumption of a lost first-century account that was both in Greek and ambiguously worded.

2 Woods 2018a, 879.

3 See Saller 1980, 74–9; Power 2014a, 73–4.

4 Cf. Simcox 1883, 211: 'all the stories which he [Suetonius] gives might have been or ought to have been true. They illustrate a sound view of the character which is under discussion.' See also above, Chapter 9, for Suetonius' similar treatment of possibly apocryphal material on Roman writers in the *Illustrious Men*.

5 See the references above, p. 187, n. 27. Woods 2018a, 874 n. 4 himself merely considers the possibility that this tale was invented by the common source, not by Suetonius. On the general reluctance of scholars to impute any creativity to Suetonius, see also below, Chapter 32.

introduction to this list of incidents, but does not seem to have similar doubts concerning earlier alleged omens.[6]

Woods then muses in the same footnote that the original source must have attributed these particular omens to rumour, which resolves the difficulty by adhering to his own simplistic argument for Suetonius' misunderstanding of his source.

However, the more convincing reason is that the biographer evidently did not wish to claim responsibility for the item, which thus permitted him to appropriate it as he wished, giving himself room to manoeuvre: if it is dubious, it need not be as accurately reported, especially since, as Hurley notes, this kind of omen was a *topos* that was suspect as a probable invention anyway in the first place.[7] Suetonius' introduction to these omens ambiguously casts doubt not only on whether it was an actual omen, but also on whether it ever really happened, accidentally or not. Writing that the blood splatter was something 'even perceived' (*habita sunt etiam*) to portend death only because it happened 'by chance' – or indeed 'perhaps' (*forte*) – on that day is tantamount to disavowing the information. As often, Suetonius' authorial statements point the way to what he is doing to his historical material, or rather getting away with doing.[8] Suetonius is assumed to have misunderstood his source on this omen before the assassination of Caligula, but it is more probable that he is here not merely bowdlerizing his source, but personally altering it to maintain his narrow biographical focus on the emperor.[9]

6 Woods 2018a, 874 n. 4.
7 See Hurley 1993, 205 (ad loc.).
8 For Suetonius' disavowal of certainty as a rhetorical strategy, see above, pp. 44–5, 91–2.
9 On the biographer's especially precise focus on his subject, see Power 2014b, 4–8 with further references.

29 Jesus' Flight into Egypt in Suetonius

Iudaeos impulsore Chresto assidue tumultuantis Roma expulit.

He banished the Jews from Rome for their continual rioting that was led by Christ.

(Claud. 25.4)

This is not only the most famous line that Suetonius ever wrote, but also one of the briefest and most puzzling.[1] It causes no apparent grammatical difficulty, but poses at least one problem of historical interpretation in the word *impulsore*. How could Claudius have 'expelled the Jews from Rome for constantly making disturbances *at the instigation of* Christ', when Jesus had already died during the reign of Tiberius?[2] Some have tried to strain the

---

1 See e.g. Dunn 2011, 3: 'a confused reference'. The sentence has been much discussed by scholars; for bibliography, see Botermann 1996, 104–7; Slingerland 1997, 98–9; M. H. Williams 2004, 39–40, n. 22 = 2013, 40 n. 37. In this chapter, I use the translation of Suetonius by Rolfe 1913–14, with the sole exception of my adaptations of the passage under discussion; that of Cassius Dio by Cary 1924–25; and the King James Version of the Holy Bible.

2 Cf. Mottershead 1986, 149. The date of the expulsion is usually taken as either AD 41 or 49; see, respectively, Dio Cass. 60.6.6; Acts 18:2; and Oros. 7.6.15; with e.g. Hurley 2001, 176–7. Hurley's commentary describes well the issue of contradiction in Suetonius' phrase, but she dismisses it as a possible error: 'The historical Jesus was, of course, not inciting riots in Rome, but Christian missionaries were beginning to arrive … [Suetonius] was capable of inconsistency and simple carelessness and cannot be presumed to have had a clear understanding of the pesky group's origins – nor, perhaps, did his source' (177). Her conclusion seems at odds with the concession a page later (178) that this Chrestus is probably a famous figure, and therefore Jesus; cf. Momigliano 1934, 31–3 and below, n. 8. If Suetonius considered the facts of Jesus' life so commonplace, he would certainly have been aware of the well-known time of his death during the prefecture of Pontius Pilate, which was clearly in his first-century sources, as Tacitus attests (*Ann.* 15.44.3). Cf. also Pliny's reference without explanation to *Christiani* ('Christians', *Ep.* 10.96.1), on which see Ash 2018, 205: 'This suggests terminology familiar to contemporaries.' For the reference as a chronological error on the part of Suetonius, who was allegedly confused by his source, see also Cook 2020, 253 with further bibliography.

meaning of *impulsor* to mean simply 'because of',[3] but that is not how it is usually found in such contexts as an uproar (*tumultus*), rebellion (*seditio*), murder (*caedes*), or war (*bellum*), where it clearly implies the person's direct inciting of the act. The *Augustan History*, to take one example, uses the related word *impulsus* in this way when it reports that in the conspiracy to assassinate Caracalla, several on the staff of Marcius Agrippa had been made accomplices '*through the urging of* Martialis' (impulsu *Martialis, M. Ant.* 6.6), while Eutropius tells us how Numerian 'was murdered in a plot of which *the ring-leader* was Aper' (impulsore *Apro ... per insidias occisus est*, 9.18).[4] In other words, if Suetonius had wished to convey that these disturbances were merely 'due to Christ' or 'due to Christian preaching' more generally, he did a very poor job, misleading countless readers for centuries, who naturally assumed that the man in question must have actually been alive and present at Rome during this time, because that is what the Latin undeniably suggests, at least as it stands.

For this reason, editors have been reluctant to change *Chresto*, which is found in the manuscripts, to *Christo*, as Orosius appears to have done in his *History against the Pagans* (7.6.15),[5] since they believed that this man could not possibly have been Jesus, but was rather a different instigator by the name of Chrestus who lived under Claudius.[6] Yet as scholars have noted, it would be very unlike Suetonius not to identify such a person more clearly by writing *quodam Chresto* ('a certain Chrestus') to distinguish his anonymity.[7] On the other hand, if it is indeed Jesus whom Suetonius mentions in reference to this unrest among the Jews, why does he not make that fact clearer, as Tacitus does when he describes him as 'the founder of the name' (*auctor nominis*) of the Christian religion (*Ann.* 15.44.3)? Moreover, the historian's description proves that a reference to Christ at least appeared in the first-century source material that he shared with Suetonius, making it all the more likely that Suetonius' 'Chrestus' is Jesus. When one considers that the biographer rarely includes a name unless he can reasonably expect the reader to know the person's significance, it is uniquely odd that he should have been so obscure on this occasion.[8] His later reference to Christians in the *Nero* (16.2) seems predicated on the view that Christ's identity

---

3 See e.g. Stern 1980, 117; Spence 2004, 76–8, 105–7 with further references; cf. Riesner 1998, 166.
4 For other examples, see Cook 2010, 20–1.
5 On Orosius' probable alteration of the name, see Boman 2011, 369.
6 See e.g. Benko 1969, 412; Van Voorst 2000, 32; Gruen 2002, 39; Carrier 2014, 271–2.
7 Baumgarten-Crusius 1816, 2.55; Rolfe 1913–14, 2.52; Janne 1934, 540; Bruce 1962, 316; 1982, 338 = 1990, 82; Stern 1980, 116; Cook 2010, 18–19.
8 Mottershead 1986, 150. On Suetonius' deliberate use of names, see Baldwin 1983, 177; Wardle 1992, 475; Jones 2002. Townend 1967, 84 even went so far as to call Suetonius' seemingly ambiguous reference to Jesus 'infuriating'; cf. id. 1970, 1021. I am not convinced by the argument of Carrier 2014 that the Tacitean passage is a spurious interpolation.

should already be taken for granted, so that 'Christians' do not require the same explanation as when they appear in the *Annals*.[9] This is not even to mention the obvious fact that the Bible contains no story about Jesus causing Jewish disturbances in Rome.[10] Besides these problems, the only evidence that Chrestus may have been a misspelling or alternative spelling of Christus is found in authors who are later than Suetonius (Tert. *Apol.* 3; Lactant. *Div. inst.* 4.7.5), and possibly dependent on this very passage of the *Claudius*. At any rate, the different meanings of the two names (*Chrestus*/Χρηστός, 'good, sweet'; *Christus*/Χριστός, 'anointed, Messiah') appear to have been quite distinctly known before late antiquity, and by no means confused.[11] Because of these contradictions and the lack of overall sense in the line, there may be a more serious problem with the text, especially in the presence of at least one misspelled word.[12]

The corrupt part of the text is probably found in the words that do not logically fit. If one presumes that this man is Jesus, he could in no way have been the 'instigator' of disturbances at Rome that took place after his death. In place of the paradosis *impulsore Chresto*, which is historically incorrect, I suggest printing <*en*>*im pulso orbe Christo*, thus connecting the whole line to the end of the previous sentence, which should now be signified with a semicolon.[13] One common kind of scribal error is the incorrect division of words due to manuscripts being written in a running script without spaces, or *scriptio continua*. To give some instances of this phenomenon, Petronius' *ab asse creuit* (*Sat.* 43.1) became *abbas secreuit*, which is the result in the first place of dividing the words improperly (*abas/secreuit*, rather than *ab/asse/creuit*). This original text was at last restored

---

9 There was thus probably a clear reference to Jesus in an earlier biography. For how Suetonius expects the reader to have prior knowledge of much generally historical material, owing to his especially biographical focus, see Townend 1967, 84; Power 2014b, 13. He also hardly ever repeats himself, so that the reader may cross-refer to other parts of the *Caesars* for more information; see above, p. 209. On the brevity of his style, see e.g. Williams 1989, 774 = 2013, 71; above, pp. 143, 176.

10 See May 1938, 38–9.

11 See esp. Benko 1969, 408–10; Edwards 1991, 232–3.

12 Housman 1913, 110 n. 1 = 1972, 2.868 n. 1 suspected a corruption in a different passage of Suetonius (*Aug.* 94.5), which may be similarly textual, on the sole basis of historical inaccuracy. See also Kaster 2014, 149–50 on the fifteenth-century correction of *praedicator* to *pedicator* at *Iul.* 49.1, which is supported only by context and historical logic; cf. id. 2016b, 128–9.

13 A less likely conjecture is *enim* with a noun such as *pastore* ('shepherd') or *praeceptore* ('teacher'), since Jesus is referred to by both titles in the Gospels; see John 10:11, 14 (ποιμήν); cf. Matthew 9:36; and id. 23:10 (καθηγητής), respectively. But the sense of these possibilities remains unclear, and we would be left with a no less vaguely causal meaning, such as 'on account of the shepherd Christ', or 'following the guidance of Christ', which still implies his contemporary presence in Rome. They are also not as close to the *ductus litterarum* as the above conjecture, which could most easily have been misread as *impulsore*.

from the manuscript reading only by the scholarly conjecture of Scheffer in the seventeenth century, while Juvenal's *illic aeluros* (15.7) was clearly corrupted to *illicaeruleos*, which was later only partially corrected to *illic caeruleos*; it was not until the mid-sixteenth century that Brodeau suggested *aeluros*, understanding that the middle letters *lur* had also become transposed into *rul*.[14] Another similar example of the textual difficulties caused by word divisions is a sentence that appears in one manuscript of Tacitus rightly as <u>*Corbulo, ne* irritum bellum</u> ... <u>*exscindere parat*</u> castella (*Ann.* 13.39.1), but in another manuscript has been misconstrued, with the first pair of underlined words wrongly combined together as a single word, and the second pair incorrectly separated: <u>*Corbulone* irritum bellum</u> ... <u>*exinde repetit*</u> castella.[15] Without a correct version surviving in another manuscript for comparison, as here, such mistakes can sometimes be difficult to discern with the different spaces between words in our modern texts, but once they are recognized, the new coherence that is brought by the restoration makes the new reading obvious.

If Suetonius' *en* ('look!') had been read separately from the *im* of *impulsore* as its own word, it may well have been deleted by a scribe as out of context, but at any rate the loss of small particles such as *en* is a regular enough occurrence in the transmission of ancient texts that it need not detain us. It is noteworthy that the letters *b* and *r* were liable to confusion in some medieval scripts.[16] This would give us *im pulso orre*, from which haplography would produce *impulsore*. A second error seems to have occurred in the corruption of *Christo* into *Chresto*, since Christus could easily have been mistaken for Chrestus, and the letters *i* and *e* were often confused in Latin transcriptions.[17] Read the fully emended sentence, including my change in punctuation, as follows:

> Iliensibus quasi Romanae gentis auctoribus tributa in perpetuum remisit recitata uetere epistula Graeca senatus populique R. Seleuco regi amicitiam et societatem ita demum pollicentis si consanguineos suos Ilienses ab omni onere immunes praestitisset; Iudaeos <u><en>im pulso orbe Christo</u> assidue tumultuantis Roma expulit.
>
> <en>im pulso orbe Christo *scripsi*: impulsore Chresto *mss*.

> He allowed the people of Ilium perpetual exemption from tribute, on the ground that they were the founders of the Roman race, reading an ancient letter of the senate and people of Rome written in Greek to king Seleucus, in which they promised him their friendship and alliance only

---

14 See Tarrant 2016, 11, 74, respectively. On the former error, see also Reynolds and Wilson 2013, 224.
15 Reynolds and Wilson 2013, 234.
16 Dyck 2017, 311.
17 Hunt, Smith, and Stok 2017, 74.

on condition that he should keep their kinsfolk of Ilium free from every burden; <u>for indeed</u> when the Jews, <u>after they had driven Christ from their region,</u> constantly made disturbances, he expelled them from Rome.

(Claud. 25.3–4)

The corruption of this phrase into *impulsore Chresto* would have occurred before Orosius' comment in the early fifth century, which no doubt perpetuated the mistake that found its way into M, our earliest manuscript of the *Caesars* that was copied in the ninth century, and the one that best represents the archetype from which all others descend.[18] If we accept that Suetonius expected the reader to know the person in question, and that it is therefore most likely Jesus, then the biographer would probably have spelled the name correctly with an 'i', just as he does in the *Nero* (*Christiani, Ner.* 16.2). It is also spelled this way by his contemporaries such as Tacitus (*Christianos ... Christus, Ann.* 15.44.3), who shared common sources with Suetonius, and such as Pliny the Younger (*Christo ... Christiani, Ep.* 10.96.5), so that *Christo* could easily have been the original text that was simply misread by a scribe as *Chresto*, since Chrestus was a very common name in the ancient world.[19]

An objection could be raised that Tacitus' eleventh-century manuscript M2, on which all subsequent manuscripts for Books 11–16 of the *Annals* depend, actually has *Chrestiani* (*Ann.* 15.44.3), which some editors choose to retain. However, this is our sole manuscript to survive from before the fourteenth century for this passage, and *Christiani* was favoured by Fisher as a cogent emendation in his OCT.[20] Equally cogent was the correction of Suetonius' *Chrestus* to *Christus* by Orosius, who influenced a number of subsequent Christian discussions of this passage from the *Claudius*.[21] Shaw has suggested that the correct spelling in Tacitus' *Annals* is indeed *Chrestiani*, and even proposes that the historian's other word *Christus* may be wrong, appealing directly to Orosius' alteration of Suetonius: 'I believe that the *Christus* of M2 has similarly been corrected ... it makes the most

---

18 Cf. *mimum* at *Aug.* 99.1, which had already been corrupted into *minimum* prior to the composition of M; see above, Chapter 19. As with the common name *Chrestus* (on which see below), this is another easily made, and therefore likely, mistake. In his new OCT, Kaster (2016a) has now accepted my argument for *mimum*, and also emends his earlier text (1995) of Suetonius' *Grammarians*, due to my defence of Vahlen's conjecture *nam erat* for *nametra* (*Gramm.* 13.1), which is based on similar stylistic grounds to those used in this chapter; see above, Chapter 17.

19 See Benko 1969, 410–12; Cook 2020, 255–7; also the references above, n. 11. Conversely, the name Christus is rare in Latin, and thus prone to being misread; see Cook 2010, 16–17, who speculatively attributes the reading *Chrestus* to confusion on the part of both Suetonius and his source (21).

20 Fisher 1906. On the manuscript tradition of Tacitus, see Tarrant and Winterbottom 1983.

21 See Boman 2011, 358–69.

logical sense for Tacitus to say that *Chrestianus* would come from *Chres-tus*.'[22] Although Shaw at least partly accepts my argument that Pliny's con-temporary circle, at least with regard to Suetonius and Tacitus, was not as close as many have assumed,[23] he still sees a confluence of orthogra-phy between Tacitus and Suetonius that bespeaks a supposedly authentic Roman usage of *Chrestiani*, which must be refuted here.[24] Edwards, who is apparently unknown to Shaw, put it best: 'Even if we were to accept ... Chrestiani at Annales XV.44, there is still no evidence for Chrestus in the circle to which Suetonius belonged.'[25] As Edwards demonstrates, Pliny has *Christiani* seven times (*Ep.* 10.96.1–3, 5–6), twice more in his reply from Trajan (10.97.1–2), and *Christus* three times (10.96.5–7); Tacitus has at least *Christus* once; and Suetonius has at least *Christiani* once. Ergo, Tacitus' *Chrestiani* and Suetonius' *Chrestus* are the odd men out, with no confirming parallels in the other authors, and in both cases with reasons to suspect that the earliest surviving manuscript may be in error. The argu-ment should thus be the other way around, because the preponderance of literary evidence actually points us towards the 'i' spelling. Orosius rightly knew at least to correct the misspelled title Christus (which could have been unknown to earlier pagan scribes), but not the first part of the cor-rupt phrase, *impulsore*, since as is unfortunately often the case with textual errors, it already gave a grammatically complete sense to the line, if none-theless a confusing one, as he admits through the phrase *nequaquam dis-cernitur* ('in no way clear', Oros. 7.6.16). However, that one of Suetonius' earliest extant readers suspected the need for an emendation here suggests how problematic the manuscript tradition is for this section of the passage. Orosius' word *Christo* is not, therefore, an example of an error due to the spread of Christianity, which was another palaeographical tendency,[26] but rather of Christian thinking actually helping an author to restore a text through its quotation.

According to my recovered text, Suetonius notes the ironic fact that the Jews, after they themselves had forced a man out of Judaea, were exiled by Claudius for the same kind of internal strife within their own commu-nity. There is not necessarily any implication that these riots had to do with the belief that Jesus was indeed *Christus*, that is, the Messiah; all we know is that Suetonius simply referred to him as Christ rather than Jesus of Nazareth, probably because that is how he was named in his source. To

22 Shaw 2015, 80–1, following Fuchs 1950, 68–74; cf. Shaw 2018, 239. Shaw's (2015) larger argument against Nero's persecution of the Christians has since been challenged by Jones 2017, who, in turn, has also been swiftly answered, if not fully refuted, by Shaw (2018). *Contra* the view of Shaw more broadly, see also Cook 2020.
23 See Chapter 25, cited in its earlier form by Shaw 2015, 89 n. 77.
24 Shaw 2015, 84.
25 Edwards 1991, 232 n. 3.
26 See Reynolds and Wilson 2013, 232–3.

infer that these disturbances must obviously have related to the spread of Christianity is to make an *a priori* assumption in the face of other known examples of Jewish expulsions from Rome on various other grounds, albeit before Jesus (Val. Max. 1.3.3; Joseph. *AJ* 18.83; Dio Cass. 57.18.5).[27] My emendation does at least eliminate the evidence for an absent distinction between Christianity and Judaism in the Greco-Roman world of the second century, which had been based on Jesus' allegedly being a leader (*impulsor*) of the Jews, making them his followers,[28] although the exact nature of the disturbances in the *Claudius*, which the biographer only tells us were 'frequent' (*assidue*), remains a matter of conjecture.

However, one conjecture is especially desirable. The report of the historian Cassius Dio on the measures taken against the Jews in AD 41, despite its different interpretation of the events, is possibly the same one described here by Suetonius, because of the very close contexts of expulsion from Rome and especially the two authors' mutual reference to the idea of a 'disturbance' (ταραχή ~ *tumultus*).[29] In Dio's passage, the reason given for imposing restrictions on the Jews, rather than driving them out, is that they 'had again increased so greatly that by reason of their multitude it would have been hard without raising a tumult to bar them from the city' (πλεονάσαντας αὖθις, ὥστε χαλεπῶς ἂν ἄνευ ταραχῆς ὑπὸ τοῦ ὄχλου σφῶν τῆς πόλεως εἰρχθῆναι, 60.6.6), which points to the same concern over the danger of disorderly behaviour. We know that the Jewish population at Rome had grown to about 40,000 Jews by the early imperial period,[30] and that Tiberius famously issued a ban on Jews in AD 19, which Claudius seems to have been reinstating.[31] According to Suetonius' description of the original ban by Tiberius, the emperor 'removed from the city' (*urbe summouit*) all of the Jews except those who could serve in the military (*Tib.* 36). Tiberius was at least partly motivated to control the Roman borders in the first place by the growing number of Jews in the city, especially the threat that they posed not only to law and order due to their constant uprisings,[32] but also to Roman culture more generally.[33] Claudius' expulsion may therefore have resulted from similar concerns. As one scholar has put it, the ban by

27 Benko 1969, 407, 409, 412–13.
28 See Paget 2010, 10.
29 Slingerland 1997, 98, 105; cf. Stern 1980, 115–16, who similarly finds the two reports historically reconcilable; also above, n. 2. On the date of AD 41 for the expulsion in Suetonius as certainly preferable over that of AD 49, see Mottershead 1986, 151–3.
30 See Williams 1989, 769 n. 19 = 2013, 66 n. 19 with further references. It is noteworthy that the references in Josephus (*AJ* 18.3.5) and Tacitus (*Ann.* 2.85) to Tiberius' expulsion of the Jews both mention their considerable number in Rome, which is no doubt based on a common source that was contemporary with the event; see Merrill 1919, 366–8, 371; Benko 1969, 417.
31 Cf. Benko 1969, 413.
32 Williams 1989, 779–80 = 2013, 75–7.
33 See van der Lans 2015, 39–42.

Claudius 'responded to *tumultus* among the Jewish population – a word with political overtones'.[34] By expelling the Jews, Claudius was seen to be a strong emperor who kept the public peace by removing potentially violent or criminal elements from Roman society.[35]

The biographer's brief report about Jesus' flight from Judaea, as we can now understand it, is supported by evidence at the beginning of the Gospel of Matthew in the story of the flight into Egypt that forms part of the infancy narrative. Matthew (2:16) tells us that Jesus was driven from his native Jewish province into Egypt because of Herod the Great, who had issued an edict that the infants of Bethlehem should be killed. In fact, according to this first gospel, Jesus had to remain an exile from Judaea even during the reign of Herod's son Archelaus, growing up instead in the nearby province of Galilee, where he was taken by his parents Joseph and Mary:

Ἀναχωρησάντων δὲ αὐτῶν ἰδοὺ ἄγγελος Κυρίου φαίνεται κατ᾽ ὄναρ τῷ Ἰωσὴφ λέγων Ἐγερθεὶς παράλαβε τὸ παιδίον καὶ τὴν μητέρα αὐτοῦ καὶ φεῦγε εἰς Αἴγυπτον, καὶ ἴσθι ἐκεῖ ἕως ἂν εἴπω σοι· μέλλει γὰρ Ἡρῴδης ζητεῖν τὸ παιδίον τοῦ ἀπολέσαι αὐτό. ... ἀκούσας δὲ ὅτι Ἀρχέλαος βασιλεύει τῆς Ἰουδαίας ἀντὶ τοῦ πατρὸς αὐτοῦ Ἡρῴδου ἐφοβήθη ἐκεῖ ἀπελθεῖν· χρηματισθεὶς δὲ κατ᾽ ὄναρ ἀνεχώρησεν εἰς τὰ μέρη τῆς Γαλιλαίας, καὶ ἐλθὼν κατῴκησεν εἰς πόλιν λεγομένην Ναζαρέτ, ὅπως πληρωθῇ τὸ ῥηθὲν διὰ τῶν προφητῶν ὅτι Ναζωραῖος κληθήσεται.

And when they were departed, behold, the angel of the Lord appeareth to Joseph in a dream, saying, 'Arise, and take the young child and his mother, and flee into Egypt, and be thou there until I bring thee word: for Herod will seek the young child to destroy him.' ... But when he heard that Archelaus did reign in Judaea in the room of his father Herod, he was afraid to go thither: notwithstanding, being warned of God in a dream, he turned aside into the parts of Galilee. And he came and dwelt in a city called Nazareth: that it might be fulfilled which was spoken by the prophets, 'He shall be called a Nazarene.'

(Matthew 2:13, 22–3 KJV)

The language of 'flight' (φεῦγε) and 'destruction' (ἀπολέσαι) in the Lord's command suggests an equivalent kind of exile to the one described in our emended sentence of Suetonius, and the second dream sent to Joseph essentially extended this exile, which was not self-imposed, but forced upon Jesus and his parents as a *de facto* expulsion, due to the threat of death

34 Ibid. 67–71 (quotation at 67–8). Cf. Riesner 1998, 166 (citing the verb form of the word also at *Iul.* 69, *Calig.* 9, 17.1, 51.3, 55.1, *Galb.* 9.2, 19.2): 'the situation must have resulted in incidents that the Roman authorities viewed as disturbances of public order'; also Mottershead 1986, 150–1.
35 Suetonius also categorizes Nero's persecution of the Christians (*Ner.* 16.2) among his positive deeds; see Simcox 1883, 218.

from Herod that made them seek refuge in Egypt. The family's eventual resettlement in Galilee, rather than Judaea, was not simply a precaution, but a submission to the will of the Lord, who was keeping Jesus safe from being murdered. It is implied that if Jesus had indeed returned to Judaea, he would not have survived. Why else would Joseph have been guided instead to Nazareth? This view of the resettlement in Nazareth as an exile is especially strengthened if we understand Matthew's ironic allusions through this chapter to the sons of Israel who were slaughtered by Pharaoh (Exodus 1:22), and to the exile of Moses from Egypt (Exodus 2), to which he would eventually return after Pharaoh's death (Exodus 4:20).[36]

The Gospel of Matthew is an earlier work than the *Caesars*, having been dated to *c.* AD 85–95, and demonstrates that Jesus' flight on account of Herod had been part of a widely known tradition for at least two decades before Suetonius' collection of imperial biographies appeared around AD 120.[37] The specific reference to a man named Christ who had to leave the region of the Jews removes the ambiguity that was previously in the anecdote as it was preserved by our extant manuscripts, making it now a much clearer and more sensible reference to Jesus. It is unlikely to be a later Christian forgery that also became quickly corrupted before Orosius, not only because the coincidence of two such fates befalling exactly the same sentence of the manuscripts in so small a timeframe is beyond belief, but more importantly because it is confirmed through comparison with the biographer's typical style, which corroborates the emended text as genuinely Suetonian. The word *enim* ('for indeed') explains the thematic connection between these Jewish 'disturbances' (*tumultuantis*) and the 'every burden' (*omni onere*) from which Claudius wished to spare the Trojans due to their shared ancestry with the Romans, and from which he also spared the Romans themselves, according to Suetonius, by exiling the Jews. Suetonius portrays Claudius not only as equating the Trojans and the Romans – since he believed that all Romans, including the Trojans who shared their blood and were therefore Romans too, should be free from the constraint of taxation – but also as likening taxes and disturbances, through the equally burdensome quality of these two kinds of problems for the Romans; hence, Suetonius' emphasis on 'every' in the phrase 'every burden'. With these

---

36 See McDaniel 2013, 75–7. Matthew's infancy narrative (1–2) conflicts on several events, including Jesus' flight into Egypt, with the version in the Gospel of Luke (1–2), particularly the presentation of Jesus at the temple in Luke, but these discrepancies are best seen as variant traditions, with the two evangelists' particular selections and omissions explained by their respective agendas; see MacEwen 2015, 125–6. Matthew's inclusion of the exile from Judaea at least shows that it was a well-known part of the historical material on Jesus, and appeared in sources early enough to have been available also to Suetonius. Despite the lack of any mention of Herod's edict to slaughter the infants of Bethlehem in Josephus' account of the king in his *Jewish Antiquities* (14.158–17.190), the story cannot be historically discounted based simply on this absence or on other differing sources; cf. Griggs 1990, 35 n. 2; *pace* Toher 2011, 212.

37 For the date of the Gospel of Matthew, see Sim 1998, 40 with bibliography.

specific details, the biographer shows how Claudius was such a great leader that he brought both more money and greater peace to his own people.

Moreover, as I shall now show through some other examples of Suetonius' prose style, some missing connective such as *enim* seems required by the rhetorical demands of the biographer's point in the brief add-on *Iudaeos … expulit*. Suetonius often uses the conjunction *enim* in this explanatory way to offer another illustration of the same point (e.g. *Vita Verg.* 29, *Iul.* 50.2, 69, *Aug.* 56.3, 66.1, 66.3, 82.2, *Calig.* 9, 12.3, 34.2, *Otho* 5.1, *Vit.* 17.2, *Vesp.* 6.2, 22, *Dom.* 4.4), and most prominently to justify the condemning verdicts of the *Julius* (76.1) and *Otho* (12.1) with immediate examples of the vices in their character that were considered more significant than the virtues.[38] One of the closest examples of his tendency to explain a point further with *enim* is found in a section of the *Augustus*, which resembles the structure of our passage through a brief final elaboration:

> quin etiam quondam iuxta cubiculum eius lixa quidam ex Illyrico exercitu, ianitoribus deceptis, noctu deprehensus est cultro uenatorio cinctus, imposne mentis an simulata dementia, *incertum*: nihil *enim* exprimi quaestione potuit.

> Even a soldier's servant from the army in Illyricum, who had escaped the vigilance of the door-keepers, was caught at night near the emperor's bedroom, armed with a hunting knife; but whether the fellow was crazy or feigned madness is *a question, since* nothing could be wrung from him by torture.

> (*Aug.* 19.2)

A second apt comparison may be made with a later part of the *Claudius*, where Suetonius in his customary manner disapprovingly recounts the extreme lengths to which the emperor's fearful nature led him:

> reliquo autem tempore salutatoribus scrutatores semper apposuit, *et quidem omnibus et acerbissimos*. sero *enim* ac uix remisit ne feminae praetextatique pueri et puellae contrectarentur et ne cuius comiti aut librario calamariae et graphiariae thecae adimerentur.

> Afterwards he even subjected those who came to pay their morning calls to search, *sparing none the strictest examination. Indeed*, it was not until late, and then reluctantly, that he gave up having women and young boys and girls grossly mishandled, and the cases for pens and styles taken from every man's attendant or scribe.

> (*Claud.* 35.1–2)

---

38 The word *enim* is such a regular feature of Suetonius' style that he also sometimes uses it as an interjection in the middle of a sentence, rather than at the end; see *Aug.* 35.1, 58.2, 99.2, *Tib.* 1.1, 13.1, *Calig.* 4, 8.4, 26.1, *Galb.* 3.3, 19.1, *Dom.* 11.3.

In the context of these two passages, the detail about Claudius' expulsion of the Jews expands on his affirmation that the Roman people should be saved from undue hardships such as taxes and disturbances, picking up on the phrase *omni onere* in the same way that these other passages build, respectively, on the words *incertum* and *et quidem omnibus et acerbissimos* that are italicized above. The Jews in this passage are considered an *onus* to the Roman people because of their constant disturbances, and Suetonius categorizes them as such in his *Life* of Claudius. This thematic correlation was formerly obscured, but is now made characteristically more explicit by the biographer's recaptured grammar.

The larger context of the surrounding parts of this chapter on Claudius' treatment of foreign peoples likewise supports my textual conjecture, since Achaea and Macedonia are mentioned together earlier in the same chapter (*Claud.* 25.3). The Lycians and Rhodians are also syntactically paired through the parallel structure of the sentence just before the one about Jesus, in a similar way to the Trojans and Jews, since the emperor took independence from the Lycians, but gave it to the Rhodians, with the word *libertatem* serving to connect the two reports:

> Lyciis ob exitiabiles inter se discordias *libertatem* ademit, Rhodiis ob paenitentiam ueterum delictorum reddidit.

> He deprived the Lycians of their *independence* because of deadly intestine feuds, and restored theirs to the Rhodians, since they had given up their former faults.

> (*Claud.* 25.3)

In the sentence that follows our passage, the Germans are even explicitly compared to the Parthians and Armenians (*Claud.* 25.4). Furthermore, Suetonius then carries the same kind of assessment of different populations against each other into the next section on religious groups, drawing a contrast between Claudius' opposite handlings of the Druids in one case, and the believers in the Eleusinian rites (or cult of Venus Erycina) in another, through the adverb *contra* ('on the other hand'):[39]

> Druidarum religionem apud Gallos dirae immanitatis et tantum ciuibus sub Augusto interdictam penitus aboleuit, *contra* sacra Eleusinia etiam transferre ex Attica Romam conatus est templumque in Sicilia Veneris Erycinae uetustate conlapsum ut ex aerario pop. R. reficeretur auctor fuit.

> He utterly abolished the cruel and inhuman religion of the Druids among the Gauls, which under Augustus had merely been prohibited

---

39 See Hurley 2001, 179 (ad loc.).

to Roman citizens; *on the other hand* he even attempted to transfer
the Eleusinian rites from Attica to Rome, and had the temple of Venus
Erycina in Sicily, which had fallen to ruin through age, restored at the
expense of the treasury of the Roman people.

(Claud. 25.5)

If Suetonius is connecting various peoples to one another thematically and
grammatically throughout this chapter, whether by comparison or contrast, it follows that the Trojans and Jews, the only two such groups who
had oddly appeared to stand juxtaposed yet separate in this chapter, are
actually part of one linked discussion that similarly hangs on a common
topic. The conjunction *enim* finally makes this relationship clear, whereas
formerly the search for any direct relevance in our sentence to the preceding text had been confounding, other than simply vis-à-vis the Trojans and
Jews' respectively different treatments by Claudius. Now we can see the
point of that difference to Suetonius in the connective *enim*.

 This consistency with Suetonian style applies to the diction and grammar of the rest of the conjecture too. The word *orbis* is sometimes used
generally in Latin literature without *terrarum* to mean simply a 'part of
the world, region' (*OLD* 13a), or even 'zone' (13b), rather than the whole
world itself (12b), which the Romans often viewed as synonymous with
the city of Rome (*orbis/urbs*).[40] This is why when *orbis* is found by itself, it
more often means the entire empire, as when Pliny the Elder writes of 'our
empire' (*nostro orbe*, *HN* 12.98), or when Suetonius himself in the *Vespasian* refers to *plurimas per totum orbem ciuitates* ('many cities throughout
the empire', *Vesp.* 17). Virgil writes of 'the Britons who are divided from
the whole world' (*toto diuisos orbe Britannos*, *Ecl.* 1.66), and yet we understand that he means that they are divided from *his* whole world, because logically Britain still exists; it is merely not part of the *Roman* world.
In other words, *orbis* is common geographical language in Latin for the
wide territory of a certain group such as the Romans, who were a separate race from the Britons, and therefore suits the context of our sentence,
which is about the expulsion of people from specific lands. In fact, there
are even more limiting uses of this word, and Suetonius' sentence about
Jesus would seem to qualify, because it already contains the word *Roma*
towards the end, so that *orbe* must suggest another meaning. This follows
from both the logic of the sentence (Jesus was highly associated with his
crucifixion in Judaea, not Rome) and the probability that the biographer
would otherwise have put things more succinctly: his famous brevity,
which favours an economically parallel sentence structure, would not have
abided two separate nouns to represent the same geographical location.
The presence of *Roma* points us towards construing *orbe* as a different

40 See e.g. Fielding 2017, 77.

territory of the world, and since *orbe* follows *Iudaeos* ('the Jews'), it may reasonably be translated as 'their region', from which they expelled Christ (*pulso orbe Chresto*). For this usage of *orbis*, we might compare Ovid's *Heroides*, where Penelope laments to her missing husband Odysseus: 'I am not permitted to know the reason for your delaying, or in what *part of the world* you are uncaringly hidden!' (*nec scire mihi, quae causa morandi | aut in quo lateas ferreus* orbe, *licet! Her.* 1.58). Although this poet's words are supposedly those of a woman from archaic Greece, his own audience was Roman, and clearly could be expected to have no trouble understanding from these Latin lines merely a place within the world, rather than all of it, just as readers of Suetonius may easily comprehend by *orbe* a particular region, not the entire earth.[41]

Nonetheless, the word *orbis* is dramatic, and its use here almost a poetic touch ('from their orb'), since it is found in this sense mostly in poetry, and when prose writers do use it in this way, it tends to be done as emphatic language (e.g. Sen. *Q Nat.* 5.18.10). The biographer thus ends this section with a pithy reference to a well-known figure that is punctuated by an artistic flourish.[42] Suetonius is often lauded for such occasional moments of drama, especially around the important divisions of his biographies like the one towards vices that is begun just after our passage in *Claudius* 25.5, such as when he suddenly claims in his *Life* of Nero that 'the earth' (*terrarum orbis*) itself finally 'abandoned' (*destituit, Ner.* 40.1) the emperor, referring to his death, which is a surprising turn of phrase.[43] Therefore, although the word *orbe* does not signify the death of leaving the earth, it is a little more sweeping than 'province' (*prouincia*), suggesting an expulsion not merely from Judaea, but from the whole Jewish realm – a banishment from the entire dominion of the Jews which foreshadows their alleged later complicity, as also related by Matthew (27:22–5), in Jesus' eventual trial and crucifixion under Pontius Pilate. Just as Matthew mitigates the responsibility of Pilate for Jesus' execution, so too Suetonius erases the role in his exile that was played by Herod, who was already marginalized to some extent in Matthew's source by the dreams sent to Joseph. Indeed, due to this consistent bias against the Jews, the two authors may well be following a common source for the flight into Egypt.[44] The sense of Suetonius' statement is that he had been compelled to move out of the territory of Judaea that was ruled by Herod, that is, out of his own Jewish place of birth, which explains the origin of how he came to be known as Jesus of Nazareth. Suetonius omits

---

41 The word *orbis* means simply 'a part of the world' also in e.g. Verg. *Aen.* 7.224; Ov. *Met.* 8.100, 10.305, *Fast.* 3.466; Mart. 7.8.2; cf. Ov. *Her.* 18.175, with Heyworth 2016, 147.

42 Suetonius at times uses poetic language elsewhere in the *Caesars*; see e.g. *Tit.* 7.2, with MacRae 2015; Ambühl 2016, 168–9.

43 As Montesquieu famously observed; see above, pp. 1–2.

44 The evangelists' sharing of source material with Suetonius is suggested by Billings 2009, 74–5.

Herod altogether because he considers him a minor character, as he is accustomed to do even with such major figures from history, so that the Jews are essentially portrayed as having exiled one of their own. The biographer would almost certainly have known that it was Herod who ruled this province and had caused the exile, but Suetonius' brevity here is in keeping with his propensity for generalizations.[45]

It is a misleading description, since Herod did not expel Jesus, but on the contrary wished for him to remain in Judaea, where he could be found and put to death. But Herod's edict brought about his journey into Egypt, where his family was driven by the hostility of their own people, at least according to the view put forth in the *Claudius*. Whether it was done by the Jewish people themselves, or by their king Herod, is beside the point to Suetonius. For an example of a similar use of the verb *pello* in a passive construction that leaves out the agent of the action, which is obviously understood to be the emperor (although in our context, the Jews are the agent), we may offer this line from the next biography in Suetonius' collection: 'The *children* of those who were condemned *were banished* or put to death by poison or starvation' (*damnatorum* liberi urbe pulsi *enectique ueneno aut fame*, Ner. 36.2). Just as in the sentence about Jesus, we have here the same kind of ablative of separation in the middle of a participial phrase again using *pello* to denote someone being forced into exile (*liberi urbe pulsi*).[46] Such ablatives are common with this verb, and we might compare another sentence in the epitome of one of Livy's lost books: '*Lucius Cornelius Cinna … was driven from the city* by his colleague Gnaeus Octavius' (L. Cornelius Cinna … pulsus urbe *a Cn. Octauio collega*, Liv. Epit. 79).

The position of this item about Jesus among Claudius' accomplishments can now be appreciated. It is part of the climax of a biographical crescendo, before it is announced that these great deeds should not in fact be credited to the emperor, since he was controlled by his wives and freedmen (*Claud.* 25.5), a statement which begins the major division in the *Life* between virtuous acts and those qualities of character that Suetonius will go on to denounce.[47] As readers, we are clearly meant to agree from a Roman perspective that the expulsion of the Jews was a positive achievement, although in the version recorded by the existing manuscripts, the story had

45 On Suetonius' exclusion of secondary historical figures and his tendency to generalize instead, see Bradley 1978, 204–5; above, pp. 45, n. 96, 155, n. 21, 180, n. 10, 187.

46 Cf. *Aug.* 13.3, where Suetonius relates the claim by landowners that they were 'driven from their homes' (*pelli se*), and *Tib.* 49.2, where he reports that the Parthian king Vononus was 'dethroned by his subjects' (*Vononem … pulsus a suis*); also *Iul.* 33, *Calig.* 44.2, *Dom.* 13.1. This word is used in a different sense at *Iul.* 36, where Suetonius reports how Caesar was 'put to flight' (*pulsus*) in battle. On the biographer's fondness for participial constructions to include a subordinate fact or event, see Wallace-Hadrill 1983, 19; Power 2014b, 4.

47 For Suetonius' use of such crescendos, see above, pp. 121, 154–5, 195, 207; below, p. 236, n. 13.

formerly been the only seemingly arbitrary fact that is presented neutrally in this chapter. With the text finally restored, it is made more grammatically clear through *enim* that the Jews' uproars were viewed as burdensome to the Roman people, even if they were not actually violent acts against the state.[48] Suetonius approves of the emperor's action against them as much as his protection of the Trojans, and notes the anecdote about Jesus as an illustration of the very kind of internal turmoil that had existed among the Jews for some time.[49]

This is the first known example of a narrative from the Bible besides Jesus' crucifixion being confirmed by a Roman author whose sources date to the time of his life. Unlike Tacitus, who mentions Jesus in relation to his death and to his founding of the Christian religion that was opposed by many Romans, Suetonius instead chooses to mention the different detail of his exile in Egypt and Galilee, taking his fame as a religious leader for granted and comparing his persecution to that of the Jews by Claudius. By removing the anecdote from its historical context during Jesus' childhood, Suetonius instead draws attention only to the point that he was driven from Judaea, omitting the detail that the flight occurred when he was still a mere infant and posed no real threat, except as foretold in the future. In this omission is the implication that Suetonius expects his reader to understand Jesus' later significance as an adult. The troublesomeness of the Jews and their own ironic treatment of a troublesome figure are the only significant facts for Suetonius, and the ones that he decides to emphasize. As often, his use of the earlier historical tradition takes on a smaller, more biographical purpose, and he disregards chronology and arranges his material out of context through his selection and suppression of details for a unique thematic effect.

This emendation should be accepted especially when we consider the usual cause-and-effect order of Suetonius' sentences,[50] suggesting the tit-for-tat nature of the emperor's expulsion of the Jews. The restored text implies that Claudius' decision to banish them may have been influenced by the consideration that this punishment seemed suitable for a group who were themselves were known for exiling a controversial religious figure from their land.[51] This also coheres well with what we know about the 'impulsive' character, as it were, of Claudius himself, who appears to have

---

48 See Spence 2004, 92: 'Of course, it involves a disturbance of the established order, but the penalty of expulsion rather than mass executions points unarguably to communal unrest rather than communal rebellion.'
49 Cf. ibid. 80: 'The adverb *assidue*, "constantly", suggests not a major and sudden eruption of tumults which would have necessitated an immediate and decisive response but rather a building of pressure ...'
50 See Power 2013a, 128.
51 This point is rhetorically underscored by verbal repetition not in the wordplay of antanaclasis (*impulsore ... expulit*), but in the symmetry of paregmenon (*pulso ... expulit*).

believed that the punishment should fit the crime through poetic justice, which can be inferred from the example told by Suetonius of the emperor's approval of the suggestion that a forger's hands be cut off, and his immediate order that it be done (*Claud.* 15.2).[52] So too the Jews, in Claudius' view, were hoisted on their own petard. The restored clause *enim pulso orbe Christo* is not in fact the beginning of a separate sentence, but rather of an ironic side-note, which Suetonius often provides, as we have shown through the above examples. The discovery of this textual emendation solves the mysterious crux of an ancient passage, offering significant new evidence for the historical life of Jesus that confirms an important story from the Bible. Suetonius' perspective on the tale is particularly Matthean, indicating a larger role of the Jews in the ordeals of Jesus, and possibly suggesting that Suetonius had a common source with the evangelist. The flight into Egypt that is recorded in the first gospel has now been verified by an independent Roman source.

52 On Claudius' rather subjective view of justice, see Tuori 2016, 230.

30 Nero's Cannibal (Suetonius, *Nero* 37.2)[*]

In his biography of the emperor Nero, Suetonius mentions a story about an 'all-consuming man' (*polyphagus*) from Egypt. Nero knew of his reputation and considered employing him, so that this man could tear people apart and cannibalize them to death in front of him:[1]

> creditur etiam polyphago cuidam Aegypti generis crudam carnem et quidquid daretur mandere assueto concupisse uiuos homines laniandos absumendosque obicere.

> It is even believed that to a certain all-consuming man of Egyptian origin, who was accustomed to eating raw flesh and whatever was given to him, he wished men to be thrown, so that they could be torn to pieces and consumed alive.

> (*Ner.* 37.2)

The story is confirmed by an account of Nero's reign in the Chronography of 354, which provides other details not found in Suetonius:

> hoc imp. fuit polyfagus natione Alexandrinus nomine Arpocras, qui manducauit pauca: aprum coctum, gallinam uiuam cum suas sibi pinnas, oua C, pineas C, clauos galligares, uitrea fracta, thallos de scopa palmea, mappas IIII, porcellum lactantem, manipulum feni, et adhuc esuriens esse uidebatur.

---

[*] This chapter was first published in *HSCP* 107 (2013), 323–30.
[1] For Egyptians as cannibals, cf. Juv. 15.12, 78–83; Dio Cass. 71.4.1; with e.g. Fredericks 1976; Baldwin 1977, 408 = 1985, 503. On accusations of cannibalism as linked to racism in the ancient world, see Isaac 2004, 207–11. For a similar anecdote about the emperor Aurelian, see SHA, *Aurel.* 50.4, which is probably an invention based on our passage of Suetonius' *Nero*; see Woods 2004, 219, citing Paschoud 1996, 224, who was anticipated by Baldwin 1977, 408–9 = 1985, 503–4. On the *Historia Augusta*'s use of Suetonius for fiction, see e.g. Bird 1971; Arbo 2010; Fry 2010. For another reinvention of this Suetonian passage by Marvell, see Patterson 2000, 471.

> In this reign there was an all-consuming man of Alexandrian birth named Arpocras, who ate a few things: a cooked boar, a live hen along with its feathers, 100 eggs, 100 pine nuts, hobnails, broken glass, the brush from a broomstick, 4 table napkins, a suckling baby pig, a handful of hay, and still seemed hungry.
>
> (*Chron. Min.* s.v. *Nero*)

As the chronographer makes clear, Arpocras was not actually a cannibal, but was simply known for consuming anything, including uncooked meat and even living animals. Nero's idea was to turn him into a cannibal by making him eat people, that is, to use him as one. Suetonius' anecdote has generally been viewed as a 'curious and far-fetched item',[2] but it is not so strange when we see that the point is the extensive cruelty of Nero's plans, rather than the existence at Rome of an Egyptian who already ate men alive of his own volition. The emperor wished to pervert Arpocras' omnivorous gluttony for his own sadistic crimes.

A different interpretation has been offered by Woods, who makes the case that Suetonius here misunderstands his source, who by *polyphagus* actually meant either a 'crocodile' or 'hippopotamus', and probably the latter, since that animal was famous for having – or appearing to have (they are herbivores) – an insatiable and indiscriminate appetite.[3] Although Woods does not seem aware of their articles, he had been anticipated some twenty-eight years earlier by Littman's conjecture of 'crocodile', which Baldwin swiftly refuted in an important note.[4] Woods' argument for 'hippopotamus' has some evidence to speak for it, but also fails to convince. First, Woods' discounting of the evidence from the Chronography of 354 is not cogent: he suggests that it is an elaboration of an ambiguous report of a *polyphagus* under *Nero*, and that the invented material is drawn from a similar story about a later glutton recorded by the same writer under the emperor Severus Alexander.[5] This view supposes that both Suetonius and the chronographer independently misconstrued the Neronian *polyphagus* as a human rather than an animal, and freely embellished their passages. Such a coincidence of mistakes seems unlikely, unless the chronographer is dependent on the Suetonian passage, a possibility which is precluded by their differing content. Each author includes details not found in the other, including a birthplace (*Alexandrinus*) for Arpocras that may have

2 Bradley 1978, 225 (ad loc.).
3 Woods 2004. Against his own case, Woods (2004, 220) cites Strabo 4.5.4 and 11.5.7, where the term πολυφάγοι is used of humans, and in the former passage even associated with cannibals (ἀνθρωποφάγοι).
4 Littman 1976; Baldwin 1977 = 1985, 501–4.
5 Woods 2004, 220 n. 6. For a similar kind of transposition of detail, see Woodman 1979 = 1998b, 70–85.

interested Suetonius,[6] and Nero's plan to turn him into a cannibal, which the chronographer would hardly have omitted.

Second, the use of the term *polyphagus*, instead of the proper word *hippopotamus*, is explained by Woods through the conjecture that Suetonius' source was clearly interested in unusual details, and may therefore also have wished to use less obvious terminology. According to this view, Suetonius' interest in technical language prompts him to retain the original Greek term,[7] which was supposedly ambiguous and misunderstood by Suetonius as a gluttonous person by whom Nero wanted humans to be devoured. However, this would have been a major leap to make if the passage had been ambiguous, especially for a writer who himself appears to have been an expert in the terms for animals, as evidenced by his lost work *Natures of Animals* (*De animantium naturis*), which is attested by Gerald of Wales (*Itinerar. Cambr.* 1.7).[8] The following fragments appear to have been preserved from that work:[9]

ponti belua: crocodilus; canis Aegyptius lambit et fugit. dicit Suetonius.

meropes: galbeoli, ut putat Tranquillus. hae genitores suos recondunt iam senes et alere dicuntur in similitudinem ripariae auis, quae in specu ripae nidificat, ut in libro X ostenditur.

sea monster: a crocodile; an Egyptian creature that snaps and runs away. So says Suetonius.

bee-eaters: birds that eat bees, as thinks Tranquillus. These consume their own parents when they get too old and are said to feed like the sand martin, which builds its nest in a tunnel of the shore, as shown in Book 10.

(Suet. frr. 163–4 Reiff.)

According to these citations by scholiasts, Suetonius was an authority on strange beasts and other wildlife, particularly the crocodile. It is not a

---

6 See Baldwin 1977, 406 = 1985, 501. For Suetonius' interest in the birthplaces of at least his biographical subjects, see e.g. Steidle 1951, 68–70.

7 For Suetonius' tendency to preserve language from his sources, see e.g. Baldwin 1983, 327–8, 388, 485–7; Wallace-Hadrill 1983, 21–2.

8 See Reifferscheid 1860, 247–65, 439–40, 443, although it is doubtful that the list of animal sounds that Reifferscheid attributes to the work (fr. 161 Reiff.) is Suetonian; see Marcovich 1971; *pace* Schmidt 1991, 3813. Marcovich also casts doubt on the view of Finch (1969) that Suetonius is the author of the similar catalogue in Vat. lat. 6018 (pp. 250–1 Reiff.). Reifferscheid 1860, 439–40 agrees with Roth (1858, xciv) that *Natures of Animals* was part of Suetonius' larger work, the *Prata*. It probably formed Book 10 (see below). The claim by König and Woolf (2013, 54) that '[i]t is unclear ... how much, if anything, [the *Prata*] included on the natural world' is erroneous, since two nominatim fragments survive from the work on this very subject (Isid. *De nat.* 38, 44 = Suet. frr. 152, 157 Reiff.), to mention merely those explicitly ascribed to it.

9 *Schol. Luc.* 8.764 and *Schol. Bern.* ad *G.* 4.14, respectively. With the former fragment, cf. Plin. *HN* 8.148; Phaedr. 1.25; with the latter, Plin. *HN* 10.99, 30.33.

stretch to think that Suetonius' work also included mention of the hippopotamus, which was deemed important by, for example, Pliny the Elder in his section on animals, since it was a creature of the Nile River (*HN* 8.95–6), just like the crocodile (8.89).[10] Suetonius' general interest in the precision of language therefore actually directs us against interpreting Nero's *polyphagus* as an animal.

Finally, Woods notes especially the stereotypical *topos* of the cruel tyrant feeding men to wild beasts to support his theory,[11] but he fails to observe how this scene combines cruelty not so much with entertainment as with food. The language of 'eating' in our passage (*mandere*, *Ner.* 37.2) suggests Suetonius' moral category of dining practices, which often points to the virtuous or vicious character of an emperor:[12] we might compare Augustus' related verb *manduco*, which is quoted by Suetonius in the section of the *Life* devoted to food, as part of his emphasis on how little the emperor ate (*manducaui*, *Aug.* 76.2). Whereas Augustus' eating habits only reveal his modest lifestyle, those of Vitellius (*Vit.* 13.2), for example, symbolize his lack of restraint.[13] Nero's too serve to underline his unbridled appetite for physical pleasures, including banquets, drinking, and prostitutes (*Ner.* 27.2–3). Just as Nero's scene with his mother's corpse in Suetonius (*Ner.* 34.2) may be read as a perverse form of one of his banquets,[14] so too Nero's cannibal brings out the same idea of his unbounded lust for both food and killing.

In conclusion, the conjectures of 'crocodile' and 'hippopotamus' for *polyphagus* at *Nero* 37.2 are not only contradicted by a clear parallel in an independent source, but also ignore Suetonius' expert knowledge of animals. Suetonius was in an especially good position to suspect a description of a crocodile or hippopotamus in his source on Nero, but he did not judge the anecdote to contain either. We should therefore revert to the standard acceptance of the more horrific tale that Nero did indeed wish to seek out this *polyphagus* to be his personal cannibal, which is in keeping with the biographer's particularly high capacity for the sordid, especially descriptions

---

10 However, it cannot be said for certain that Suetonius read Pliny's work, even though the *Vita Plini* shows that he at least knew of it; see Kaster 1995, 344–5; Gibson 2011, 189, 204. For the Romans' familiarity with the Nile, see Schrijvers 2007, 224–9; with these animals in particular, Draycott 2012, esp. 45–8.

11 Woods 2004, 221. For the use of this punishment in Roman public shows, see Coleman 1990; Kyle 1998, 52–5, 184–7, 249–50. In fact, the stock figure of the tyrant is himself often associated with a wild beast; see Dunkle 1971, 14.

12 Baldwin 1983, 257–8; Wallace-Hadrill 1983, 68, 78, 91, 172, 175, 179; Goddard 1994; Stein-Hölkeskamp 2002, 481–5 with bibliography. On this moral theme in Pliny's *Panegyric*, see S. Braund 1996.

13 Gowers 1993, 20–1; cf. Donahue 2004, 66–9.

14 See Vössing 2004, 452–5.

of extreme violence,[15] and also with his interest in the moral theme of imperial dining. The story is not unlike other strange forms of cruelty told by Suetonius that combine the theme of food with that of a tyrant's pleasure from watching people being slain, such as Caligula's wish to have a professional decapitator on hand to kill men in front of him for his amusement during his meals (*Calig.* 32), or Vitellius' appetite for death as he 'feasted his eyes' (*pascere oculos*, *Vit.* 14.2) on a man specifically brought before him for execution.[16]

15 E.g. *Calig.* 27.4, *Ner.* 29, *Galb.* 20.2, *Vit.* 16–17. On such sordid material in Suetonius, see e.g. Martin 1981, 73; Goodyear 1982, 663; Oakley 1997–2005, 2.137 n. 1; 2009b, 206–11; below, Chapter 32. For violence in Suetonius, including torture and murder, see Gale and Scourfield 2018a, 10.
16 Kyle 1998, 195 n. 4: 'cannibalistic rhetoric'. On this detail about Vitellius, see also Burke 1998, 89–90, comparing the similar phrase at *Vit.* 10.3. We might contrast the less gastronomic, and more visual, emphases placed on Vitellius' cruelty by Tacitus at *Hist.* 2.61, 2.70, 3.39.1; see e.g. Keitel 1992, 343–4; 2007; Ash 2007, 245–6, 271–2. For Tacitus' more sympathetic treatment of cannibalism generally, see *Agr.* 28, with Ash 2010a, 284–5.

31 Nero's Amazons, Sporus, and Alexander

in praeparanda expeditione primam curam habuit deligendi uehicula portandis scaenicis organis concubinasque quas secum educeret tondendi ad uirilem modum et securibus peltisque Amazonicis instruendi.

In his preparations for this expedition, his first concern was for carts to be selected for the transportation of his theatrical instruments, and, so that he could take his concubines with him, for them to be given haircuts of a masculine length and equipped with Amazonian axes and light shields.

(*Ner.* 44.1)

This story about Nero's planned expedition against Vindex has generally been viewed as portraying the emperor's overzealous concern for theatricality in his troop of concubines dressed up as Amazonian warriors. According to this view, it was possibly invented by an earlier hostile source to parody Nero's unmilitary reign, with the concubines simply satisfying his fondness for Hellenistic re-enactments.[1] Champlin even sees these details as suggesting a mythological parallel with Hercules, who famously conquered the Amazons.[2] Nero certainly wished to take his concubines with him for the purpose of celebrating his expected victory over Vindex, just as he clearly did the equipment for his stage entertainments (*scaenicis organis*),[3] but the point of this particular costume's amusement and the nature of Nero's intended festivities have not been fully understood. In this chapter, I offer an alternative reading of the concubines' outfit, which suggests that their attire was in keeping with Nero's perverse lust, as portrayed by Suetonius. As a consequence, the anecdote's factual credibility is renewed.

---

1 See Edwards 1994, 90; Warmington 1999, 80; Champlin 2003, 163–4; Malitz 2005, 104; Brandão 2009, 386; Pollard 2010, 216; Starbatty 2010, 227. The tale is doubted on far more speculative grounds, including an unfounded textual misreading of Suetonius' word *Amazonicis*, by Woods 2006, 138–47. Nero is reported to have owned a small statue of an Amazon (Plin. *HN* 34.82).
2 Champlin 2003, 136; *contra*, see Woods 2006, 139–40.
3 M. Griffin 1984, 233; Leigh 2017, 26.

Suetonius never states that Nero gave Amazon costumes to his concubines, only *secures* and *peltae*. These smaller weapons were synonymous
with the Amazons in Suetonius' day,[4] and the description 'Amazonian'
(*Amazonicis*) therefore simply designates that they were lighter arms befit-
ting female combatants. This makes sense if Nero had intended real weapons to be carried by the women as he 'led them with him' (*secum educeret*).
However, focus on these weapons has distracted readers from the more telling detail that the emperor had the concubines' 'hair shortened in the style
of a man' (*tondendi ad uirilem modum*).[5] The Amazons did not have male
haircuts; on the contrary, femininity was among their defining attributes,
including long hair.[6] Earlier in the *Caesars*, Suetonius even records how
Augustus once had an actor whipped for dressing a woman with hair of extremely short, masculine length (*Aug.* 45.4), because it violated traditional
morality by diminishing a noticeable aspect of her female gender.[7] So the
interpretation that Nero outfitted his concubines as Amazonian warriors
must be false. If Nero had wished to portray them as such, he could have
displayed the women on horseback, or else bare-breasted – two hallmarks
of the Amazonian myth exploited earlier by Caligula in the exhibition of
his wife Caesonia (*Calig.* 25.3).[8] Instead, the emperor furnishes them with
practical weaponry and makes them look, if anything, like men. By truly
equipping the concubines for warfare in this way, and shortening their hair,
Nero appears to have dressed them up not as Amazons, but as Roman soldiers (not as women, but as men).

This new interpretation of the passage is consistent with the sexual incli-
nations of Nero, who was fond of role play and gender reversal. He forced
men to perform oral sex on him (*Ner.* 35.4), but also raped women with
cunnilingus (*Ner.* 29; see above, Chapter 20). The boy Sporus was turned
into a eunuch by Nero, and was even dressed in his late wife's jewellery, so
that he would be practically changed into a woman (*in muliebrem naturam*

---

4 See Hor. *Carm.* 4.4.20; Plut. *Pomp.* 35.5; Mart. 9.101.5; Arr. *Anab.* 7.13.2; with Thomas
   2011, 136; Woods 2014, 29–30.
5 Cf. Rolfe 1913–14, 2.167: 'to have the hair of his concubines … trimmed man-fashion'.
6 See Woods 2006, 146. For the long hair of the Amazons generally, see e.g. Blok 1995,
   30–1; Gera 1997, 18.
7 Wardle 2014, 339 (ad loc.).
8 On the passage in the *Caligula*, see Hurley 1993, 105, who in my view wrongly compares
   this part of the *Nero*; for scepticism of the identification of Caesonia as an Amazon, see
   Wardle 1994, 235. Less likely is the suggestion that she is supposed to be Venus Victrix,
   which is made by Woods 2014, 31; *pace* Barrett 2015, 152 n. 25. This passage was later
   a model for Joyce (who clearly regarded Caesonia as an Amazon), as was Suetonius'
   portrayal of Caligula's horse Incitatus, particularly the emperor's intention to make the
   horse consul (*Calig.* 55.3); see Power 2016, 288–90. The latter anecdote was also used
   by Marvell and Swift, as has been shown by Pritchard 1990. On the Amazons' fame as
   horse riders, and thus their appropriateness to an emperor such as Caligula who was fond
   of horses, see e.g. Roscher 1884–6, 271–2.

transfigurare, *Ner.* 28.1).[9] As Suetonius tells us in his work *Insults*, under the entry for the word 'fair-cheeked' (εἰδομαλίδης), homosexual male prostitutes in antiquity were sometimes dressed up as women and forced to wear makeup (Suet. *Blasph.* 52). After his own marriage as a bride to the freedman Pythagoras, the emperor simulated 'the cries and lamentations of a maiden being deflowered' (*uoces quoque et heiulatus uim patientium uirginum*, *Ner.* 29).[10] His role play even extended to procuring a courtesan who looked like his own mother (*Ner.* 28.2; see above, Chapter 7). The emperor was presumably supplied with his concubines by Tigellinus, who kept just such a retinue (Plut. *Galb.* 17.7; Tac. *Hist.* 1.72.3).[11] But since Vindex was soon defeated by Verginius Rufus, Nero's plans proved unnecessary.[12]

The dressed-up concubines remind us of Nero's own assuming the role of bride with Pythagoras, which the biographer tells us was done 'in the same way that he himself had married Sporus' (*sicut ipsi Sporus, ita ipse denupsit*, *Ner.* 29), including wearing a 'bridal veil' (*flammeo*, 28.1), so that he could have sex in this role, complete with feminine clothing.[13] His treatment of his eunuch was similarly theatrical, and he renamed this freed slave-boy 'Sporus'. Champlin's point that Sporus' name means 'seed' in Greek is significant, since he suggests an ironic pun on the young boy's inability to reproduce: 'calling a boy Sporus after cutting off his testicles was meant as a joke.'[14] There also appears to be a more immediate and logical reason for the humour. The nickname 'Sporus' was likely a play on words to denote the boy's sexual use, which was to receive the emperor's 'semen'. Nero was better known for crudely obvious, rather than cleverly subtle, puns on Greek words.[15] But there is no need to select one interpreta-

---

9 See Kapparis 2011, 246.

10 On Nero's erotic contradictions, see Hendry 1995–6, 283. The emperor Otho was likened to Nero in his similar preference for opposite sexual roles; see Charles and Anagnostou-Laoutides 2013–14, 206–7, 210.

11 *Pace* Woods 2006, 145–6. The famous banquet on the Lake of Agrippa was similarly bedecked by Tigellinus with nude prostitutes (Tac. *Ann.* 15.37.3; Dio Cass. 62.15.4).

12 Like the story of Caligula's intention to make his horse consul (see above, n. 8), or Nero's plan to keep a cannibal at the imperial court discussed in the previous chapter, this tale is thus yet another example of counterfactual or 'virtual' history reported by Suetonius that never actually happened; on this topic, see e.g. Pelling 2013a. For one of the most famous examples, see the Alexander digression in Livy 9.17–19, with Oakley 1997–2005, 3.184–261 (ad loc.).

13 Although Nero's marriage to Pythagoras occurred before his one with Sporus, Suetonius places it afterwards for a crescendo of shocking effect; see Ormand 2009, 233–4. For the change of roles in the Suetonian passage, see Ash 2018, 176.

14 Champlin 2003, 150; cf. Ormand 2009, 233: 'a rather grim joke'. However, such an alleged joke may have been difficult for anyone to get; see Crawford 2017, 147. The far-fetched suggestion of Woods (2009, 79–80) that the eunuch's name was instead 'Spurius', which was meant to denote his illegitimacy as Nero's potential heir, has since been refuted by Charles 2014.

15 Cf. *Ner.* 33.1, discussed above, p. 47, n. 7.

tion: Nero's pun probably encompasses on array of such perverse meanings, evoking not only the castration of Sporus but also his passive position as a sexual partner.

Comparison with the only other example that Suetonius provides for Nero's military record, or lack thereof, reinforces my argument for a more obvious reference in his troop of concubines, where his earlier potential feats as a solider also prove damning. Like the devised action against Vindex, this example is an expedition intended to highlight the emperor's own personal leadership, but was again simply envisaged, rather than ever made.[16] It was planned sometime around AD 66–7 to assert control over the borders between the Romans and a neighbouring people called the Alani (or Rhoxolani).[17] Suetonius records a unique detail, which is not found in Cassius Dio's account (63.8.1–2), about the legion that Nero created specifically for this expedition:

> parabat et ad Caspias portas expeditionem conscripta ex Italicis senum pedum tironibus noua legione, quam Magni Alexandri 'phalanga' appellabat.

> He was also preparing an expedition to the Caspian Gates, having levied a new legion out of Italians standing six feet tall each, which he called the 'phalanx of Alexander the Great'.

> (*Ner.* 19.2)

This name that Nero gives his new legion has usually been seen as a homage to Alexander the Great (*imitatio Alexandri*), which was common among the Roman emperors, particularly Nero.[18] An intention to travel into the East was certainly a natural point of comparison between the emperor and Alexander, and the Macedonian phalanx was a well-known *exemplum* of indomitability at Rome.[19] Nero is also implicitly likened to Alexander by

---

16 Saddington 2004, 24, 35–6. For Nero as unmilitary, see Van Overmeire 2012a, 759–60; 2012b, 485; Hurley 2013, 32–4; Grau 2017, 273. On war in Suetonius, see also Saddington 2005; Wardle 2019.

17 See M. Griffin 1984, 228–9, 299; Edmondson 1992, 235 (ad loc.); Braund 2013, 88, 97–8. For the date of this anecdote, see Murison 1993, 24 n. 83. The Alani, rather than the Albani (Tac. *Hist.* 1.6.2), were convincingly conjectured by Mommsen 1886, 62 n. 1; *pace* Ash 2007, 106. On their identification with the Rhoxolani, see Bosworth 1977, 222; cf. Syme 1987, 58–61 = *RP* 6.282–5.

18 See e.g. Chilver 1979, 55; Shotter 2008, 104–5; Van Overmeire 2012a, 775; Doody 2013, 298–9. For earlier bibliography, see Champlin 2003, 139, 307 nn. 89–90. Woods 2006, 148–50 questions the standard interpretation also of this passage, but again on dubious grounds; cf. above, n. 1. On *imitatio Alexandri* and the emperors, see e.g. Baynham 1998, 10–11 n. 37; Spawforth 2006, 20–1; Asirvatham 2010, 109–11, 114–15; on Nero's specifically, Perron 1990; Morgan 1997a, 213; Van Overmeire 2012a, 766–9, 778; Mratschek 2013, 46, 49, 57.

19 For another 'phalanx of Alexander' created by the emperor Caracalla, see Dio Cass. 77.7.1; on *phalanges* in antiquity generally, Echeverría 2012, 303–13.

Curtius Rufus (10.9.1–6), since he equates the civil strife during the two aftermaths of their deaths (see Chapter 8).[20]

One point has escaped notice: the height of the men, which Suetonius explicitly mentions, as though it were an explanation for the ensuing description. This is typical of the cause-and-effect order of Suetonius' prose structure.[21] Nero's soldiers were all six Roman feet tall (*senum pedum*), which is roughly equivalent to five feet and nine inches by today's measurements – an ideal height by ancient standards.[22] This would have especially lent them to such a grand comparison, despite Alexander's own modest height.[23] Just as Nero's concubine soldiers have been misinterpreted as Amazons, and Sporus' name misconstrued as referring to his own semen or lack thereof, so too the specific reason for the name of Nero's phalanx has been missed, despite its obviousness. He gave his concubines 'Amazonian' or female-fitting weapons in the process of turning them into military men, and nicknamed his troop of six-foot warriors on account of their 'Macedonian' stature. What could emphasize Suetonius' point better about Nero's lack of military achievements than his comparing himself to such an accomplished general as Alexander, during one of his only two expeditions, which he never even made? The answer, as we discover later in the biography, is his plan to dress his concubines as Roman soldiers, so that he could satisfy his lust with them after the victory, rather than lead them into battle.

20 Cf. Champlin 2003, 9–10, 235.
21 See above, p. 227.
22 Cowan 2003, 9–10. For the Macedonian phalanx as especially tall, see Bar-Kochva 1989, 91–2 n. 4; cf. Tarn 1948, 170. The conjecture *senum milium peditum* ('of six thousand footmen') is preserved by Holland (1899, 2.112 n. 3), although from no manuscript tradition known to me. On the accepted reading, cf. Caes. *B Civ.* 2.15; Columella, *Rust.* 3.13.4; on the conjecture in Holland, Gronovius 1824, 1498 (on Gell. *NA* 16.4.4).
23 Cf. Bradley 1978, 119 (ad loc.): 'there is no need to assume excessive symbolism'; also Warmington 1999, 47 (ad loc.): 'the remark quoted by Suetonius could have been a joke.' Alexander in reality is known to have been of only average physical stature; see esp. Curt. 7.8.9 (cf. also e.g. 5.2.3). On Alexander in Suetonius, see Baldwin 1983, 84, 225, 230; Brandão 2009, 98–9, 106, 116, 139–40, 181, 208, 212, 241, 320, 355.

32 Vitellius and the Baker and Cook

Rousseau once wrote:

> Propriety, no less strict in literature than in life, no longer permits us to say anything in public which we might not do in public … The lives of kings may be written a hundred times, but to no purpose; we shall never have another Suetonius.[1]

Tacitus may have boasted of living in an age when you could 'think what you like, and say what you think' (*sentire quae uelis, et quae sentias dicere*, *Hist.* 1.1.4), but his own freedom did not extend to the use of graphic language in his historical works. It is rather the biographer Suetonius, not Tacitus, who takes advantage of their era's permissibility, which has detracted from his reputation as a historian to an unwarranted extent. The quintessential example of the alleged superiority of Tacitus to Suetonius with respect to history is the vicious death of Vitellius as told by both authors (Tac. *Hist.* 3.84.5–85; Suet. *Vit.* 16–18), which a number of scholars since Syme have touted.[2] As a classic example for contrasting the styles of Tacitus and Suetonius, I should compare it to the famous duel between Manlius and the Gaul in Livy (7.9.6–10.14), which is often set against the extant parallel account by Quadrigarius.[3] The gruesome murder of Vitellius is also recounted

---

1 Foxley 1911, 202.
2 E.g. Syme 1958, 189–90; Leeman 1963, 351; Goodyear 1970, 27–8; 1982, 663; Cizek 1975; Sage 1979, 510; Newbold 1984, 120; Lounsbury 1987, 104–5; 1991, 3779 n. 47; Braun 1990, 206–7; Richter 1992, 227; Gorringe 1993, 418–29; Shotter 1993, 12; Levene 1997, 144–5; Burke 1998; Pausch 2004, 305–9, 316; Pomeroy 2006, 188–9; Oakley 2009b, 206–11.
3 See Oakley 1997–2005, 2.113–23 (ad loc.). Tacitus and Suetonius' respective versions of other events, including the banquets of Vitellius (Tac. *Hist.* 2.62; Suet. *Vit.* 13), have instead been discussed by Ash (2009, xxx), who illustrates the two writers' differing standards with regard to the truth, bringing out well that they are not always to Tacitus' credit. Simcox (1883, 215–17) observes that the *Life* of Tiberius in particular allows for a very close comparison with Tacitus, in which he finds Suetonius 'almost always' (215) the better historian. Where Suetonius can be checked, we do not find any more errors in his biographies of the early Roman emperors than in our parallel accounts for the same period of history; see esp. Krause 1831; cf. Butler and Cary 1927, xii–xiii; Syme 2016b, 188; also Nelson 1942 for a comparison of epigraphical evidence with Suetonius' *Nero*.

by Cassius Dio (65.20.1–21.2), and all three writers appear to have drawn independently on a common source or sources, offering usefully extensive points of comparison (the brief and negative account of Vitellius' assassination by Josephus at *BJ* 4.11.4 contributes little). But while this scene does ably illustrate differences of style between Tacitus and Suetonius, it by no means necessarily elevates Tacitus as the better historical account of this event, as scholars have almost universally contended.

Allow me to make a few points that dismantle the simple notion that the vaunted Tacitus is any more historically factual about this brutal event than the purportedly distasteful Suetonius. Although the biographer includes sordid details, we shall see that they serve a literary purpose of moral condemnation, as is customary in the biographical genre, which often provides a deterrent example against the uncommendable behaviour to future readers. Of our three major authorities, Suetonius' version is by far the most hostile to the emperor, completely portraying in death the tyrant that Vitellius was in life. Syme found Suetonius' account of Vitellius' end 'revolting' in its graphic detail, as opposed to the more 'reticent' version of Tacitus, which avoids 'the squalid and disgusting'.[4] Subsequent scholars have generally agreed with the doyen of Tacitean studies, assuming that the more sordid details of the Suetonian passage were in the common source, not because they have exact parallels in the other two accounts, but because they do not. This view of Suetonius is particularly paradoxical: he is thought to be uncritical, and therefore historically unreliable, but this is also what makes him reliable, since whatever truth he does preserve is therefore untouched. Even Suetonian scholars tend to patronize him as tralatitious and unwittingly useful, due to an alleged absence of literary treatment that is ironically one of his virtues.[5] They search his text for small gems of truth amid what they view as the contemptible gossip and rumours from ancient Rome.

The particular issue of Vitellius' death scene that I wish to discuss here is Suetonius' comment that in Vitellius' final hours, the emperor found himself 'with only two companions, a baker and cook' (*duobus solis comitibus, pistore et coco, Vit.* 16). In Tacitus, these companions appear to be represented by the phrase 'the lowest of slaves' (*infimis seruitiorum, Hist.* 3.84), and they are entirely absent from Dio. The usual assumption of scholars is that the baker and cook were in the common source, but that the

---

4   Syme 1958, 189. Cf. Damon 2020, 126–7 on Suetonius as 'indecorous' (126) in his portrayal of Tiberius compared to the parallel ancient accounts of his reign.
5   See e.g. Townend 1967, 95: 'Suetonius gains immensely from this lack of refinement'; Hurley 2001, 2: 'his lack of discrimination turns out to be a blessing'; cf. ead. 2011, xxvii–xxix. Both were echoing contemporary views on Latin literature; cf. e.g. Duff 1960, 508: 'Compared with Tacitus, he is as a photograph to a picture or a finished engraving'; Goodyear 1982, 663: 'he retails every sordid detail.' Damon (2020, 126) likewise presumes discreet omission on the part of Tacitus and Dio when they do not include certain details that are found in Suetonius.

dignity of Tacitus' endeavour forced him to conceal them, while Suetonius
retained them. This is part of the usual tendency of scholars, when faced
with a variant in the parallel tradition, to view Suetonius as the one who
is sticking closer to his source – a bias which has precluded consideration
of other possibilities.[6] In this case, it has been noticed that the detail of
Vitellius' servants being a baker and cook is perhaps significant, when one
considers this emperor's notorious vice of gluttony. Murison in his note on
this passage writes: 'Tacitus omits the number and occupations of Vitellius'
companions. The *pistor* and *cocus* seem unlikely but [Suetonius] cannot
resist one last stab at Vitellius' gluttony.'[7] The commentator would seem to
imply that this detail was in the common tradition, and that Tacitus left it
out not only because it was trivial, but because he is a more critical writer,
and knew that it seemed too good to be true.

Such praise of Tacitus at Suetonius' expense is by no means irrational,
since the historian does sometimes turn specifics from his sources into more
poetically generalized language (see e.g. above, Chapter 21). However, it
does not necessarily follow that he must always be doing this. Burke likewise sees the biographer's description of the emperor's companions as part
of his development of the theme of gluttony, but he too implies throughout
his discussion that these are careful selections from his sources, not inventions.[8] I should submit that Suetonius' account is the only one to emphasize
Vitellius' gluttony within the death scene by developing what was clearly
an event in the shared earlier material (since it occurs in both Tacitus and
Dio) – namely, the mockery of the emperor's obesity by the assassins – into
a full sketch of his appearance (*Vit.* 17.2). In his *Life* of Vitellius, Suetonius
encases the physical rubric within the death scene itself, and it seems no
less likely that the baker and cook are not simply a clever embellishment
by Suetonius from a supplementary source that he uniquely discovered, but
rather his own invented elaboration to suit his theme of physical attributes,
such as the emperor's appearance and intake of food and wine.[9]

These more specific occupations may have seemed to Suetonius a fittingly
vivid gloss for 'the lowest of slaves', which is perhaps how the common
source actually put it in the first place after all. And yet, this possibility
has never even been explicated. It would not be the only known instance
of Suetonius finessing his source material.[10] At the very least, we should

6 See above, p. 187, n. 27.
7 Murison 1992, 172.
8 Burke 1998, 84, 92.
9 Nevertheless, my argument is certainly supported by Burke's (1998) more general point
   about the development of this theme of gluttony throughout the *Life*.
10 See Schmidt 1989, arguing that Otho's letter to Statilia Messalina (*Otho* 10.2), which is
   known only from Suetonius, was contrived as part of a literary parallel with Nero, *pace*
   Murison 1992, 172; also above, Chapters 14–15 on an allusion to Virgil in the *Galba*,
   and Chapter 28 on a likely embellishment in the *Caligula*.

sceptically question who is the more faithful reporter in this case, Tacitus or Suetonius. If my interpretation is correct, it is neither that Tacitus is being especially dignified nor Suetonius especially honest for that matter, only that they each serve an entirely different kind of reader: one seeks flamboyant art, the other gritty realism. Both authors can write, but they do so for different ends and effects. The fashionability of Tacitus is a relatively recent phenomenon: as Ammianus (28.4.14) tells us, his historical works quickly failed to find an audience in late antiquity.[11] Suetonian biography, however, while less thought-proving and profound, remained popular with all kinds of readers and was frequently quoted in subsequent literature – which the self-serving Ammianus unconvincingly attributes to a growingly trivial readership, but which actually indicates ongoing admiration by the public.

There is more literary licence in Suetonius' *Lives* than readers have allowed. Just as he should not be disbelieved where he clashes with Tacitus unless there is a good reason to doubt him,[12] so too the truth should not be taken for granted in his writings any more than in such obviously rhetorical historians, with regard to his divergences from other ancient accounts or the fantastical quality of some of his anecdotes. Suetonius not only preserves facts unavailable elsewhere but is himself a brilliant writer who manipulates his material to create specific impressions on the reader. Neither history nor biography has any superior moral ground: both can be composed by good and bad men alike. Suetonius' authorial purpose may differ from that of Tacitus, but it does not naturally follow that the latter is higher-minded; rather, his focus is simply broader. With regard to Vitellius and the other rulers of the Roman Empire, the two genres complement each other well, but they are not equal with regard to their ability to remain relevant over time. Suetonius' biographies continue to fascinate readers through the ages by their revealing anecdotes and shocking stories, which are not subject to changing fashions. Styles come and go, but facts last.

11 See also above, p. 184, n. 19.
12 This more common-sense standard is espoused by Baldwin 1989a with regard to the *Life* of Virgil.

Bibliography

Abramenko, A. 1994. 'Zeitkritik bei Sueton: Zur Datierung der *Vitae Caesarum*', *Hermes* 122: 80–94.

Adams, J. N. 1982. *The Latin Sexual Vocabulary*. London.

———. 1995. *Pelagonius and Latin Veterinary Terminology in the Roman Empire*. Leiden.

———. 2003. *Bilingualism and the Latin Language*. Cambridge.

Ailloud, H., ed. 1931–2. *Suétone: Vies des douze Césars*, 3 vols. Paris.

Aleshire, S. B. 1991. *Asklepios at Athens: Epigraphic and Prosopographic Essays on the Athenian Healing Cults*. Amsterdam.

Allen, A. W. 1950. '"Sincerity" and the Roman Elegists', *CP* 45: 145–60.

Allen, W. 1958. 'Imperial Mementos in Suetonius', *CB* 35: 1–4.

Ambühl, A. 2016. 'Literary Love Triangles: Berenice at Alexandria and Rome', *PLLS* 16: 155–84.

Aparicio, L. M. M. 2008. 'Homero en *Las vidas de los Césares* de Suetonio'. In Dorado et al. 2008, 443–53.

Arbo, A. M. 2010. 'Histoire d'un palimpseste: le *Nero* et le *Caligula* de Suétone dans la *Vita Commodi* de l'*Histoire Auguste*', *DHA Suppl.* 4: 201–21.

Armstrong, D. 1986. '*Horatius eques et scriba*: Satires 1.6 and 2.7', *TAPA* 116: 255–88.

———. 2010. 'The Biographical and Social Foundations of Horace's Poetic Voice'. In Davis 2010, 7–33.

———. 2012. '*Juvenalis eques*: A Dissident Voice from the Lower Tier of the Roman Elite'. In S. Braund and J. Osgood, eds., *A Companion to Persius and Juvenal*, 59–78. Malden, MA.

Armstrong, J. 2013. '"Bands of Brothers": Warfare and Fraternity in Early Rome', *JAH* 1: 53–69.

Arrighetti, G. 1994. 'Riflessione sulla letteratura e biografia presso i Greci'. In F. Montanari, ed., *La philologie grecque à l'époque hellénistique et romaine: sept exposés suivis de discussions*, 211–62. Geneva.

Ash, R. 1997a. 'Severed Heads: Individual Portraits and Irrational Forces in Plutarch's *Galba* and *Otho*'. In Mossman 1997, 189–214.

———. 1997b. 'Warped Intertextualities: Naevius and Sallust at Tacitus *Histories* 2.12.2', *Histos* 1: 42–50.

———. 1999. *Ordering Anarchies: Armies and Leaders in Tacitus' Histories*. London.

———. 2003. '"*Aliud est enim epistulam, aliud historiam … scribere*" (*Epistles* 6.16.22): Pliny the Historian?', *Arethusa* 36: 211–25.

———, ed. 2007. *Tacitus: Histories Book II*. Cambridge.

———. 2009. 'Introduction'. In K. Wellesley, *Tacitus: The Histories*, rev. ed., xv–xxxiv. London.

———. 2010a. 'The Great Escape: Tacitus on the Mutiny of the Usipi (*Agricola* 28)'. In Kraus, Marincola, and Pelling 2010, 275–93.

———. 2010b. 'Rhoxolani Blues (Tacitus, *Histories* 1.79): Virgil's Scythian Ethnography Revisited'. In Miller and Woodman 2010, 141–54.

———, ed. 2012. *Tacitus*. Oxford.

———. 2016. 'Never Say Die! Assassinating Emperors in Suetonius' *Lives of the Caesars*'. In De Temmerman and Demoen 2016, 200–16.

———, ed. 2018. *Tacitus: Annals Book XV*. Cambridge.

Asirvatham, S. R. 2010. 'Perspectives on the Macedonians from Greece, Rome, and beyond'. In J. Roisman and I. Worthington, eds., *A Companion to Ancient Macedonia*, 99–124. Malden, MA.

Atkinson, J. E. 1980. *A Commentary on Q. Curtius Rufus' Historiae Alexandri Magni Books 3 and 4*. Amsterdam.

———. 1994. *A Commentary on Q. Curtius Rufus' Historiae Alexandri Magni Books 5 and 7,2*. Amsterdam.

———. 1998. 'Q. Curtius Rufus' "Historiae Alexandri Magni"', *ANRW* 2.34.4: 3447–83.

Atkinson, J. E., and Yardley, J. C. 2009. *Curtius Rufus: Histories of Alexander the Great, Book 10*. Oxford.

Augoustakis, A. 2004–5. '*Nequaquam historia digna*? Plinian Style in *Ep.* 6.20', *CJ* 100: 265–73.

Augoustakis, A., and Traill, A. 2013. 'Introduction'. In A. Augoustakis and A. Traill, eds., *A Companion to Terence*, 1–14. Malden, MA.

Austin, R. G., ed. 1964. *P. Vergili Maronis Aeneidos liber secundus*. Oxford.

Averintsev, S. S. 2002. 'From Biography to Hagiography: Some Stable Patterns in the Greek and Latin Tradition of Lives, Including Lives of the Saints'. In P. France and W. St Clair, eds., *Mapping Lives: The Uses of Biography*, 19–36. Oxford.

Baar, M. 1990. *Das Bild des Kaisers Tiberius bei Tacitus, Sueton und Cassius Dio*. Stuttgart.

Babcock, C. L. 1981. '*Carmina operosa*: Critical Approaches to the "Odes" of Horace, 1945–1975', *ANRW* 2.31.3: 1560–611.

Badian, E. 1971. 'Alexander the Great, 1948–67', *CW* 65: 37–83.

Baier, T. 2003. 'Κτῆμα oder ἀγώνισμα: Plinius über historischen und rhetorischen Stil (*Epist.* 5, 8)'. In L. Catagna and E. Lefèvre, eds., *Plinius der Jüngere und seine Zeit*, 69–81. Munich.

Bakola, E. 2010. *Cratinus and the Art of Comedy*. Oxford.

Baldwin, B. 1973a. 'Lucian on Poetry', *Prudentia* 5: 117–26. Repr. in Baldwin 1985, 343–52.

———. 1973b. *Studies in Lucian*. Amsterdam.

———. 1975a. 'Suetonius: Birth, Disgrace and Death', *AClass* 18: 61–70. Repr. in Baldwin 1989b, 30–9.

———. 1975b. 'Was Suetonius Disgraced?', *EMC* 19: 22–6.

————. 1975–6. 'The Women of Greece and Rome', *Helikon* 15–16: 130–45. Repr. in Baldwin 1989b, 122–37.

————. 1977. 'Polyphagus: Glutton or Crocodile?', *AJP* 98: 406–9. Repr. in Baldwin 1985, 501–4.

————. 1979a. 'Biography at Rome'. In *SLLRH* 1.100–18. Repr. in Baldwin 1983, 66–100; also in Baldwin 1989b, 11–29.

————. 1979b. 'Nero and His Mother's Corpse', *Mnemosyne* 32: 380–1. Repr. in Baldwin 1985, 280–1.

————. 1979c. 'Some Alleged Greek Sources of the *Historia Augusta*', *LCM* 4: 19–23. Repr. in Baldwin 1984, 45–9.

————. 1980. *The Roman Emperors*. Montreal.

————. 1982a. 'Continuity and Change: The Practical Genius of Early Byzantine Civilisation'. In R. L. Hohlfelder, ed., *City, Town and Countryside in the Early Byzantine Era*, 1–24. New York. Repr. in Baldwin 1989b, 224–47.

————. 1982b. 'Vergil in Byzantium', *A&A* 28: 81–93. Repr. in Baldwin 1984, 445–57.

————. 1983. *Suetonius*. Amsterdam.

————. 1984. *Studies on Late Roman and Byzantine History, Literature and Language*. Amsterdam.

————. 1985. *Studies on Greek and Roman History and Literature*. Amsterdam.

————. 1989a. 'Ancient Lives of Virgil'. In Baldwin 1989b, 467–90.

————. 1989b. *Roman and Byzantine Papers*. Amsterdam.

————. 1993. 'Half-lines in Virgil: Old and New Ideas', *SO* 68: 144–51.

————. 1995. 'Roman Emperors in the Elder Pliny', *Scholia* 4: 56–78.

————. 1997. 'Hadrian's Dismissal of Suetonius: A Reasoned Response', *Historia* 46: 254–6.

————. 2002. 'Augustus the Poet'. In P. Defosse, ed., *Hommages à Carl Deroux*, vol. 1, 40–7. Brussels.

————. 2005. 'Nero the Poet'. In *SLLRH* 12.307–18.

————. 2006. 'Aspects of the Suda', *Byzantion* 76: 11–31.

————. 2010. '"Contemporary" Allusions in the *Historia Augusta*'. In *SSLRH* 15.446–62.

Baltussen, H. 2002. 'Matricide Revisited: Dramatic and Rhetorical Allusion in Tacitus, Suetonius and Cassius Dio', *Antichthon* 36: 30–40.

Bannon, C. J. 1997. *The Brothers of Romulus: Fraternal Pietas in Roman Law, Literature, and Society*. Princeton, NJ.

Baraz, Y. 2012a. 'Pliny's Epistolary Dreams and the Ghosts of Domitian', *TAPA* 142: 105–32.

————. 2012b. *A Written Republic: Cicero's Philosophical Politics*. Princeton, NJ.

Barchiesi, A., and Cucchiarelli, A. 2005. 'Satire and the Poet: The Body as Self-Referential Symbol'. In K. Freudenburg, ed., *The Cambridge Companion to Roman Satire*, 207–23. Cambridge.

Bar-Kochva, B. 1989. *Judas Maccabaeus: The Jewish Struggle against the Seleucids*. Cambridge.

Barrett, A. A. 1989. *Caligula: The Corruption of Power*. London.

————. 1996. *Agrippina: Sex, Power, and Politics in the Early Empire*. New Haven, CT.

————. 2005. 'Vespasian's Wife', *Latomus* 64: 385–96.

——. 2015. *Caligula: The Abuse of Power*, 2nd ed. Abingdon.

Bartera, S. 2011. 'Year-Beginnings in the Neronian Books of Tacitus' *Annals*', *MH* 68: 161–81.

Barton, T. S. 1994. 'The *inventio* of Nero: Suetonius'. In Elsner and Masters 1994, 48–63.

Bartsch, S. 1994. *Actors in the Audience: Theatricality and Doublespeak from Nero to Hadrian*. Cambridge.

——. 1997. *Ideology in Cold Blood: A Reading of Lucan's Civil War*. Cambridge, MA.

Bartsch, S., Freudenburg, K., and Littlewood, C., eds. 2017. *The Cambridge Companion to the Age of Nero*. Cambridge.

Barzanò, A. 1985. 'Curzio Rufo e la sua epoca', *MIL* 38: 71–100.

——. 1988. 'Tiberio Giulio Alessandro, Prefetto d'Egitto (66/70)', *ANRW* 2.10.1: 518–80.

Batstone, W. 1997. 'Virgilian Didaxis: Value and Meaning in the *Georgics*'. In C. Martindale, ed., *The Cambridge Companion to Virgil*, 125–44. Cambridge.

Bauman, R. A. 1983. *Lawyers in Roman Republican Politics: A Study of the Roman Jurists in Their Political Setting, 316–82 BC*. Munich.

Baumgarten-Crusius, D. K. W., ed. 1816. *C. Suetonii Tranquilli opera*, 3 vols. Leipzig.

Bayer, K., ed. 1995, *Vergil: Landleben, Cata lepton, Bucolica, Georgica*, 6th ed., ed. J. and M. Götte. Zurich.

——. 2002. *Suetons Vergilvita: Versuch einer Rekonstruktion*. Tübingen.

Baynham, E. 1998. *Alexander the Great: The Unique History of Quintus Curtius*. Ann Arbor, MI.

Beare, W. 1942. 'The Life of Terence', *Hermathena* 59: 20–9.

Beagon, M. 2005a. *The Elder Pliny on the Human Animal: Natural History, Book 7*. Oxford.

——. 2005b. '*Mors repetina* and the Roman Art of Dying', *SyllClass* 16: 85–137.

Beck, M., ed. 2014. *A Companion to Plutarch*. Malden, MA.

Beecroft, A. 2011. 'Blindness and Literacy in the *Lives* of Homer', *CQ* 61: 1–18.

Bellandi, F. 2006. 'La *turpis fuga* di Nerone (*Octauia* 620 e Tacito, *hist*. 3, 68)', *Latomus* 65: 634–40.

Belmont, D. E. 1980. 'The Vergilius of Horace, *Ode* 4.12', *TAPA* 110: 1–20.

Benario, H. W. 1972. 'Priam and Galba', *CW* 65: 146–7.

——. 1975. *An Introduction to Tacitus*. Athens, GA.

——. 2012. 'The *Annals*'. In Pagán 2012a, 101–22.

Benediktson, D. T. 1992. 'Nero and Agrippina's Goodbye Kiss: *papillas* or *pupillas*?', *Maia* 44: 161–3.

——. 1996–7. 'Structure and Fate in Suetonius' *Life of Galba*', *CJ* 92: 167–73.

Beneker, J. 2012. *The Passionate Statesman: Eros and Politics in Plutarch's Lives*. Oxford.

Benko, S. 1969. 'The Edict of Claudius of A.D. 49 and the Instigator Chrestus', *ThZ* 25: 406–18.

Bennett, E. N. 1891. 'Spartian. *Vit. Hadr.* xi', *CR* 5: 68.

Bennett, J. 2001. *Trajan: optimus princeps*, 2nd ed. London.

Beroaldo, F., ed. 1493. *Commentationes conditae a Philippo Beroaldo in Suetonium Tranquillum*. Bologna.

Berry, D. H. 2008. 'Letters from an Advocate: Pliny's "Vesuvius" Narratives (*Epistles* 6.16, 6.20)', *PLLS* 13: 297–313.

Berthet, J.-F. 1978. 'La culture Homérique des Césars d'après Suétone', *REL* 56: 314–34.

Berthold, H. 2008. *'Ihrem Originale nachzudenken': Zu Lessings Übersetzungen.* Tübingen.

Bessone, L. 1979. 'Pitagora e Sporo, non dorifori', *GFF* 2: 105–14.

Best, E. E. 1977. 'Suetonius: The Use of Greek among the Julio-Claudian Emperors', *CB* 53: 39–4.

Billerbeck, M. 1990. 'Philology at the Imperial Court', *G&R* 37: 191–203.

Billings, B. S. 2009. '"At the Age of 12": The Boy Jesus in the Temple (Luke 2:41–52), the Emperor Augustus, and the Social Setting of the Third Gospel', *JThS* 60: 70–89.

Bird, H. W. 1971. 'Suetonian Influence in the Later Lives of the Historia Augusta', *Hermes* 99: 129–34.

———. 1973. 'Germanicus mytheroicus', *EMC* 17: 94–101.

———. 1984. *Sextus Aurelius Victor: A Historiographical Study.* Liverpool.

———. 1994. *Aurelius Victor: De Caesaribus.* Liverpool.

Birley, A. R. 1976. *Lives of the Later Caesars.* Harmondsworth.

———. 1984. Review of Baldwin 1983, de Coninck 1983, and Wallace-Hadrill 1983, *JRS* 74: 245–51.

———. 1997. *Hadrian: The Restless Emperor.* London.

———. 2000. 'The Life and Death of Cornelius Tacitus', *Historia* 49: 230–47.

———. 2005. *The Roman Government of Britain.* Oxford.

Bitschofsky, R. 1888. 'Kritisch-exegetische Studien zu den Scriptores Historiae Augustae'. In *Jahresbericht über das K.K. Staatsgymnasium im II. Bezirke in Wien*, 3–44. Vienna.

Bittarello, M. B. 2011. 'Otho, Elagabalus and the Judgement of Paris: The Literary Construction of the Unmanly Emperor', *DHA* 37: 93–113.

Blanshard, A. J. L. 2010. *Sex: Vice and Love from Antiquity to Modernity.* Oxford.

Blok, J. H. 1995. *The Early Amazons: Modern and Ancient Perspectives on a Persistent Myth.* Leiden.

Boedefeld, H. 1982. *Untersuchungen zur Datierung der Alexandergeschichte des Q. Curtius Rufus.* Diss., University of Düsseldorf.

Bollansée, J., ed. 1999a. *Hermippos of Smyrna.* Leiden.

———. 1999b. *Hermippos of Smyrna and His Biographical Writings: A Reappraisal.* Leuven.

Boman, J. 2011. 'Inpulsore Cherestro? Suetonius' *Divus Claudius* 25.4 in Sources and Manuscripts', *Liber Annuus* 61: 355–76.

Borzsák, S., ed. 1984. *Q. Horati Flacci opera.* Leipzig.

Bosworth, A. B. 1977. 'Arrian and the Alani', *HSCP* 81: 217–55.

———. 1983. 'History and Rhetoric in Curtius Rufus', *CP* 78: 150–61.

———. 2004. 'Mountain and Molehill? Cornelius Tacitus and Quintus Curtius', *CQ* 54: 551–67.

Botermann, H. 1996. *Das Judenedikt des Kaisers Claudius: Römischer Staat und Christiani im 1. Jahrhundert.* Stuttgart.

Bowditch, P. L. 2001. *Horace and the Gift Economy of Patronage.* Berkeley, CA.

Bowersock, G. W. 1969. 'Suetonius and Trajan'. In J. Bibauw, ed., *Hommages à Marcel Renard*, vol. 1, 119–25. Brussels.

———. 1990. 'The Pontificate of Augustus'. In K. A. Raaflaub and M. Toher, eds., *Between Republic and Empire: Interpretations of Augustus and His Principate*, 380–94. Berkeley, CA.

———. 1998. '*Vita Caesarum*: Remembering and Forgetting the Past'. In S. M. Maul and W.-W. Ehlers, eds., *La biographie antique: huit exposés suivis de discussions*, 193–210. Geneva.

Bowie, E. 2008. 'Plutarch's Habits of Citation: Aspects of Difference'. In Nikolaidis 2008, 143–58.

Bradley, K. R. 1973. 'The Composition of Suetonius' *Caesares* Again', *JIES* 1: 257–63.

———. 1976. 'Imperial Virtues in Suetonius' *Caesares*', *JIES* 4: 245–53.

———. 1978. *Suetonius' Life of Nero: An Historical Commentary*. Brussels.

———. 1985. Review of Baldwin 1983 and Wallace-Hadrill 1983, *CP* 80: 254–65.

———. 1987. *Slaves and Masters in the Roman World: A Study in Social Control*. Oxford.

———. 1991. 'The Imperial Ideal in Suetonius' "Caesares"', *ANRW* 2.33.5: 3701–32.

———. 1998. 'Introduction'. In J. C. Rolfe, ed., *Suetonius*, vol. 1, 2nd ed., 1–34. Cambridge, MA.

———. 2012. 'Suetonius'. In S. Hornblower, A. Spawforth, and E. Eidinow, eds., *The Oxford Classical Dictionary*, 4th ed., 1409–10. Oxford.

———. 2016. 'Yourcenar's Suetonius: Grasping for the Wind', *Phoenix* 70: 147–69.

———. 2019. 'Publilius Syrus and the Anxiety of Continuity', *Mouseion* 16: 65–89.

Bradshaw, A. 2002. 'Horace's Birthday and Deathday'. In T. Woodman and D. Feeney, eds., *Traditions and Contexts in the Poetry of Horace*, 1–16. Cambridge.

Braithwaite, A. W., ed. 1927. *C. Suetoni Tranquilli Divus Vespasianus*. Oxford.

Brandão, J. L. 2006. 'Vida suetoniana de Terêncio: estrutura e estratégias de defesa do poeta'. In A. Pociña, B. Rabaza, and M. de F. Silva, eds., *Estudios sobre Terencio*, 111–23. Granada.

———. 2009. *Máscaras dos Césares: teatro e moralidade nas Vidas suetonianas*. Coimbra.

———. 2010. *Plutarco: Vidas de Galba e Otão*. Coimbra.

Braun, L. 1990. 'Vitellius und Tiberius bei Tacitus und Sueton', *WJA* 16: 205–19.

Braund, D. 1996. 'The Politics of Catullus 10: Memmius, Caesar and the Bithynians', *Hermathena* 160: 45–57.

———. 2013. 'Apollo in Arms: Nero at the Frontier'. In Buckley and Dinter 2013, 83–101.

Braund, S. 1988. *Beyond Anger: A Study of Juvenal's Third Book of Satires*. Cambridge.

———. 1996. 'The Solitary Feast: A Contradiction in Terms?', *BICS* 41: 37–52.

Bravi, A. 1996. 'Gli imperatori della *Historia Augusta* e il *luxus* nelle arti', *Xenia antiqua* 5: 5–104.

Brenk, F. E. 1977. *In Mist Apparelled: Religious Themes in Plutarch's Moralia and Lives*. Leiden.

———. 1992. 'Plurarch's Life "Markos Antonios": A Literary and Cultural Study', *ANRW* 2.33.6: 4347–469.

Brennan, T. C. 2018. *Sabina Augusta: An Imperial Journey*. Oxford.

Bright, D. F. 1978. *Haec mihi fingebam: Tibullus in His World*. Leiden.

———. 1981. 'Ovid vs. Apuleius', *ICS* 6: 356–66.

Brink, C. O., ed. 1963–82. *Horace on Poetry*, 3 vols. Cambridge.

Briscoe, J. 2008. *A Commentary on Livy Books 38–40*. Oxford.

———. 2012. *A Commentary on Livy Books 41–45*. Oxford.

Brown, E. L. 1963. *Numeri Virgiliani: Studies in Eclogues and Georgics*. Brussels.

Brown, P. M., ed. 1993. *Horace: Satires I*. Warminster.

Brown, V. 1972. *The Textual Transmission of Caesar's Civil War*. Leiden.

Bruce, F. F. 1962. 'Christianity under Claudius', *BJRL* 44: 309–26.

———. 1982. 'The Romans Debate – Continued', *BJRL* 64: 334–59. Repr. in Bruce 1990, 79–97.

———. 1990. *A Mind for What Matters: Collected Essays of F. F. Bruce*. Grand Rapids, MI.

Brugnoli, G. 1960. 'Suetoniana I: De grammaticis et rhetoribus', *AFLC* 28: 337–61. Repr. in Brugnoli 1968a, 97–127, 131–4.

———. 1963. 'Coniectanea XI–XX', *RCCM* 5: 255–65.

———. 1964. 'Problematica suetoniana', *C&S* 3: 63–7.

———. 1968a. *Studi suetoniani*. Lecce.

———, ed. 1968b. *Suetonio: Vita di Orazio*. Rome.

———. 1985. '"Opes cum dignatione": arricchimento e ascesa sociale dei ceti subalterni nell'ideologia di Svetonio', *Index* 13: 327–51.

———. 1993. 'Svetonio *eques Romanus*'. In *Atti: giornate filologiche 'Francesco Della Corte'*, 47–61. Genoa.

———. 1996. 'Per il testo del *De grammaticis* di Suetonio', *GIF* 48: 189–221.

Brunet, S. 2004. 'Female and Dwarf Gladiators', *Mouseion* 4: 145–70.

Bruun, C., and Edmondson, J. 2015. 'The Epigrapher at Work'. In C. Bruun and J. Edmondson, eds., *The Oxford Handbook of Roman Epigraphy*, 3–20. Oxford.

Buckley, E. 2018. 'Flavian Epic and Trajanic Historiography: Speaking into Silence'. In König and Whitton 2018, 86–107.

Buckley, E., and Dinter, M., eds. 2013. *A Companion to the Neronian Age*. Malden, MA.

Buckwald, C. 2020. 'Shameous Caesar: Suetonius and *Finnegans Wake* I.7', *Joyce Studies Annual*: 115–50.

Buongiovanni, C. 2016. 'Augusto "letterato" nella biografia svetoniana e la dimensione pubblica dell'*otium*', *Maia* 68: 362–73.

Burden-Strevens, C. 2020. *Cassius Dio's Speeches and the Collapse of the Roman Republic: The Roman History, Books 3–56*. Leiden.

Burke, J. W. 1993. *Suetonius' De vita Caesarum: A Study in the Literary Iconography of Power*. Diss., University of Wisconsin.

———. 1998. 'Emblematic Scenes in Suetonius' *Vitellius*', *Histos* 2: 83–94.

Burke, P. F. 2019. 'Saint Pilate and the Conversion of Tiberius'. In M. C. English and L. M. Fratantuono, eds., *Pushing the Boundaries of Historia*, 264–8. Abingdon.

Burman, P., ed. 1736. *C. Suetonius Tranquillus cum notis integris*, vol. 1. Amsterdam.

Burridge, R. A. 2004. *What Are the Gospels? A Comparison with Graeco-Roman Biography*, 2nd ed. Grand Rapids, MI.

Busto de Lezica, M. N. 2008. '¿Le temía Claudio a la muerte? (Suetonio, *Claudio* 43–46)', *Auster* 13: 73–86.

Butler, H. E., and Cary, M., eds. 1927. *Suetonius: Divus Julius*. Oxford.

Büttner, R. 1893. *Porcius Licinus und der litterarische Kreis des Q. Lutatius Catulus*. Leipzig.

Cairns, F. 2006–7. '"Titius" at Tibullus 1.4.73–4: A Double Reference?', *Eranos* 104: 28–30.

Calder, W. M. 1988. 'F. G. Welcker's Sapphobild and Its Reception in Wilamowitz'. In W. M. Calder et al., eds., *Friedrich Gottlieb Welcker: Werk und Wirkung*, 131–56. Stuttgart.

Callu, J.-P., ed. 1992. *Histoire Auguste*, vol. 1.1. Paris.

Cameron, A. 2004. *Greek Mythography in the Roman World*. Oxford.

———. 2010. 'The Date of the Scholia vetustiora on Juvenal', *CQ* 60: 569–76.

Carlsen, J. 2016. 'Alexander the Great in Cassius Dio'. In Lange and Madsen 2016, 316–31.

Carney, T. F., ed. 1963. *P. Terenti Afri Hecyra*. Pretoria.

———. 1968. 'How Suetonius' Lives Reflect on Hadrian', *PACA* 11: 7–24.

Carrier, R. 2014. 'The Prospect of a Christian Interpolation in Tacitus, *Annals* 15.44', *VChr* 68: 264–83.

Carter, J. M., ed. 1982. *Suetonius: Divus Augustus*. London.

Carter, M. A. S. 2002. '*Vergilium vestigare: Aeneid* 12.587–8', *CQ* 52: 615–17.

Cary, E. 1924–5. *Dio's Roman History*, vols. 7–8. London.

Cels-Saint-Hilaire, J. 1999. 'Horace, *libertino patre natus*'. In C. Petitfrère, ed., *Construction, reproduction et représentation des patriciats urbains de l'Antiquité au XXe siècle*, 23–46. Tours.

Champlin, E. 1989. 'The Life and Times of Calpurnius Piso', *MH* 46: 101–24.

———. 2003. *Nero*. Cambridge, MA.

———. 2008. 'Tiberius the Wise', *Historia* 57: 408–25.

———. 2011. 'Sex on Capri', *TAPA* 141: 315–32.

Charles, M. B. 2014. 'Nero and Sporus Again', *Latomus* 73: 667–85.

Charles, M. B., and Anagnostou-Laoutides, E. 2010a. 'The Sexual Hypocrisy of Domitian: Suet., *Dom.* 8, 3', *AC* 79: 173–87.

———. 2010b. 'Suetonius *Vespasianus* 3: The Status of Flavia Domitilla', *AClass* 53: 125–43.

———. 2012a. 'Galba in the Bedroom: Sexual Allusions in Suetonius' *Galba*', *Latomus* 71: 1077–87.

———. 2012b. 'Vespasian, Caenis and Suetonius'. In *SLLRH* 16.530–47.

———. 2013–14. 'Unmanning the Emperor: Otho in the Literary Tradition', *CJ* 109: 199–222.

Cheesman, C. 2009. 'Names in -por and Slave Naming in Republican Rome', *CQ* 59: 511–31.

Chiai, G. F. 2019. 'Good Emperors, Bad Emperors: The Function of Physiognomic Representation in Suetonius' *De vita Caesarum* and Common Sense Physiognomics'. In J. C. Johnson and A. Stavru, eds., *Visualizing the Invisible with the Human Body: Physiognomy and Ekphrasis in the Ancient World*, 203–26. Berlin.

Chilver, G. E. F. 1979. *A Historical Commentary on Tacitus' Histories I and II*. Oxford.

Chong-Gossard, K. O. 2010. 'Who Slept with Whom in the Roman Empire? Women, Sex, and Scandal in Suetonius' *Caesares*'. In A. J. Turner, K. O. Chong-Gossard, and F. J. Vervaet, eds., *Private and Public Lies: The Discourse of Despotism and Deceit in the Graeco-Roman World*, 295–327. Leiden.

Citroni, M. 2006. 'The Concept of the Classical and the Canons of Model Authors in Roman Literature'. In J. I. Porter, ed., *Classical Pasts: The Classical Traditions of Greece and Rome*, 204–34. Princeton, NJ.

Cizek, E. 1975. 'La mort de Vitellius dans les Vies des douze Césars de Suétone', *REA* 77: 125–30.

———. 1977. *Structures et idéologie dans 'Les vies des douze Césars' de Suétone.* Paris.

Clarke, K. 1997. 'In Search of the Author of Strabo's *Geography*', *JRS* 87: 92–110.

———. 2002. '*In arto et inglorius labor*: Tacitus's Anti-History'. In A. K. Bowman et al., eds., *Representations of Empire: Rome and the Mediterranean World*, 83–103. Oxford.

Clauss, J. J. 1983. *Allusion and the Narrative Style of Apollonius Rhodius: A Detailed Study of Book 1 of the Argonautica*. Diss., University of California, Berkeley.

Coffee, N. 2009. *The Commerce of War: Exchange and Social Order in Latin Epic.* Chicago.

Coleman, K. M. 1986. 'The Emperor Domitian and Literature', *ANRW* 2.32.5: 3087–115.

———. 1990. 'Fatal Charades: Roman Executions Staged as Mythological Enactments', *JRS* 80: 44–73.

———, ed. 2006. *M. Valerii Martialis Liber Spectaculorum.* Oxford.

———. 2011. 'Public Entertainments'. In M. Peachin, ed., *The Oxford Handbook of Social Relations in the Roman World*, 335–57. Oxford.

Cook, J. G. 2010. *Roman Attitudes toward the Christians: From Claudius to Hadrian.* Tübingen.

———. 2020. '*Chrestiani, Christiani*, Χριστιανοί: A Second Century Anachronism?', *VChr* 74: 237–64.

Cornell, T. J. 2013a. 'Suetonius'. In Cornell 2013b, 125–9.

———, ed. 2013b. *The Fragments of the Roman Historians*, vol. 1. Oxford.

Courtney, E. 1990. 'Greek and Latin Acrostichs', *Philologus* 134: 3–13.

———, ed. 1993. *The Fragmentary Latin Poets.* Oxford.

———. 2009. 'Housman's Manilius'. In D. J. Butterfield and C. A. Stray, eds., *A.E. Housman: Classical Scholar*, 29–44. London.

———. 2013. 'The Two Books of Satires'. In Günther 2013a, 63–168.

Cova, P. V. 1966. *La critica letteraria di Plinio il Giovane.* Brescia.

Cowan, R. 2003. *Roman Legionary: 58 BC–AD 69.* Oxford.

Cowan, R. 2011. 'Lucan's Thunder-Box: Scatology, Epic, and Satire in Suetonius' *Vita Lucani*', *HSCP* 106: 301–13.

Crawford, K. 2017. 'Sporus in the Renaissance: The Eunuch as Straight Man'. In W. Caferro, ed., *The Routledge History of the Renaissance*, 140–51. London.

Crompton, L. 2003. *Homosexuality and Civilization.* Cambridge, MA.

Crook, J. A. 1956-7. 'Suetonius "ab epistulis"', *PCPS* 4: 18–22.

———. 1969. Review of F. Della Corte, *Svetonio: eques Romanus*, 2nd ed. (Florence, 1967), *CR* 19: 62–3.

Crowther, N. B. 1971. 'Valerius Cato, Furius Bibaculus, and Ticidas', *CP* 66: 108–9.

Curry, S. A. 2014. 'Nero *quadripes*: Animalizing the Emperor in Suetonius's *Nero*', *Arethusa* 47: 197–230.

Dalmasso, L. 1906. *La Grammatica di C. Svetonio Tranquillo.* Turin.

Damon, C., ed. 2003. *Tacitus: Histories Book I*. Cambridge.

———. 2010. 'Déjà vu or déjà lu? History as Intertext', *PLLS* 14: 375–88.

———. 2014. 'Suetonius the Ventriloquist'. In Power and Gibson 2014, 38–57.

———. 2018. 'Death by Narrative in Suetonius' *Lives*', *PLLS* 17: 107–27.

———. 2020. 'Looking for Seneca's *Historiae* in Suetonius' *Life of Tiberius*'. In Scappaticcio 2020, 123–42.

D'Anna, G. 1954. *Le idee letterarie di Suetonio*. Florence.

———. 1956. 'Sulla vita suetoniana di Terenzio', *RIL* 89: 31–46.

———. 1963. 'Osservazioni sulle fonti della morte di Agrippina minore', *Athenaeum* 41: 111–17.

———. 1988. 'Suetonio grammatico?', *C&S* 107: 62–7.

Davenport, C. 2014. 'The Conduct of Vitellius in Cassius Dio's *Roman History*', *Historia* 63: 96–116.

———. 2019. *A History of the Roman Equestrian Order*. Cambridge.

Davies, J. P. 2004. *Rome's Religious History: Livy, Tacitus and Ammianus on Their Gods*. Cambridge.

Davis, G., ed. 2010. *A Companion to Horace*. Malden, MA.

Davis, J. E. 2014. 'Terence Interrupted: Literary Biography and the Reception of the Terentian Canon', *AJP* 135: 387–409.

Davis, P. J. 1999. '"Since My Part Has Been Well Played": Conflicting Evaluations of Augustus', *Ramus* 28: 1–15.

de Climent, M. B., ed. 1964–70. *C. Suetonio Tranquillo: Vida de los doce Césares*, 4 vols. Barcelona.

de Coninck, L. 1980–1. 'Un projet d'études sur les sources primaires littéraires et documentaires des historiens à Rome', *AncSoc* 11–12: 387–407.

———. 1983. *Suetonius en de Archivalia*. Brussels.

———. 1991. 'Les sources documentaires de Suétone, "Les XII Césars": 1900–1990', *ANRW* 2.33.5: 3675–700.

de Gubernatis, M. L., ed. 1945. *Q. Horati Flacci opera*. Turin.

de Heredia, J.-M. 1898. *Sonnets*, trans. E. R. Taylor. San Francisco, CA.

de la Cerda, J. L., ed. 1612. *P. Vergilii Maronis priores sex libri Aeneidos argumentis, explicationibus notis illustrati*. Lyon.

Delarue, F. 1995. 'Suétone et l'hypotypose', *Lalies* 15: 291–300.

del Castillo, A. 2002. 'The Emperor Galba's Assumption of Power: Some Chronological Considerations', *Historia* 51: 449–61.

Della Corte, F. 1956. 'Suspiciones II'. In *Antidoron U. E. Paoli oblatum*, 82–95. Genoa. Repr. in *Op*. 9.249–62.

———. 1958. *Svetonio: eques Romanus*. Milan.

den Hengst, D. 2009. *Emperors and Historiography: Collected Essays on the Literature of the Roman Empire*, eds. D. W. P. Burgersdijk and J. A. van Waarden. Leiden.

Desideri, P. 2017. 'Plutarch's *Lives*'. In D. S. Richter and W. A. Johnson, eds., *The Oxford Handbook of the Second Sophistic*, 311–26, 707–9. Oxford.

de Souza, P. 2008. '*Parta victoriis pax*: Roman Emperors as Peacemakers'. In P. de Souza and J. France, eds., *War and Peace in Ancient and Medieval History*, 76–106. Cambridge.

De Temmerman, K. 2016. 'Ancient Biography and Formalities of Fiction'. In De Temmerman and Demoen 2016, 3–25.

De Temmerman, K., and Demoen, K., eds. 2016. *Writing Biography in Greece and Rome: Narrative Technique and Fictionalization*. Cambridge.

Devillers, O. 2003. *Tacite et les sources des Annales: enquêtes sur la méthode historique.* Leuven.

Devine, A. M. 1979. 'The *Parthi*, the Tyranny of Tiberius, and the Date of Q. Curtius Rufus', *Phoenix* 33: 142–59.

Dihle, A. 1956. *Studien zur griechischen Biographie.* Göttingen.

Dilke, O. A. W. 1957. 'The Literary Output of the Roman Emperors', *G&R* 4: 78–97.

Donahue, J. F. 2004. *The Roman Community at Table during the Principate.* Ann Arbor, MI.

Doody, A. 2013. 'Literature of the World: Seneca's *Natural Questions* and Pliny's *Natural History*'. In Buckley and Dinter 2013, 288–301.

Dorado, A. C. et al., eds. 2008. *Donum amicitiae: estudios en homenaje al profesor Vicente Picón García.* Madrid.

Dorey, T. A., ed. 1967. *Latin Biography.* London.

Draycott, J. 2012. 'The Symbol of Cleopatra Selene: Reading Crocodiles on Coins in the Late Republic and Early Principate', *AClass* 55: 42–56.

Drinkwater, J. F. 2019. *Nero: Emperor and Court.* Cambridge.

Dubuisson, M. 2003. 'Suétone et la fausse impartialité de l'érudit'. In Lachenaud and Longrée 2003, 249–61.

———. 2004. 'Le portrait de César chez Suétone: un cas de persuasion'. In P.-A. Deproost and A. Meurant, eds., *Images d'origines, origines d'une image: hommages à Jacques Poucet*, 289–96. Louvain-la-Neuve.

Duchêne, P. 2016. 'Suetonius' Construction of His Historiographical *auctoritas*'. In V. Liotsakis and S. Farrington, eds., *The Art of Historiography: Literary Perspectives on Greek and Roman Historiography*, 271–88. Berlin.

Duckworth, G. E. 1952. *The Nature of Roman Comedy: A Study in Popular Entertainment.* Princeton, NJ.

Dueck, D. 2009. 'Poetic Citations in Latin Prose Works of Historiography and Biography', *Hermes* 137: 170–89.

Duff, J. D. 1914. 'Suetonius', *JPh* 33: 161–71.

Duff, J. W. 1916. Review of Rolfe 1913–14, *CR* 30: 166–9.

———. 1960. *A Literary History of Rome in the Silver Age: From Tiberius to Hadrian*, 2nd ed. London.

Duff, T. E. 1999. *Plutarch's Lives: Exploring Virtue and Vice.* Oxford.

———. 2003a. *The Greek and Roman Historians.* London.

———. 2003b. 'Plutarch on the Childhood of Alkibiades (*Alk.* 2–3)', *PCPS* 49: 89–117.

———. 2008. 'How *Lives* Begin'. In Nikolaidis 2008, 187–207.

Dugan, J. 2001. 'Preventing Ciceronianism: C. Licinius Calvus' Regimens for Sexual and Oratorical Self-Mastery', *CP* 96: 400–28.

Dunkle, J. R. 1971. 'The Rhetorical Tyrant in Roman Historiography: Sallust, Livy and Tacitus', *CW* 65: 12–20.

Dunn, J. D. G. 2011. *Jesus, Paul, and the Gospels.* Grand Rapids, MI.

Dyck, A. R. 2017. 'Three Textual Problems in Cicero's *Philosophica*', *CQ* 67: 310–12.

Eaton, J. 2011. 'The Political Significance of the Imperial Watchword in the Early Empire', *G&R* 58: 48–63.

Echeverría, F. 2012. 'Hoplite and Phalanx in Archaic and Classical Greece: A Reassessment', *CP* 107: 291–318.

Eck, W. 2000. 'The Emperor and His Advisors'. In A. K. Bowman, P. Garnsey, and D. Rathbone, eds., *The Cambridge Ancient History*, vol. 11, 2nd ed., 195–213. Cambridge.

Eden, P. T., ed. 1984. *Seneca: Apocolocyntosis*. Cambridge.

Edmondson, J. 1992. *Dio: The Julio-Claudians*. London.

Edwards, C. 1994. 'Beware of Imitations: Theatre and the Subversion of Imperial Identity'. In Elsner and Masters 1994, 83–97.

———. 2000. *Suetonius: Lives of the Caesars*. Oxford.

———. 2007. *Death in Ancient Rome*. New Haven, CT.

Edwards, M. J. 1991. 'Χρηστός in a Magical Papyrus', *ZPE* 85: 232–6.

Edwards, R. 2008. 'Hunting for Boars with Pliny and Tacitus', *ClAnt* 27: 35–58.

———. 2018. 'Pliny's Tacitus: The Politics of Representation', *BICS* 61: 66–77.

Ektor, J. 1980. 'L'impassibilité et l'objectivité de Suétone: confrontation avec Tacite', *LEC* 48: 317–26.

Elder, O., and Mullen, A. 2019. *The Language of Roman Letters: Bilingual Epistolography from Cicero to Fronto*. Cambridge.

Elsner, J., and Masters, J., eds. 1994. *Reflections of Nero: Culture, History & Representation*. Chapel Hill, NC.

Erler, M., and Schorn, S., eds. 2007. *Die griechische Biographie in hellenistischer Zeit: Akten des internationalen Kongresses vom 26.–29. Juli 2006 in Würzburg*. Berlin.

Evans, E. C. 1950. 'Physiognomics in the Roman Empire', *CJ* 45: 277–82.

———. 1969. 'Physiognomics in the Ancient World', *TAPS* 59.5: 1–101.

Fabia, P. 1898. *Les sources de Tacite dans les Histoires et les Annales*. Paris.

Fagan, G. G. 2011. *The Lure of the Arena: Social Psychology and the Crowd at the Roman Games*. Cambridge.

Fagles, R. 2006. *Virgil: The Aeneid*. New York.

Fairweather, J. 1974. 'Fiction in the Biographies of Ancient Writers', *AncSoc* 5: 231–75.

———. 1983. 'Traditional Narrative, Inference and Truth in the *Lives* of Greek Poets', *PLLS* 4: 315–69.

Falkner, T. M. 1989. 'Ἐπὶ γήραος οὐδῷ: Homeric Heroism, Old Age and the End of the *Odyssey*'. In T. M. Falkner and J. de Luce, eds., *Old Age in Greek and Latin Literature*, 21–67. Albany, NY.

Fantham, E. 1999. 'Two Levels of Orality in the Genesis of Pliny's *Panegyricus*'. In E. A. Mackay, ed., *Sings of Orality: The Oral Tradition and Its Influence in the Greek and Roman World*, 221–37. Leiden. Repr. in Rees 2012a, 109–25.

———. 2013a. 'The Fourth Book of *Odes*'. In Günther 2013a, 445–66.

———. 2013b. 'The Performing Prince'. In Buckley and Dinter 2013, 17–28.

———. 2013c. *Roman Literary Culture: From Plautus to Macrobius*, 2nd ed. Baltimore, MD.

Fantuzzi, M. 2013. 'Achilles and the *improba virgo*: Ovid, *Ars am.* 1.681–704 and Statius, *Ach.* 1.514–35 on Achilles at Scyros'. In T. D. Papanghelis, S. J. Harrison, and S. Frangoulidis, eds., *Generic Interfaces in Latin Literature: Encounters, Interactions and Transformations*, 151–68. Berlin.

Farrell, J. 2009. 'The Impermanent Text in Catullus and Other Roman Poets'. In Johnson and Parker 2009, 164–85.

Farrell, J., and Putnam, M. J. C., eds. 2010. *A Companion to Vergil's Aeneid and Its Tradition*. Malden, MA.

Feeney, D., and Nelis, D. 2005. 'Two Virgilian Acrostics: *certissima signa?*', *CQ* 55: 644–6.

Ferrero, I. M. 1997. 'Pragmatismo plutarquiano y dramatismo suetoniano en las Vitae Caesarum'. In C. Schrader, V. Ramón, and J. Vela, eds., *Plutarco y la historia: actas del V Simposio español sobre Plutarco, Zaragoza 20–22 de junio de 1996*, 315–27. Zaragoza.

Fielding, I. 2017. *Transformations of Ovid in Late Antiquity*. Cambridge.

Fields, D. 2020. 'Patronage, Cultural Difference and Literary Interactivity'. In König, Langlands, and Uden 2020, 95–113.

Finch, C. E. 1969. 'Suetonius' Catalogue of Animal Sounds in Codex Vat. Lat. 6018', *AJP* 90: 459–63.

Finglass, P. J., ed. 2007. *Sophocles: Electra*. Cambridge.

———, ed. 2018. *Sophocles: Oedipus the King*. Cambridge.

Fisher, C. D., ed. 1906. *Cornelii Taciti Annalium ab excessu Divi Augusti libri*. Oxford.

Flach, D. 1972. 'Zum Quellenwert der Kaiserbiographien Suetons', *Gymnasium* 79: 273–89.

Fletcher, R., and Hanink, J., eds. 2016. *Creative Lives in Classical Antiquity: Poets, Artists and Biography*. Cambridge.

Flory, M. B. 1989. 'Octavian and the Omen of the *gallina alba*', *CJ* 84: 343–56.

Fowler, D. P. 1983. 'An Acrostic in Vergil (*Aeneid* 7. 601–4)?', *CQ* 33: 298.

Foxley, B. 1911. *Jean Jacques Rousseau: Émile*. London.

Fraenkel, E. 1933. 'Lucili quam sis mendosus', *Hermes* 68: 392–9. Repr. in Fraenkel 1964, 199–208.

———. 1957. *Horace*. Oxford.

———. 1964. *Kleine Beiträge zur klassischen Philologie*, vol. 2. Rome.

Frangoulidis, S. A. 1990. 'Tacitus (*Hist.* 1.40–43), Plutarch (*Galba* 26–27) and Suetonius (*Galba* 7.20) on the Death of Galba', *Favonius* 3: 1–10.

Fredericks, S. G. 1976. 'Juvenal's Fifteenth Satire', *ICS* 1: 174–89.

Freisenbruch, A. 2010. *Caesars' Wives: Sex, Power, and Politics in the Roman Empire*. New York.

Freudenburg, K. 2001. *Satires of Rome: Threatening Poses from Lucilius to Juvenal*. Cambridge.

———. 2010. '*Horatius anceps*: Persona and Self-Revelation in Satire and Song'. In Davis 2010, 271–90.

Freyburger-Galland, M.-L. 2009. 'Dion Cassius et Suétone'. In Poignault 2009, 147–62.

Fry, C. 2010. '*Suetonianus quidam*: l'auteur de l'*Histoire Auguste* en utilisateur du style suétonien'. In L. Galli Milić and N. Hecquet-Noti, eds., *Historiae Augustae: colloquium Genevense in honorem F. Paschoud septuagenarii*, 135–52. Bari.

Fuchs, H. 1950. 'Tacitus über die Christen', *VChr* 4: 65–93.

Fugmann, J. 1995. 'Zum Problem der Datierung der "Historiae Alexandri Magni" des Curtius Rufus', *Hermes* 123: 233–43.

Funaioli, G. 1927. 'I Cesari di Svetonio'. In *Raccolta di scritti in onore di Felice Ramorino*, 1–26. Milan. Repr. in Funaioli 1947, 147–79.

———. 1931. 'Suetonius', *RE* 4 A1: 593–641.

———. 1947. *Studi di letteratura antica: spiriti e forme, figure e problemi delle letterature classiche*, vol. 2.2. Bologna.

Fündling, J. 2006. *Kommentar zur Vita Hadriani der Historia Augusta*, 2 vols. Bonn.

Gale, M. R., and Scourfield, J. H. D. 2018a. 'Introduction: Reading Roman Violence'. In Gale and Scourfield 2018b, 1–43.

———, eds. 2018b. *Texts and Violence in the Roman World*. Cambridge.

Galinsky, K. 1996. *Augustan Culture: An Interpretive Introduction*. Princeton, NJ.

Galli, F. 1991. *Svetonio: Vita di Domiziano*. Rome.

Galtier, F. 2011. *L'image tragique de l'Histoire chez Tacite: étude des schèmes tragiques dans les Histoires et les Annales*. Brussels.

Gamberini, F. 1983. *Stylistic Theory and Practice in the Younger Pliny*. Hildesheim.

Gangloff, A. 2011. 'Le *princeps* et le bon roi selon Homère'. In S. Benoist et al., eds., *Figures d'empire, fragments de mémoire: pouvoirs et identités dans le monde romain impérial (IIe s. av. n. è. – VIe s. de n. è.)*, 105–22. Villeneuve d'Ascq.

Garbrah, K. A. 1981. 'Terence and Scipio: An Echo of Terence in the Oratorical Fragments of Scipio Aemilianus?', *Athenaeum* 59: 188–91.

Garraty, J. A. 1958. *The Nature of Biography*. London.

Garrett, P. 2015. 'Reconstructing the Lost Beginning of Suetonius' *Divus Iulius*', *Antichthon* 49: 110–34.

———. 2018a. '*Sit in medio*: Family and Status in Suetonius' *Vitellius*', *AClass* 61: 53–68.

———. 2018b. 'Structure and Persuasion in Suetonius' *De uita Caesarum*', *Ramus* 47: 197–215.

———. 2019. 'Foreshadowing and Flashback: Childhood Anecdotes in Suetonius' *Caesars*', *CQ* 69: 378–83.

Gascou, J. 1976. 'Suétone et l'ordre équestre', *REL* 54: 257–77.

———. 1984. *Suétone historien*. Rome.

———. 1994. 'L'utilisation de documents de première main dans les *Vies des Douze Césars* de Suétone', *VL* 133: 7–21.

———. 2001. 'Histoire et biographie: Suétone'. In J. Leclant and F. Chamoux, eds., *Histoire et historiographie dans l'antiquité: actes du 11e colloque de la villa Kérylos à Beauliue-sur-Mer, les 13 & 14 octobre 2000*, 155–65. Paris.

Geiger, J. 1985. *Cornelius Nepos and Ancient Political Biography*. Stuttgart.

———. 2008. *The First Hall of Fame: A Study of the Statues in the Forum Augustum*. Leiden.

———. 2014. 'The Project of the *Parallel Lives*: Plutarch's Conception of Biography'. In Beck 2014, 292–303.

Gelzer, M. 1968. *Caesar: Politician and Statesman*. Oxford.

Georgiadou, A. 1988. 'The *Lives of the Caesars* and Plutarch's Other *Lives*', *ICS* 13: 349–56.

———. 2014. 'The *Lives of the Caesars*'. In Beck 2014, 251–66.

Gera, D. 1997. *Warrior Women: The Anonymous Tractatus de mulieribus*. Leiden.

Geue, T. 2019. *Author Unknown: The Power of Anonymity in Ancient Rome*. Cambridge, MA.

———. 2020. 'Keeping/Losing Records, Keeping/Losing Faith: Suetonius and Justin Do the Document'. In König, Langlands, and Uden 2020, 203–22.

Gibson, R. K., ed. 2003. *Ovid: Ars amatoria Book 3*. Cambridge.

———. 2011. 'Elder and Better: The *Naturalis Historia* and the *Letters* of the Younger Pliny'. In Gibson and Morello 2011, 187–205.

———. 2014. 'Suetonius and the *uiri illustres* of Pliny the Younger'. In Power and Gibson 2014, 199–230.

———. 2015. 'Not Dark Yet …: Reading to the End of Pliny's Nine-Book Collection'. In I. Marchesi, ed., *Pliny the Book-Maker: Betting on Posterity in the Epistles*, 187–224. Oxford.

———. 2018. 'Pliny and Plutarch's Practical Ethics: A Newly Rediscovered Dialogue'. In König and Whitton 2018, 402–21.

———. 2020. *Man of High Empire: The Life of Pliny the Younger.* New York.

Gibson, R. K., and Morello, R., eds. 2011. *Pliny the Elder: Themes and Contexts.* Leiden.

———. 2012. *Reading the Letters of Pliny the Younger: An Introduction.* Cambridge.

Gibson, R., and Steel, C. 2010. 'The Indistinct Literary Careers of Cicero and Pliny the Younger'. In P. Hardie and H. Moore, eds., *Classical Literary Careers and Their Reception*, 118–37. Cambridge.

Gibson, R. K., and Whitton, C., eds. 2016. *The Epistles of Pliny.* Oxford.

Ginsberg, L. D. 2020. 'Allusive *prodigia*: Caesar's Comets in Neronian Rome (Tac. *Ann.* 15.47)', *TAPA* 150: 231–49.

Giordano, L. 2000. 'Ottaviano Augusto scrittore: le lettere private', *MAT* 24: 3–52.

Goddard, J. 1994. 'The Tyrant at Table'. In Elsner and Masters 1994, 67–82.

Godolphin, F. R. B. 1935. 'The Source of Plutarch's Thesis in the Lives of Galba and Otho', *AJP* 56: 324–8.

Goodyear, F. R. D. 1970. *Tacitus.* Oxford.

———, ed. 1972. *The Annals of Tacitus Books 1–6*, vol. 1. Cambridge.

———, ed. 1981. *The Annals of Tacitus Books 1–6*, vol. 2. Cambridge.

———. 1982. 'Suetonius'. In Kenney 1982, 661–4.

———. 1984. 'Tiberius and Gaius: Their Influence and Views on Literature', *ANRW* 2.32.1: 603–10.

Gordon, A. E. 1968. 'Notes on the Res Gestae of Augustus', *CSCA* 1: 125–38.

Gore, J., and Kershaw, A. 2008. 'An Unnoticed Acrostic in Apuleius *Metamorphoses* and Cicero *De divinatione* 2.111–12', *CQ* 58: 393–4.

Görler, W. 1999. 'Rowing Strokes: Tentative Considerations on "Shifting" Objects in Virgil and Elsewhere'. In J. N. Adams and R. G. Mayer, eds., *Aspects of the Language of Latin Poetry*, 269–86. Oxford.

Gorringe, C. F. 1993. *A Study of the Death-Narratives in Suetonius' De Vita Caesarum.* Diss., University of Queensland.

Gowers, E. 1993. *The Loaded Table: Representations of Food in Roman Literature.* Oxford.

———. 2003. 'Fragments of Autobiography in Horace *Satires* 1', *ClAnt* 22: 55–92.

———. 2004. 'The Plot Thickens: Hidden Outlines in Terence's Prologues', *Ramus* 33: 150–66.

———. 2009a. 'A Cat May Look at a King: Difference and Indifference in Horace, *Satire* 6'. In G. Urso, ed., *Ordine e sovversione nel mondo greco e romano*, 301–16. Pisa.

———. 2009b. 'Eupolitics: Horace, Sermones I, 4'. In F. Felgentreu, F. Mundt, and N. Rücker, eds., *Per attentam Caesaris aurem: Satire – die unpolitische Gattung?* 85–98. Berlin.

———. ed. 2012. *Horace: Satires Book I.* Cambridge.

Gowing, A. M. 1992. *The Triumviral Narratives of Appian and Cassius Dio*. Ann Arbor, MI.

Gransden, K. W. 2004. *Virgil: The Aeneid*, 2nd ed., ed. S. J. Harrison. Cambridge.

Grant, M. 1954. *Roman Literature*. Cambridge.

———. 1970. *The Ancient Historians*. London.

———. 1979. 'Foreword'. In Graves 1979, 8–11.

Gratwick, A. S. 1982. 'Terentius Afer, Publius'. In Kenney 1982, 814–20.

Grau, D. 2017. 'Nero: The Making of the Historical Narrative'. In Bartsch, Freudenburg, and Littlewood 2017, 261–75.

Graves, R. 1979. *Suetonius: The Twelve Caesars*, 2nd ed., ed. M. Grant. London.

Graziosi, B. 2002. *Inventing Homer: The Early Reception of Epic*. Cambridge.

———. 2006. 'Il rapporto tra autore ed opera nella tradizione biografica greca'. In F. Roscalla, ed., *L'autore e l'opera: attribuzioni, appropriazioni, apocrifi nella Grecia antica*, 155–74. Pisa.

———. 2009. 'Horace, Suetonius, and the *Lives* of the Greek Poets'. In Houghton and Wyke 2009, 140–60.

Grazzini, S., ed. 2011. *Scholia in Iuvenalem recentiora: secundum recensiones φ et χ tomus I (satt. 1–6)*. Pisa.

Griffin, J. 1984. 'Augustus and the Poets: "Caesar qui cogere posset"'. In F. Millar and E. Segal, eds., *Caesar Augustus: Seven Aspects*, 189–218. Oxford.

———. 1986. 'Introduction'. In C. D. Lewis, *Virgil: The Aeneid*, ix–xxiv. Oxford.

Griffin, M. 1984. *Nero: The End of a Dynasty*. London.

———. 1999. 'Pliny and Tacitus', *SCI* 18: 139–58. Repr. in Gibson and Whitton 2016, 355–77; also in Griffin 2018, 248–62.

———. 2018. *Politics and Philosophy at Rome: Collected Papers*, ed. C. Balmaceda. Oxford.

Griggs, C. W. 1990. *Early Egyptian Christianity: From Its Origins to 451 C.E.* Leiden.

Grilli, A. 1976. 'Il "saeculum" di Curzio Rufo', *PP* 31: 215–23.

Grillo, L. 2012. *The Art of Caesar's Bellum Civile: Literature, Ideology, and Community*. Cambridge.

Grishin, A. A. 2008. '*Ludus in undis*: An Acrostic in *Eclogue 9*', *HSCP* 104: 237–40.

Gronovius, J., ed. 1824. *Auli Gellii Noctes Atticae*, vol. 3, 2nd ed. London.

Groot, H. 2008. *Zur Bedeutung der öffentlichen Spiele bei Tacitus, Sueton und Cassius Dio: Überlegungen zur Selbstbeschreibung der römischen Gesellschaft*. Münster.

Grosso, F. 1959. 'L'epigrafe di Ippona e la vita di Svetonio: con i fasti dei pontefici di Vulcano a Ostia', *RAL* 14: 263–96.

Gruen, E. S. 1967. 'Cicero and Licinius Calvus', *HSCP* 71: 215–33.

———. 1996. 'The Expansion of the Empire under Augustus'. In A. K. Bowman, E. Champlin, and A. Lintott, eds., *The Cambridge Ancient History*, vol. 10, 2nd ed., 147–97. Cambridge.

———. 2002. *Diaspora: Jews amidst Greeks and Romans*. Cambridge, MA.

Guastella, G., ed. 1992. *Gaio Svetonio Tranquillo: La vita di Caligola*. Rome.

Gudeman, A. 1889. 'A New Source in Plutarch's Life of Cicero', *TAPA* 20: 139–58.

———. 1902. *The Sources of Plutarch's Life of Cicero*. Philadelphia, PA.

Günther, H.-C., ed. 2013a. *Brill's Companion to Horace*. Leiden.

———. 2013b. 'The First Collection of Odes: *Carmina I–III*'. In Günther 2013a, 211–406.

———. 2013c. 'Horace's Life and Work'. In Günther 2013a, 1–62.

Haaland, G. 2005. 'Josephus and the Philosophers of Rome: Does *Contra Apionem* Mirror Domitian's Crushing of the "Stoic Opposition"?'. In J. Sievers and G. Lembi, eds., *Josephus and Jewish History in Flavian Rome and beyond*, 297–316. Leiden.

Habinek, T. N. 1990. 'Lucius' Rite of Passage', *MD* 25: 49–69.

———. 1998. *The Politics of Latin Literature: Writing, Identity, and Empire in Ancient Rome*. Princeton, NJ.

Hägg, T. 2012. *The Art of Biography in Antiquity*. Cambridge.

Hamilton, J. R. 1988. 'The Date of Quintus Curtius Rufus', *Historia* 37: 445–56.

Hanink, J. 2010. 'The *Life* of the Author in the Letters of "Euripides"', *GRBS* 50: 537–64.

Hardie, A. 1990. 'Juvenal and the Condition of Letters: The Seventh Satire', *PLLS* 6: 145–209.

Hardy, E. G., ed. 1890. *Plutarch's Lives of Galba and Otho*. London.

———. 1906. *Studies in Roman History*. London.

Harrer, G. A. 1918. 'Senatorial Speeches and Letters in Tacitus' Annals', *SPh* 15: 333–43.

Harrill, J. A. 2017. 'Saint Paul and the Christian Communities of Nero's Rome'. In Bartsch, Freudenburg, and Littlewood 2017, 276–89.

Harrison, S., ed. 2007a. *The Cambridge Companion to Horace*. Cambridge.

———. 2007b. *Generic Enrichment in Vergil and Horace*. Oxford.

———. 2014. *Horace*. Cambridge.

Haverfield, F. 1916. 'Tacitus during the Late Roman Period and the Middle Ages', *JRS* 6: 196–201.

Hawkins, S. 2011. 'Catullus' Furius', *CP* 106: 254–60.

Heeren, A. H. L. 1820. *De fontibus et auctoritate Vitarum parallelarum Plutarchi commentationes quatuor*. Göttingen.

Heinze, R. 1993. *Vergil's Epic Technique*. London.

Helm, R. 1929. *Hieronymus' Zusätze in Eusebius' Chronik und ihr Wert für die Literaturgeschichte*. Leipzig.

Hemelrijk, E. A. 1999. *Matrona docta: Educated Women in the Roman Élite from Cornelia to Julia Domna*. London.

Henderson, J. 1989. 'Tacitus/The World in Pieces', *Ramus* 18: 167–210.

———. 2002. *Pliny's Statue: The Letters, Self-Portraiture and Classical Art*. Exeter.

———. 2014. 'Was Suetonius' *Julius* a Caesar?'. In Power and Gibson 2014, 81–110.

Hendrickson, T. 2013. 'Poetry and Biography in the *Athēnaiōn Politeia*: The Case of Solon', *CJ* 109: 1–19.

Hendry, M. 1995–6. 'Two Notes on Suetonius', *MCr* 30–1: 281–3.

Herbert-Brown, G. 1999. 'Jerome's Dates for Gaius Lucilius, *satyrarum scriptor*', *CQ* 49: 535–43.

Herrmann, L. 1955. 'La vie amoureuse d'Horace', *Latomus* 14: 3–30.

Heyworth, S. J. 2016. 'Authenticity and Other Textual Problems in *Heroides* 16'. In Hunter and Oakley 2016, 142–70.

Highet, G. 1973. 'Libertino patre natus', *AJP* 94: 268–81. Repr. in Highet 1983, 165–76.

———. 1983. *The Classical Papers of Gilbert Highet*, ed. R. J. Ball. New York.

Hills, P. D. 2001. 'Ennius, Suetonius and the Genesis of Horace, *Odes* 4', *CQ* 51: 613–16.

Hinds, S. 1998. *Allusion and Intertext: Dynamics of Appropriation in Roman Poetry.* Cambridge.

Hoffer, S. E., 1999. *The Anxieties of Pliny the Younger.* Atlanta, GA.

Hofstee, C., ed. 1898. *C. Suetonii Tranquilli Vitae Galbae, Othonis, Vitelli.* Groningen.

Hohl, E., ed. 1927. *Scriptores Historiae Augustae*, vol. 1. Leipzig.

Holford-Strevens, L. 2003. *Aulus Gellius: An Antonine Scholar and His Achievement*, 2nd ed. Oxford.

Holland, P. 1899. *Suetonius: History of Twelve Caesars*, 2 vols. London.

Hollis, A. S., ed. 2007. *Fragments of Roman Poetry c.60 BC–AD 20.* Oxford.

Horsfall, N. 1994. 'Problemi della biografia letteraria: Terenzio; Orazio; Virgilio', *AAPel* 68: 41–53.

———. 1995. 'Virgil: His Life and Times'. In N. Horsfall, ed., *A Companion to the Study of Virgil*, 1–25. Leiden.

———. 1998. 'The First Person Singular in Horace's *Carmina*'. In P. E. Knox and C. Foss, eds., *Style and Tradition: Studies in Honour of Wendell Clausen*, 40–54. Stuttgart.

———. 2000. *Virgil, Aeneid 7: A Commentary.* Leiden.

———. 2006–7. 'Fraud as Scholarship: The Helen Episode and the Appendix Vergiliana', *ICS* 31–2: 1–27. Repr. in Horsfall 2020, 426–45.

———. 2008. *Virgil, Aeneid 2: A Commentary.* Leiden.

———. 2010. 'Pictures from an Execution'. In J. Dijkstra, J. Kroesen, and Y. Kuiper, eds., *Myths, Martyrs, and Modernity: Studies in the History of Religions in Honour of Jan N. Bremmer*, 237–47. Leiden.

———. 2016. *The Epic Distilled: Studies in the Composition of the Aeneid.* Oxford.

———. 2020. *Fifty Years at the Sibyl's Heels: Selected Papers on Virgil and Rome.* Oxford.

Horváth, A. 1996. 'Griechische Zitate im ersten Jahrhundert der Kaiserzeit im Spiegel der Kaiserbiographien Suetons', *ACD* 32: 71–83.

Houghton, L. B. T., and Wyke, M., eds. 2009. *Perceptions of Horace: A Roman Poet and His Readers.* Cambridge.

Housman, A. E. 1913. 'Manilius, Augustus, Tiberius, Capricornus, and Libra', *CQ* 7: 109–14. Repr. in Housman 1972, 2.867–72.

———. 1972. *The Classical Papers of A. E. Housman*, 3 vols, eds. J. Diggle and F. R. D. Goodyear. Cambridge.

Houston, G. W. 2014. *Inside Roman Libraries: Book Collections and Their Management in Antiquity.* Chapel Hill, NC.

Howard, A. A., and Jackson, C. N. 1922. *Index verborum C. Suetoni Tranquilli stilique eius proprietatum nonnullarum.* Cambridge, MA.

Howley, J. A. 2014. '"Heus tu, rhetorisce": Gellius, Cicero, Plutarch, and Roman Study Abroad'. In J. M. Madsen and R. Rees, eds., *Roman Rule in Greek and Latin Writing: Double Vision*, 163–92. Leiden.

———. 2018. *Aulus Gellius and Roman Reading Culture: Text, Presence, and Imperial Knowledge in the Noctes Atticae.* Cambridge.

Hulls, J.-M. 2014. 'The Mirror in the Text: Privacy, Performance, and the Power of Suetonius' *Domitian*'. In Power and Gibson 2014, 178–96.

———. 2019. 'Building Meaning: Constructions of Imperial Power in Domitianic Architecture, Visual Culture, and Literary Sources', *ICS* 44: 268–96.

Hunink, V. 2006. 'Some Cases of Genre Confusion in Apuleius'. In R. R. Nauta, ed., *Desultoria scientia: Genre in Apuleius' Metamorphoses and Related Texts*, 33–42. Leuven.

Hunt, J. M., Smith, R. A., and Stok, F. 2017. *Classics from Papyrus to the Internet: An Introduction to Transmission and Reception*. Austin, TX.

Hunter, I. Q. 2020. '*Caligula*, History, and the Erotic Imagination'. In D. Cartmell and A. D. Polasek, eds., *A Companion to the Biopic*, 159–89. Hoboken, NJ.

Hunter, R., and Oakley, S. P., eds. 2016. *Latin Literature and Its Transmission*. Cambridge.

Hurley, D. W. 1989. 'Gaius Caligula in the Germanicus Tradition', *AJP* 110: 316–38.

———. 1993. *An Historical and Historiographical Commentary on Suetonius' Life of C. Caligula*. Atlanta, GA.

———, ed. 2001. *Suetonius: Diuus Claudius*. Cambridge.

———. 2003. 'The Politics of Agrippina the Younger's Birthplace', *AJAH* 2.1: 95–117.

———. 2011. *Suetonius: The Caesars*. Indianapolis, IN.

———. 2013. 'Biographies of Nero'. In Buckley and Dinter 2013, 29–44.

———. 2014a. 'Rhetorics of Assassination: Ironic Reversal and the Emperor Gaius'. In Power and Gibson 2014, 146–58.

———. 2014b. 'Suetonius' Rubric Sandwich'. In Power and Gibson 2014, 21–37.

Hutton, M. et al. 1914–37. *Tacitus*, 5 vols. London.

Iddeng, J. W. 2000. 'Juvenal, Satire and the Persona Theory: Some Critical Remarks', *SO* 75: 107–29.

———. 2006. '*Publica aut peri!* The Releasing and Distribution of Roman Books', *SO* 81: 58–84.

Ihm, M., ed. 1907. *C. Suetoni Tranquilli opera*, vol. 1. Leipzig.

———, ed. 1908. *C. Suetoni Tranquilli opera*, vol. 1. Leipzig.

Ingleheart, J. 2009. 'Writing to the Emperor: Horace's Presence in Ovid's *Tristia* 2'. In Houghton and Wyke 2009, 123–39.

Innes, M. 1997. 'The Classical Tradition in the Carolingian Renaissance: Ninth-Century Encounters with Suetonius', *IJCT* 3: 265–82.

Irwin, E. 1998. 'Biography, Fiction, and the Archilochean *ainos*', *JHS* 118: 117–83.

———. 2005. *Solon and Early Greek Poetry: The Politics of Exhortation*. Cambridge.

———. 2006. 'The Biographies of Poets: The Case of Solon'. In McGing and Mossman 2006, 13–30.

Isaac, B. 2004. *The Invention of Racism in Classical Antiquity*. Princeton, NJ.

Jahn, O., ed. 1851. *D. Iunii Iuvenalis Saturarum libri V*, vol. 1. Berlin.

Janne, H. 1934. 'Impulsore Chresto', *AIPhO* 2: 531–53.

Janson, T. 1964. *Latin Prose Prefaces: Studies in Literary Conventions*. Stockholm.

Jenkyns, R. 1998. *Virgil's Experience: Nature and History; Times, Names, and Places*. Oxford.

Johnson, W. A., and Parker, H. N., eds. 2009. *Ancient Literacies: The Culture of Reading in Greece and Rome*. Oxford.

Johnson, W. R. 2010. 'The Epistles'. In Davis 2010, 319–33.

Jones, B. W. 1992. *The Emperor Domitian*. London.

———, ed. 1996. *Suetonius: Domitian*. London.

————. 2002. 'Domitian, Nerva and the Bias of Suetonius'. In P. Defosse, ed., *Hommages à Carl Deroux*, vol. 2, 236–9. Brussels.

Jones, B. W., and Milns, R. D. 2002. *Suetonius: The Flavian Emperors; A Historical Commentary*. London.

Jones, C. P. 1966. 'Towards a Chronology of Plutarch's Works', *JRS* 56: 61–74.

————. 1971. *Plutarch and Rome*. Oxford.

————. 1986. 'Suetonius in the Probus of Giorgio Valla', *HSCP* 90: 245–51.

————. 2017. 'The Historicity of the Neronian Persecution: A Response to Brent Shaw', *NTS* 63: 146–52.

Jones, J. W. 1965. 'Trojan Legend: Who Is Sinon?', *CJ* 61: 122–8.

Joseph, T. A. 2012. *Tacitus the Epic Successor: Virgil, Lucan, and the Narrative of Civil War in the Histories*. Leiden.

Kapparis, K. K. 2011. 'The Terminology of Prostitution in the Ancient Greek World'. In A. Glazebrook and M. M. Henry, eds., *Greek Prostitutes in the Ancient Mediterranean, 800 BCE–200 CE*, 222–55. Madison, WI.

Kaster, R. A. 1992. *Studies on the Text of Suetonius De grammaticis et rhetoribus*. Atlanta, GA.

————, ed. 1995. *C. Suetonius Tranquillus: De grammaticis et rhetoribus*. Oxford.

————. 2010. 'Scholarship'. In A. Barchiesi and W. Scheidel, eds., *The Oxford Handbook of Roman Studies*, 492–504. Oxford.

————. 2014. 'The Transmission of Suetonius's *Caesars* in the Middle Ages', *TAPA* 144: 133–86.

————, ed. 2016a. *C. Suetoni Tranquilli De uita Caesarum libri VIII et De grammaticis et rhetoribus liber*. Oxford.

————. 2016b. 'Making Sense of Suetonius in the Twelfth Century'. In A. Grafton and G. W. Most, eds., *Canonical Texts and Scholarly Practices: A Global Comparative Approach*, 110–35. Cambridge.

————. 2016c. *Studies on the Text of Suetonius' De uita Caesarum*. Oxford.

Katz, J. T. 2007. 'An Acrostic Ant Road in Aeneid 4', *MD* 59: 77–86.

————. 2008. 'Vergil Translates Aratus: Phaenomena 1–2 and Georgics 1.1–2', *MD* 60: 105–23.

Kavanagh, B. 2010. 'The Identity and Fate of Caligula's Assassin, Aquila', *Latomus* 69: 1007–17.

Keitel, E. 1992. '*Foedum spectaculum* and Related Motifs in Tacitus *Histories* II-III', *RhM* 135: 342–51.

————. 1995. 'Plutarch's Tragedy Tyrants: Galba and Otho', *PLLS* 8: 275–88.

————. 2007. 'Feats Your Eyes on This: Vitellius as a Stock Tyrant (Tac. *Hist.* 3.36–69)'. In Marincola, 2007, 441–6.

————. 2010. 'The Art of Losing: Tacitus and the Disaster Narrative'. In Kraus, Marincola, and Pelling 2010, 331–52.

Kelly, G. 2008. *Ammianus Marcellinus: The Allusive Historian*. Cambridge.

Kemezis, A. M. 2016. '*Inglorius labor*? The Rhetoric of Glory and Utility in Plutarch's *Precepts* and Tacitus' *Agricola*', *CW* 110: 87–117.

Kendall, P. M. 1965. *The Art of Biography*. London.

Kenney, E. J., ed. 1982. *The Cambridge History of Classical Literature*, vol. 2. Cambridge.

Kessissoglu, A. I. 1988. 'Mimus vitae', *Mnemosyne* 41: 385–8.

Kilpatrick, R. S. 1990. *The Poetry of Criticism: Horace, Epistles II and Ars Poetica*. Edmonton.

Kindstrand, J. F., ed. 1976. *Bion of Borysthenes: A Collection of the Fragments with Introduction and Commentary.* Uppsala.

Kivilo, M. 2010. *Early Greek Poets' Lives: The Shaping of the Tradition.* Leiden.

Klingner, F., ed. 1959. *Q. Horati Flacci opera.* Leipzig.

König, A., Langlands, R., and Uden, J., eds. 2020. *Literature and Culture in the Roman Empire, 96–235: Cross-Cultural Interactions.* Cambridge.

König, A., and Whitton, C., eds. 2018. *Roman Literature under Nerva, Trajan and Hadrian: Literary Interactions, AD 96–138.* Cambridge.

König, J., and Woolf, G., eds. 2013. *Encyclopaedism from Antiquity to the Renaissance.* Cambridge.

Konstan, D. 2009. 'Reading Politics in Suetonius'. In W. J. Dominik, J. Garthwaite, and P. A. Roche, eds., *Writing Politics in Imperial Rome*, 447–62. Leiden.

Konstan, D., and Walsh, R. 2016. 'Civic and Subversive Biography in Antiquity'. In De Temmerman and Demoen 2016, 26–43.

Korzeniewski, D. 1959. *Die Zeit des Quintus Curtius Rufus.* Diss., University of Cologne.

Köster, I. K. 2021. 'Flamingos and Perverted Sacrifices in Suetonius' *Life of Caligula*', *Mnemosyne* 74: 299–317.

Kraggerud, E. 2017. *Vergiliana: Critical Studies on the Texts of Publius Vergilius Maro.* Abingdon.

Kraus, C. S., ed. 1994. *Livy: Ab urbe condita Book VI.* Cambridge.

Kraus, C. S., Marincola, J., and C. Pelling, eds. 2010. *Ancient Historiography and Its Contexts: Studies in Honour of A. J. Woodman.* Oxford.

Krause, A. 1831. *De C. Suetonii Tranquilli fontibus et auctoritate.* Berlin.

Krebs, C. B. 2018. 'A Style of Choice'. In L. Grillo and C. B. Krebs, eds., *The Cambridge Companion to the Writings of Julius Caesar*, 110–30. Cambridge.

Krostenko, B. A. 2001. *Cicero, Catullus, and the Language of Social Performance.* Chicago.

Kyle, D. G. 1998. *Spectacles of Death in Ancient Rome.* London.

Lachenaud, G., and Longrée, D., eds. 2003. *Grecs et Romains aux prises avec l'histoire: représentations, récits et idéologie*, vol. 1. Rennes.

Lana, I. 1998. 'Svetonio'. In I. Lana and E. V. Maltese, eds., *Storia della civiltà letteraria greca e latina*, vol. 2, 1030–5. Turin.

Landrobe, H. S. 2008. 'Suetoni "Vita Horati": retrato metatextual frustrante'. In Dorado et al. 2008, 431–6.

Lange, C. H., and Madsen, J. M., eds. 2016. *Cassius Dio: Greek Intellectual and Roman Politician.* Leiden.

Langlands, R. 2006. *Sexual Morality in Ancient Rome.* Cambridge.

———. 2018a. *Exemplary Ethics in Ancient Rome.* Cambridge.

———. 2018b. 'Extratextuality: Literary Interactions with Oral Culture and Exemplary Ethics'. In König and Whitton 2018, 330–46.

La Penna, A. 1996. 'Il viaggio di Terenzio in Asia: un errore della tradizione manoscritta?', *RFIC* 124: 282–4.

Lavan, M. 2020. 'Beyond Romans and Others: Identities in the Long Second Century'. In König, Langlands, and Uden 2020, 37–57.

Lavelle, B. M. 2005. *Fame, Money, and Power: The Rise of Peisistratos and 'Democratic' Tyranny at Athens.* Ann Arbor, MI.

Leach, E. W. 2012. 'Pliny's Diffident Suetonius: A Profile in Five *epistulae*', *NECJ* 39: 87–98.

Leeman, A. D. 1963. *Orationis ratio: The Stylistic Theories and Practice of the Roman Orators, Historians, and Philosophers*, 2 vols. Amsterdam.

Lee-Stecum, P. 2013. 'Tibullus in First Place'. In T. S. Thorsen, ed., *The Cambridge Companion to Latin Love Elegy*, 68–82. Cambridge.

Lefebvre, L. 2010. 'L'optimus princeps et les lettres'. In Y. Perrin, ed., *Néronia VIII: bibliothèques, livres et culture écrite dans l'empire romain de César à Hadrien*, 290–300. Brussels.

Lefèvre, E. 2009. *Vom Römertum zum Ästhetizismus: Studien zu den Briefen des jüngeren Plinius*. Berlin.

Lefkowitz, M. R. 1976. 'Fictions in Literary Biography: The New Poem and the Archilochus Legend', *Arethusa* 9: 181–9.

———. 1978. 'The Poet as Hero: Fifth-Century Autobiography and Subsequent Biographical Fiction', *CQ* 28: 459–69.

———. 1984. 'Satyrus the Historian'. In *Atti del XVII congresso internazionale di papirologia (Napoli, 19–26 maggio 1983)*, 3 vols, 339–43. Naples.

———. 1987. 'Was Euripides an Atheist?', *SIFC* 5: 149–66.

———. 2007. 'Visits to Egypt in the Biographical Tradition'. In Erler and Schorn 2007, 101–13.

———. 2009. 'Biographical Mythology'. In U. Dill and C. Walde, eds., *Antike Mythen: Medien, Transformationen und Konstruktionen*, 516–31. Berlin.

———. 2012. *Lives of the Greek Poets*, 2nd ed. Baltimore, MD.

Lehmann, H. 1858. *Claudius und Nero und ihre Zeit*, vol. 1. Gotha.

Leigh, M. 2017. 'Nero the Performer'. In Bartsch, Freudenburg, and Littlewood 2017, 21–33.

Leitão, D. D. 1998. 'Senecan Catoptrics and the Passion of Hostius Quadra (Sen. Nat. 1)', *MD* 41: 127–60.

Lendon, J. E. 1997. *Empire of Honour: The Art of Government in the Roman World*. Oxford.

Leo, F. 1901. *Die griechisch-römische Biographie nach ihrer litterarischen Form*. Leipzig.

Lessing, G. E. 1754. *Schrifften*, vol. 3. Berlin.

———. 1890. *Sämtliche Schriften*, vol. 5, 3rd ed., ed. K. Lachmann. Stuttgart.

Levene, D. S. 1997. 'Pity, Fear and the Historical Audience: Tacitus on the Fall of Vitellius'. In S. M. Braund and C. Gill, eds., *The Passions in Roman Literature and Thought*, 128–49. Cambridge. Repr. in Ash 2012, 209–33.

———. 2004. 'Tacitus' *Dialogus* as Literary History', *TAPA* 134: 157–200.

———. 2010. *Livy on the Hannibalic War*. Oxford.

Levi, M. A. 1937. 'Dopo Azio: appunti sulle fonti augustee; Svetonio', *RFIC* 16: 1–24. Repr. in Levi 1951, xxiv–lxiv.

———, ed. 1951. *C. Suetoni Tranquilli Divus Augustus*. Florence.

Levick, B. 1989. 'Claudius Speaks: Two Imperial Contretemps', *Historia* 38: 112–16.

———. 1990. *Claudius*. New Haven, CT.

———. 2002. 'Women, Power, and Philosophy at Rome and beyond'. In G. Clarke and T. Rajak, eds., *Philosophy and Power in the Graeco-Roman World: Essays in Honour of Miriam Griffin*, 134–55. Oxford.

———. 2012. 'Tacitus in the Twenty-first Century: The Struggle for Truth in *Annals* 1–6'. In Pagán 2012a, 260–81.

———. 2013. 'Cluvius Rufus'. In Cornell 2013b, 549–60.

Lewis, R. G. 1991. 'Suetonius' "Caesares" and Their Literary Antecedents', *ANRW* 2.33.5: 3623–74.

———. 1993. 'Imperial Autobiography, Augustus to Hadrian', *ANRW* 2.34.1: 629–706.

L'Hoir, F. S. 2006. *Tragedy, Rhetoric, and the Historiography of Tacitus' Annales.* Ann Arbor, MI.

Lindsay, H., ed. 1993. *Suetonius: Caligula.* London.

———. 1994. 'Suetonius as *ab epistulis* to Hadrian and the Early History of the Imperial Correspondence', *Historia* 43: 454–68.

———. 1995a. 'Suetonius on the Character of Horace', *AUMLA* 83: 69–82.

———. 1995b. *Suetonius: Tiberius.* London.

———. 2009. 'Suetonius *De Poetis*: The Project and the Life of Vergil', *Classicum* 35: 2–7.

Littman, R. J. 1976. 'The Meaning of Polyphagus', *AJP* 97: 369.

Lloyd-Jones, H., ed. 1994. *Sophocles: Ajax, Electra, Oedipus Tyrannus.* Cambridge, MA.

Longrée, D. 2003. 'Tacite et Suétone: linguistique comparative et genres littéraires'. In Lachenaud and Longrée 2003, 315–26.

Loomis, J. W. 1969. 'M. Furius Bibaculus and Catullus', *CW* 63: 112–14.

Louis, N. 2010. *Commentaire historique et traduction du Diuus Augustus de Suétone.* Brussels.

Lounsbury, R. C. 1986–7. Review of Baldwin 1983 and Wallace-Hadrill 1983, *CJ* 82: 159–62.

———. 1987. *The Arts of Suetonius: An Introduction.* New York.

———. 1991. '*Inter quos Sporus erat*: The Making of Suetonius' "Nero"', *ANRW* 2.33.5: 3748–79.

———. 2006. Review of Hurley 2001, *CW* 100: 79–80.

Lowrie, M. 2009. *Writing, Performance, and Authority in Augustan Rome.* Oxford.

———. 2010a. 'Horace'. In M. Gagarin and E. Fantham, eds., *The Oxford Encyclopedia of Ancient Greece and Rome*, vol. 4, 29–36. Oxford.

———. 2010b. 'Horace: *Odes* 4'. In Davis 2010, 210–30.

Luce, T. J., and Woodman, A. J., eds. 1993. *Tacitus and the Tacitean Tradition.* Princeton, NJ.

Luck, G. 1964. 'Über Suetons "Divus Titus"', *RhM* 107: 63–75.

Ludolph, M. 1997. *Epistolographie und Selbstdarstellung: Untersuchungen zu den 'Paradebriefen' Plinius des Jüngeren.* Tübingen.

Lyne, R. O. A. M. 1980. *The Latin Love Poets: From Catullus to Horace.* Oxford.

McDaniel, K. 2013. *Experiencing Irony in the First Gospel: Suspense, Surprise, and Curiosity.* London.

Macé, A. 1900. *Essai sur Suétone.* Paris.

MacEwen, R. K. 2015. *Matthean Posteriority: An Exploration of Matthew's Use of Mark and Luke as a Solution to the Synoptic Problem.* London.

Mackail, J. W. 1895. *Latin Literature.* London.

MacLean, R. 2018. *Freed Slaves and Roman Imperial Culture: Social Integration and the Transformation of Values.* Cambridge.

MacRae, D. E. 2015. '*Invitus invitam*: A Window Allusion in Suetonius' *Titus*', *CQ* 65: 415–18.

Magie, D., ed. 1921. *The Scriptores Historiae Augustae*, vol. 1. London.

Malitz, J. 2005. *Nero*. Oxford.

Malloch, S. J. V. 2004. 'The End of the Rhine Mutiny in Tacitus, Suetonius, and Dio', *CQ* 54: 198–210.

———, ed. 2013. *The Annals of Tacitus Book 11*. Cambridge.

Manolaraki, E., and Augoustakis, A. 2012. 'Silius Italicus and Tacitus on the Tragic Hero: The Case of Germanicus'. In Pagán 2012a, 386–402.

Marchesi, I. 2008. *The Art of Pliny's Letters: A Poetics of Allusion in the Private Correspondence*. Cambridge.

Marcovich, M. 1971. 'Voces animantium and Suetonius', *ZAnt* 21: 399–416.

Marec, E. 1954. 'Le forum d'Hippone', *Libyca* 2: 363–416.

Marec, E., and Pflaum, H. G. 1952. 'Nouvelle inscription sur la carrière de Suétone, l'historien', *CRAI*: 76–85.

Marincola, J. 2005. 'Concluding Narratives: Looking to the End in Classical Historiography', *PLLS* 12: 285–320.

———, ed. 2007. *A Companion to Greek and Roman Historiography*, 2 vols. Malden, MA.

Marrone, G. C. 2002. 'La cena dei dodici dèi', *RCCM* 44: 25–33.

Marshall, R. M. A. 2019. 'Suetonius the Bibliographer'. In S. A. Adams, ed., *Scholastic Culture in the Hellenistic and Roman Eras: Greek, Latin, and Jewish*, 119–46. Berlin.

Martin, R. 2009. 'Les grands crimes de Néron vus par Tacite et Suétone'. In Poignault 2009, 73–84.

Martin, R. H. 1981. *Tacitus*. Berkeley, CA.

Martin, R. H., and Woodman, A. J., eds. 1989. *Tacitus: Annals Book IV*. Cambridge.

Martina, M. 1984. 'Le vite antiche di Lucano e Persio', *CCC* 5: 155–89. Repr. in Martina 2004, 206–30.

———. 2004. *Scritti di filologia classica e storia antica*, eds. G. Bandelli, M. Fernandelli, L. Galasso, and L. Toneatto. Trieste.

Matthews, J. 2010. *Roman Perspectives: Studies in the Social, Political and Cultural History of the First to Fifth Centuries*. Swansea.

May, G. 1938. 'La politique religieuse de l'empereur Claude', *RD* 17: 1–46.

Mayer, R., ed. 1994. *Horace: Epistles Book I*. Cambridge.

———, ed. 2001. *Tacitus: Dialogus de oratoribus*. Cambridge.

———. 2003a. 'A Lost Allusion Recovered: Tacitus, *Histories* 3.37.1 and Homer, *Iliad* 19.301–2', *CQ* 53: 313–15.

———. 2003b. 'Pliny and *gloria dicendi*', *Arethusa* 36: 227–34.

McCarter, S. 2015. *Horace between Freedom and Slavery: The First Book of Epistles*. Madison, WI.

McDermott, W. C. 1969. Review of Dorey 1967, *CJ* 64: 188–9.

———. 1971a. 'Pliny the Younger and Inscriptions', *CW* 65: 84–94.

———. 1971b. 'Suetonius and Cicero', *CW* 64: 213–14.

———. 1972a. 'M. Cicero and M. Tiro', *Historia* 21: 259–86.

———. 1972b. 'Suetonius and the Second Proscription', *Gymnasium* 79: 495–9.

———. 1980. 'Suetonius and Cicero', *Gymnasium* 87: 485–95.

McGing, B., and Mossman, J., eds. 2006. *The Limits of Ancient Biography*. Swansea.

McKeown, J. C. 1987–98. *Ovid: Amores*, 3 vols. Liverpool and Leeds.

McNeill, R. L. B. 2001. *Horace: Image, Identity, and Audience*. Baltimore, MD.

McNelis, C. 2007. 'Grammarians and Rhetoricians'. In W. Dominik and J. Hall, eds., *A Companion to Roman Rhetoric*. Malden, MA.

McQueen, E. I. 1967. 'Quintus Curtius Rufus'. In Dorey 1967, 17–43.

Mehl, A. 2011. *Roman Historiography: An Introduction to Its Basic Aspects and Development*. Oxford.

Meister, J. 2014. 'Reports about the "Sex Life" of Early Roman Emperors: A Case of Character Assassination?'. In E. Shiraev and M. Icks, eds., *Character Assassination throughout the Ages*, 59–81. New York.

Mellor, R. 1993. *Tacitus*. London.

———. 1999. *The Roman Historians*. London.

———. 2011. *Tacitus' Annals*. New York.

Merrill, E. T. 1919. 'The Expulsion of the Jews from Rome under Tiberius', *CP* 14: 365–72.

Méthy, N. 2009. 'Suétone vu par un contemporain: les débuts de l'historien dans la correspondance de Pline le Jeune', *Gerión* 27: 219–29.

Meulder, M. 2002. 'Histoire et mythe dans la *Vita Neronis* de Suétone', *Latomus* 61: 362–87.

Millar, F. 1964. *A Study of Cassius Dio*. Oxford.

———. 1977. *The Emperor in the Roman World (31 BC–AD 337)*. London.

———. 2004. *Rome, the Greek World, and the East*, vol. 2, ed. H. M. Cotton and G. M. Rogers. Chapel Hill, NC.

Mills, D. H. 1978. 'Vergil's Tragic Vision: The Death of Priam', *CW* 72: 159–66.

Milns, R. D. 1966. 'The Date of Curtius Rufus and the *Historiae Alexandri*', *Latomus* 25: 490–507.

———. 2010. 'Suetonius and Vespasian's Humour', *AClass* 53: 117–23.

Mitchell, E. 2010. 'Timer for an Emperor: Old Age and the Future of the Empire in Horace *Odes* 4', *MD* 64: 43–76.

Mitchell, J. 2015. 'Literary Quotation as Literary Performance in Suetonius', *CJ* 110: 333–55.

Moles, J. 1983a. 'Some "Last Words" of M. Iunius Brutus', *Latomus* 42: 763–79.

———. 1983b. 'Virgil, Pompey, and the *Histories* of Asinius Pollio', *CW* 76: 287–8.

———. 1997. 'Plutarch, Brutus and Brutus' Greek and Latin Letters'. In Mossman 1997, 141–68.

———. 2007. 'Philosophy and Ethics'. In Harrison 2007a, 165–80.

———. 2017. *A Commentary on Plutarch's Brutus*, ed. C. Pelling. Newcastle upon Tyne.

Momigliano, A. 1931. 'Vitellio', *SIFC* 9: 117–87. Repr. in Momigliano 1992, 129–81.

———. 1934. *Claudius: The Emperor and His Achievement*. Oxford.

———. 1968–9. 'Ammiano Marcellino e la *Historia Augusta* (a proposito del libro di Ronald Syme)', *AAT* 103: 423–36. Repr. in Momigliano 1975, 93–103.

———. 1975. *Quinto contributo alla storia degli studi classici e del mondo antico*, 2 vols. Rome.

———. 1984. Review of R. Syme, *Historia Augusta Papers* (Oxford, 1983) and *RP* 3, *TLS* (12 Oct.), 1147–8. Repr. in Momigliano 1987, 392–8.

———. 1987. *Ottavo contributo alla storia degli studi classici e del mondo antico*. Rome.

———. 1992. *Nono contributo alla storia degli studi classici e del mondo antico*, ed. R. Di Donato. Rome.

———. 1993. *The Development of Greek Biography*, 2nd ed. Cambridge, MA.

Mommsen, T. 1869. 'Zur Lebensgeschichte des jüngeren Plinius', *Hermes* 3: 31–136. Repr. in Mommsen 1906, 366–468.

———. 1886. *Provinces of the Roman Empire: From Caesar to Diocletian*, vol. 2. London.

———. 1906. *Gesammelte Schriften*, vol. 4. Berlin.

Montesquieu, C. de S. 1777. *Complete Works*, vol. 4. London.

———. 1879. *Oeuvres complètes de Montesquieu*, vol. 7, ed. É. Laboulaye. Paris.

Mooney, G. W., ed. 1930. *C. Suetoni Tranquilli De Vita Caesarum libri VII–VIII: Galba, Otho, Vitellius, Divus Vespasianus, Divus Titus, Domitianus.* Dublin.

Morford, M. 1985. 'Nero's Patronage and Participation in Literature and the Arts', *ANRW* 2.32.3: 2003–31.

Morgan, G. 1993a. '*Nullam, Vare* ... Chance or Choice in *Odes* 1.18?', *Philologus* 137: 142–5.

———. 1993b. 'Tacitus, *Histories* 1.58.2', *Hermes* 121: 371–4.

———. 1993c. 'The Unity of Tacitus, *Histories* 1, 12–20', *Athenaeum* 81: 567–86.

———. 1994. 'A Lugubrious Prospect: Tacitus, *Histories* 1.40', *CQ* 44: 236–44.

———. 1998. '*Indulgentia* in Tacitus'. In *SLLRH* 9.411–24.

———. 2004. 'Eight Notes on Suetonius' Galba', *Philologus* 148: 305–24.

———. 2005. 'Martius Macer's Raid and Its Consequences: Tacitus, *Histories* 2.23', *CQ* 55: 572–81.

Morgan, L. 1997a. '*Achilleae comae*: Hair and Heroism according to Domitian', *CQ* 47: 209–14.

———. 1997b. '"Levi quidem de re ...": Julius Caesar as Tyrant and Pedant', *JRS* 87: 23–40.

———. 1999. *Patterns of Redemption in Virgil's Georgics*. Cambridge.

———. 2000. 'The Autopsy of C. Asinius Pollio', *JRS* 90: 51–69.

Morrison, A. D. 2020. *Apollonius Rhodius, Herodotus and Historiography.* Cambridge.

Mossman, J., ed. 1997. *Plutarch and His Intellectual World*. London.

Mottershead, J., ed. 1986. *Suetonius: Claudius*. Bristol.

Mouchová, B. 1968. *Studie zu Kaiserbiographien Suetons*. Prague.

———. 1986–7. 'Einige Bemerkungen zum Wortschatz Suetons', *ZJKF* 28–9: 48–52.

———. 1991. 'Die Ausdrücke populus, plebs und vulgus bei Sueton', *GLP* 13: 87–101.

Mouritsen, H. 2011. *The Freedman in the Roman World*. Cambridge.

Mratschek, S. 2013. 'Nero the Imperial Misfit: Philhellenism in a Rich Man's World'. In Buckley and Dinter 2013, 45–62.

Munro, H. A. J. 1869. 'Catullus' 29th poem', *JPh* 2: 1–34.

Murgatroyd, P. 1975. '*Militia amoris* and the Roman Elegists', *Latomus* 34: 59–79.

Murgia, C. E. 2002. 'Critica varia'. In J. F. Miller, C. Damon, and K. S. Myers, eds., *Vertis in usum: Studies in Honor of Edward Courtney*, 67–75. Munich.

Murison, C. L., ed. 1992. *Suetonius: Galba, Otho, Vitellius*. London.

———. 1993. *Galba, Otho and Vitellius: Careers and Controversies*. Hildesheim.

———. 1999. *Rebellion and Reconstruction: Galba to Domitian; An Historical Commentary on Cassius Dio's Roman History Books 64–67 (A.D. 68–69).* Atlanta, GA.

Mynors, R. A. B., ed. 1990. *Virgil: Georgics*. Oxford.

Nagy, B. 2003. '*Imbellis ac firmus parum*: The Poet as Military Tribune', *NECJ* 30: 117–27.

Naumann, H. 1979. 'Lücken und Einfügungen in den Dichter-Viten Suetons', *WS* 13: 151–65.

Nauta, R. R. 2006. 'The *recusatio* in Flavian Poetry'. In Nauta, van Dam, and Smolenaars 2006, 21–40.

Nauta, R. R., van Dam, H.-J. and Smolenaars, J. J. L., eds. 2006. *Flavian Poetry*. Leiden.

Nelson, N. 1942. 'The Value of Epigraphic Evidence in the Interpretation of Latin Historical Literature', *CJ* 37: 281–90.

Newbold, R. F. 1984. 'Suetonius' Boundaries', *Latomus* 43: 118–32.

Newman, J. K. 2011. *Horace as Outsider*. Hildesheim.

Nichols, M. F. 2017. *Author and Audience in Vitruvius' De architectura*. Cambridge.

Niebuhr, B. G. 1848. *Vorträge über römische Geschichte*. Berlin.

Nikolaidis, A. G., ed. 2008. *The Unity of Plutarch's Work: 'Moralia' Themes in the 'Lives', Features of the 'Lives' in the 'Moralia'*. Berlin.

Nisbet, R. G. M. 2007. 'Horace: Life and Chronology'. In Harrison 2007a, 7–21.

Nisbet, R. G. M., and Hubbard, M. 1970. *A Commentary on Horace: Odes, Book I*. Oxford.

Nisbet, R. G. M., and Rudd, N. 2004. *A Commentary on Horace: Odes, Book III*. Oxford.

Nogara, B., ed. 1912. *Codices Vaticani Latini*, vol. 3.1: *Codices 1461–2059*. Rome.

Noguerol, É. L. 2003. *Pline le Jeune: la 'persona', ses masques ou l'envers du décor*. Lille.

Norden, E. 1898. *Die antike Kunstprosa vom VI. Jahrhundert vor Christi bis in die Zeit der Renaissance*, 2 vols. Leipzig.

Nutting, H. C. 1928. 'Miscella', *CP* 23: 287–9.

———. 1933. 'Suetonius, Galba 20.2', *CW* 27: 45.

Oakley, S. P. 1991. Review of Martin and Woodman 1989. In *CR* 41: 341–5.

———. 1997–2005. *A Commentary on Livy Books VI–X*, 4 vols. Oxford.

———. 2009a. '*Res olim dissociabiles*: Emperors, Senators and Liberty'. In Woodman 2009a, 184–194.

———. 2009b. 'Style and Language'. In Woodman 2009a, 195–211.

———. 2020. 'Point and Periodicity: The Style of Velleius Paterculus and Other Latin Historians Writing in the Early Principate'. In Scappaticcio 2020, 199–234.

O'Brien, P. 2006. 'Ammianus epicus: Virgilian Allusion in the *Res Gestae*', *Phoenix* 60: 274–303.

———. 2007. 'An Unnoticed Reminiscence of the *Aeneid* 10.517–20 at Ammianus Marcellinus 22.12.6', *Mnemosyne* 60: 662–8.

Ogilvie, R. M. 1980. *Roman Literature and Society*. Harmondsworth.

Ogilvie, R. M., and Richmond, I., eds. 1967. *Cornelii Taciti De vita Agricolae*. Oxford.

O'Gorman, E. 2011. 'Imperial History and Biography at Rome'. In A. Feldherr and G. Hardy, eds., *The Oxford History of Historical Writing*, vol. 1, 291–315. Oxford.

O'Hara, J. J. 2010. 'The Unfinished *Aeneid*?'. In Farrell and Putnam 2010, 96–106.

Oliensis, E. 1998. *Horace and the Rhetoric of Authority*. Cambridge.

Orelli, J. K. von 1852. *Q. Horatius Flaccus*, vol. 2. Turici.

Ormand, K. 2009. *Controlling Desires: Sexuality in Ancient Greece and Rome.* Westport, CT.

Osgood, J. 2006. *Caesar's Legacy: Civil War and the Emergence of the Roman Empire.* Cambridge.

———. 2008. 'Caesar and Nicomedes', *CQ* 58: 687–91.

———, ed. 2011. *A Suetonius Reader: Selections from the Lives of the Caesars and the Life of Horace.* Mundelein, IL.

———. 2013. 'Suetonius and the Succession to Augustus'. In A. G. G. Gibson, ed., *The Julio-Claudian Succession: Reality and Perception of the 'Augustan Model',* 19–40. Leiden.

———. 2019. 'Family History in Augustan Rome'. In I. Gildenhard et al., eds., *Augustus and the Destruction of History: The Politics of the Past in Early Imperial Rome,* 135–55. Cambridge.

O'Sullivan, T. M. 2009. 'Death *ante ora parentum* in Virgil's *Aeneid*', *TAPA* 139: 447–86.

Otis, B. 1964. *Virgil: A Study in Civilized Poetry.* Oxford.

Pade, M. 2007. *The Reception of Plutarch's Lives in Fifteenth-Century Italy*, vol. 1. Copenhagen.

Paget, J. C. 2010. *Jews, Christians and Jewish Christians and Antiquity.* Tübingen.

Pagán, V. E. 2002. Review of Hurley 2001, *JRS* 92: 252–3.

———, ed. 2012a. *A Companion to Tacitus.* Malden, MA.

———. 2012b. *Conspiracy Theory in Latin Literature.* Austin, TX.

Paratore, E. 1950. *Storia della letteratura latina.* Florence.

———. 1959. 'Claude et Néron chez Suétone', *RCCM* 1: 326–41.

———. 1970. *La letteratura latina dell'età imperiale.* Florence.

———. 2007. *Una nuova ricostruzione del 'De poetis' di Suetonio*, 3rd ed., eds. C. Questa, L. Bravi, G. Clementi, and A. Torino. Urbino.

Parker, H. N. 2009. 'Books and Reading Latin Poetry'. In Johnson and Parker 2009, 186–229.

Parkin, T. G. 2003. *Old Age in the Roman World: A Cultural and Social History.* Baltimore, MD.

Paschoud, F., ed. 1996. *Histoire Auguste*, vol. 5.1. Paris.

Pastor, L. B. 2018. 'Quintus Curtius' *novum sidus* (10.9.3–6)', *Hermes* 146: 381–5.

Paterson, J. J. 1986. Review of Gascou 1984, *G&R* 33: 96.

Patterson, A. 2000. 'A Restoration Suetonius: A New Marvell Text?', *MLQ* 61: 463–80.

Pausch, D. 2004. *Biographie und Bildungskultur: Personendarstellungen bei Plinius dem Jüngeren, Gellius und Sueton.* Berlin.

———. 2013. 'Kaiser, Künstler, Kitharöde: Das Bild Neros bei Sueton'. In C. Walde, ed., *Neros Wirklichkeiten: zur Rezeption einer umstrittenen Gestalt,* 45–79. Rahden.

Pauw, D. A. 1980. 'Impersonal Expressions and Unidentified Spokesmen in Greek and Roman Historiography and Biography', *AClass* 22: 115–30.

Pelling, C. 1979. 'Plutarch's Method of Work in the Roman Lives', *JHS* 99: 74–96. Repr. in Pelling 2002b, 1–44.

———, ed. 1988. *Plutarch: Life of Antony.* Cambridge.

———. 1990a. 'Childhood and Personality in Greek Biography'. In C. Pelling, ed., *Characterization and Individuality in Greek Literature*, 213–44. Oxford. Repr. in Pelling 2002b, 301–38.

———. 1990b. 'Truth and Fiction in Plutarch's *Lives*'. In D. A. Russell, ed., *Antonine Literature*, 19–54. Oxford. Repr. in Pelling 2002b, 143–70.

———. 1993. 'Tacitus and Germanicus'. In Luce and Woodman 1993, 59–85. Repr. in Ash 2012, 281–313.

———. 1997a. 'Is Death the End? Closure in Plutarch's *Lives*'. In D. H. Roberts, F. M. Dunn, and D. Fowler, eds., *Classical Closure: Reading the End in Greek and Latin Literature*, 228–50. Princeton, NJ. Repr. in Pelling 2002b, 365–86.

———. 1997b. 'Plutarch on Caesar's Fall'. In Mossman 1997, 215–32.

———. 2002a. 'Duplices tabellae: A Reading – and Rereading – of Propertius 3, 23', *SIFC* 20: 171–81.

———. 2002b. *Plutarch and History: Eighteen Studies*. London.

———. 2002c. 'Plutarch's *Caesar*: A *Caesar* for the Caesars?'. In P. Stadter and L. Van der Stockt, eds., *Sage and Emperor: Plutarch, Greek Intellectuals, and Roman Power in the Time of Trajan (98–117 A.D.)*, 213–26. Leuven. Repr. in Pelling 2002b, 253–66.

———. 2009. 'The First Biographers: Plutarch and Suetonius'. In M. Griffin, ed., *A Companion to Julius Caesar*, 252–66. Malden, MA.

———. 2010. 'The Spur of Fame: *Annals* 4.37–8'. In Kraus, Marincola, and Pelling 2010, 364–84.

———. 2011. *Plutarch: Caesar*. Oxford.

———. 2013a. 'Historical Explanation and What Didn't Happen: The Virtues of Virtual History'. In A. Powell, ed., *Hindsight in Greek and Roman History*, 1–24. Swansea.

———. 2013b. 'Intertextuality, Plausibility, and Interpretation', *Histos* 7: 1–20.

———. 2015. 'The Rhetoric of *The Roman Revolution*', *SyllClass* 26: 207–47.

———. 2020. 'Intertextuality in Plutarch: What's the Point?'. In T. S. Schmidt, M. Vamvouri, and R. Hirsch-Luipold, eds., *The Dynamics of Intertextuality in Plutarch*, 11–27. Leiden.

Penella, R. J. 2018. 'The Fathers of the Emperors Caligula and Claudius in Suetonius' *Lives of the Caesars*', *Phoenix* 72: 161–5.

Perkins, C. A., 1993. 'Tacitus on Otho', *Latomus* 52: 848–55.

Perron, Y. 1990. 'D'Alexandre à Néron: le motif de la tente d'apparat'. In J. M. Croisille, ed., *Neronia IV: Alejandro Magna, modelo de los emperadores romanos*, 211–29. Brussels.

Peter, H., ed. 1884. *Scriptores Historiae Augustae*, vol. 1, 2nd ed. Leipzig.

Petschenig, M. 1879. 'Beiträge zur Textkritik der Scriptores Historiae Augustae', *SKAW* 93: 355–418.

Pettinger, A. 2012. *The Republic in Danger: Drusus Libo and the Succession of Tiberius*. Oxford.

Pigoń, J. 1993. 'Drusus imperator? An Episode in the Fall of Sejanus in Tacitus, Suetonius, and Cassius Dio', *Antiquitas* 18: 183–90.

Pike, J. B. 1903. *Gai Suetoni Tranquilli De vita Caesarum libri III–VI: Tiberius, Caligula, Claudius, Nero*. Boston, MA.

Pipitone, G. 2015. 'Sulle nozze di Nerone con Pitagora/Doriforo: nota a Suet. *Nero* 29', *REA* 117: 77–85.

Plass, P. 1988. *Wit and the Writing of History: The Rhetoric of Historiography in Imperial Rome*. Madison, WI.

Poignault, R. 2001. 'Les fleuves dans le récit militaire tacitéen', *Latomus* 60: 414–32.

———, ed. 2009. *Présence de Suétone: actes du colloque tenu à Clermont-Ferrand (25–27 novembre 2004)*. Clermont-Ferrand.

Pollard, N. 2010. 'The Roman Army'. In D. S. Potter, ed., *A Companion to the Roman Empire*, 206–27. Malden, MA.

Pomeroy, A. J. 2006. 'Theatricality in Tacitus' *Histories*', *Arethusa* 39: 171–91.

———. 2017. 'Fabius and Minucius in Tacitus: Intertextuality and Allusion in *Annals* Book 15', *CQ* 67: 583–96.

Potter, D. S. 2012. 'Tacitus' Sources'. In Pagán 2012a, 125–40.

Poulle, B. 2016. 'À quoi servent les éloges et les blâmes dans les biographies de Tacite et Suétone?', *REL* 94: 141–50.

Powell, A. 2017a. 'The Harvard School, Virgil, and Political History: Pure Innocence or Pure in No Sense?', *CW* 111: 96–101.

———. 2017b. 'Sinning against Philology? Method and the Suetonian-Donatan Life of Virgil'. In Powell and Hardie 2017, 173–98.

Powell, A., and Hardie, P., eds. 2017. *The Ancient Lives of Virgil: Literary and Historical Studies*. Swansea.

Powell, C. A. 1972. '*Deum ira, hominum rabies*', *Latomus* 31: 833–48.

Power, T. 2009. Review of Paratore 2007, *CR* 59: 302–3.

———. 2011. Review of Poignault 2009, *CR* 61: 485–7.

———. 2013a. Review of Hurley 2011, *CR* 63: 127–9.

———. 2013b. Review of Louis 2010, *JRS* 103: 341–2.

———. 2014a. 'The Endings of Suetonius' *Caesars*'. In Power and Gibson 2014, 58–77.

———. 2014b. 'Introduction: The Originality of Suetonius'. In Power and Gibson 2014, 1–18.

———. 2014c. 'Suetonius' *Famous Courtesans*'. In Power and Gibson 2014, 231–55.

———. 2016. 'Bloom and Caligula', *N&Q* 63: 288–91.

Power, T., and Gibson, R. K., eds. 2014. *Suetonius the Biographer: Studies in Roman Lives*. Oxford.

Prauscello, L. 2004. 'Rehearsing her Own Death: A Note on Bassilla's Epitaph', *ZPE* 147: 56–8.

Preud'homme, L. 1904. *Troisième étude sur l'histoire du texte de Suétone: classification des manuscrits*. Brussels.

Priestley, J. 2014. *Herodotus and Hellenistic Culture: Literary Studies in the Reception of the Histories*. Oxford.

Pritchard, A. 1990. 'The Houyhnhnms: Swift, Suetonius, and Marvell', *N&Q* 37: 305–6.

Putnam, M. C. J. 2006. *Poetic Interplay: Catullus and Horace*. Princeton, NJ.

Questa, C. 1957. 'Tecnica biografica e tecnica annalistica nei libri LIII–LXIII di Cassio Dione', *StudUrb* 31: 37–53.

———. 1963. *Studi sulle fonti degli Annales di Tacito*, 2nd ed. Rome.

Quinn, K. 1973. *Catullus: The Poems*, 2nd ed. London.

———. 1982. 'The Poet and His Audience in the Augustan Age', *ANRW* 2.30.1: 75–180.

Radice, B., ed. 1969. *Pliny: Letters and Panegyricus*, 2 vols. Cambridge, MA.

Ramage, E. S. 1987. *The Nature and Purpose of Augustus' Res Gestae*. Stuttgart.

Ramondetti, P. 2002. 'Una lente sul dettaglio: una particolare struttura sintattica nelle *Vite dei Cesari* di Svetonio', *Paideia* 57: 379–427.

Reed, J. D. 2007. *Virgil's Gaze: Nation and Poetry in the Aeneid*. Princeton, NJ.

Reekmans, T. 1992. 'Verbal Humour in Plutarch and Suetonius' Lives', *AncSoc* 23: 189–232.

Rees, R. 2007. 'Letters of Recommendation and the Rhetoric of Praise'. In R. Morello and A. D. Morrison, eds., *Ancient Letters: Classical and Antique Epistolography*, 149–68. Oxford.

———, ed. 2012a. *Latin Panegyric*. Oxford.

———. 2012b. 'The Modern History of Latin Panegyric'. In Rees 2012a, 3–48.

Reeve, M. 2011. 'The *Vita Plinii*'. In Gibson and Morello 2011, 207–22.

Reichel, M. 2007. 'Xenophon als Biograph'. In Erler and Schorn 2007, 25–43.

Reifferscheid, A., ed. 1860. *C. Suetoni Tranquilli praeter Caesarum libros reliquiae*. Leipzig.

Reynolds, L. D., ed. 1983. *Texts and Transmission: A Survey of the Latin Classics*. Oxford.

Reynolds, L. D., and Wilson, N. G., eds. 2013. *Scribes and Scholars: A Guide to the Transmission of Greek and Latin Literature*, 4th ed. Oxford.

Reynolds, R. W. 1943. 'Criticism of Individuals in Roman Popular Comedy', *CQ* 37: 37–45.

Richlin, A. 1992. *The Garden of Priapus: Sexuality and Aggression in Roman Humor*, 2nd ed. Oxford.

Richter, B. 1992. *Vitellius: ein Zerrbild der Geschichtsschreibung; Untersuchungen zum Prinzipat des A. Vitellius*. Frankfurt a. M.

Riesner, R. 1998. *Paul's Early Period: Chronology, Mission Strategy, Theology*. Grand Rapids, MI.

Ripat, P. 2006. 'Roman Omens, Roman Audiences, and Roman History', *G&R* 53: 155–74.

Ritter, F., ed. 1857. *Q. Horatius Flaccus*, vol. 2. Leipzig.

Robinson, R. P. 1920. *De fragmenti Suetoniani De grammaticis et rhetoribus codicum nexu et fide*. Urbana, IL.

Roche, P. 2011. 'Pliny's Thanksgiving: An Introduction to the *Panegyricus*'. In P. Roche, ed., *Pliny's Praise: The Panegyricus in the Roman World*, 1–28. Cambridge.

———. 2018. 'Pliny and Suetonius on Giving and Returning Imperial Power'. In König and Whitton 2018, 146–59.

Rochette, B. 2015. 'Suétone et le bilinguisme des Julio-Claudiens'. In O. Devillers, ed., *Autour de Pline le Jeune: en hommage à Nicole Méthy*, 155–68. Bordeaux.

Rodeghiero, M. M. 2012. 'Frammenti "erratici" di propaganda pompeiana nella *Vita di Augusto* di Svetonio', *RCCM* 54: 95–132.

Rohrbacher, D. 2009. 'Enmann's *Kaisergeschichte* from Augustus to Domitian', *Latomus* 68: 709–19.

———. 2010. 'Physiognomics in Imperial Latin Biography', *ClAnt* 29: 92–116.

———. 2013. 'The Sources of the *Historia Augusta* Re-Examined', *Histos* 7: 146–80.

Rolfe, J. C. 1913. 'Suetonius and His Biographies', *PAPHS* 52: 206–25.

———, ed. 1913–14. *Suetonius*, 2 vols. London.

———. 1915. 'The Use of 'gens' and 'familia' by Suetonius', *CP* 10: 445–9.

Roller, M. B. 1998. 'Pliny's Catullus: The Politics of Literary Appropriation', *TAPA* 128: 265–304. Repr. in Gibson and Whitton 2016, 246–88.

Rollo, A. 2015–16. 'La tradition des passages grecs dans le *De vita Caesarum* de Suétone entre le Moyen Âge et la Renaissance', *EPHE* 148: 51–68.

———. 2018. 'Notes on Suetonius' *Graeca*', *CQ* 68: 612–20.

Roman, L. 2006. 'A History of Lost Tablets', *ClAnt* 25: 351–88.

Roscher, W. H., ed. 1884–6. *Ausführliches Lexikon der griechischen und römischen Mythologie*, vol. 1. Leipzig.

Rostagni, A., ed. 1944. *Svetonio: De poetis e biografi minori*. Turin.

Roth, C. L., ed. 1858. *C. Suetoni Tranquilli quae supersunt omnia*. Leipzig.

Roth, J. P. 1998. *The Logistics of the Roman Army at War (264 B.C.–A.D. 235)*. Leiden.

Rowland, M. 2010. 'Effeminacy as Imperial Vice in Suetonius' Nero and Caligula', *Classicum* 36: 23–30.

Rudich, V. 1993. *Political Dissidence under Nero: The Price of Dissimulation*. London.

Rudd, N., ed. 1989. *Horace: Epistles Book II and Epistle to the Pisones ('Ars Poetica')*. Cambridge.

Ruhnken, D. 1828. *Scholia in Suetonii Vitas Caesarum*, ed. J. Geel. Leiden.

Rutledge, S. H. 2001. *Imperial Inquisitions: Prosecutors and Informants from Tiberius to Domitian*. London.

———, ed. 2014. *A Tacitus Reader: Selections from Annales, Historiae, Germania, Agricola, and Dialogus*. Mundelein, IL.

Ryder, K. C. 1984. 'The *senex amator* in Plautus', *G&R* 31: 181–9.

Saddington, D. B. 2004. 'Suetonius on Military Matters – The Julio-Claudian Period', *REMA* 1: 23–43.

———. 2005. 'Suetonius on Military Matters: A.D. 68/9 and the Flavian Period', *REMA* 2: 89–104.

Sage, P. 1979. 'L'expression narrative dans les *XII Césars* de Suétone: analyse d'une structure de phrase', *Latomus* 38: 499–524.

Saller, R. P. 1980. 'Anecdotes as Historical Evidence for the Principate', *G&R* 27: 69–83.

———. 1982. *Personal Patronage under the Early Empire*. Cambridge.

Sanders, H. A. 1944. 'Suetonius in the Civil Service under Hadrian', *AJP* 65: 113–23.

Sansone, D. 1993. 'Nero's Final Hours', *ICS* 18: 179–89.

Scantamburlo, C. 2011. *Svetonio: Vita di Cesare*. Pisa.

Scappaticcio, M. C., ed. 2020. *Seneca the Elder and His Rediscovered Historiae ab initio bellorum civilium: New Perspectives on Early-Imperial Roman Historiography*. Berlin.

Schierl, P. 2006. *Die Tragödien des Pacuvius: ein Kommentar zu den Fragmenten mit Einleitung, Text und Übersetzung*. Berlin.

Schlegel, C. 2000. 'Horace and His Fathers: Satires 1.4 and 1.6', *AJP* 121: 93–119.

Schmidt, M. G. 1989. 'Ein Brief Kaisers Othos an die Witwe Neros (Suet. Otho 10,2)', *Historia* 38: 503–8.

Schmidt, P. L. 1991. 'Suetons "Pratum" seit Wessner (1917)', *ANRW* 2.33.5: 3794–825.

Schmidt, W. 1983. *Vergil-Probleme*. Göppingen.

Schorn, S., ed. 2004. *Satyros aus Kallatis: Sammlung der Fragmente emit Kommentar.* Basel.

Schrijvers, P. H. 2007. 'A Literary View of the Nile Mosaic at Praeneste'. In L. Bricault, M. J. Versluys, and P. G. P. Meyboom, eds., *Nile into Tiber: Egypt in the Roman World*, 223–39. Leiden.

Schropp, J. W. G. 2017. '*Nonnulli Graecorum [...] tradiderunt* (Suet. Iul. 52,2): Kannte Sueton die Caesar-Vita Plutarchs?', *Hermes* 145: 41–60.

Schulz, V. 2016. 'Historiography and Panegyric: The Deconstruction of Imperial Representation in Cassius Dio's *Roman History*'. In Lange and Madsen 2016, 276–96.

———. 2019a. *Deconstructing Imperial Representation: Tacitus, Cassius Dio, and Suetonius on Nero and Domitian.* Leiden.

———. 2019b. 'Defining the Good Ruler: Early Kings as Proto-Imperial Figures in Cassius Dio'. In C. Burden-Strevens and M. O. Lindholmer, eds., *Cassius Dio's Forgotten History of Early Rome: The Roman History, Books 1–21*, 311–32. Leiden.

———. 2020. 'Material to Remember? "Tyrannical" Space in Roman Imperial Historiography and Biography', *Mnemosyne* 73: 296–319.

Schwartz, S. 1990. *Josephus and Judaean Politics.* Leiden.

Scott, R. T. 2010. 'There's Nothing Wrong with Horace, *Odes* 4'. In *SLLRH* 15.258–70.

Selden, D. L. 1992. '*Caveat lector*: Catullus and the Rhetoric of Performance'. In R. Hexter and D. Selden, eds., *Innovations of Antiquity*, 461–512. New York. Repr. in J. H. Gaisser, ed., *Catullus* (Oxford, 2007), 490–559.

Seo, J. M. 2009. 'Plagiarism and Poetic Identity in Martial', *AJP* 130: 567–93.

Sharrock, A., and Ash, R. 2002. *Fifty Key Classical Authors.* London.

Shaw, B. D. 2015. 'The Myth of the Neronian Persecution', *JRS* 105: 73–100.

———. 2018. 'Response to Christopher Jones: The Historicity of the Neronian Persecution', *NTS* 64: 231–42.

Shelton, J. A. 2013. *The Women of Pliny's Letters.* Abingdon.

Sherwin-White, A. N. 1966. *The Letters of the Pliny: A Historical and Social Commentary.* Oxford.

Shochat, Y. 1981. 'Tacitus' Attitude to Galba', *Athenaeum* 59: 199–204.

Shotter, D., ed. 1993. *Suetonius: Lives of Galba, Otho & Vitellius.* Warminster.

———. 2005. *Nero*, 2nd ed. Abingdon.

———. 2008. *Nero Caesar Augustus: Emperor of Rome.* Harlow.

Shuckburgh, E. S., ed. 1896. *C. Suetoni Tranquilli Divus Augustus.* Cambridge.

Sikes, E. E. 1936. 'C. Suetonius Tranquillus (*c.* A.D. 75–140)'. In S. A. Cook, F. E. Adcock, and M. P. Charlesworth, eds., *The Cambridge Ancient History*, vol. 11, 741–2. Cambridge.

Sim, D. C. 1998. *The Gospel of Matthew and Christian Judaism: The History and Social Setting of the Matthean Community.* Edinburgh.

Simcox, G. A. 1883. *A History of Latin Literature from Ennius to Boethius*, vol. 2. London.

Siwicki, C. 2020. 'Architectural Criticism in the Roman World and the Limits of Literary Interaction'. In König, Langlands, and Uden 2020, 247–68.

Slater, N. W. 2014. 'Speaking Verse to Power: Circulation of Oral and Written Critique in the *Lives of the Caesars*'. In R. Scodel, ed., *Between Orality and Literacy: Communication and Adaptation in Antiquity*, 289–308. Leiden.

Slater, W. J. 1971. 'Pindar's House', *GRBS* 12: 141–52.

Slingerland, H. D. 1997. *Claudian Policymaking and the Early Imperial Repression of Judaism at Rome*. Atlanta, GA.

Slootjes, D. 2020. 'Augustus and His Presentation of the People in the *Res gestae*', *CW* 113: 279–98.

Smith, B. H. 1968. *Poetic Closure: A Study of How Poems End*. Chicago.

Smith, R. A. 1997. *Poetic Allusion and Poetic Embrace in Ovid and Virgil*. Ann Arbor, MI.

Smolenaars, H. 2017. 'The Historical Truth of Vergil's Recital of the *Georgics* at Atella (*VSD* § 27)'. In Powell and Hardie 2017, 153–72.

Solin, H. 1982. *Die griechischen Personennamen in Rom: ein Namenbuch*, 3 vols. Berlin.

———. 1996. *Die stadtrömischen Sklavennamen: ein Namenbuch*, 3 vols. Stuttgart.

———. 2001. 'Griechische und römische Sklavennamen: eine vergleichende Untersuchung'. In H. Bellen and H. Heinen, eds., *Fünfzig Jahre Forschungen zur antiken Sklaverei an der Mainzer Akademie, 1950–2000: Miscellanea zum Jubilaeum*, 307–30. Stuttgart.

Somerville, T. 2010. 'Note on a Reversed Acrostic in Vergil *Georgics* 1.429–33', *CP* 105: 202–9.

Southern, R. W. 1970. 'Aspects of the European Tradition of Historical Writing 1: The Classical Tradition from Einhard to Geoffrey of Monmouth', *TRHS* 20: 173–96. Repr. in Southern 2004, 11–29.

———. 2004. *History and Historians: Selected Papers of R. W. Southern*, ed. R. J. Bartlett. Oxford.

Spawforth, A. J. S. 2006. '"Macedonian Times": Hellenistic Memories in the Provinces of the Roman Near East'. In D. Konstan and S. Saïd, eds., *Greeks on Greekness: Viewing the Greek Past under the Roman Empire*, 1–26. Cambridge.

Speller, E. 2003. *Following Hadrian: A Second-Century Journey through the Roman Empire*. Oxford.

Spence, S. 2004. *The Parting of the Ways: The Roman Church as a Case Study*. Leuven.

Stadter, P. A. 1988. 'The Proems of Plutarch's *Lives*', *ICS* 13: 275–95.

———. 1996. 'Anecdotes and the Thematic Structure of Plutarchean Biography'. In J. A. Fernández Delgado, J. Antonio, and F. Pordomingo Pardo, eds., *Estudios sobre Plutarco: Aspectos Formales*, 291–303. Madrid.

———. 2005. 'Revisiting Plutarch's *Lives of the Caesars*'. In A. P. Jiménez and F. Titchener, eds., *Valori letterari delle opera di Plutarco: studi offerti al Professore Italo Gallo dall'International Plutarch Society*, 419–35. Málaga. Repr. in Stadter 2014, 56–69.

———. 2007. 'History and Biography'. In Marincola 2007, 528–40.

———. 2014. *Plutarch and His Roman Readers*. Oxford.

Starbatty, A. 2010. *Aussehen ist Ansichtssache: Kleidung in der Kommunikation der römischen Antike*. Munich.

Steffen, W. 1960. 'Kritische Bemerkungen zu Suetons Vita Horati'. In J. Irmscher and K. F. Kumaniecki, eds., *Römische Literatur der augusteischen Zeit: eine Aufsatzsammlung*, 18–25. Berlin.

Steidle, W. 1951. *Sueton und die antike Biographie*. Munich.

Stein-Hölkeskamp, E. 2002. 'Culinarische Codes: Das ideale Bankett bei Plinius d. Jüngeren und seinen Zeitgenossen', *Klio* 84: 465–90.

Stem, R. 2012. *The Political Biographies of Cornelius Nepos.* Ann Arbor, MI.

Stern, M., ed. 1980. *Greek and Latin Authors on Jews and Judaism*, vol. 2. Jerusalem.

Stevenson, T. 2013. 'The Succession Planning of Augustus', *Antichthon* 47: 118–39.

Stok, F. 1994. 'Sulla datazione del *De poetis* di Svetonio', *Vichiana* 5: 193–202. Repr. in G. Brugnoli and F. Stok, eds., *Studi sulle Vitae Vergilianae* (Pisa, 2006), 47–57.

———. 2010. 'The Life of Vergil before Donatus'. In Farrell and Putnam 2010, 107–20.

Stroup, S. C. 2010. *Catullus, Cicero, and a Society of Patrons: The Generation of the Text.* Cambridge.

Strunk, T. E. 2012. 'Pliny the Pessimist', *G&R* 59: 178–92.

———. 2014. 'Rape and Revolution: Livia and Augustus in Tacitus' *Annales*', *Latomus* 73: 126–48.

———. 2017. *History after Liberty: Tacitus on Tyrant, Sycophants, and Republicans.* Ann Arbor, MI.

Stuart, D. R. 1928. *Epochs of Greek and Roman Biography.* Berkeley, CA.

Suerbaum, W. 2004. 'Tacitus schreibt eine unpolitische Geisterstory des Plinius in eine Aufsteigergeschichte um: Aufstieg und Fall des Curtius Rufus bei Plin. epist. 7,27,2f. und bei Tac. ann. 11,20f'. In H. Heftner and K. Tomaschitz, eds., *Ad fontes! Festschrift für Gerhard Dobesch zum 65; Geburtstag am 15. September 2004*, 493–504. Vienna.

———. 2015. *Skepsis und Suggestion: Tacitus als Historiker und als Literat.* Heidelberg.

Sumi, G. S. 2002. 'Impersonating the Dead: Mimes at Roman Funerals', *AJP* 123: 559–85.

Sumner, G. V. 1961. 'Curtius Rufus and the "Historiae Alexandri"', *AUMLA* 15: 30–9.

———. 1982. 'The *coitio* of 54 BC, or Waiting for Caesar', *HSCP* 86: 133–9.

Swan, P. M. 1987. 'Cassius Dio on Augustus: A Poverty of Annalistic Sources?', *Phoenix* 41: 272–91.

———. 2004. *The Augustan Succession: An Historical Commentary on Cassius Dio's Roman History Books 55–56 (9 B.C.–A.D. 14).* Oxford.

Syme, R. 1939. *The Roman Revolution.* Oxford.

———. 1958. *Tacitus*, 2 vols. Oxford.

———. 1960. 'Pliny's Less Successful Friends', *Historia* 9: 362–79. Repr. in *RP* 2.477–95; also in Gibson and Whitton 2016, 67–88.

———. 1968. *Ammianus and the Historia Augusta.* Oxford.

———. 1971. *Emperors and Biography: Studies in the Historia Augusta.* Oxford.

———. 1977. 'The Enigmatic Sospes', *JRS* 67: 34–49. Repr. in *RP* 3.1043–61.

———. 1980a. 'Biographers of the Caesars', *MH* 37: 104–28. Repr. in *RP* 3.1251–75.

———. 1980b. 'Guard Prefects of Trajan and Hadrian', *JRS* 70: 64–80. Repr. in *RP* 3.1276–302.

———. 1980c. 'Minor Emendations in Pliny and Tacitus', *CQ* 30: 426–8. Repr. in *RP* 3.1233–5.

———. 1981. 'The Travels of Suetonius Tranquillus', *Hermes* 109: 105–17. Repr. in *RP* 3.1337–49.

———. 1987. 'Exotic Names, Notably in Seneca's Tragedies', *AClass* 30: 49–64. Repr. in *RP* 6.269–86.

———. 1991. 'A Political Group'. In *RP* 7.568–87.

———. 1995. *Anatolica: Studies in Strabo*, ed. A. R. Birley. Oxford.

———. 2016a. *Approaching the Roman Revolution: Papers on Republican History*, ed. F. Santangelo. Oxford.

———. 2016b. 'Caesar as *pontifex maximus*'. In Syme 2016a, 186–95.

Szoke, M. 2019. 'Condemning Domitian or Un-Damning Themselves? Tacitus and Pliny on the Domitianic "Reign of Terror"', *ICS* 44: 430–52.

Taillardat, J., ed. 1967. *Suétone: Περὶ βλασφημιῶν, Περὶ παιδιῶν*. Paris.

Tarn, W. W. 1948. *Alexander the Great*, vol. 2. Cambridge.

Tarrant, R. 2007. 'Horace and Roman Literary History'. In Harrison 2007a, 63–76.

———. 2016. *Texts, Editors, and Readers: Methods and Problems in Latin Textual Criticism*. Cambridge.

Tarrant, R., and Winterbottom, M. 1983. 'Tacitus'. In Reynolds 1983, 406–11.

Tatum, W. J. 2014. 'Another Look at Suetonius' *Titus*'. In Power and Gibson 2014, 159–77.

Teuffel, W. S. 1891–2. *History of Roman Literature*, 2 vols. London.

Thom, S. 2001. 'Horace on Horace *Odes* 4', *Akroterion* 46: 43–59.

Thomas, R. F. 1986. 'Virgil's *Georgics* and the Art of Reference', *HSCP* 90: 171–98. Repr. in P. Hardie, ed., *Virgil*, vol. 2 (London, 1999), 58–82.

———, ed. 1988. *Virgil: Georgics*, 2 vols. Cambridge.

———. 2001. *Virgil and the Augustan Reception*. Cambridge.

———, ed. 2011. *Horace: Odes IV and Carmen saeculare*. Cambridge.

Tibbetts, S. J., and Winterbottom, M. 1983. 'Suetonius'. In Reynolds 1983, 399–405.

Tilg, S. 2008. 'Augustus and Orestes: Two Literary Clues', *CQ* 58: 368–70.

Toher, M. 2011. 'Herod's Last Days', *HSCP* 106: 209–28.

———. 2012. 'The *exitus* of Augustus', *Hermes* 140: 37–44.

———, ed. 2017. *Nicolaus of Damascus: The Life of Augustus and The Autobiography*. Cambridge.

Townend, G. B. 1959. 'The Date of Composition of Suetonius' *Caesares*', *CQ* 9: 285–93.

———. 1960. 'The Sources of the Greek in Suetonius', *Hermes* 88: 98–120.

———. 1961. 'The Hippo Inscription and the Career of Suetonius', *Historia* 10: 99–109.

———. 1964. 'Cluvius Rufus and the *Histories* of Tacitus', *AJP* 85: 337–77.

———. 1967. 'Suetonius and His Influence'. In Dorey 1967, 79–111.

———. 1970. 'Suetonius'. In N. G. L. Hammond and H. H. Scullard, eds., *The Oxford Classical Dictionary*, 2nd ed., 1020–1. Oxford.

———. 1972a. 'The Earliest Scholiast on Juvenal', *CQ* 22: 376–87.

———. 1972b. 'Suetonius and Literary Biography', *PCA* 69: 27.

———. 1973. 'The Literary Substrata to Juvenal's Satires', *JRS* 63: 148–60.

———. 1982a. 'Introduction'. In H. E. Butler, M. Cary, and G. B. Townend, eds., *Suetonius: Divus Julius*, 2nd ed., vii–xv. London.

———. 1982b. 'Suetonius'. In T. J. Luce, ed., *Ancient Writers: Greece and Rome*, 2 vols., 1049–61. New York.

Traub, H. W. 1955. 'Pliny's Treatment of History in Epistolary Form', *TAPA* 86: 213–32. Repr. in Gibson and Whitton 2016, 123–45.

Treggiari, S. 1969. 'Pompeius' Freedman Biographer Again', *CR* 19: 264–6.

Trimble, J. 2014. '*Corpore enormi*: The Rhetoric of Physical Appearance in Suetonius and Imperial Portrait Statuary'. In J. Elsner and M. Meyer, eds., *Art and Rhetoric in Roman Culture*, 115–54. Cambridge.

Trinacty, C. 2009. 'Like Father, like Son? Selected Examples of Intertextuality in Seneca the Younger and Seneca the Elder', *Phoenix* 63: 260–77.

Tuori, K. 2016. *The Emperor of Law: The Emergence of Roman Imperial Adjudication*. Oxford.

Turner, A. 1943. 'A Vergilian Anecdote in Suetonius and Dio', *CP* 38: 261.

Tzounakas, S. 2007. '*Neque enim historiam componebam*: Pliny's First Epistle and His Attitude towards Historiography', *MH* 64: 42–54.

Uden, J. 2007. 'Impersonating Priapus', *AJP* 128: 1–26.

———. 2015. *The Invisible Satirist: Juvenal and Second-Century Rome*. Oxford.

———. 2020. 'The Margins of Satire: Suetonius, *satura*, and Scholarly Outsiders in Ancient Rome', *AJP* 141: 575–601.

Vacher, M. C., ed. 1993. *Suétone: Grammairiens et rhéteurs*. Paris.

van der Lans, B. 2015. 'The Politics of Exclusion: Expulsion of Jews and Others from Rome'. In M. Labahn and O. Lehtipuu, eds., *People under Power: Early Jewish and Christian Responses to the Roman Empire*, 33–77. Amsterdam.

van Hooff, A. 2003. 'The Imperial Art of Dying'. In L. de Blois et al., eds., *The Representation and Perception of Roman Imperial Power*, 99–116. Amsterdam.

Van Overmeire, S. 2012a. 'According to the Habit of Foreign Kings: Nero, Ruler Ideology and the Hellenistic Monarchs', *Latomus* 71: 753–79.

———. 2012b. 'Nero, the Senate and People of Rome: Reactions to an Emperor's Image'. In *SLLRH* 16.472–91.

Van Voorst, R. E. 2000. *Jesus outside the New Testament: An Introduction to Ancient Evidence*. Grand Rapids, MI.

van Wassenhove B. 2008. 'The Representation of Galba in Suetonius', *Athenaeum* 96: 623–34.

Vasaly, A. 2015. *Livy's Political Philosophy: Power and Personality in Early Rome*. Cambridge.

Velaza, J. 1993. 'Elementos para una cronología literaria de Suetonio', *EClás* 35: 37–50.

Venini, P., ed. 1977. *C. Svetonio Tranquillo: Vite di Galba, Otone, Vitellio*. Turin.

———. 1988. 'Svetonio'. In F. Della Corte, ed., *Dizionario degli Scrittori Greci e Latini*, vol. 3, 2145–51. Settimo milanese.

Verdière, R. 1960. 'Le baiser d'adieu de Néron'. In *Hommages à Léon Herrmann*, 774–6. Brussels.

———. 1975. 'À verser du dossier sexuel de Néron', *PP* 30: 5–22.

Verhoeff, H. 1984. 'Does Oedipus Have His Complex?', *Style* 18: 261–83.

Vernant, J.-P. 1991. 'A "Beautiful Death" and the Disfigured Corpse in Homeric Epic'. In *Mortals and Immortals: Collected Essays*, ed. F. I. Zeitlin, 50–74. Princeton, NJ. Repr. in D. L. Cairns, ed., *Homer's Iliad* (Oxford, 2001), 311–41.

Viljamaa, T. 1991. 'Suetonius on Roman Teachers of Grammar', *ANRW* 2.33.5: 3826–51.

Ville, G. 1981. *La gladiature en occident des origines à la mort de Domitien*. Rome.

Vlaardingerbroek, M. 1999. 'Hadrianus en Suetonius: De keizer en de kamerge-leerde', *Hermeneus* 71: 220–5.

Vollmer, F., ed. 1907. *Q. Horati Flacci carmina*. Leipzig.

———, ed. 1908. *Q. Horati Flacci carmina*. Leipzig.

von Albrecht, M. 1997. *A History of Roman Literature: From Livius Andronicus to Boethius*, 2 vols. Leiden.

von Büren, V. 2010. 'Le Juvénal des Carolingiens à la lumière du Ms Cambridge King's College 52', *AntTard* 18: 115–37.

Vössing, K. 2004. *Mensa regia: Das Bankett beim hellenistischen König und beim römischen Kaiser*. Munich.

Vout, C. 2007. *Power and Eroticism in Imperial Rome*. Cambridge.

Wallace-Hadrill, A. 1982. '*Civilis princeps*: Between Citizen and King', *JRS* 72: 32–48.

———. 1983. *Suetonius: The Scholar and His Caesars*. London.

———. 1986. Review of Gascou 1984, *CR* 36: 243–5.

Walsh, P. G. 2006. *Pliny the Younger: Complete Letters*. Oxford.

Wardle, D. 1992. 'Cluvius Rufus and Suetonius', *Hermes* 120: 466–82.

———. 1993. 'Did Suetonius Write in Greek?', *AClass* 36: 91–103.

———. 1994. *Suetonius' Life of Caligula: A Commentary*. Brussels.

———. 1998a. 'Suetonius and His Own Day'. In *SLLRH* 9.425–47.

———. 1998b. *Valerius Maximus: Memorable Deeds and Sayings Book I*. Oxford.

———. 2001. 'Suetonius: The "Change" in, and the "Generosity" of Titus', *Antichthon* 35: 64–9.

———. 2002. 'Suetonius as *ab epistulis*: An African Connection', *Historia* 51: 462–80.

———. 2005. 'Unimpeachable Sponsors of Imperial Autocracy, or Augustus' Dream Team (Suetonius *Divus Augustus* 94.8–9 and Dio Cassius 45.2.2–4)', *Antichthon* 39: 29–47.

———. 2007. 'A Perfect Send-off: Suetonius and the Dying Art of Augustus (Suetonius, *Aug.* 99)', *Mnemosyne* 60: 443–63.

———. 2008. 'Further Thoughts on the Death of Augustus', *AClass* 51: 187–91.

———. 2012. 'Suetonius on Augustus as God and Man', *CQ* 62: 307–26.

———. 2014. *Suetonius: Life of Augustus*. Oxford.

———. 2015. 'Suetonius and Galba's Taste in Men: A Note', *Latomus* 74: 1006–13.

———. 2019. 'Suetonius on the Civil Wars of the Late Republic'. In C. H. Lange and F. J. Vervaet, eds., *The Historiography of Late Republican Civil War*, 376–410. Leiden.

———. 2020. 'Suetonius, Caesar and a Dream of World-Domination', *Athenaeum* 108: 72–88.

Wardman, A. 1967. 'Descriptions of Personal Appearance in Plutarch and Suetonius: The Use of Statues as Evidence', *CQ* 17: 414–20.

Warmington, B. H., ed. 1999. *Suetonius: Nero*, 2nd ed. London.

Watson, L. 2005. 'Catullan Recycling? *Cacata carta*', *Mnemosyne* 58: 270–7.

Watson, L., and Watson, P., eds. 2003. *Martial: Select Epigrams*. Cambridge.

Watson, P. 2006. 'Contextualising Martial's Metres'. In Nauta, van Dam, and Smolenaars 2006, 285–97.

Weaver, P. R. C., and Wilkins, P. I. 1993. 'A Lost alumna', *ZPE* 99: 241–4.

Wessner, P., ed. 1902. *Aeli Donati Commentum Terenti*, vol. 1. Leipzig.

———, ed. 1931. *Scholia in Iuvenalem vetustiora*. Leipzig.

Westall, R. 2016. 'The Sources of Cassius Dio for the Roman Civil Wars of 49–30 BC'. In Lange and Madsen 2016, 51–75.

———. 2018. *Caesar's Civil War: Historical Reality and Fabrication*. Leiden.

White, P. 1993. *Promised Verse: Poets in the Society of Augustan Rome*. Cambridge.

Whittaker, H. 2000. 'Temples to Proconsuls? Some Remarks on Suetonius' *Divus Augustus* LII', *SO* 75: 99–106.

Whitton, C. 2010. 'Pliny, *Epistles* 8.14: Senate, Slavery and the *Agricola*', *JRS* 100: 118–39.

———. 2012. '"Let Us Tread Our Path Together": Tacitus and the Younger Pliny'. In Pagán 2012a, 345–68.

———, ed. 2013. *Pliny the Younger: Epistles Book II*. Cambridge.

———. 2018a. '*Alius aliud*: Context, Commentary and Pliny (*Epistles* 9,3)'. In U. Tischer, A. Forst, and U. Gärtner, eds., *Text, Kontext, Kontextualisierung: Moderne Kontextkonzepte und antike Liteartur*, 137–59. Hildesheim.

———. 2018b. 'Quintilian, Pliny, Tacitus'. In König and Whitton 2018, 37–62.

———. 2019a. *The Arts of Imitation in Latin Prose: Pliny's Epistles/Quintilian in Brief*. Cambridge.

———. 2019b. 'The Arts of Self-Imitation in Pliny (and the Date of *Panegyricus*)', *Maia* 71: 339–79.

Wilkes, J. 1972. 'Julio-Claudian Historians', *CW* 65: 177–203.

Wilkinson, L. P. 1949. 'Lucretius and the Love-Philtre', *CR* 64: 47–8.

Williams, C. A., ed. 2004. *Martial: Epigrams Book Two*. Oxford.

———. 2010. *Roman Homosexuality*, 2nd ed. Oxford.

Williams, G. 1995. '*Libertino patre natus*: True or False?'. In S. J. Harrison, ed., *Homage to Horace: A Bimillenary Celebration*, 296–313. Oxford. Repr. in K. Freudenburg, ed., *Horace: Satires and Epistles* (Oxford, 2009), 138–55.

Williams, G. D. 2017. 'Lucan's *Civil War* in Nero's Rome'. In Bartsch, Freudenburg, and Littlewood 2017, 93–106.

Williams, M. H. 1989. 'The Expulsion of the Jews from Rome in A.D. 19', *Latomus* 48: 765–84. Repr. in Williams 2013, 63–80.

———. 2004. 'The Shaping of the Identity of the Jewish Community in Rome in Antiquity'. In J. Zangenberg and M. Labahn, eds., *Christians as a Religious Minority in a Multicultural City*, 33–46. London. Repr. in Williams 2013, 33–48.

———. 2013. *Jews in a Graeco-Roman Environment*. Tübingen.

Wills, J. 1996. *Repetition in Latin Poetry: Figures of Allusion*. Oxford.

Wilmart, A., ed. 1937–45. *Codices Reginenses Latini*, vols. 1–2. Vatican City.

Winterling, A. 2011. *Caligula: A Biography*. Berkeley, CA.

Wiseman, T. P. 1969. *Catullan Questions*. Leicester.

———. 1979. *Clio's Cosmetics: Three Studies in Greco-Roman Literature*. Leicester.

———. 1985. *Catullus and His World: A Reappraisal*. Cambridge.

———. 2009. 'Augustus, Sulla and the Supernatural'. In C. Smith and A. Powell, eds., *The Lost Memoirs of Augustus and the Development of Roman Autobiography*, 111–23. Swansea.

———. 2013. *The Death of Caligula: Josephus Ant. Iud. XIX 1–273*, 2nd ed. Liverpool.

———. 2014. 'Suetonius and the Origin of Pantomime'. In Power and Gibson 2014, 256–72.

Woodman, A. J. 1979. 'Self-Imitation and the Substance of History: Tacitus, *Annals* 1.61–5 and *Histories* 2.70, 5.14–15'. In D. A. West and T. Woodman, eds., *Creative Imitation and Latin Literature*, 143–55. Cambridge. Repr. in Woodman 1998b, 70–85.

———. 1992. 'Nero's Alien Capital: Tacitus as Paradoxographer (*Annals* 15.36–7)'. In A. J. Woodman and J. Powell, eds., *Author and Audience in Latin Literature*, 173–88. Cambridge. Repr. in Woodman 1998b, 168–89; also in Ash 2012, 315–37.

———. 1993. 'Amateur Dramatics at the Court of Nero: *Annals* 15.48–74'. In Luce and Woodman 1993, 104–28. Repr. in Woodman 1998b, 190–217.

———. 1998a. 'Epilogue: *lectorum incuria*?'. In Woodman 1998b, 218–43.

———. 1998b. *Tacitus Reviewed*. Oxford.

———, ed. 2009a. *The Cambridge Companion to Tacitus*. Cambridge.

———. 2009b. 'Horace and Historians', *CCJ* 55: 157–67. Repr. in Woodman 2012, 112–20.

———. 2009c. 'Introduction'. In Woodman 2009a, 1–14.

———. 2009d. 'Tacitus and the Contemporary Scene'. In Woodman 2009a, 31–43. Repr. in Woodman 2012, 243–56.

———. 2012. *From Poetry to History: Selected Papers*. Oxford.

———, ed. 2017. *The Annals of Tacitus Books 5 and 6*. Cambridge.

———, ed. 2018. *The Annals of Tacitus Book 4*. Cambridge.

Woods, D. 2004. 'Nero's Pet Hippopotamus (Suet. *Nero* 37,2)', *Arctos* 38: 219–22.

———. 2006. 'Three Notes on Military Affairs under Nero', *REMA* 3: 133–50.

———. 2006–7. 'Nero, "Doryphorus", and the Christians', *Eranos* 104: 49–59.

———. 2009. 'Nero and Sporus', *Latomus* 68: 73–82.

———. 2011. 'Which Gaius Julius Caesar (Suet., *Calig.* 8.1)?', *MH* 68: 154–60.

———. 2012. 'Seven Notes on the Reign of Caligula'. In *SLLRH* 16.437–71.

———. 2014. 'Caligula Displays Caesonia (Suet. Calig. 25.3)', *RhM* 157: 27–36.

———. 2018a. 'Caligula, Asprenas, and the Bloodied Robe', *Mnemosyne* 71: 873–80.

———. 2018b. 'Caligula as Venus (Suet. Calig. 52)', *RhM* 161: 422–32.

———. 2019. 'Caligula's Sexual Desire for the Moon (Suet. *Calig.* 22.4)', *MH* 76: 235–41.

Wright, A. 2001. 'The Death of Cicero: Forming a Tradition; The Contamination of History', *Historia* 50: 436–52.

Yakobson, A., and Cotton, H. M. 1985. 'Caligula's *recusatio imperii*', *Historia* 34: 497–503.

Yardley, J. C. 2008. *Tacitus: The Annals; The Reigns of Tiberius, Claudius, and Nero*. Oxford.

Zadorojnyi, A. V. 2005. '"Stabbed with Large Pens": Trajectories of Literacy in Plutarch's *Lives*'. In L. de Blois et al., eds., *The Statesman in Plutarch's Works*, vol. 2, 113–37. Leiden.

———. 2006. 'Lord of the Flies: Literacy and Tyranny in Imperial Biography'. In McGing and Mossman 2006, 351–94.

Zeiner, N. K. 2005. *Nothing Ordinary Here: Statius as Creator of Distinction in the Silvae*. New York.

Ziogas, I. 2016. 'Famous Last Words: Caesar's Prophecy on the Ides of March', *Antichthon* 50: 134–53.

Index

Note: Page numbers followed by 'n' denote footnotes.

For Product Safety Concerns and Information please contact our EU
representative GPSR@taylorandfrancis.com
Taylor & Francis Verlag GmbH, Kaufingerstraße 24, 80331 München, Germany

9780367560010